<creative html design>

lynda weinman
william weinman

design: ali karp

Creative HTML Design

By Lynda Weinman and William E. Weinman

Published by: New Riders Publishing
201 West 103rd Street
Indianapolis, IN 46290 USA

© 1998 by Lynda Weinman and William E. Weinman
Printed in the United States of America 1 2 3 4 5 6 7 8 9 0
Library of Congress Cataloging-in-Publication Data
•••CIP data available upon request•••
ISBN: 1-56205-704-9

Warning and Disclaimer: This book is designed to provide information about HTML and web design. Every effort has been made to make this book as complete and accurate as possible, but no warranty or fitness is implied.

Trademark Acknowledgments: All terms mentioned in this book that are known to be trademarks or service marks have been appropriately capitalized. New Riders Publishing cannot attest to the accuracy of this information. Use of a term in this book should not be regarded as affecting the validity of any trademark or service mark. The information is provided on an "as is" basis. The authors and New Riders Publishing shall have neither liability nor responsibility to any person or entity with respect to any loss or damages arising from the information contained in this book or from the use of the discs or programs that may accompany it.

Publisher: Jordan Gold
Brand Manager: Alan Bower
Managing Editor: Brice Gosnell

Credits

Executive Editor:
Beth Millett

Development Editor:
Jennifer Eberhardt

Project Editor:
Dayna Isley

Technical Editor:
Joe Tennis

Manufacturing Coordinator:
Paul Gilchrist

Book Designer:
Ali Karp "Alink Newmedia"
alink@earthlink.net

Cover Designer:
Bruce Heavin
bruce@stink.com

Ducks In A Row, Illustrator:
Joan Farber

Production Department
Director: Larry Klein
Supervisor: Vic Peterson
Team: Angela Perry
          Elizabeth San Miguel

Indexer:
Christine Nelsen

About the Authors

Lynda Weinman is a writer, designer, animator, teacher, and mom. She lives in southern California with her daughter, her daughter's numerous pets, her husband Bruce (who painted the wonderful book cover to this and Lynda's other books), and her dad. She writes for a lot of magazines, lectures at a lot of schools and conferences, and writes a lot of books. Oh yeah, in her alleged free time she updates her web site: http://www.lynda.com.

William E. Weinman is a musician, electronics engineer, programmer, writer, father, son, and abuser of commas. Unlike his brother-in-law, Bruce Heavin, who lives in a cave under the Santa Monica Mountains, Bill was born in southern California and now lives in Texas with his wife and partner Lee Harrington, stepdaughter Megan Bristow, and cats Max and Brooke. As co-founder of the web hosting service WebMonster Networks, he builds and maintains web servers. In his alleged spare time, he writes music in his home studio and plays guitar at blues jams around the country. On a good day, Bill's web site is here: http://www.weinman.com/wew/ (wouldn't it be neat if you could click on a book?).

Creative HTML Design's **book web site:**
http://www.htmlbook.com/

Dedication

This book is dedicated to our grandmother, Lillian Weinman (who would have been 99 years old at this book's publication). Always a strong example of strength and courage, thanks for reinforcing our positive self-image. We wish you were here to read the fruits of your labor with us!
—Lynda and Bill

Bill's Acknowledgments:

Thanks to my **wife and partner Lee**, for putting up with my door being closed (and for picking up all the extra work with our business) while I wrote and wrote and wrote,

To my **son David**, who brings a bright smile with him wherever he goes,

to my **stepdaughter Megan**, for bringing boundless energy and enthusiasm into my life,

to my **Dad**, for his wonderful introduction and for being so involved in our lives,

to **my agent David Rogelberg**, whose honesty and integrity is so rare and precious in this business,

to **David Dwyer**, and the **folks at New Riders**, for believing us when we told them there was nothing like this book on the market; and finally,

to my amazing **sister Lynda**, for working with me to make this a far better book than either of us could have done alone.

Lynda's Acknowledgments:

Special thanks to my **daughter Jamie**, who asked once if she could have "jamie-dot-com," only to change her mind, "Mom, I'm not calm. I should be Jamie-dot-excited!"

Extremely special thanks to my wonderful **husband Bruce**, who is the most supportive person I've ever known and helps me more than I can convey.

More special thanks to our **book designer Ali Karp**, who finally had time to go on a date after designing six straight books with me, and met the love of her life. Way to go, Ali! Congrats to you and Barak—"Mazel Tov" on your upcoming marriage. I plan to stop writing long enough to be her matron of honor ;-).

A sad farewell to **David Dwyer**, who is no longer on my publishing team, but who had a huge hand in the success of my books by lending his vision and trust.

Last but not least, major thanks to our favorite awesome **development editor Jennifer Eberhardt**, who went beyond the call of duty time and again to help make this book (and my other books) as good as we all wanted.

Our favorite book designer Ali, and her love Barak. Congratulations on your upcoming marriage—we all wish you great happiness!

A Special Thank You To:

Forté (http://www.forteinc.com/), for the Agent Newsreader.

Adobe (http://www.adobe.com/), for Photoshop, Illustrator, and so much else!

Macromedia (http://www.macromedia.com/), for Director, Flash, Dreamweaver, and Freehand.

WebMonster Networks (http://www.webmonster.net/), for giving us a place to pass files back and forth and for hosting the site for this book (http://www.htmlbook.com/).

Joan Farber and, Ducks In A Row (http://ducks.htmlbook.com/), for being the guinea pig and letting us use their web site project for this book.

Web Design & Web Programming Lists Members (http://www.webmonster.net/lists/), for so much insight into the way web professionals work!

Our grandmother Lillian with our Dad (1935).

Lynda and Bill before they wrote *Creative HTML Design*.

After they wrote *Creative HTML Design* (shown with Dad). You be the judge.

▶ table of contents

3   Speedy Graphics   31

5 Clickable 83

6   Tiles   109

13   Style Sheets   227

14   Navigation   247

15   Rollovers   267

‣ contents at a glance

Dad's Foreword
a reputable source

When they were children, my son Bill and his sister Lynda already demonstrated clear signs of the exceptional talents they later revealed. Lynda, even in third grade, demanded every available color of Crayola the company offered, and later in her teens, purchased sets of Magic Markers with exotic and unusual shades.

Bill, on the other hand, quickly outshone his poor father whose successful construction of a HeathKit High Fidelity amplifier, tuner, and speakers gave himself such pride of accomplishment. Bill proceeded to build better and more powerful units from scratch, using parts he purchased at Henry's Radio.

All of us have been involved with computers from an early date. Bill owned an Altair, the first Personal Computer, built from a kit and described and featured in the July, 1975 issue of Popular Electronics. Lynda learned to hack on an Apple II Plus, and eventually bought the first available Macintosh in 1984. Bill became a DOS wizard, and I bought a Commodore 64 myself.

I was thrilled and proud of the opportunity to write a foreword to their book, and I read the chapters one by one as they emerged from the printer. As a casual computer user, not very deeply involved in the programming or technical side of it, I found this book amazingly clear and instructive.

I have "surfed" the web since being introduced to it about three years ago. But the details of just how and through what magic process I could find myself visiting the Louvre or researching the works of Shakespeare were a complete mystery to me. Now, they are not that big a mystery.

My hope is that you will enjoy reading this book as much as I did.

Introduction

Lynda's Introduction

Can HTML Be Creative?

One of the coolest things to happen to me in 1993 was my discovery of the web. One of the uncoolest things was the simultaneous discovery that I had to learn HTML in order to create web content. I was the product of the GUI generation (raised and bred on the **G**raphical **U**ser Interface), and in no way associated myself with programming languages or command line interfaces.

I'd always heard programming was a creative act, though as a visual-type person, I was highly suspicious of people who claimed this. I knew I kept wanting to do things with HTML that it wouldn't easily let me do, and the process of working with it felt far from "creative."

And yet, look at the web today, a mere few years later, and you'll find a creative playing field in full force. My brother and I hope to get you to the point where that's how it feels, and where HTML is a willing vehicle to help you communicate what you want to say effectively and creatively.

The web has an amazing way of bringing together divergent technologies, people, and practices. My brother and I qualify as part of this weird phenomenon. We barely knew each other as we were growing up. I mean, he was a boy! Another species…but that's another story! He was the build-MITS-kit, teach-yourself-assembly-language and hack-your-way-through-music-and-programming-type. I was the I-have-my-Mac-hear-me-roar-try-to-outdo-this type. We both viewed each other in the nose-up position, and rarely discussed computers when we spoke.

So the web caught us off guard. Each of us at opposite ends of computer careers (myself a digital designer/animator, and he a programmer) the web let us face each other squarely eye-to-eye to say, "Hey, I want to learn what you do! You're not so uncool after all!" I wrote some design books, he wrote some programming books, and we finally said, "Let's do one together!" And here it is.

When I wrote my first book in 1995 (*Designing Web Graphics*), I could barely get publishers to understand that graphic designers would ever want to publish on the web. It was not considered at that point to be a design medium. Things have changed—look around the web today, and you'll find stellar examples of beautiful visual design. (You'll also see some not-so-stellar examples, but more about that later.)

To be honest, there hasn't been an HTML book until now that I could wholeheartedly recommend. I like some of the visual quickstart guides, and the teach yourself guides, but they always raised more questions for me than they answered. It seemed to me that a different kind of HTML book was needed—one that walked the reader through the web site creation process which contained lessons and source files handy to try out. Even though there are a glut of HTML books in the bookstores, I saw a glaring need for a different type of HTML book that offered a more holistic approach to teaching the subject matter. I've never met anyone more knowledgeable about HTML than my brother, so when he agreed to partner with me on this book, I was thrilled.

Mitchell Waite (Waite Group Press and Waite Online) once pegged me perfectly. He said, "Oh, I get what you do! You write books for yourself!" He couldn't have been more correct. I write books in a way in which I would want things explained to me. There's a certain amount of required organization, a certain amount of required detail and background information, and a whole lot of concrete, "Oh, so THAT's how you do it!" To be concise, I'm the practical type, not the theoretical type.

My brother and I are both well-worn travelers in this weird HTML/Web landscape, and hope to share our hard-earned lessons with you. We hope you get down, get dirty, and get creative with this HTML/Web stuff. We've learned a lot of tricks and techniques that will help you get past the tools and into the creative process.

Lynda's Goals for This Book

My area of expertise is graphics, and my brother's is programming. To date, my books have included tips, techniques, and exercises to learn how to create web graphics. I look at the HTML books on the market and don't think they include enough information about graphics, but also see the necessity to focus on HTML as the main subject when first starting in web publishing. It's my hope with *Creative HTML Design* that we've bridged the two worlds—graphics and programming—and created a single resource that can get people started on the right track.

My brother and I really enjoy sharing knowledge with each other. This has been a fantastic opportunity for us to blend our knowledge, get it down on paper, and put it in one place. We both write conversationally, and in some respects, this book invites you to witness our lively and educated conversation about web design and web programming.

Artists care about how things look, that colors match, and that artwork aligns exactly the way we planned. The web is a disconcerting medium because it's been designed to be customizable by the end user and the browsers, creating a situation where the results of your design efforts can easily look different than you planned. This book will help artists and programmers control what they can and accept and identify what they can't.

Bill's Introduction

Can Programming Be Creative?

Conventional wisdom says that programming is technical, and graphics is creative. That's the sort of thinking that got us into this mess. If more programmers (and project managers) understood that programming is first a creative act (not unlike painting or music), we would have more innovative software and less "me too" bloatware screaming at us to believe that, contrary to appearance, it's actually innovative.

It's worth repeating: Programming is first a creative act.

Technology is "The knowledge and means used to produce the material necessities of a society" (Webster's, 1981). Programming is much more than that—it's a tool of expression, a set of skills with which you can create the reality of a vision. It is an art that will not be recognized as such until our children are grown because our contemporaries don't understand it. That makes it a technology in their eyes.

I've spent most of my life in the creative application of new technologies. I'm a fundamentally creative person, who just happens to love playing with new technology. I started out life as a musician, playing guitar, keyboards, and drums in rock-and-roll bands. On the side, I built custom synthesizers and designed sound reinforcement systems. I never drew that much of a distinction between all of those activities because I see them all as creative pursuits.

When the web came along, I saw a new way to explore the creative application of emerging technology. With transistors getting smaller and faster, processor speed being measured in hundreds of MIPS (**M**illions of **I**nstructions **P**er **S**econd), memory prices falling and high-end graphics display hardware following suit, the web couldn't have happened at a better time. Now we can start really having fun!

The other exciting thing about the web is that, in bringing together the visual arts with the programmatic arts, it has also brought me together with my long-lost sister. Lynda didn't mention the part where she spent 18 years in the Himalayas spinning yak wool with the Swami Bawgdhagda Dhogdhoo. But upon her return, with the web exploding like Krakatau on a bad hair day, it became necessary for her to finally look up her propeller-head brother. Isn't life strange?

Us programmers are so terribly misunderstood.

Bill's Goals for This Book

Computers are obstinate about precision. Miss a period here or a semi-colon there, and you'll get pistachios instead of caviar every time. That's why it's important to know how a language works before you try to write something in it.

Before we wrote this book, I had not yet seen a thorough and accurate book on HTML and its associated disciplines. There were some good books on graphics, but their HTML was weak; there were some technically accurate books on HTML, but they weren't really complete, or they just didn't teach the subject well. So when Lynda and I realized that we each wanted to write the same book, we both got really excited about combining our disparate skills and perspectives to create a uniquely useful book about HTML and how to build a web site.

Building a web site is more than just HTML. If you want to learn how to use tables to stitch irregular parts of a graphic together, you need to also learn how to make the graphic; or, if you want to learn how to use JavaScript to make rollover controls, it's good to also know how to make rollover graphics that invite the user to engage them.

My sister Lynda is the undisputed master of on-line graphics, and she has added generous tips, tricks, and insights where necessary to help you accomplish your ultimate goal: a web site that says what you want it to say—with compelling graphics and flawless HTML.

Lynda and Bill rode together long before they wrote together.

In the process of writing this book, I have learned what a wonderful teacher my sister is. She has a knack for teaching like Mozart had a knack for a catchy tune (I don't hear too many people whistling Mahler on their way to work). Combined with my propensity for bits and bytes, I hope we have created a book that will inspire you as much as it educates you.

In short, I want to see some more innovation. Make something new, and send me the URL.

How This Book Works

This book is designed to work on a number of levels. It can be read in linear order, or it can be surfed, much the way you would gather information on the web. Everyone learns differently—some people learn from theoretical books, others from manuals, others from step-by-step exercises, and some from simply diving in head first and doing. We have tackled this book from all these angles. We wanted to do more than a how-to book, more than an exercise book, and more than a theory book. Our goal was not simply to present information, but to also explain why it was necessary, how you would do it, and where could you find resources related to it.

Creative HTML Design walks you through building a real working web site, specially created for the lesson plans in this book. In the process, you will have a chance to read about all the phases of site design. This book includes a complete HTML 4.0 reference with details on all current HTML elements.

Web Site Information and Email Contacts

The ***Creative HTML Design*** web site (http://www.htmlbook.com) is there to help you by providing updates to the book and tips and pointers that will be kept current as new technology emerges.

The **Ducks In A Row** web site (http://ducks.htmlbook.com) is a live implementation of the examples and exercises in this book. In fact, this book represents the actual process that we went through in building this site.

Lynda and **Bill** both live active email lives. Lynda's email address is lynda@lynda.com; and Bill's is wew@bearnet.com. Please feel free to contact us with questions, comments, complaints, and even kudos. We love kudos.

We hope you enjoy reading this book as much as we've enjoyed writing it. We both learned a ton from each other, and it's our hope that you will benefit from the results.

Our Lesson Approach

Once you're up to speed on web publishing, you would design your site in the following stages:

- Concept

- Planning

- Collecting Assets (artwork, text, media, etc.)

- Producing Graphics and Layouts

- Writing Code/HTML Editing/Scripting, Etc.

- Publishing to a Server

We did not choose to teach you how to create your web site in this order because we agreed that it would not be the best order to learn from. How can you develop a concept if you don't understand the limitations of the medium? How can you plan a site if you've never built one before? How can you collect assets if you don't understand what you need? How can you produce graphics and layouts if you've never authored for the web? How can you publish something you don't know how to make yet?

For this reason, we organized the materials in a logical manner for learning web publishing with HTML and graphics. If you find that there's something you already know, feel free to skip ahead to the next section or chapter. If you're curious about something that hasn't been discussed, turn to the Index to locate it and flip ahead.

You'll find all the related files to each exercise in its respective chapter folder on the <chd> CD-ROM.

About the Ducks In A Row Site

The Ducks In A Row web site (http://www.ducks.htmlbook.com) was designed for the educational purpose of this book. The rubber stamp company is real and is owned by Mainway, Inc. The Ducks In A Row artwork on the <chd> CD-ROM was created by Joan Farber, and can be used for the exercises in this book only. You may post this artwork to the web in the context of following our exercises, but you may not freely distribute this art or resell the artwork in any form or manner. **Hint:** If you like Joan's artwork, she is an independent illustrator and will be happy to consider any projects you might want to hire her for. Joan Farber's artists representative for national/international advertising campaigns and private commissioned fine art is:

Vicki Prentice Associates Inc.
630 5th Avenue (20th floor)
Rockefeller Center, NY NY 100111
212.332.3460 / fax: 212.332.3401

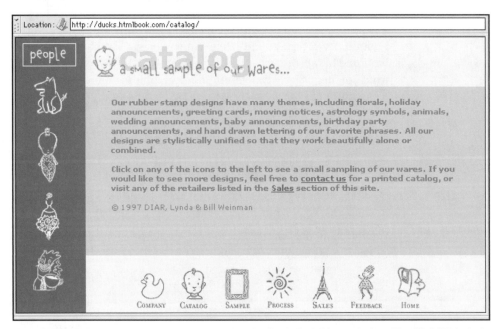

Creative HTML Design walks you through creating the Ducks In A Row web site. The CD-ROM includes all the art and programming files needed for the book's step-by-step exercises. In the process, you'll learn about seamless tiles, rollover buttons, navigation bars, frames, tables, cascading style sheets, fragments, animation, sound, transparency, web typography, site organization, and more. The lessons in the book start simple, and advance to more complex assignments. In the end, you will create a real working web site, and will be able to apply the process to your own site design projects. The Ducks In A Row website is located at http://www.ducks.htmlbook.com.

▶ contents at a glance

Here's a breakdown of the subjects this book:

Continues …

▶ contents at a glance *continued...*

In the beginning, there was this fish ...
—The Firesign Theater

Start
tips and advice

If you have never created a web site before, you'll likely find yourself in the market for an internet connection and a home for your web site. Our advice in this area is targeted to help you make informed choices based on the size and scope of your web site publishing needs.

Because this is an HTML book, as well as a design book, we know you're also interested in understanding which types of HTML editors and learning methods exist to get you up to speed fast. This chapter includes our opinions and recommendations about WYSIWYG (What You See Is What You Get) editors, HTML editors, and plain vanilla text editors.

Types of Internet Providers

Selecting an Internet provider can be a frustrating experience. Most of the hype you hear is nothing more than the technological equivalent of the double-speak in George Orwell's *1984*, and what little accurate information is available is so technical that it may as well be double-speak. To head off disappointment, don't expect selecting an Internet provider to be easy, and don't expect to be satisfied with your initial choice.

First, you need to understand the difference between an **I**nternet **S**ervice **P**rovider (ISP) and a **P**resence **P**rovider (PP).

Your computer's modem connects to a phone line, which dials your ISP's "dialup" lines and connects to the Internet through their computers and routers.

Internet Service Provider (ISP): This is the company that you use to connect your computer to the Internet. An Internet connection enables you to look at web pages, get email, and send your artwork, media, and code to your own web site.

Presence Provider (PP): This is a company that hosts your actual web site, and that is its sole purpose. To use a presence provider, you also need an ISP so that you have someplace to dial in to in order to send your files to the Presence Provider, receive email, browse the web, and so on.

ISP OR PP?

If you're just starting with your first web page, you may decide for economic reasons to have your **I**nternet **S**ervice **P**rovider also host your web site. ISPs typically have a less expensive rate when providing connection services and web hosting services as a bundled deal. While this makes sense for a first-time, casual web publisher, it may not make sense if you are creating a site that you expect to have high traffic and visibility. This section evaluates the decision process between going with an all purpose ISP or dedicated PP.

Most ISPs will gladly host your web site, but this usually is not the best choice. More often than not, an ISP will host your web site on the same machines that perform many other tasks, such as email, usenet news, and other services. That's because the ISP's primary business is to host dialup users, and hosting your web site is just another service they provide. Choosing to house your web site with an ISP can result in a slower web site, which may not be reliably available to your users. If you have a high-traffic site, or if your web site is critical to your business, we recommend that you find a good Presence Provider, in addition to your ISP.

A company that hosts web sites as its primary business is in a better position to do a good job than a company that hosts web sites as a side business. The dedicated hosting company runs dedicated machines that do nothing but host web sites and provide more bandwidth and overhead so that your visitors get a better response. By not sharing its resources with literally thousands of dialup users, the likelihood of sluggish server response time is greatly reduced.

While it's important that your ISP be local to your physical location (so that it's a local phone call to connect), there is no need to restrict yourself to local businesses for your web hosting. Instead, consider the following issues that actually affect your service.

Does Your Provider Have Enough Bandwidth?

Bandwidth is the measure of how much data a service can deliver in a given amount of time. It is one of the most important measurements of the quality of online service. If your ISP is short on bandwidth, you might not know because you are connected directly to their network with your modem, but those who connect to your service will know because they connect through the Internet. There is no effective way of measuring the bandwidth of your provider. We recommend that you test your provider's speed by accessing their site from a connection that is not dialed right into their network. This will give you an objective evaluation of the speed of their service.

Do They Have Enough Overhead?

Overhead is the measure of how much computing resources are allocated to your web site. Unless your site is large enough and busy enough to warrant a dedicated computer on a dedicated connection, you are probably sharing your computing resources with other web sites. That's not necessarily a bad thing. The problem occurs if the computer you are sharing becomes overloaded.

Just like with bandwidth, there is probably no way to know from the provider's advertising materials if the provider has enough overhead. The only way to find out is to compare the response times of the other sites that are hosted on the same machine. Check some of those sites, preferably from some different locations and at different times of the day. Get a feel for how responsive they are. Try to use sites that are about as busy as yours will be. Again, these are very subjective measurements, but they are really all you have to go on.

Other Services

You may also want to consider if you will need other services from your provider. If any of the following are important to you, be sure to discuss them up front with your potential provider. Some of these items may be unfamiliar to you, but don't despair. They will all be explained later in this book:

- Do you need the ability to write and/or install your own CGI programs? (See Chapter 16, "Forms," for more details about CGI.)

- Do you need access to SSI (**S**erver-**S**ide **I**ncludes)? (See Chapter 14, "Navigation," for more details about SSI.)

- Does your provider have CGI scripts, such as email, guestbooks, and counters?

- If you need multiple email accounts, does your provider support it?

- Do you need access to mail-filtering scripts for your domain? These scripts give you control over your mail and allow for separate mailboxes, autoresponders, and mail-controlled web services such as list archives and databases.

- Do you need access to raw server logs to run your own statistics?

- How much space will they give you for the price you're being quoted? If you plan to put up movies, sound, or interactive content, you may need at least 10mb of storage. Is there an extra charge if you exceed your space allotment?

- Is there a restriction to how much traffic the provider allows on its site? What are the charges if your traffic exceeds its limits?

♦ tip

ISP Comparison Study

The company C|Net runs an ongoing comparison of ISPs by area. You may want to look at this before deciding on an ISP. Note, however, that dedicated Presence Providers are not included in this survey:

http://www.cnet.com/Content/Reviews/Compare/ISP/area.html

♦ note

How the Authors Do It

We live in different states (Lynda's in California and Bill's in Texas), but we both house our web sites on a Presence Provider called WebMonster Networks (http://www.webmonster.net/), which was co-founded by Bill and his partner Lee Harrington. Lynda uses an ISP in California and Bill uses an ISP in Texas. We opted to use a dedicated Presence Provider because we both have very busy sites. Compare our sites' speed to other web sites you visit as an example of how this choice has sped up our site's performance:

http://www.lynda.com

http://www.weinman.com/wew/

HTML Software

HTML stands for **HyperText Markup Language**. It's the language with which web pages are written and designed, although most designers would cringe at the thought of calling HTML design a layout language.

And that's precisely the point: HTML was not written to be a design language. It was written to be a display language, with the intent that it might display differently on different machines and operating systems. Ever notice how browser software enables you to change your fonts and their sizes, and whether images and links are turned on or off? HTML was supposed to be a transportable language that could be customized to the end user machine's liking.

Many of the chapters in this book teach you how to trick HTML into obedience, but the starting point is HTML, whether we like it or not. HTML is the language of the web. Do you have to know HTML to design web pages? No, but it sure helps. Frankly, some of our all-time favorite sites were in fact designed by artists who never touched the code. They teamed up with an HTML programmer and did what they knew best—design.

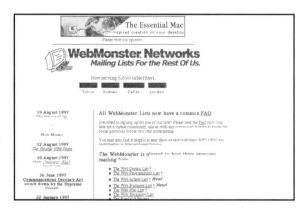

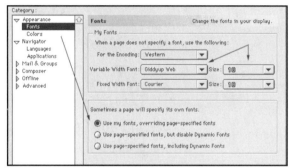

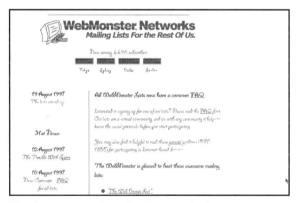

The three screens show the discrepancies between a page that was designed with certain settings and the results of the end user changing his or her browser preferences.

HTML Versus Design

A good description of designers is that we are control freaks. It is in our nature to want to control how our artwork looks; that's why we are good at what we do. Most of us, in fact, are passionate about making our artwork look just exactly to our liking. Web page design is definitely full of intense challenges, and you can decide to take them on or pass the buck to a programmer.

HTML is what made the web possible, but HTML has also become known as a designer's nightmare. There has never been a design medium that allowed its audience to change the content at whim. If you have ever created computer graphics before, you're used to having a sense of comfort that what you see as the final result is what everyone will see. When it's finished, it can never be changed. HTML plays havoc with a designer's quest for control. It is one of the strangest design mediums ever unleashed upon us, and that is because it was never intended to be a design medium in the first place.

 note

Should You Learn HTML?

It is great to know HTML, but it's not necessary in all cases. The advantage to knowing and understanding HTML is that you are in better control of knowing what is possible and what is not. You won't have to hear "No" from someone who might not care about your design as much as you do.

If you want to learn HTML, there are a few different camps to subscribe to:

Text-based editors: For those who want to learn HTML and understand what the tags do and mean.

Dedicated HTML editors: For those who want to use an HTML editor with automated tags.

WYSIWYG HTML editors: For those who use a WYSIWYG HTML editor and don't want to know why anything works, but do want to get finished web pages anyway.

Text-Based Editors

This book teaches you to code in HTML inside a text editor, regardless of whether you plan to use one. Let's examine the options, pitfalls, and advantages of using different ways for creating HTML.

It's possible to learn HTML by using any off-the-shelf text editor. Try viewing the source of pages you like and learning from them as a starting point. It's perfectly acceptable to learn HTML this way. In fact, you'll find that most HTML pros used this learning method.

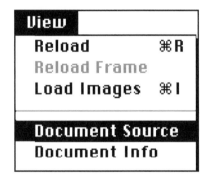

Most browsers allow you to "view the source" of HTML.

An example of viewing the source inside the Macintosh version of Netscape 4.0. Studying others' pages is a good way of picking up coding techniques.

Different people have different learning methods, different aptitudes, different needs, and different goals. There is no right or wrong way to learn HTML. If you really want to understand what you're doing and why, writing code by hand works great as a starting point. It requires patience and persistence and the acceptance that you'll make mistakes and won't get instant results. The payoff is that you'll understand what you're doing and will approach this medium with a greater degree of confidence.

In addition to the lessons in this book and CD-ROM, there are great online tutorials for learning HTML. A few of our favorites are:

Network Communication Design in Japan: (an excellent visual online HTML reference)
http://ncdesign.kyushu-id.ac.jp/

Netscape's "Creating Netsites":
http://help.netscape.com/links.html

Microsoft's Design & Layout site:
http://www.microsoft.com/workshop/design/default.asp#general

Brian Wilson's Index DOT HTML:
http://home.webmonster.net/mirrors/bloo-html/

Dedicated HTML Editors

HTML editors are similar to dedicated word processors that have automated tags built in. Normally, these tags are accessible via menu commands or handy toolbars. If you don't know a word of HTML, these types of editors certainly may baffle you. What good is an automated tag if you don't understand what tags do in the first place?

If you practice the methods of teaching yourself HTML in a standard text editor that were described earlier, you will eventually want and appreciate a text-based HTML editor. Some of them have spell-checkers, HTML checkers (to ensure that you've written correct HTML), broken-link checkers, as well as search-and-replace functionality.

Most HTML editors are found on the web and can be downloaded for free or for free trial periods. The best way to find HTML editors is on the web itself. Here are some good starting points:

http://www.shareware.com

http://www.yahoo.com/Computers_and_Internet/Internet/World_Wide_Web/ HTML_Editors/Macintosh/

http://www.yahoo.com/Computers_and_Internet/Internet/World_Wide_Web/ HTML_Editors/MS_Windows/

Here are some online reviews and comparisons of popular HTML editors:

http://www.cnet.com/Content/Reviews/Compare/11htmleds/

http://www.dsport.com/sjm/resources.html

http://www.pcmag.com/iu/features/1520/_open.htm

If you are new to HTML, we suggest that you follow the exercises in this book using a text-editing tool, as opposed to an HTML editor. The lessons here enable you to graduate to an HTML editor and understand what you are doing, which will make working with an HTML editor much easier in the long run.

WYSIWYG HTML Editors

WYSIWYG (**W**hat **Y**ou **S**ee **I**s **W**hat **Y**ou **G**et) stands for a new breed of HTML editors that profess to take the pain out of writing this stuff. At least that's the claim. WYSI-WYG editors don't require that you know a word of HTML. In fact, many of them shield you from it so successfully that you may author pages and never understand or learn a single word of code.

In principle, there's nothing wrong with that! How many people write their own word processing software or PostScript commands? People who like and understand how to program really enjoy this stuff, and very few of the rest of us enjoy it much at all.

One problem is that HTML tags change frequently. New file formats, plug-ins, and browser features make this a changing landscape unparalleled by typical word pro-cessing or PostScript software. Web design and development is an emerging medium, and most of us are eager guinea pigs to propel it further!

The only way that WYSIWYG editors could truly keep pace would be if they changed on a weekly basis. This is not to suggest that they aren't useful at all. They can be wonderful. Anyone who has ever programmed frames or a complicated nested table will be in ecstasy letting a program do it for them without coding. WSYIWYG editors can be especially useful when you're in a hurry. They are fantastic time-savers that help you get your ideas out quickly without being bogged down by programming strange tags and adding slashes and opening and closing brackets everywhere.

The problem is that once you've been bitten by the web design bug, you'll want to try new things, such as newly introduced tags, plug-ins, or file formats, that the WSYI-WYG editor won't support. And, if you've relied exclusively on the editor to compose pages, you won't have the necessary skills to understand how to extend its capabili-ties. WYSIWIG editors offer an easier programming environment, but often limit what you can accomplish.

Another problem with WSYIWYG editors (at least the current crop of them) is that the HTML they churn out is so bad that the pages generated by them often stop working or begin working very badly when viewed on a new browser or a new version of a browser. WYSIWYG editors often throw in their own HTML tags that certain browsers don't recognize. This has been the case recently (as we write this). When the latest version of Netscape Navigator became available, a large number of sites lost their background colors because they had used a popular WSYIWYG editor that inserted an extra BODY tag. This bug didn't cause a problem with the previous version of Netscape, even though it's definitely incorrect HTML.

In the perfect world, the browser would also be the HTML editor. Every time the browser changed, the HTML editor would change too. Well, without naming names, even the most popular browser's built-in editor doesn't fully support its own tags. These editors still have some growing up to do, and in the meantime, your site may be the victim of tags that don't work properly.

Chapter 19, "Good HTML," discusses proper HTML vs. WYSIWYG HTML. It will help you identify how to clean up HTML that is created by outdated editors and should enable you to correct problems in your code that may haunt you down the ever-changing technology road.

‣ chapter one summary

Being prepared for web publishing involves a lot of decision making in areas that might be new to you. Weigh your options carefully and make informed decisions. Often, there is no single correct way to go about doing this work. Diversity on the web is prevalent, and agreed upon standards are rare. As much as we'd love to tell you otherwise, web publishing is a challenging—and changing—business!

2

*"If you can just get your mind together
then come on across to me
We'll watch the sunrise from the bottom of the sea
But first, are you experienced"*
—Jimi Hendrix, 1967

First Page

▶ this chapter

how the web works
creating your first page
viewing it locally
uploading to a server

First Page
easy steps to follow

This chapter offers a number of short exercises that teach the fundamental principles of making web pages. We know you're anxious to get going, even though there might be a lot of holes in your knowledge of HTML and web design. In this chapter we encourage you to get your feet wet and leave more advanced concepts and techniques for later.

Throughout this book, we created a web site design for a rubber stamp company called Ducks In A Row. The `chap02` folder of the <chd> CD-ROM includes all the image and text files you'll need to follow the exercises in this chapter. We'll quickly walk you through how to construct web pages, how to test them from your hard drive, and how to upload the files to your server. These exercises may raise a lot of unanswered questions for you, as HTML and web design cannot be taught in a single chapter. Our goal is to start simple and build on this chapter as an introduction to the rest of the book. If you want to skip around, feel free to consult the Table of Contents, Index, Glossary, and theHTML Reference at any time.

How Does the Web Work?

Many people are confused by the distinction between the Internet and the World Wide Web. The web is a subset of the larger set called the Internet. For the purpose of this book, the web is defined as "anything on the Internet that you can access via a hyperlink." Many things that are available through a web interface are also available through more traditional Internet programs, such as ftp, gopher, and wais.

Stated another way, the World Wide Web is a collection of documents on the Internet that are loosely knit through a concept called hypertext. Hypertext documents connect to each other by hyperlinks (or hotlinks) in a completely free-form manner. Any document can have links to any other document in the world. That's why it's called a web. There are no restrictions limiting any document from linking to any other.

 note

Definitions

Some of the terms used in this chapter may be unfamiliar to you, so here's a handy definition list. These terms are also listed in the Glossary at the back of this book.

Hypertext: Text that is linked to documents on the web

Hyperlink: Linked text, images, or media

Document: Any individual object (text, image, media) on the web

Element: An object in an HTML file

Object: Any distinct component, such as a tag, attribute, image, text file, etc.

Tag: An HTML directive, enclosed in "`<"example">`"

Attribute: A modifier to an HTML tag, for example, `<TAG ATTRIBUTE>`

Container: An element that encloses other objects, for example, `<STRONG> </STRONG>`

Hyperlinks—Web-Like Relationships

Each site on the web is made up of a collection of different pages. These pages are usually viewed with an application called a web browser. If you are interested in creating your own web site, you probably already have a browser, such as Netscape Navigator, Microsoft Internet Explorer, Mosaic, or any number of less common browsers. (Many sites on the web use specific features of specific browsers; as a result, not all sites will work right on all browsers. We will do our best to note where this effect is significant within our lesson plan.)

The tangled web we weave ...

When people want to see your web site, they connect to it with their browser. They may type in the URL (**U**niform **R**esource **L**ocator, a unique address assigned to each object on the web, such as http://www.blablabla.com/object-name) for your site, or, more likely, they will select it via a hyperlink from another page somewhere. The sequence of events from that point are helpful to understand as you create your web site:

- The browser connects with a server that contains your page.

- The browser sends a command to the server, asking for the page.

- The server sends the page, actually a file, containing code in a language called HTML (**H**yper**T**ext **M**arkup **L**anguage).

- The browser reads the HTML and finds references to all the other objects on that page (for example, pictures, sounds, animation, and so on).

- One-by-one, the browser retrieves each of those other objects in the same way it got the page of HTML from the server.

- The browser assembles the page according to the instructions in the HTML and displays it for the viewer.

Following the Exercises

To do this exercise, and most of the exercises in this book, you will need a computer capable of viewing and creating both graphics and text. The system requirements are not stringent; they are actually quite flexible. Virtually any system with color graphics capability will work fine, although a faster computer with a high-end graphics adapter is always more fun.

We need not have any particular operating system. We know of people who create and view web sites on Macintosh, MS Windows, UNIX, Amiga, and many other systems. (We also know people who will swear to you that the system they are using is the only viable system).

Creating Your First Page

Step 1: Create a folder on your hard drive called ducks. Transfer the ylogo1.gif file from the chap02 folder of the <chd> CD-ROM to your new folder. Open your text editor and type the following code exactly as it appears below.

```
<HTML>
<HEAD>
<TITLE>Ducks in a Row Homepage</TITLE>
</HEAD>
<BODY>
<H1>Welcome to Ducks in a Row Online!</H1>
<P>Feel free to splash around . . .
<P><IMG SRC="ylogo1.gif">
</BODY>
</HTML>
```

Step 2: Inside the ducks folder you created, save the document as index.html or, if your system doesn't allow four-letter file name extensions, index.htm. Make sure you save it in text format and not a proprietary word processor format. See the note on this page for background information about HTML naming conventions.

Step 3: Open your browser of choice (preferably Netscape Navigator, Internet Explorer, or Mosaic). Under **File**, choose **Open File** and locate the index.html document that you just created. This process is called "viewing a file locally," or from your local hard drive. Later in this chapter, we'll cover uploading this file to a web server so it can be "viewed globally" on the World Wide Web.

Here's what the results of the HTML would produce when displayed in Netscape Navigator.

Troubleshooting Note: If your file doesn't look like this, make sure you saved the document with the proper .htm or .html extension and that it was saved in **Text Only** mode, and not a proprietary word processing file format.

Understanding What You Just Did

In the HTML that you just wrote, notice the words that are placed within angle-brackets (for example, <HTML>). These are called tags. Tags are the instructions that tell the browser how you want certain parts of the page to be displayed.

Some HTML tags come in pairs. The second of the pair, called the end-tag, has a slash (/) right after the left angle-bracket (for example, <TITLE> and </TITLE>). Tags that come in pairs are called containers because they enclose other objects. Everything between the begin-tag and the end tag is said to be within the container.

Let's look at the code from the preceding exercise to break down what each element is doing:

```
1.  <HTML>
2.  <HEAD>
3.  <TITLE>Ducks in a Row Homepage
    </TITLE></HEAD>
4.  <BODY>
5.  <H1>Welcome to Ducks in a Row Online!
    </H1>
6.  <P>Feel free to splash around . . .
    <P>
7.  <IMG SRC="ylogo1.gif">
    </BODY>
    </HTML>
```

1. The entire HTML document is within the HTML container. The document begins with <HTML> and ends with </HTML>.

2. The first element (every distinct object in an HTML document is called an element) within the HTML container is a HEAD container, and within that is a TITLE container. The HEAD element contains all the supplemental elements that don't belong in the body of the document, such as TITLE.

3. The text included inside the TITLE element will appear at the top of your browser window.

4. The BODY element contains all the content of the page, such as text, graphics, multimedia, and for-matting specifications.

5. The line that says, <H1>Welcome to Ducks in a Row Online!</H1> is called a heading. The typeface displayed on the browser will be different for headings. In most browsers, headings appear bigger and bolder than the normal type used in paragraphs of text. Notice the text Feel free to splash around... is outside of the H1 container. It appears in the default browser font for this reason. Generally, the header ele-ments (H1-H6) will insert a line break before and after without requiring any additional code.

6. A paragraph is marked with a P tag. In most browsers, paragraphs are separated from each other by an empty line. The P tag is a container, but it is different than some other containers in that it does not require an end tag (/P). You can leave out the end tag if the paragraph is fol-lowed by another paragraph. (In other words, you may want to use an explicit end tag </P> if what follows is not another paragraph.)

7. The line that says <IMG SRC="ylogo1.gif"> shows an example of a tag and attribute combina-tion. The tag is IMG, and the attribute is SRC=ylogo1.gif. The IMG tag is used to place an image on the page. The SRC attribute tells the browser where to find the file to display as the image. IMG is not a container, so an end tag is not only unnecessary, it's not allowed. If you feel confused about which tags require end tags and which do not, never fear. The HTML reference at the end of this book clearly states which ele-ments require end tags.

Carriage Returns in HTML

HTML can be very rigid in some areas and flexible in others. For the most part, HTML doesn't make any distinction between an end-of-line (what happens when you press the return key to make a new line on the computer) and a space (what happens when you press the spacebar). You could write the following code like this:

```
<HTML>
<HEAD>
<TITLE>Ducks in a Row Homepage</TITLE>
</HEAD>
<BODY>
<H1>Welcome to Ducks in a Row
Online!</H1>
<P>Feel free to splash around . . .
<P><IMG SRC="ylogo1.gif">
</BODY>
</HTML>
```

or like this:

```
<HTML><HEAD>
<TITLE>Ducks in a Row Homepage</TITLE>
</HEAD>
<BODY><H1>Welcome to Ducks in a Row
Online!</H1><P>Feel free to splash around
. . . <P>
<IMG SRC="ylogo1.gif">
</BODY>
</HTML>
```

We have placed line breaks in the book to help separate elements so they can be more clearly understood. It's a good rule of thumb to keep your lines within 80 characters wide because that is the lowest common denominator for text editors and computer screens. This means if someone needs to look at your code, they won't have to scroll sideways, and the text won't wrap. Use a fixed-space font in your editor, so you can easily tell when lines get too long.

HTML Capitalization

HTML tags are not case sensitive. All the following versions of code will work the same:

```
<HTML>
<HEAD>
<TITLE>Ducks in a Row Homepage</TITLE>
</HEAD>
<BODY>
<H1>Welcome to Ducks in a Row
Online!</H1>
<P>Feel free to splash around . . .
<P><IMG SRC="ylogo1.gif">
</BODY>
</HTML>
```

All caps: We have chosen this convention for the book in order to differentiate easily between code and content.

```
<html>
<head>
<title>Ducks in a Row Homepage</title>
</head>
<body>
<h1>Welcome to Ducks in a Row
Online!</h1>
<p>Feel free to splash around . . .
<p><img src="ylogo1.gif">
</body>
</html>
```

All lowercase: This will also work just fine.

```
<HTML>
<head>
<title>Ducks in a Row Homepage</TITLE>
</HEAD>
<body>
<H1>Welcome to Ducks in a Row
Online!</H1>
<p>Feel free to splash around . . .
<P><IMG src="ylogo1.gif">
</BODY>
</HTML>
```

A mixture of **lowercase** and **uppercase** code will also work. HTML tags are not case sensitive.

File Naming Conventions

The part of the file name after the period is called the file name **extension**. This part of the file name is often used to distinguish different uses for files. For example, in the file name `index.html`, `.html` is the extension. Files containing HTML must end in the `.html` extension (or `.htm` if your system doesn't allow extensions longer than three letters). In most cases, browsers will not recognize your file as HTML without this extension.

It's a very good idea to avoid capital letters and spaces in file names when you're working with objects for use on the web. Your web pages will likely be uploaded to a UNIX server someday, and UNIX systems distinguish between lowercase and uppercase letters in file names. For example, if you create a file called `Index.html` and someone tries to retrieve it as `index.html`, they get an error message instead of your web page. If your file is named `index.html` and your HTML code has different capitalization, such as `Index.html`, the file will not work either.

Spaces within file names such as `my index.html` are problematic as well and will likely cause errors. Instead of `my index.html`, name it `my-index.html` or `my_index.html` by using a dash or an underscore instead of a space.

If new to writing code, you may be shocked at how sensitive computers can be to otherwise insignificant things like case and syntax. Trust us, a seemingly minor capitalization or spacing error will bring your web page functionality to an abrupt halt.

Spaces in Tags and Attributes

Spaces are never allowed between the initial "<" and the name of the tag. On the other hand, spaces are allowed before the closing ">" at the end of a tag.

For example, this is not legal: `< IMG SRC="ylogo.gif">`

But this example would work: `<IMG SRC="ylogo.gif" >`

According to the HTML specification, spaces are allowed around the equals sign (=) in HTML attributes. We have found, however, that some older browsers occasionally have problems with them.

In other words, while this is legal: `<IMG SRC = "ylogo.gif">`

it's probably better to write it like this: `<IMG SRC="ylogo.gif">`

▶ note

HTML Template

It's a good practice to keep a minimal document around that you can use as a template whenever you want to create a new web page.

Here's an example of a template you can use (we have provided a file named template.html in the chap02 folder of the <chd> CD-ROM):

```
<HTML>
<HEAD>
<TITLE></TITLE>
</HEAD>
<BODY>
</BODY>
</HTML>
```

▶ e x e r c i s e

Uploading the Page

The last exercise taught you how to view the HTML document from your hard drive. This is called viewing the site locally. Next, it's time to learn how to post the page for the world to see by using an ftp program.

PC FTP Instructions

If you're using a PC, you can use the WS_FTP program that we have included in the software/pc folder of the <chd> CD-ROM. First, install the program by unzipping it into a temporary directory and running install.exe. Then, following these instructions, you will set up the connection with the information you got from your web site provider for your ftp connection.

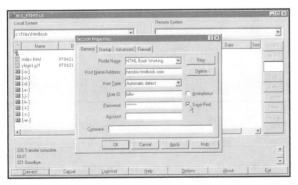

You'll need to consult your Internet or Presence Provider for the session property settings.

Step 1: Click on the **Connect** button to get the Session Properties dialog box.

Note: Only select the **Save Pwd** check box if you're sure that no one else has access to your computer!

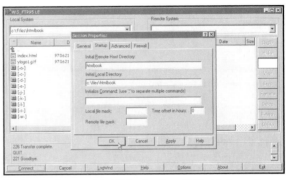

Under the Startup tab, fill in directory (folder) information.

Step 2: Select the **Startup** tab to enter directory (folder) information. (You can skip this step if you want to select your directories manually.) Press the **OK** button.

▶ continued

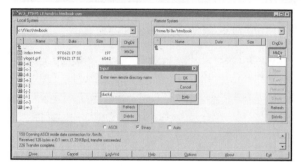

Create a new directory called ducks.

Step 3: Press the **MkDir** button on the Remote System side of the screen and enter the name **ducks** for the new directory.

Double-click to open the ducks directory.

Step 4: Double-click on the new ducks directory to open it.

Make sure you select ASCII mode for HTML files and Binary mode for images.

Step 5: To transfer your files, first select the appropriate transfer mode for the file. Always use ASCII mode for HTML files and Binary mode for images.

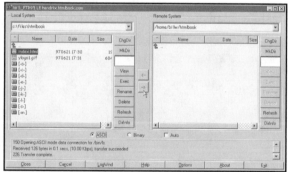

Press the right arrow button to upload to the server.

Step 6: Now you are ready to transfer your files. Select the file in the left window and press the right arrow button to upload the file to the server.

MAC FTP Instructions

For Mac users, download the program FETCH:
ftp://mac.archive.umich.edu/mac/util/comm/fetch3.03.sit.

Open Connection...

Enter host name, user name, and password (or choose from the shortcut menu):

Host:	hendrix.htmlbook.com
User ID:	lyndaw
Password:	••••
Directory:	
Shortcuts:	▼ [Cancel] [OK]

You'll need to consult your ISP to find out how to fill in the FETCH connection settings.

Step 1: Launch FETCH. You will need to ask your ISP (Internet Service Provider) about how to fill out the host and password information. Once connected, choose **Put File**. You are prompted to locate the file. For the example above, find the index.html document inside your ducks folder.

Directories
Change Directory... ⌘D
Create New Directory..

Enter a name for the new directory:
ducks
[Cancel] [OK]

Step 2: Create a new directory named ducks. Once the directory is created it, double click on it to open the folder.

Save file on hendrix.htmlbook.com

bar.gif

Format: [Raw Data ▼] [Cancel] [OK]

Step 3: Set the **Format** to **Raw Data** when you upload images or media. Press **OK**.

Save file on hendrix.htmlbook.com

company.html

Format: [Text ▼] [Cancel] [OK]

Step 4: When you save the file, set the **Format** to **Text** when you upload HTML.

Note: Make sure you replicate your ducks folder exactly onto your web server. If you have your files inside a directory called ducks, for example, make sure you create a directory on the web server called ducks too. This enables all your HTML links, images, and media to perform as they did on your hard drive. For more information on directory structure for HTML and the web, see Chapter 12, "Organization."

Now that you've uploaded the files, try viewing them from the web. We don't know what your exact URL will be because you have to get that information from your web administrator. Here's how the URL would look if it was on our server:

http://www.htmlbook.com/ducks/index.html

◀ e x e r c i s e

Link Me Up

The most visible feature of the web is the ability to jump from one page to another just by pressing on an object with your mouse pointer. By using these "hyperlinks," it is possible to surf sites in the far corners of the earth, sometimes without even realizing that you've left one site and connected to another.

An example of the Ducks In A Row home page with hyperlinks:

```
       <HTML>
       <HEAD>
       <TITLE>Ducks in a Row Homepage</TITLE>
       </HEAD>
       <BODY>
       <H1>Welcome to Ducks in a Row
       Online!</H1>
       <P> Rubber stamps or rubber duckies?
       Feel free to splash around to find out
       what we're about...
       <P><IMG SRC="ylogo1.gif">
       <P>Check out the
  1.   <A HREF="http://www.stampzone.com/">
       RUBBER STAMP ZONE</A> - an out-of-site
       rubber stamp page
       </BODY>
       </HTML>
```

1. This creates a link on your page that uses the text RUBBER STAMP ZONE to anchor the link. (The anchor text is usually rendered by the browser with an underline and/or a different color text). Clicking on the link displays the page at http:// www.stampzone.com/.

Step 1: To create a link to another site, insert the A tag in your HTML document. It will look like this:

```
<P>Check out the
<A HREF="http://www.stampzone.com/">
RUBBER STAMPZONE
</A> - an out-of-site rubber stamp page
```

Save this file as index.html to replace the preceding exercise file. You can open the file in your browser locally from your hard drive or upload it to your server to check the results.

You'll find an in-depth look at linked graphics in Chapter 5, "Clickable."

Here's how the linked RUBBER STAMP ZONE **text would appear inside the Netscape browser.**

▶ e x e r c i s e

Linking with Images

Your links don't have to be text. You can also use
graphics for hyperlinks. Let's say you'd like to link
the ylogo1.gif image to another page about the
company Ducks In A Row. We've created a document called "company.html," which is located in
the chap02 folder of the <chd> CD-ROM. Copy it
to your hard drive's ducks folder.

Step 1: Put the IMG tag in place of the text for the
link, and you will create a hyperlinked graphic.

```
<HTML>
<HEAD>
<TITLE>Ducks in a Row Homepage</TITLE>
</HEAD>
<BODY>
<H1>Welcome to Ducks in a Row
Online!</H1>
<P> Rubber stamps or rubber duckies?
Feel free to splash around to find out
what we're about...
<P><A HREF="company.html">
<IMG SRC=vylogo1.gif"></A>
<P>Check out the
<A HREF="http://www.stampzone.com/">
RUBBER STAMPZONE</A> - an out-of-site
rubber stamp page
</BODY>
</HTML>
```

1. By placing the <IMG SRC> element inside the
anchor element (that is, between the <A> and
the </A>), the graphic within the IMG tag will
beinked to the specified URL (company.html).

Now you have a graphic for the link. Be sure to
copy the files ylogo1.gif and company.html to the
ducks folder. You can open the file from a browser locally from your hard drive or upload it to
your server to check the results.

Here's an example of the linked graphic. If you click on the
graphic, the document company.html should appear.

Troubleshooting tips: If your file doesn't appear
as we've described, make sure you saved your files
in ASCII text, used the .html (or .htm) extension,
and that the files index.html, company.html, and
ylogo1.gif are inside your ducks folder.

Adding Color to the Page

HTML 4.0 allows you to make your pages more attractive by specifying particular colors for different elements on the page. You can change the background color, the color of the text, and color of links from their default colors with attributes to the BODY tag. The following BODY tag shows how:

```
<BODY TEXT="#FFFFCC" BGCOLOR="#669999" LINK="#CCCC66"
ALINK="#FFFF00" VLINK="#330033">
```

> **note**
>
> ### Hash Marks
>
> When you specify hexadecimal values in HTML (for example, for colors in the BODY tag), the # symbol (called pound, hash, or that tic-tac-toe-looking thingy) is required, as are the quotation marks. Yes, we know it usually works fine without all of that, but since it's required by the language, it's a good idea to just do it. That way, when the browser makers start enforcing the standard, your code will continue to work!

Colors in HTML are specified in hexadecimal (or, hex; base 16). Each color is represented as three pairs of hex digits for the Red, Green, and Blue components, respectively. Hexadecimal digits range from 0 to F. In other words, if you were to count from 0 to 15 in hex (assuming you had sixteen fingers), you would count:

```
0 1 2 3 4 5 6 7 8 9 A B C D E F
```

In the above BODY tag example, the background is a blue-green color. The Red part is 66 (or 102 decimal), the Green part is 99 (or 153 decimal), and the Blue part is also 99.

If you find all this talk about hex color confusing, don't fret yet. We have devoted an entire chapter to color (Chapter 4, "Web Color"), where HTML color is explained further.

▶ exercise

Add Some Color!

Step 1: To add color to the earlier example, type this HTML:

```
<HTML>
<HEAD>
<TITLE>Ducks in a Row Homepage</TITLE>
</HEAD>
<BODY BGCOLOR="#669999"
TEXT="#FFFFCC" LINK="#CCCC66"
ALINK="#FFFF00" VLINK="#330033">
<H1>Welcome to Ducks in a Row
 Online!</H1>
<P> Rubber stamps or rubber duckies?
Feel free to splash around to find out
what we're about...
<P><A HREF="company.html">
<IMG SRC="ylogo1.gif" BORDER=0></A>
<P>Check out the
<A HREF="http://www.stampzone.com/">
RUBBER STAMP ZONE</A> - an out-of-site
rubber stamp page
</BODY>
</HTML>
```

1. `BGCOLOR`, `TEXT`, `LINK`, `ALINK`, and `VLINK` are attributes to the `BODY` tag. They control the following design elements:

    `BGCOLOR`: The background color of your page.

    `TEXT`: The color of text.

    `LINK`: The color of linked text, and the border around linked graphics that have not been visited yet.

    `ALINK`: Stands for **A**ctive **L**ink; it controls the color of the link while the mouse is pressed.

    `VLINK`: Stands for **V**isited **L**ink; the color tells your users which of the sites they have visited and which may be new to them.

Step 2: Save this file as index.html to replace the preceding exercise file. You can open the file from a browser locally from your hard drive or upload it to your server to check the results.

Chapter 4, "Web Color," goes into greater detail about color issues and aesthetics on the web.

Here's what the page looks like in Netscape when we use the `BODY` tag. If this figure were printed in color, you would notice that some of the links are yellow, and some are blue. These colors are controlled by the `LINK` and `VLINK` attributes in the `BODY` tag. `LINK` is for links that have not yet been visited, and `VLINK` is for links that have already been visited by the user's browser.

Using a Background Pattern

You can also use a pattern for a background instead of just a flat color. This is done with the BACKGROUND attribute to the BODY tag. When you use a background image, it is displayed repeatedly as tiles until the entire display area is filled. This presents both challenges and opportunities for web designers. We'll teach you how to include a background pattern in the following exercise, and you can learn all the nuances and variations of this technique in Chapter 6, "Tiles."

With a background graphic, the BODY tag looks like this:

```
<BODY TEXT="#FFFFCC" BGCOLOR="#669999" LINK="#CCCC66"
ALINK="#FFFF00" VLINK="#330033" BACKGROUND="tile.gif">
```

Notice that we didn't remove the BGCOLOR attribute. It still serves two purposes:

- Although certain browsers do not render background images, these browsers may still render the background color; and

- In some browsers, the page starts to display before the background image is loaded. Leaving in a BGCOLOR ensures that the page displays with a background color that is close to the background image's dominant color, so there is less of a shock to the user when the image finally appears.

▶ e x e r c i s e

Adding a Background Tile

Copy the tile.gif from the chap02 folder of the
<chd> CD-ROM into the ducks folder on your hard
drive. Type in the following HTML (or change your
existing "index.html" file):

```
<HTML>
<HEAD>
<TITLE>Ducks in a Row Homepage</TITLE>
</HEAD>
<BODY TEXT="#FFFFCC" BGCOLOR="#669999"
LINK="#CCCC66" ALINK="#FFFF00"
VLINK="#330033" BACKGROUND="tile.gif">
<H1>Welcome to Ducks in a Row
Online!</H1>
<P> Rubber stamps or rubber duckies? Feel
free to splash around to find out what
we're about...
<P><A HREF="company.html">
<IMG SRC="ylogo1.gif" BORDER=0></A>
<P>Check out the <A HREF="http://www.
stampzone.com/">
RUBBER STAMP ZONE</A> - an out-of-site
rubber stamp page
</BODY>
</HTML>
```

Save this file as index.html to replace the preceding
exercise file. You can open the file from a browser
locally from your hard drive or upload it to your
server to check the results.

Here's the page with the background image installed.

Troubleshooting Tip: If this exercise didn't work,
be sure that the file tile.gif is copied into the active
ducks folder or directory.

Chapter 6, "Tiles," covers tile creation and aesthetic issues in much greater depth.

▸ chapter two summary

Now that you have a basic idea of what HTML is and how it works, take some time to experiment with the page. Change things around. Add text and different graphics. This is the best way to learn any new language.

When you've taken time to learn about the elements that were covered in this chapter, you will be anxious to learn about all the rest of the tags and features that HTML supports.

Subsequent chapters cover all the major groups of HTML tags and cover many of the areas we touched upon in this chapter in much greater depth.

*"If I ever get out of here,
I'm going to Katmandu."*
—*Bob Seger*

Speedy Graphics
small, fast, and good

Authoring for the web is the first time most computer artists have to be concerned about file sizes. What this boils down to is that most people understandably don't know how to make small graphics, so most of the graphics found on the web are too big. Large file sizes equal slow downloading speeds. A useful rule-of-thumb (albeit, not 100% accurate) is that every kilobyte of data takes about a second to download for the average user. For example, using this measurement, a 30k file would take approximately 1/2 minute to download. This is more true on slower connections (28.8 and lower) than on faster connections (ISDN and higher), but as much as high bandwidth and faster connection options are hyped and touted in the industry, the majority of the web audience is still in the slow connection category.

You've surely explored the web and run into pages that take too long to load. Don't let your pages commit the same mistake! It doesn't matter if your site has stunning graphics; if they are too slow, very few people will stick around long enough to wait for them to load.

Speedy Graphics

How to Read the True File Size

A new web design activity will include measuring web images by kilobytes. For those who like number crunching, a **kilobyte** is 1,024 bytes; a **megabyte** is 1,048,576 bytes (1,024k); and a **gigabyte** is 1,073,741,824 bytes (1,024mb). Graphics measuring in megabytes and gigabytes are obviously not acceptable for web delivery. Because of this, you'll often get the directive from a client to keep page sizes within a certain file size limit. Or you might have an internal goal of not exceeding 30k per page (another good rule-of-thumb). There's no set rule about how many kilobytes a single image should contain, but it's often necessary to understand how to read the file size of a document if you're trying to make it fall within a certain target range of acceptability.

```
584K/733K     ▶
```

How can you be sure of the number of kilobytes in an image? Most Photoshop users think the readout in the lower-left corner of a document informs them about the file size. Not true! These numbers relate to the amount of RAM Photoshop is using internally for the entire, uncompressed image.

	rilly small		
Name	**Size**	**Kind**	**Label**
ps numbers	11K	Adobe Photoshop™...	—
radio.pict	132K	Adobe Photoshop™...	—
radiopict.dump	33K	Adobe Photoshop™...	—
radiopict.get info	44K	Adobe Photoshop™...	—

You also might look to your hard drive for the file size. Notice that the file size numbers are all nicely rounded figures: 11k, 33k, and 132k. Your computer rounds up the size of a file to the next largest number depending on how large your hard drive partition is. Have you ever had a file read two different file sizes on a hard drive and a floppy? That's because the computer allocates space in larger chunks on your hard disk.

radiopict.get info Info

radiopict.get info

Kind : Adobe Photoshop™ 3.0.4 document
Size : 44K on disk (36,152 bytes used)

Where : Homegrrrl: .Graphics For the Web: .chapters: C/05 Rilly Rilly Sm ƒ: rilly small:

On a Mac, the only way to get information about the true byte size of a file is to do a Get Info command. First, highlight the file you want to check in the Finder, go to the File menu, and then choose Get Info.

Name	Size	Type	Modified
▢ Psp		File Folder	8/11/95 2:02 PM
_mssetup.exe	10KB	Application	3/23/92 12:00 AM
_mstest.exe	88KB	Application	3/23/92 12:00 AM
216.gif	14KB	Corel PHOTO-PAIN...	10/3/96 9:39 AM
acset.BMP	2,305KB	Bitmap Image	6/23/96 4:30 PM
acset.PCX	444KB	Corel PHOTO-PAIN...	6/23/96 5:01 PM
aolaln1.PCT	106KB	PCT File	10/15/95 7:53 AM
aolaln2.PCT	103KB	PCT File	10/15/95 7:53 AM
aolaln3.PCT	101KB	PCT File	10/15/95 7:53 AM
aolbgtx.PCT	112KB	PCT File	10/15/95 7:52 AM
aolpat.PCT	124KB	PCT File	10/15/95 7:52 AM
aoltb.PCT	95KB	PCT File	10/15/95 7:51 AM

When using Windows NT or 95, the file size shown in the folder directory is rounded to the nearest kilobyte.

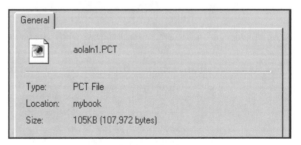

General

aolaln1.PCT

Type: PCT File
Location: mybook
Size: 105KB (107,972 bytes)

To get the most accurate reading, click the file name using the right mouse button and select Properties from the popup menu. Here you will find the true byte size.

◗ note

To Icon or Not to Icon?

On a Macintosh, Photoshop typically saves images with an icon. The icon is a small, visual representation of what the image looks like, which the file references. Photoshop icons take up a little extra room on your hard drive. This ultimately won't matter because when you send the files to your server, you'll transmit them as raw data, which will strip off the icon anyway. If your goal is to get a more accurate reading of the true file size, however, you should set your preferences in Photoshop to not save an icon.

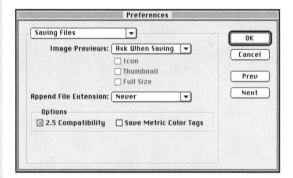

To set your preferences to not save the icon, choose File:Preferences:General. In the General dialog box, set the Image Previews to Ask When Saving.

▶ **note**

GIF Pronunciation

The definitive last word on the pronunciation of GIF from the author himself!

Sent: Wednesday, August 06, 1997 2:37 AM
To: Steve Wilhite
Subject: GIF pronunciation

Hello Steve,
Hope you don't mind that I've contacted you—
I got your email address from Jack Paulus, who
heard me speak about the GIF pronunciation
controversy at SIGGRAPH. I'm the author of a
series of books on web graphics, and am very
curious if you would end the controversy for
me and my readers. Is it a soft G as in "jiffy" or
a hard g, as in "gift"? Enquiring minds want to
know! Thanks.
Lynda

From: Steve Wilhite
To: 'Lynda Weinman'
Subject: RE: GIF pronunciation
Date: Mon, 11 Aug 1997 17:04:55 -0400

a soft G as in "jiffy"

From: lynda@lynda.com
SMTP: lynda@lynda.com]
Sent: Monday, August 11, 1997 11:53 PM
To: Steve Wilhite
Subject: RE: GIF pronunciation

Thanks so much. Now, for another question—
if you don't mind. Why a soft G, if the G in GIF
stands for Graphics? I get asked this question
often as well ;-)
-lynda

From: Steve Wilhite
To: "Lynda Weinman"
Subject: RE: GIF pronunciation
Date: Tue, 12 Aug 1997 09:44:05 -0400

That is the way I pronounced from day one
and it stuck. No other reason.

How GIF Compression Works

The GIF file-compression algorithm offers impressive file size reduction, but the degree of file size savings has a lot to do with how you create your GIF images. Understanding how GIF's internal compression scheme (LZW—Lempel **Z**iv **W**elch) works is the first step in this process.

LZW compression looks for repeated patterns that it can represent with small tokens of data. When it encounters areas in an image that repeat or don't change, it can implement much higher compression. This process is similar to another type of compression called **r**un-**l**ength **e**ncoding (RLE—used in BMP, TIFF, and PCX formats), but LZW writes, stores, and retrieves its code a little differently. Because GIF images are stored in horizontal rows of pixels, the compression algorithm will find more uniform runs to compress when the image has repeating horizontal patterns.

 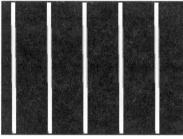 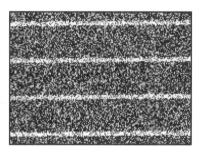

Here's an original image saved as a GIF that contains horizontal lines. It is 6.7k.

Here's the same image flipped on its side so that the lines are vertical. It's a whopping 42% bigger at 11.5k!

Try adding noise to the original. You'll be adding 88% to the file size. This one is 56k!

So what does the line test really teach?

- Artwork that has horizontal regularity compresses better than artwork that doesn't.

- Anything with noise will more than quadruple a GIF image's file size.

- Large areas of flat color compress well, although complicated line work and dithering do not.

Making Small GIFs

The GIF file format works best on images that are composed of line art or flat color. In terms of making small GIF files, what can you do to ensure that you have large areas of flat color? Several factors can produce large GIF files, and we will look at these culprits: too many colors, anti-aliasing, and dithering.

Reducing Colors in GIFs

The two most valuable techniques for making small GIF files is to use the least amount of colors necessary and the least amount of dithering. The following exercises teach you how to do this. Compare the results of your efforts to our handy, full-color compression tables, which can be found in the chap03 folder of the <chd> CD-ROM, inside the folder titled compression.tables.

▶ exercise

Reducing Colors Using Photoshop 4.0

The image01.pct file seen to the right is located in the chap03 folder on the <chd> CD-ROM.

Step 1: In Photoshop, open image01.pct file from the chap03 folder.

Step 2: Select **Image:Mode:Indexed Color**.

Step 3: Choose **Palette:Adaptive**.

Step 4: Choose **Diffusion:None**.

Step 5: Type in a value lower than 256 in the **Colors** field.

Step 6: Choose **Edit:Save a Copy:Format: Compuserve GIF.**

Step 7: Be sure to put the .gif extension at the end of the file name.

Step 8: Read the true file size of the resulting image. Have you made it as small an image as you could have? Check your results against the compression.tables folder inside the chap03 folder of the <chd> CD-ROM.

image01.pct **is located in the** chap03 **folder on the <chd> CD-ROM. Experiment with this file to see how small you can make it using the techniques covered in this exercise.**

▶ exercise

Reducing Colors Using Paint Shop Pro

The image01.pict file seen in the previous exercise to the left is located inside the chap03 folder on the <chd> CD-ROM.

Step 1: From Paint Shop Pro, open the image01.pct file from the chap03 folder.

Step 2: Select **Colors:Decrease Color Depth**: **X Colors**.

Step 3: Reduction Method:Nearest Neighbor.

Step 4: Leave the check boxes empty for Boost **Marked Colors**, **Include Windows Colors**, and **Reduce Color Bleeding**.

Step 5: Type a different value lower than 256 in the **Palette** field.

Step 6: Choose **Edit:Save As:List of File Type**: **GIF-Compuserve:File Sub-Format**: **Version89a-Non Interlaced**.

Step 7: Read the true file size of the resulting image. Have you made as small an image as you could have? Check your results against the compression.tables folder inside the chap03 folder of the <chd> CD-ROM.

▶ note

Bit Depth Dilemma?

When you enter custom values into bit-depth settings, it isn't necessary to round up or down to the nearest fixed value:

> **8-bit**=256 colors
>
> **7-bit**=128 colors
>
> **6-bit**=64 colors
>
> **5-bit**=32 colors
>
> **4-bit**=16 colors
>
> **3-bit**=8 colors
>
> **2-bit**=4 colors
>
> **1-bit**=2 colors

An acceptable custom value can be any integer, such as 57 colors, or 93, but insignificant file savings will occur between the bit-depth fixed values. In other words, a value of 93 will still create a 7-bit graphic palettebecause it's higher than the value 64, which defines 6-bit. The file savings between saving a GIF with a value of 93 colors instead of 128 colors will not be significant. The rule of thumb? There isn't one. Don't stress about reducing colors between the bit-depth fixed settings. If you do arrive at a custom number, it won't hurt anything.

Anti-Aliasing Versus Aliasing

We've established that the number of colors in an image affects file size. Great, you may be saying to yourself, but how do I really put this to practice when I'm creating artwork? One technique that greatly reduces the number of colors in an image is choosing to create aliased graphics instead of anti-aliased.

Here's an example of aliased text. The file totaled 3.8k when saved as a GIF.

Here's an example of anti-aliased text. The file totaled 5k when saved as a GIF. The anti-aliasing caused the file to be 24% larger!

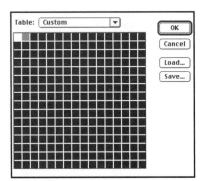

A close-up view: Aliasing does not disguise the jaggy nature of pixel-based artwork.

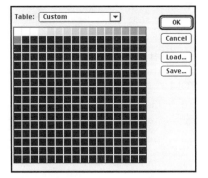

A close-up view: This close-up shows that anti-aliasing creates a blended edge. This blending disguises the square-pixel-based nature of computer artwork.

The aliased artwork used only 4 colors.

The anti-aliased artwork used 18 colors.

It's often assumed that artwork will always look better if it has anti-aliased edges. This is simply not true! Artists have never had to factor size of files into their design considerations. Having a file load 24% faster is nothing to balk at. In many cases, aliased artwork looks just as good as anti-aliased artwork, and choosing between the two approaches is something that web designers should consider when necessary.

This image is 571 x 499 pixels and only takes up 9k. Why? It has only two colors due to using aliased artwork.

Here's the aliased graphic in the context of a finished page. Not bad for a very low overhead effect.

As well as considering whether to use aliased or anti-aliased graphics, you should also always work with browser-safe colors when creating illustration-based artwork for the web. Examples of how browser-safe colors improve the quality of illustrations are demonstrated in Chapter 4, "Web Color."

Photoshop Aliased Type Exercise

Try your hand at creating aliased type in Photoshop by following these steps:

Step 1: Select **File:New File**.

Step 2: Choose 500 pixels by 200 pixels, 72 dpi, Against White.

Step 3: Click on the Type tool.

Step 4: Click on the screen to establish where you will type. You will be prompted to choose a typeface.

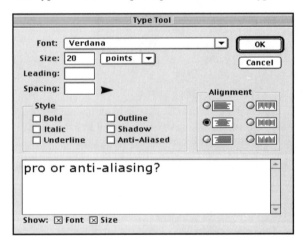

Step 5: Be sure to uncheck **Anti-Aliased**.

Step 6: Type a line of text.

Step 7: When you're done, save the file as a GIF. Read the file size.

Step 8: To compare the file savings of creating aliased type rather than anti-aliased type, you'll find a file called aatype.gif in the chap03 folder of the <chd> CD-ROM.

Paint Shop Pro Aliased Type Exercise

Try your hand at creating aliased type in Paint Shop Pro by following these steps:

Step 1: Select **File:New File**.

Step 2: Choose 500 pixels by 200 pixels, 72 dpi, Against White.

Step 3: Click on the Type tool. Click on the screen to establish where you'll type.

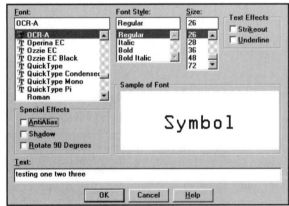

Step 4: Be sure to uncheck **Anti-Aliased**.

Step 5: Pick a font and type a line of text.

Step 6: When you're done, save the file as a GIF. Read the file size.

Step 7: To compare the file savings of creating aliased type rather than anti-aliased type, you'll find a file called aatype.gif in the chap03 folder of the <chd> CD-ROM.

To Dither or Not to Dither?

Dithering methods play a huge role in creating smaller GIFs. Any type of "visual noise", such as dithering or Photoshop noise filters, adds to the file size. Unfortunately, when you're working with photographic-based GIFs, dithering of one type or another must be employed to reduce the 24-bit color file to the 8-bit or lower bit-depth threshold of GIF.

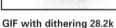

GIF with dithering 28.2k   **GIF without dithering 21.5k**

In the example above, the GIF that did not use dithering is smaller. The problem is that it looks awful! Sometimes file savings does not warrant loss of quality. When a photograph contains glows, feathered edges, or subtle gradations, you have to use dithering when converting from 24-bit to 8-bit in order to maintain quality.

GIF with dithering: 38.3k   **GIF with Photoshop's Dither None method: 27.2k**

There's almost no objectionable difference between the above two images, regardless of whether a dithering method is used to convert to 8-bit color or Photoshop's **Dither None** method was chosen. Why? This image has a lot of solid areas of color to begin with. The file savings between 38.3k and 32.3k is not huge, but the non-dither method will still yield a smaller file size.

GIF Compression Tables

These two HTML documents show the file size savings by adjusting the color depth, and choosing dithering methods. These images were compressed using Photoshop 4.0.

This page can be viewed in color by opening the file dgif.html inside the web browser of your choice. It's located inside the compression_tables folder inside the chap03 folder of the <chd> CD-ROM.

This page can be viewed in color by opening the file ngif.html inside the web browser of your choice. It's located inside the compression_tables folder inside the chap03 folder of the <chd> CD-ROM.

Dither Settings in Photoshop

In Photoshop, in order to choose whether or not to dither, you must enter the information in the Indexed Color dialog box, which is located under the **Image:Mode:Indexed Color** menu. After the Indexed Color dialog appears, the dither setting is located under the Options setting.

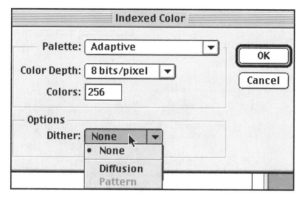

Dithering settings for Photoshop 4.0 are located under Options in the Index Color dialog box.

Dither Settings in Paint Shop Pro

When you select **Reduce Color Depth** from the **Color** menu in Paint Shop Pro, you can also set dithering and other options. Here's a definition list to help you decipher the terminology:

> **The Nearest Color:** This reduction method is the same as Dither None in Photoshop. It creates a banded appearance.

> **Error Diffusion:** This will create dithering based on the image itself.

Making Small JPEG Files

JPEGs are recommended for images that are photographic or use continuous-tone artwork. A key difference between GIF and JPEG is the fact that you can save JPEGs in a variety of compression levels. This means that more or less compression can be applied to an image, depending on which looks best.

The nuances of saving small GIFs are much more complex than the nuances of saving small JPEGs. Your single decision is how much or how little JPEG compression to apply to the image. Fewer number of colors in a JPEG could potentially increase file size because JPEG compression was designed for complex, continuous-tone images.

In Photoshop, the more compression you assign to an image (via a slider bar with values from 0-10) the smaller it becomes. Low quality indicates a high amount of compression, and maximum quality a low amount. In addition to these settings, Photoshop offers three different options for JPEG compression:

Baseline: Standard JPEG compression.

Optimized Baseline: Uses Photoshop to create maximum color optimization.

Progressive: Creates an interlaced JPEG where you can define the number of progressive scans.

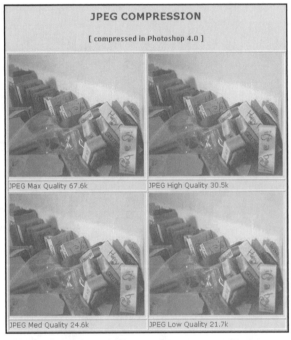

JPEG COMPRESSION

[compressed in Photoshop 4.0]

JPEG Max Quality 67.6k

JPEG High Quality 30.5k

JPEG Med Quality 24.6k

JPEG Low Quality 21.7k

You can see by this test that there's not a whole lot of difference between low quality and high quality in this example. Many people are reluctant to reduce their JPEGs to the lowest quality settings, but with most photographic images low settings work well.

▶ e x e r c i s e

JPEG Compression in Photoshop 4.0

Setting JPEG compression levels in Photoshop occurs after you save the file. It's not very intuitive, so here's an exercise to walk you through the steps.

Step 1: Open the image02.pct file from the chap03 folder of the <chd> CD-ROM.

Step 2: Select **File:Save a Copy As:JPEG**.

Step 3: You are presented with various options. Experiment with quality settings and save a variety of results.

Step 4: Open the files you just created to check file sizes and quality.

▶ e x e r c i s e

JPEG Compression in Paint Shop Pro

Setting JPEG compression levels in Paint Shop Pro occurs after you save the file. It's not very intuitive, here's an exercise to walk you through the steps.

Step 1: Open the image02.pct file from the chap03 folder of the <chd> CD-ROM.

Step 2: Select **File:Save As**.

Step 3: Select **Save As Type:JPG**.

Step 4: Press the **Options** button and make sure the **GIF/JPG** tab is selected.

Step 5: You are presented with options for the dpi (**d**ots **p**er **i**nch) and compression level. A higher numbered compression level makes files smaller with lower quality. Experiment with the settings and save a variety of results.

Step 6: Open the files to check file sizes and quality.

Note: Paint Shop Pro does not allow you to create optimized or progressive JPEGs.

▶ note

Problems with Progressive JPEGs

Progresive JPEGs render in stages, like interlaced GIFs. Many people like using them because they give the illusion of loading faster than a standard JPEG. In reality they take just as long (if not longer), but your viewer has the advantage of seeing a low res version of the image while she waits for it to fully download. The one serious drawback is if you are targeting an audience that might be looking at your site with an older browser. Any browser before a 3.0 release does not recognize progressive JPEGs. In fact, they produce the dreaded broken image icon—meaning your audience has no chance to see the image at all.

JPEG or GIF?

As we've said, use GIF for graphics and JPEG for photographs. Although there are good reasons for saving photographs as GIF (animation, transparency, and interlacing), there are no good reasons for saving graphics as JPEGs, unless the graphics are combined with photographs. With photographic content in general, don't be afraid to try low-quality settings; the file size savings is usually substantial, and the quality penalties are not too steep.

Graphic GIF

Graphic JPEG

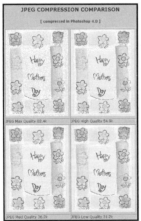

Photograph GIF

Photograph JPEG

Here is compelling evidence that proves that graphics compress better, and look better, if GIF compression is used. You can view the JPEG comparison by opening the file jpgcomp.html **from the** compression_tables **folder inside the** chap03 **directory of the <chd> CD-ROM.**

Here is compelling evidence that proves that photographs compress better, and look better, if JPEG compression is used. You can view the GIF comparison by opening the file dgifcomp.html **from the** compression_tables **folder inside the** chap03 **directory of the <chd> CD-ROM.**

DeBabelizer

Many people sing the praises of DeBabelizer because it has more features for optimizing graphics and working with palettes than Photoshop or other popular imaging programs. There are two versions of DeBabelizer: DeBabelizer for Macintosh and DeBabelizer Pro for Windows 95/NT.

DeBabelizer has, for lack of a better word, an interesting interface. It's not so much the interface that's hard to learn; it's understanding all the options that are presented—many of which use terms that are unfamiliar to the average web publisher.

Over the years, DeBabelizer has built a reputation as a must-have program for professional multimedia and web producers. In part, this is because it has so many more options than other imaging programs. DeBabelizer's reputation is well-earned for creating smaller files than other imaging programs, due to more flexible optimization capabilities.

The learning curve for either version of DeBabelizer is steep. We only recommend this program if you have lots of time on your hands to learn a program or have lots of images (as in the case of a catalog) where the extra file savings will really add up over the scope of your web site's graphics.

We have provided some exercises for learning DeBabelizer. You'll find a lite version of DeBabelizer and DeBabelizer Pro in the Software folder on the <chd> CD-ROM, if you want to try them out.

▶ e x e r c i s e

GIFs in DeBabelizer Pro for Windows

Step 1: File:Open:Image md.pct.

Step 2: Choose **Palette:Reduce Colors**.

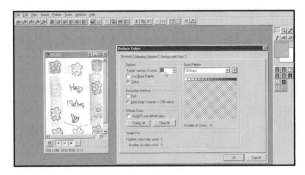

Step 3: The Reduce Colors window appears. Choose a target number of colors. We think this image looks fine at 32 colors, but the purpose of this exercise is for you to try your hand at optimizing a GIF in DeBabelizer. You can enter the value of 32, or any other value to experiment. The base palette can be either selected or ignored. What is a base palette, you may well ask? **Base palettes** are fixed colors that you can set, such as the browser-safe palette (called the **Netscape Palette** in DeBabelizer) or a grayscale palette. Many multimedia developers need base palettes in order to function properly on specific operating systems. If you don't want to use a base palette(in this case, you don't) make sure the Use **Base Palette** check box is unchecked.

Step 4: Choose a **Reduction Method**. Fast won't optimize as well as Slow. Experiment with this image to see if there's any significant difference between choosing Fast or Slow.

Step 5: Click on the **Dithering Options** tab. Select a dithering method. Diffusion is the default setting and mirrors the Photoshop diffusion dithering method. Albi is another option and results in higher contrast. The amount of dither defaults to 87%. If you don't like the results, choose **Edit: Undo Reduce Colors** (control Z) and re-adjust the slider.

Step 6: Click on the **Background Color** tab. Select the Don't dither background color option if you want to prevent a single color within your document from dithering.

Step 7: Click on **OK** to reduce the number of colors. If you don't like the results, try again.

Step 8: When you're ready to save, choose **File:Save as** and then select the **GIF** format.

JPEGs in DeBabelizer Pro for Windows

Step 1: Choose **File:Open** and then select md.pct from the chap03 folder of the <chd> CD-ROM.

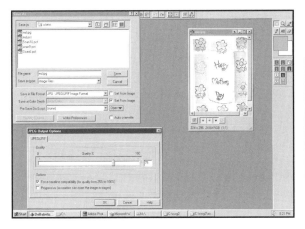

Step 2: Choose **File:Save As** and then select **JPEG**. Click on Writer Preferences and try some different compression settings on the Quality Slider.

Step 3: Check your results by re-opening the newly saved JPEG file. Try some different compression settings and check the file saving and quality results.

GIFs in DeBabelizer for Macintosh

Step 1: Upon selecting **File:Open**, a scary looking window of unknown functions and buttons appears! Click on the pull-down menu located beneath the **Desktop** button to locate the chap03 folder on the <chd> CD-ROM. Double-click on the md.pct file.

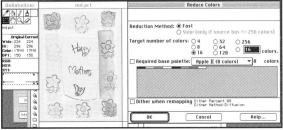

Step 2: Under the **Palette** menu, choose **Reduce Colors.**

Step 3: Choose the **Reduction Method** (Fast is the only option if the image contains more than 256 colors, like this one) and the **Target number of colors**. You will not need a base palette, so leave that check box unchecked. If you want the file to dither, choose **Dither when remapping**. **Tip:** If you want to change the dither options, choose **Palette:Dither Options** and change them before you do this step.

Step 4: Choose **File:Save As:GIF:Non-Interlaced**. Be sure to check the file sizes and experiment with different settings.

PNG

PNG (**P**ortable **N**etwork **G**raphics, or more fondly known as PNGs Not GIF) holds great promise as a new web file format. The **W3C** (**W**orld **W**ide **W**eb **C**onsortium at http://www.w3.org/pub/WWW/Press/PNG-PR.en.html) has made a formal endorsement of PNG, which strongly indicates that Netscape and MSIE will support it as an inline file format in the near future. As of this writing, PNG is supported in Netscape Navigator 4 with a plug-in from **Seigel & Gale** http://www.siegelgale.com/. Internet Explorer does recognize PNG files, but does not display PNG transparency or recognize gamma tagging.

PNG uses a lossless compression method, meaning that no quality loss is incurred when it's applied to images. PNG is compressed by using any of a number of pre-compression filters and is then decompressed when viewed. This enables PNG to retain every original detail and pixel with no loss of quality.

Unlike GIF or JPEG, PNG can be stored at many different bit depths by using different storage methods. GIF, for example, can be stored only in 8-bit or lower bit depths. JPEGs must be stored in 24-bit, no lower. PNG can be stored in 8-bit, 24-bit, or 32-bit. This makes PNG one of the most flexible formats available for web images, and also somewhat more complicated to use. Expect a learning curve before you can use PNG files effectively for your web images.

PNG Resources

The Siegel & Gale PNG Live plug-in for Netscape Navigator 4.
http://codelab.siegelgale.com/solutions/pnglive2.html

The PNG Home Page
http://www.wco.com/~png/

The PNG Specification at W3C
http://www.w3.org/TR/REC-png-multi.html

Gamma Correction

The PNG format also supports gamma correction for properly displaying images on different platforms without loosing contrast or brightness in the translation. Differences in gamma between different platforms can make an image seem darker or lighter on a platform other than the one it was created on. The PNG format has the capacity to store a value that represents the gamma of the system on which the image was created. This value then can be used by the displaying system to correct for the image's gamma value, if known.

In order for all that to work, both the creating and displaying systems must know their own gamma, which is usually not the case in today's web world. This is a case of a great feature that, at the time this chapter was written, was unsupported.

Alpha-Channel Transparency

The PNG format has the capacity to store a variable transparency value known as alpha-channel transparency. This value allows your images to have up to 256 different levels of partial transparency (or translucency). For example, the image in the accompanying screenshot uses an alpha-channel to present a drop shadow that displays correctly against this irregular background.

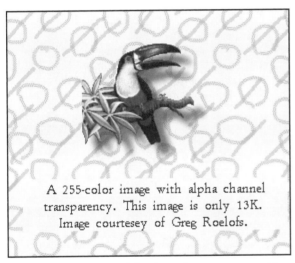

This toucan image uses alpha-channel transparency and is. from Greg Roelofs's PNG Resource at http://www.wco.com/~png/.

One common misconception about PNG images is that you must use a 32-bit palette to use alpha-channel transparency. This is not true. The PNG format allows any entry in any palette to represent any channel, either Red, Green, Blue, or Alpha (these palettes are called RGBA instead of RGB).

In fact, the image of the Toucan in the screen shot to the left is only 12.5k in size because it uses an 8-bit RGBA palette, where some of the entries are used to represent the transparency mask, instead of colors. We cover this subject in more detail in Chapter 8, "Transparency."

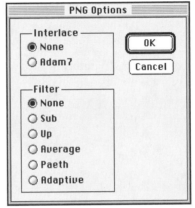

PNG Compression Options in Photoshop

Interlace

None: No Interlacing

Adam7: Adam Costello wrote the interlacing scheme, and 7 refers to the way it interlaces (7 passes over the image). This name is actually part of the PNG spec, and since PNG may someday support alternate interlacing schemes, the naming scheme used is somewhat important. In addition, the Adam7 interlace scheme differs vastly from the scan line scheme used in GIF, so it seems important to differentiate it. An interlaced GIF file comes in by lines, and a PNG file "dissolves" in. Adam7 interlacing adds somewhat to the file size.

Filters

Filters are applied to the image before compression to prepare it for optimum compression. To obtain the optimum compression for an image, you may want to experiment with these filters. PNG is a new file format, so there is little practical experience to guide us in predicting how filters affect file size.

PNG also has an adaptive filtering scheme that allows for filters to be applied separately to each scan line in an image. This means that an optimum compression can be realized when different filters are applied to different horizontal regions of an image.

None: Like the name says, this filter offers no added compression.

Sub: Transmits the difference between each byte and the value of the corresponding byte of the prior pixel. This filter may work well for images that have smooth, continuous tones, as is the case with computer-generated gradients.

Up: Is just like the Sub filter except that the pixel immediately above the current pixel, rather than just to its left, is used as the predictor. Use this filter if your continuous tones are vertical; use Sub if they are horizontal.

Average: Uses the average of the two neighboring pixels (left and above) to predict the value of a pixel.

Paeth: Is named after Alan Paeth, the originator of this compression method. The Paeth filter computes a simple linear function of the three neighboring pixels (left, above, and upper left) and then chooses the neighboring pixel closest to the computed value.

Adaptive: Strictly speaking, Adaptive is not a filter in its own right. It applies each of the other filters on a scan line-by-scan line basis and then chooses the best among them for that line. In most circumstances, this process results in the smallest files.

Note: The PNG specification recommends that 24-bit images use Adaptive, and indexed (8-bit and lower) images use None.

The major drawback of the PNG format is that none of the major browsers currently support it. Both Netscape and Microsoft have been promising PNG support for the past two versions, and so far neither has delivered the full spec (however, plug-ins are available). The reason is probably that it takes a lot of programming to properly support the format. It will be worth the wait if the support that comes includes gamma correction and alpha-channel transparency.

▶ **warning**

Large 24-bit PNG Files

On low-resolution images for the web, the quality difference between JPEG and PNG is imperceptible. The fact that PNG uses lossless compression almost always results in much larger files than JPEG for 24-bit images. Our recommendation is that you always choose JPEG over PNG for photographic material. The only time PNG compression compares favorably in terms of file size is when it is used in 8-bit and lower bit depths. PNG has two advantages over JPEG and GIF: It can store gamma information to adjust automatically for the gamma (see Glossary) of its target platform, and it supports 8-bit transparency (otherwise known as alpha channels). You can find examples of PNG transparency in the Alpha Channel section of this chapter.

▶ chapter three summary

You can create great-looking graphics that are also small and quick to download if you pay attention to what file formats you use and what options you select when saving them. In summary, remember the following:

• Try to keep your pages under 30 kilobytes total for all elements.

• Is the image a photograph? Use a JPEG file.

• Is the image flat-color? Use GIF or PNG.

• Is the image animated? Use GIF.

• Does the image need alpha-channel transparency? Use PNG (but only if your audience supports it in their browsers!).

• Make sure you use the smallest possible color palette in your GIF and PNG images, for the smallest possible file size.

• You will find occasional exceptions to all these rules, but they are an excellent place to start.

• In the next chapter, we look at the other side of the graphics equation, with a discussion of color use and the browser-safe color palette.

4

*"Now I've discovered a new palette,
a new canvas: light.
My brushes are
a keyboard and math."*
—Lee Harrington

> ▶ **this chapter**
>
> *browser-safe color*
> *hexadecimal color*
> *color for illustrations*
> *color for photographs*
> *html color tags*

Web Color
safe specs

In "real life," most people would consider choosing colors for artwork, text, and backgrounds a fun and creative act. In "web design life," choosing color is often more of a challenge, as you must field cross-platform color management differences.

Creating color artwork for the web is distinct from other color delivery mediums because you're publishing your work to people's screens instead of a printed pages. The cross-platform realities of monitor differences can cause your artwork to render differently on different operating systems.

Computer screen-based color is composed of projected light and pixels instead of ink pigments, dot patterns, and screen percentages. In some ways, working with screen-based color can be more fun than working with printed inks. No waiting for color proofs or working with CMYK values which are much less vibrant than RGB. No high-resolution files. No dot screens to deal with. While presenting graphics via a computer screen is a lot easier in some ways, don't be fooled into thinking that what you see on your screen is what other people will see on theirs. Just like its print-based counterpart, computer screen-based color has its own set of gremlins.

Designers Versus Everyone Else

A huge irony in web design is that most designers have much better systems than the general computer audience they design for. A typical graphic designer's workstation generally consists of lots of RAM, a larger-than-average monitor, a fast processor, and a video card that supports thousands or millions of colors. The majority of your web audience doesn't use their computer for graphics. They might use it for word processing, spreadsheets, or databases where lots of color, RAM, screen real estate, and fast speeds aren't critical.

The reality is that most of your audience will see your web site through 256-colored (8-bit) glasses. Even if you create artwork by using any of the millions of colors at your disposal, those visitors who have limited color systems couldn't see what you created even if they wanted to.

So, what you see on your screen might not be what everyone you design for sees on their screens. It's important to understand what havoc 8-bit web browsers can wreak on your page design so that you can build your images and color choices in a more indestructible manner.

Creating color images and screens for the web can be done without understanding the medium's limitations, but the results may not be what you are hoping for. In addition to teaching you the HTML behind web color, the focus of this chapter is to describe the web and computer color environment and to clue you in on known pitfalls and solutions that offer maximum control over how your artwork is seen.

Browser-Safe Specs

Browser software is your window to the web. You can't see web pages without the browser, so it plays a huge role in how your images are displayed, especially when viewed on 256-color systems.

In 256-color mode, most popular browsers (Netscape Navigator, Mosaic, and Internet Explorer) share a common palette. They work with the system palettes of each respective platform: Mac, Windows, and Win95. This means that any artwork you create will be forced into a variety of different palettes, depending on which operating system it is viewed from.

Mac System Palette

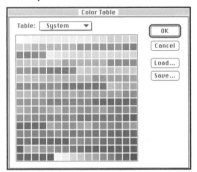

Win95 Palette

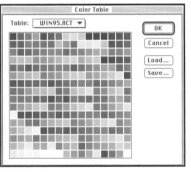

Windows Palette

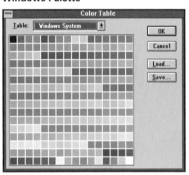

Although these three palettes look entirely different, they share 216 common colors. If you use the shared colors, referred to in this book as "browser-safe" colors, you will eliminate a lot of cross-platform inconsistencies with color artwork published over the web.

Thankfully, there are common colors found within each respective 256 system palette—216 common colors, in fact. Each operating system reserves 40 colors out of the possible 256 for its own use. This means that if you stick to the 216 common colors, they will be universally honored between browsers, operating systems, and computer platforms.

What Does the Browser-Safe Palette Look Like?

The 216-color palette for the web has only 6 red values, 6 green values, and 6 blue values—each of which range in contrast. Sometimes this palette is referred to as the 6 × 6 × 6 palette, or the 6 × 6 × 6 cube. This system represents a predetermined palette that the browsers must use—and that can't be changed—when the browsers are in 256-color mode. If you create artwork with colors outside of this system, the browsers will alter your artwork to fit the cube when displayed on systems that are limited to 8-bit color.

If you work with browser-safe colors, keep these facts in mind:

- The RGB values found within the 216-color palette have some predictable similarities: The numbers are all formed from combinations of 0, 51, 102, 153, 204, and 255.

- The regularity of these numbers is even easier to see when viewed in hexadecimal: 00, 33, 66, 99, CC, and FF.

- These colors were picked for their mathematical properties—they are equally spaced in the available range of values—not for aesthetic reasons. Knowing the pattern of the numeric values is useful because you easily can check your code or image documents to see whether they contain these values or any values.

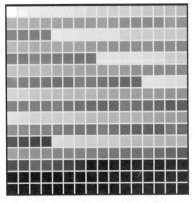

Notice how the browser-safe colors are organized by math? The organization is not useful when picking color combinations.

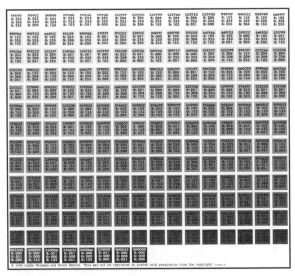

You'll find files, nhue.gif and nvalue.gif (shown here) in the chap04 folder of the <chd> CD-ROM. These files are organized by color and lights and darks, and are much more useful for aesthetic color picking.

> **note**

Do Browser-Safe Colors Really Matter?

You may think that all this hubbub over browser-safe colors does not apply to you. If you think your site will only be viewed from millions-of-color monitors (24-bit), then you might be right. It's always important to decide who your audience is before you design a site and create artwork that is appropriate for your viewers. There are some situations, such as if you have a site that might only appeal to graphic designers, or if the site is on a company intranet, where making the assumption that every visitor will be able to see 24-bit color is not unrealistic.

Our recommendation is that if you are going to pick colors for backgrounds, type, text, links, and illustrations, why not choose cross-platform compatible colors? The penalty of assuming your audience can view all the colors in the spectrum is that you loose control of how your artwork appears rather than grabbing color control before it has a chance to change what you've done. There may come a day years from now when everyone has video cards that support more than 256 colors, but today the majority of systems do not.

RGB Color

To create web page color schemes, you have to use hexadecimal (or simply, "hex") numbers in your HTML files. If you're scratching your head at this point, don't fret — most people who aren't programmers have never had to understand hex. Fortunately, it's not hard, just chalk it up to another web design skill you get to develop.

If you're used to picking color on the computer by using imaging software color pickers, chances are you have never had to pay much attention to the math used to represent the colors. If you choose RGB or CMYK, there's no reason to look at the numeric values behind your choices; instead, you're most likely used to basing your choices on personal taste, such as, "I like this blue-violetish color."

The RGB color system uses a series of three numbers to represent color. The numbers represent the intensity of the Red, Green, and Blue color components that are projected from the computer screen in each pixel. With 24-bit color, each number ranges from 0–255, which is 8 bits of storage in the computer. That's why the common color system used by designers is called 24-bit color (3 colors × 8 bits = 24 bits).

In most imaging software, including Photoshop and Paint Shop Pro, the RGB values are represented in decimal, or base-10. So when you see 164,56,146, you get that nice blue-violetish color you like so much. Those three numbers represent the Red, Green, and Blue components of the color, respectively.

You've probably never noticed that the numbers are in decimal because we have all used the decimal system so much in our lives that we consider it "normal." We have ten fingers to count on, so it is perfectly natural for us to count in base-10. Unless you took advanced math or computer science in school (or were one of the blessed few who got "new math" in the '60s), you probably never even considered the possibility of another number system.

Hexadecimal RGB

The numeric values of RGB are represented in hexadecimal for HTML. Hexadecimal is a base-16 number system. Just as the decimal system that you are already familiar with uses 10 different digits (0, 1, 2, 3, 4, 5, 6, 7, 8, and 9), the hexadecimal system uses 16 different digits (0, 1, 2, 3, 4, 5, 6, 7, 8, 9, A, B, C, D, E, and F). Letters are used for the digits over 9 rather than creating a whole new set of glyphs and pronunciations for everyone to learn.

Decimal Digits

| 0 | 1 | 2 | 3 | 4 | 5 | 6 | 7 | 8 | 9 |

Hexidecimal Digits

| 0 | 1 | 2 | 3 | 4 | 5 | 6 | 7 | 8 | 9 | A | B | C | D | E | F |

The hexadecimal digits greater than 9 have the equivalent values of the decimal numbers 10–15:

Decimal	Hex
0	0
1	1
2	2
3	3
4	4
5	5
6	6
7	7
8	8
9	9
10	A
11	B
12	C
13	D
14	E
15	F

Just as base-10 is natural for humans (who have five digits on each limb), hexadecimal is natural for computers, which readily work with multiples of two. The range of 0–F represents 16 possible different values, and 16 is as natural value for a computer as 10 is for a person.

Hexadecimal Colors in HTML

For HTML, colors are represented by three pairs of hexadecimal digits. Each pair of digits represents one of the RGB color components—Red first, then Green, and finally Blue. Just as the decimal representation of RGB colors uses a series of three values, so does the hexadecimal representation. But because the hexadecimal values are always two digits, there is no need for a comma to separate them.

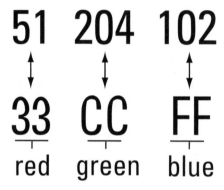

For example, the decimal color 51,204,102 would be 33CCFF in hex.

To the right is a helpful chart when converting RGB numbers (0–255) to hex. The browser-safe values are highlighted.

DEC	HEX	DEC	HEX	DEC	HEX	DEC	HEX	DEC	HEX	DEC	HEX
000	00	051	33	102	66	153	99	204	CC	255	FF
001	01	052	34	103	67	154	9A	205	CD		
002	02	053	35	104	68	155	9B	206	CE		
003	03	054	36	105	69	156	9C	207	CF		
004	04	055	37	106	6A	157	9D	208	D0		
005	05	056	38	107	6B	158	9E	209	D1		
006	06	057	39	108	6C	159	9F	210	D2		
007	07	058	3A	109	6D	160	A0	211	D3		
008	08	059	3B	110	6E	161	A1	212	D4		
009	09	060	3C	111	6F	162	A2	213	D5		
010	0A	061	3D	112	70	163	A3	214	D6		
011	0B	062	3E	113	71	164	A4	215	D7		
012	0C	063	3F	114	72	165	A5	216	D8		
013	0D	064	40	115	73	166	A6	217	D9		
014	0E	065	41	116	74	167	A7	218	DA		
015	0F	066	42	117	75	168	A8	219	DB		
016	10	067	43	118	76	169	A9	220	DC		
017	11	068	44	119	77	170	AA	221	DD		
018	12	069	45	120	78	171	AB	222	DE		
019	13	070	46	121	79	172	AC	223	DF		
020	14	071	47	122	7A	173	AD	224	E0		
021	15	072	48	123	7B	174	AE	225	E1		
022	16	073	49	124	7C	175	AF	226	E2		
023	17	074	4A	125	7D	176	B0	227	E3		
024	18	075	4B	126	7E	177	B1	228	E4		
025	19	076	4C	127	7F	178	B2	229	E5		
026	1A	077	4D	128	80	179	B3	230	E6		
027	1B	078	4E	129	81	180	B4	231	E7		
028	1C	079	4F	130	82	181	B5	232	E8		
029	1D	080	50	131	83	182	B6	233	E9		
030	1E	081	51	132	84	183	B7	234	EA		
031	1F	082	52	133	85	184	B8	235	EB		
032	20	083	53	134	86	185	B9	236	EC		
033	21	084	54	135	87	186	BA	237	ED		
034	22	085	55	136	88	187	BB	238	EE		
035	23	086	56	137	89	188	BC	239	EF		
036	24	087	57	138	8A	189	BD	240	F0		
037	25	088	58	139	8B	190	BE	241	F1		
038	26	089	59	140	8C	191	BF	242	F2		
039	27	090	5A	141	8D	192	C0	243	F3		
040	28	091	5B	142	8E	193	C1	244	F4		
041	29	092	5C	143	8F	194	C2	245	F5		
042	2A	093	5D	144	90	195	C3	246	F6		
043	2B	094	5E	145	91	196	C4	247	F7		
044	2C	095	5F	146	92	197	C5	248	F8		
045	2D	096	60	147	93	198	C6	249	F9		
046	2E	097	61	148	94	199	C7	250	FA		
047	2F	098	62	149	95	200	C8	251	FB		
048	30	099	63	150	96	201	C9	252	FC		
049	31	100	64	151	97	202	CA	253	FD		
050	32	101	65	152	98	203	CB	254	FE		

The browser-safe values appear in blue at the top of each column in this chart.

Hexadecimal Resources

Many resources for converting decimal RGB to hex exist on the web. There are two different options: Hex Charts, which typically show color swatches and their hex values, and Hex Converters, which allow a user to type decimal RGB values and then offer the hexadecimal conversion in return. Both options are covered in the following sections.

Web Hex Converters

A number of sites on the web let you plug in RGB values and then generate hex code for your values on-the-fly. This can be convenient when you're working and want a quick visualization of what a certain color scheme will look like. Some sites even go so far as to accept RGB input and then automatically output hex and HTML.

Inquisitor Mediarama's RGB-HEX Converter
http://www.echonyc.com/~xixax/Mediarama/hex.html

Test your hex color choices on-the-fly
http://www.hidaho.com/c3/

Click on any color and hex numbers appear
http://www.schnoggo.com/rgb2hex.html

Browser-Safe Color JavaScript Hex Converter
http://www.hanson-dodge.com/colors/index.html

Hex Calculators

Some hexadecimal calculators take the RGB values you enter and convert the math automatically. After you have converted your RGB, you are ready to use the resulting hex in your HTML code.

For Mac users, we have provided a great hex calculator on the <chd> CD-ROM written by Joseph Cicinelli, called Calculator II. You can also download this application from:
ftp://ftp.amug.org/pub/mirrors/info-mac/sci/calc/calculator-ii-15.hqx

PCs ship with a hex calculator, which usually is found in the Accessories group. Open the Calculator and then under View, select Scientific. This changes the standard calculator to a scientific calculator. Then, simply select the Hex option to start converting your RGB values.

When To Use Browser-Safe Colors?

We've reviewed the browser-safe colors, but we haven't really touched yet on when or how you use them. Three different types of scenarios are covered here: HTML color, illustration-type color artwork, and photographic-type color artwork.

```
<Body Text="#663300" LINK="#FF0000" VLINK="#CC6600" ALINK="#6666CC" BGCOLOR="#FFFFCC">

Sample Text

Link

Visited Link

Active Link
```

HTML color refers to programming browser-safe choices for backgrounds, text, links, and tables.

Illustration-type artwork includes line art, logos, flat-color, and cartoons.

Photographic-type artwork includes continuous-tone artwork, photographs, glows, drop shadows, and gradients.

HTML-Based Color Choices

You should always use browser-safe colors when choosing web page color schemes for backgrounds, text, or link colors. If you don't, you may be in for a rude surprise when the browser changes your colors.

This comparison demonstrates the kind of color shifting that occurs with hexadecimal-based artwork on 8-bit systems if the colors used are not browser safe.

Mac 24-bit display

PC 24-bit display

Mac 8-bit display

PC 8-bit display

Use the charts called nhue.gif and nvalue.gif from the chap04 folder of the <chd> CD-ROM to choose colors. It's helpful to pick a limited grouping of colors that work well together. This section will show how to visualize color choices in Photoshop by using layers. Putting the colors to use in HTML code follows later in the chapter.

▶ note

Shameless Plug

If you have insecurities about choosing color schemes, you may want to check out Lynda Weinman and Bruce Heavin's book, *Coloring Web Graphics.2*. It includes hundreds of pre-selected, aesthetically organized browser-safe color combinations, as well as a CD-ROM full of browser-safe background tiles to choose from.

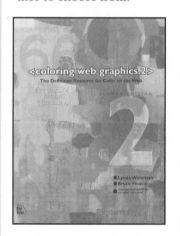

How to Load a Browser-Safe Swatch Palette into Photoshop

Palettes can be loaded into Photoshop's Swatch set. In this case, you'll load the browser-safe palette. It's possible to load other palettes or save your own palettes. If you want a palette to be compatible with Windows 95 , it must be saved with an .aco extension.

Reset Swatches: Reverts the Swatch palette to its default (Mac or Windows palette, depending on which platform you're using Photoshop).

Load Swatches: Appends a Swatch set to whichever swatches you already have loaded.

Replace Swatches: Substitutes a Swatch set with the new one you've loaded.

Save Swatches: Enables you to save your own Swatch set.

The bclut2.aco file is available from the <chd> CD-ROM inside the chap04 folder. You can load it into the Photoshop Swatch palette by following these steps:

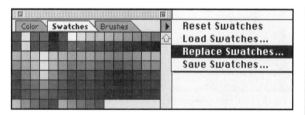 

Step 1: Choose **Windows, Palettes, Show Swatches.** Using the upper right arrow, choose **Load** or **Replace Swatches** from the pull-down menu.

Step 2: Select the bclut2.aco file. The custom Swatch set appears as a new set in the Photoshop Swatch palette.

Previsualizing Colors in Photoshop

Getting colors to work together is a very different practice than choosing individual colors that you like. A green might look great alone, but the minute you add a background color or colored text over it, the readability might suffer. So far, we have picked colors for all the exercises in this book. To see how to work with browser-safe colors and color relationships, launch Photoshop and open the ducks.psd file from the chap04 folder of the <chd> CD-ROM.

The next step is to load the browser-safe Swatch set (see the preceding exercise, "How to Load a Browser-Safe Swatch Palette into Photoshop").

Using the Eyedropper tool, select colors from the browser-safe color chart and fill the various layers to see the results of your choices. Working with Photoshop layers when choosing colors is a great way to identify browser-safe color schemes.

After you've found a color combination you like, write down the RGB values you'd like to use for your BODY tags (BGCOLOR, TEXT, LINK, VLINK, ALINK). Find the color values by selecting **Show Info** from the **Window** menu, which brings forth an interactive readout of the RGB values as you touch the colors with your eyedropper. As you identify the colors you have used, write them down. Use the conversion chart in this chapter to convert the RGB values to hex.

The background tile must be generated as a GIF file so that the colors don't shift in the browser. Follow these steps to experiment with your own color choices:

Step 1: Open the tile.psd document from the chap04 folder of the <chd> CD-ROM.

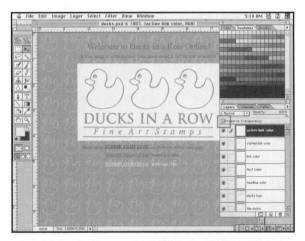

When a layer has Preserve Transparency checked, it enables you to refill that layer with a color of your choosing.

Step 2: By using the Eyedropper tool, select the colors you chose from the duck.psd file **Hint:** You can keep the tile.psd file active and eyedrop on another Photoshop file at the same time. You can also eyedrop from the swatches palette, assuming you've already loaded the bclut2.aco file from the preceding exercise.

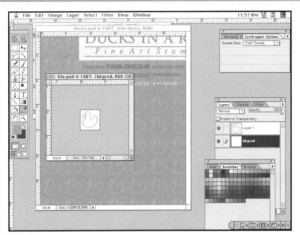

It's possible to work with two (or more) Photoshop files at once and use the eyedropper to share colors between the multiple documents.

Step 3: Choose **Edit:Fill** to fill the tile.psd layers with those color selections. Make sure the layer you want to edit is selected before you fill. When you are finished, you'll need to flatten the layers and **save a copy** as a GIF by following these steps:

Step 4: Under **Mode,** select **Index Color.**

Step 5: For the palette setting, select **Exact.** Only four colors should appear.

Step 6: Under **File**, choose **Save a Copy As**, and select **Compuserve GIF** as the file format. Name this file tile.gif. It's very important that you don't have any spaces between the words tile and gif. It should be typed as tile-dot-gif (tile.gif). Make sure the HTML requests the file spelled exactly this way, in all lowercase.

Step 7: Store the tile.gif file in the same folder as the HTML file you'll create to put everything we've just learned to practice.

Step 8: The final step is to put it all together. Here's some HTML to copy. You only have to insert your own values into the BODY tag. Make sure the ylogo1.gif file is in the same folder you save your HTML and tile.gif image to.

```
<HTML>
<HEAD>
<TITLE>Playing with Color</TITLE>
</HEAD>
<BODY BGCOLOR=" #xxxxxx"
BACKGROUND="tile.gif" TEXT=" #xxxxxx"
LINK=" #xxxxxx" ALINK=" #xxxxxx">
<IMG SRC=" ylogo1.gif">
</BODY>
</HTML>
```

Working with Color Picker-Based Applications

On the Mac, certain programs don't let you mix colors by hex or RGB values. Many HTML editors, including Adobe PageMill, Claris Homepage, and BBEdit, for example, rely on the Apple Color Picker to choose custom colors. You can type in percentages in these programs instead of hex or RGB. Here's a conversion table to help you do this:

PERCENTAGE	RGB	HEX
100	255	FF
80	204	CC
60	153	99
40	102	66
20	51	33
0	0	0

To target the browser-safe color picking problem, Pantone has come to the rescue with a Mac-only product called ColorWeb (http://www. pantone.com). Its "Internet-safe" color picking system includes two components: a printed Swatch set and a System Color Picker that displays the 216 safe colors inside the Apple Color Picker dialog box.

 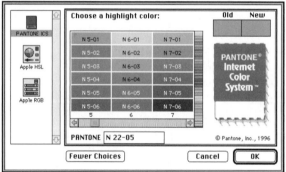

If you install Pantone's ColorWeb software, it will add another entry called Pantone ICS into the Apple Color Picker choices. Pantone ICS will enable you to pick from the 216 browser-safe colors.

The Pantone Internet Color Guide looks like a typical Pantone color swatch book, except that it has a web-color spin. The guide profiles and organizes the 216 browser-safe colors in chromatic order and lists the values for RGB, CMYK, Hexadecimal, and Hexachrome (Pantone's proprietary color format for picking printing ink colors).

The ColorWeb software is an excellent (Mac-only) tool that offers the capability to pick browser-safe colors in programs that do not support RGB decimal or RGB percentage-based values. Pricing and order information are available at the Pantone web site.

▶ note

Internet Color Picker

Macintosh System OS8 ships with a built-in "HTML Color Picker." This is the best solution we've seen so far to browser-safe color picking utilities. The picker includes a "snap-to" function that causes the sliders to automatically stop at browser-safe color choices. The greatest benefit to using this color picking system is that it includes the hexadecimal translation right in the read out! **Note:** At the time this chapter was written, the Pantone Color Web System did not work with MacOS8.

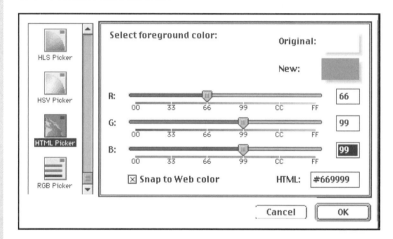

▶ warning

CMYK/RGB Conversions

There is no perfectly accurate way to convert CMYK values to RGB. The numbers that the Pantone Internet Color Guide cites for CMYK Internet-safe values are ballpark approximations that do not yield browser-safe colors when converted to RGB. The two color spaces—RGB and CMYK—do not share common colors consistently. Some RGB colors are outside of the CMYK color gamut, and there is nothing you can adjust to create a reliable conversion method.

Illustration-Based Artwork

On 256-color computers, the web browser forces your artwork into its fixed palette. Unlike HTML-based color, which shifts non-safe colors to a new color of the browser's choice, color image files dither instead. Dithering is a process where the computer attempts to display a color outside its color range by placing different colored dots next to each other. The colors are calculated mathematically and often look extremely unappealing.

If you use the browser-safe 216 color palette when creating illustration-based artwork, you will avoid unexpected and unwanted dithering.

Here's an example of what happens to the Ducks in a Row logo when it uses colors outside the safe range. Notice the unwanted dots? Those are caused by dithering.

If the graphic were prepared with browser-safe colors, it would not dither, regardless of which bit depth the end-viewer's system supports.

▸ **note**

GIFWizard

If you don't have Photoshop, or want to try a useful online utility, check out GIFWizard at http://www.raspberryhill.com. If you enter the URL of a graphic, the GIFWizard program automatically shrinks its file size. The program removes unwanted colors and uses the browser-safe color palette if you used those colors to begin with.

▶ note

Browser-Safe CLUT

The term CLUT refers to **c**olor **l**ook**u**p **t**able. Any 8-bit or lower image uses a CLUT. It is invisible to you unless you view it. You can view the CLUT of an 8-bit or lower image in Photoshop by selecting **Image:Color Table** when you have an 8-bit file loaded (a GIF, for example).

Lynda has a CLUT available from her web site for the browser-safe colors that can be used by many different imaging programs. By storing the browser-safe CLUT in a handy place, you can use it to load the 216 colors into paint programs, and paint with the colors to ensure that your artwork will not unexpectedly dither.

<http://www.lynda.com/files/CLUTS/>

▶ warning

Converting to Browser-Safe Doesn't Always Work!

There are times when you might have an existing color image that you want to convert to browser-safe colors. It's very rare for an image to look good when a CLUT with colors different from those used in the original image has been applied. Photoshop determines how to substitute the new colors, and it might not yield the results you expect. It's always best to create artwork with browser-safe colors first and not rely on post-processing techniques to fix existing artwork. Follow the exercises in this chapter to learn how to start with images using browser-safe colors rather than changing them to browser-safe colors after they've been made.

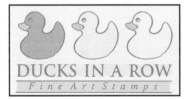
The original 24-bit image, created in colors that were not browser-safe.

Here is the image in a web browser. Notice the unwanted dithering.

You can avoid dithering by converting the image to the 216 colors without diffusion. The colors will be shifted by the computer instead of chosen by you.

How to Ensure Your Artwork Stays Browser Safe

If you work with browser-safe colors when you create artwork, you still have the important task of ensuring that those colors remain browser safe during the file format conversion and saving process.

Unfortunately, files that are saved as JPEGs do not retain precise color information. The lossy compression method used by the JPEG format throws away information, and, unfortunately, some of that information relates to color control. Because of this, there is no way to accurately control color using the JPEG file format.

Here's an example of a solid browser-safe color with the hex readout of 51, 153, 153.

When saved as a GIF file, this color stayed browser safe.

When saved as a JPEG, the color shifted from 51, 153, 153 to 54, 154, 156. It is no longer browser safe, as evidenced by the dither when displayed in Netscape Navigator under 8-bit monitor conditions.

Chapter 2, "First Page," emphasizes the point that JPEGs are not good for illustration-type graphics. Not only do they compress the graphics poorly, but they introduce artifacts into images, which alters color information.

This means that you cannot accurately match foreground GIFs to background JPEGs or foreground JPEGs to background GIFs. Even if you prepare images in browser-safe colors, they will not remain browser safe when converted to JPEG, no matter what you do. This is one more reason not to use JPEGs when dealing with flat-style illustration, logos, cartoons, or any other graphical image that does not lend itself to having unwanted dithering.

▶ e x e r c i s e

Removing Colors in Photoshop 4.0

At times you will apply the browser-safe palette to a file to ensure that the colors within the file honor the 216 color limit. The problem is that later you might want to reduce the file size even further than 216 by reducing the number of colors.

The following shows you how to apply a browser-safe palette and then reduce the color depth.

Step 1: Open the ylogo1.pct file from the chap04 folder of the <chd> CD-ROM.

duck216.gif is located inside the chap04 folder from the <chd> CD-ROM. It contains 216 colors and is too big, at 11k. When reduced to the 15 exact colors it actually contained, it was much smaller at 8k, and incurred no quality loss.

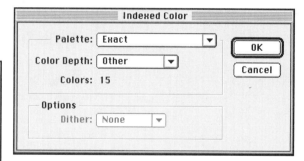

Step 2: Choose **Image:Mode:Index Color** and select the built-in 216 color table called **Web** inside the **Palette** field. The image is now browser safe, but it is also 216 colors! That's a few too many colors than necessary for this image. By leaving the image this way, it would be 11k. There's no reason for the image to include all 216 colors.

Step 3: Change the image back to RGB mode (**Image:Mode:RGB**) and then back to Indexed Color mode (**Image:Mode:Indexed Color**), and choose Exact Palette this time. This image only contains 15 different colors! When saved as a GIF with only 15 colors, the image is 8k, a 27% file size savings with no impact on the image quality at all!

Photographic-Based Artwork

Photographs are the one type of artwork that really do not benefit from using browser-safe colors. When an end user on a 256 color system sees a photograph on a web page, the browser converts it to its respective system palette. The good news is that the browser does just as good a job as you could if you had pre-built the photograph in the 216 palette. Let the browser do your dirty work for you! Not only will it save time, but if you create photographic artwork in millions, thousands, or adaptive colors, it will look better to end users who have better color systems.

▶ note

JPEGs Don't Use Palettes!

If you are saving your photograph as a JPEG, you do not need to worry about which palette to save it with. JPEGs don't use palettes or CLUTs; they can display any of 16.7 million colors. If you are saving your photographic image as a GIF, you should use an adaptive palette. An adaptive palette chooses colors from the image rather than fixed colors from an unrelated color scheme.

Photographs viewed in 24-bit

JPEG - High Quality 30.5k   8-bit Adaptive GIF 61k   Browser-Safe Color GIF 44k

Photographs viewed in 8-bit

The JPEG, which is a 24-bit file, and the adaptive file, which is an 8-bit file based on the colors within the image, exhibit the highest quality in these examples, not an outside palette as in the case of the images saved with the system or brow ser-safe palette. It is not necessary to convert photographic-based images to the browser-safe palette or even an 8-bit palette. The browser does it's dithering dirty work, regardless of how you prepare the image. It's best to leave the image in an adaptive palette or 24-bit file format so that the photographs will have the added advantage of looking better in 24-bit browser environments. JPEGs always produce the smallest file size for photographs and have the added advantage of being a 24-bit file format, unlike GIF, which cannot save images at bit-depths higher than 8-bit (256 colors).

Adding Color to a Web Page with HTML

You learned the basics of creating colored text and backgrounds in Chapter 2, "First Page." Now it's time to get deeper into the HTML tags that relate to color. The following examples and exercises run you through the numerous possibilities for color coding your pages.

Using Color Names Instead of Hex

You don't have to use hexadecimal numbers inside the color attribute tags; you can use words, too. Here's a list of color names that will work in Netscape Navigator.

Using any of the names inside the color attribute tags generates colored text in Netscape Navigator or Internet Explorer.

```
<HTML>
<HEAD>
<TITLE>Ducks in a Row Homepage</TITLE>
</HEAD>
<BODY TEXT="antiquewhite" BGCOLOR="darkcyan"
LINK="yellow" VLINK="darkorange">
<H1>Welcome to Ducks in a Row Online!</H1>
<P> Feel free to splash around...
<P><A HREF="company.html">
<IMG SRC="ylogo1.gif" BORDER=0></A>
<P>Check out the
<A HREF="http://www.stampzone.com/">
RUBBER STAMP ZONE</A> - an out-of-site
rubber stamp page
</BODY>
</HTML>
```

Here is an example of using "antiquewhite" along with "darkcyan" as color names within the BODY tag. (This file, called clrnames.html, is inside the chap04 folder on the <chd> CD-ROM.

The result of using color names instead of hex values to define color, shown in Netscape Navigator.

Coloring Individual Lines of Text

You can assign specific colors to individual lines of text by using the FONT tag.

```
<HTML>
<HEAD>
<TITLE>Ducks in a Row Homepage</TITLE>
</HEAD>
<BODY TEXT="#FFFFCC" BGCOLOR="#999966"
LINK="#006699" ALINK="#FFFF00"
VLINK="#330033">
<H1><FONT COLOR="#FFFFCC">Welcome to Ducks
in a Row Online!</FONT></H1>
<P>
<FONT COLOR="#663333">Rubber stamps or
rubber duckies? Feel free to splash around
to find out what we're about...</FONT>
<P>
<A HREF="company.html">
<IMG SRC="ylogo1.gif" WIDTH=419 HEIGHT=219
ALIGN=bottom></A>
<P>
<FONT COLOR="#FFFF99">Check out the</FONT>
<FONT COLOR="#006699">
<A HREF="http://www.stampzone.com/">
RUBBER STAMP ZONE</A></FONT>
<FONT COLOR="#FFFF99">- an out-of-site
rubber stamp page</FONT>
</BODY>
</HTML>
```

The FONT tag can contain a color attribute, which can be specified by using color names or hex numbers. It must be closed with a </FONT> tag each time you want the specific color to end.

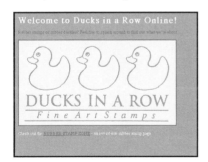

Here are the results of using the FONT **tag to insert color attributes so that individual words or letters can be colored.**

Color Names—Not Browser Safe!

While it might seem much easier to call a color by a name, the big problem is that very few color names are browser safe. Here's a list of the names that are cross-platform compatible:

Name	HEX
aqua	0000FF
black	000000
blue	0000FF
cyan	00FFFF
fuschia	FF00FF
lime	00FF00
magenta	FF00FF
red	FF0000
white	FFFFFF
yellow	FFFF00

Coloring Links

Link color can affect the border color around linked images or the color of linked text.

```
     <HTML>
     <HEAD>
     <TITLE>Ducks in a Row Homepage</TITLE>
     </HEAD>
1.   <BODY TEXT="#FFFFCC" BGCOLOR="#999966"
     LINK="#663333" ALINK="#FFFF00"
     VLINK="#330033">
     <H1>Welcome to Ducks in a Row
     Online!</H1>
     <P>Rubber stamps or rubber duckies?
     Feel free to splash around to find out
     what we're about...
     <P><A HREF="company.html">
2.   <IMG SRC="ylogo1.gif" BORDER=10></A>
     <P>Check out the
     <A HREF="http://www.stampzone.com/">
     RUBBER STAMP ZONE</A> - an out-of-site
     rubber stamp page
     </BODY>
     </HTML>
```

1. The LINK attribute within the BODY tag establishes the color for the linked text or graphic. The <A HREF></A> tag produces linked text.

2. The IMG SRC tag inserts an image, and the BORDER attribute enables you to set a width for the border, measured in pixels. **Note:** If you don't want a border, you can set this to BORDER=0.

The result of creating colored links. Make the border around the graphic wider with the BORDER **attribute.**

Adding Color to Tables

The BGCOLOR attribute works in table cells, as well as the body of the HTML document.

```
     <HTML>
     <HEAD>
     <TITLE>Ducks in a Row Homepage</TITLE>
     </HEAD>
     <BODY TEXT="#FFFFCC" BGCOLOR="#999966"
     LINK="#663333" ALINK="#FFFF00"
     VLINK="#330033">
1.   <TABLE BORDER=1 BGCOLOR="#663333">
2.   <TR><TH><FONT SIZE=5>Welcome to Ducks
     in a Row Online!</FONT>
     </TABLE>
     <P>Rubber stamps or rubber duckies?
     Feel free to splash around to find out
     what we're about...
     <P><A HREF="company.html">
     <IMG SRC="ylogo1.gif" BORDER=10></A>
     <P>Check out the
     <A HREF="http://www.stampzone.com/">
     RUBBER STAMP ZONE</A> an out-of-site
     rubber stamp page!
     </BODY>
     </HTML>
```

1. The TABLE tag establishes the beginning of the table command. The BORDER attribute assigns an embossed border to the table.

2. TR initiates a table row. The TH stands for table header. Everything within the TH tag is automatically bolded and centered. The BGCOLOR attribute sets a background color for the table by using hexadecimal or color names.

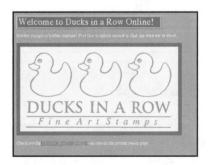

Here's an example of coloring cells within a table by using the BGCOLOR **attribute within the** TABLE **tag.**

HTML Tags That Support Color

Here's a list of all HTML tags that may affect the color of displayed elements:

Tag	Attribute(s)	Description
BODY	BGCOLOR, TEXT, LINK, VLINK, ALINK	Sets the colors for the document background/text/links/visited links/active links, respectively.
FONT[1]	COLOR	Sets the color of the font.
BASEFONT[1]	COLOR	Sets the color of the default font for the document.
TABLE[2]	BGCOLOR	Sets the background color for the entire table.
TR[2]	BGCOLOR	Sets the background color for the table row.
TD[2]	BGCOLOR	Sets the background color for the table cell.
TH[2]	BGCOLOR	Sets the background color for the table heading.

[1] The use of the FONT tag is depreciated in the HTML 4.0 specification (that is, the authors of the HTML spec. would rather you didn't use it) in favor of style sheets. This is wishful thinking on their part, as we can't really stop using the FONT tag until everyone updates their browsers to those that support style sheets.

[2] The TABLE BGCOLOR attributes are not actually a part of the HTML specification before 4.0, although they are supported by Netscape Navigator 3.0 and later and MSIE 3.0 and later (so lots of folks are using them). See the pattern?

▶ chapter four summary

In this chapter, we've taught you how to implement color in the various elements of your web pages. Our focus was on the why of the "browser-safe" color palette, how to use the hexadecimal number system with your HTML colors, and what code elements to use for applying color to your web pages.

Some of this information may be a bit more technical than what you're used to, but don't let that discourage you. Experiment with the various techniques in this chapter, and you will learn even more!

In the next chapter, we cover how to make images into links using imagemaps and other techniques.

5

Clickable

*"When you're hot, you're hot
When you're not, you're not."*
—Jerry Reed

Clickable
looking hot

When an image is "hot," it will send the viewer somewhere else after it's clicked. A hot button can link a viewer to another image, page, site, or external file, depending on how the link is programmed.

You can program a single image to be hot if you place it on the page using HTML tags that link to an outside URL. There are two types of hot images: those single images that are linked to one outside URL and those single images that have been divided into regions by using an imagemap to direct viewers to multiple URLs.

When a graphic is hot, you can also refer to it as a link, hotlink, hyperlink, or interactive button. All these words describe the same thing—clicking on such an image will result in some action, usually loading a new page.

This chapter reviews the two types of hot images: linked graphics and imagemap-based graphics. You will have a chance to explore more advanced techniques which involve JavaScript rollovers, navigation bars, as well as frames in Chapter 14, "Navigation."

Identifying Hot Images

Images that are hot may have visual cues that differentiate them from other inline graphics. Typically, a border appears around an image that links to somewhere else, and this border defaults to a blue color in most browsers. If your audience has had any experience on the web, they will already be trained to know that any time they encounter a border around an image, it means that it can be clicked as an active link.

The hand symbol and blue border are both visual cues of a linked graphic.

There are some instances where a hot image will not have the telltale border around it. If you'd prefer that your hot graphic be without one, this chapter describes how to turn the border off. The

only way a viewer knows to click on borderless hot images is if your graphic invites them to bring their cursor closer. In most browsers, as the viewer's cursor passes over a hot spot, it changes from a pointer to the pointing hand cursor shown here. This familiar symbol indicates, just like the border, that an image is a clickable button instead of a static graphic.

The pointing hand cursor indicates that text or graphics are "hot."

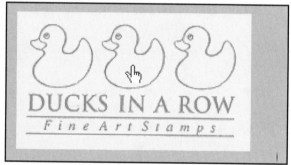

Even if a graphic doesn't have the telltale border, the pointing hand cursor indicates that it's "hot."

Creating Linked Images and Text

Remember from Chapter 1, "Start," that the IMG tag is used to insert an inline graphic on a page:

```
<IMG SRC="makingstamps.gif ">
```

The result of the above IMG **tag inserts a graphic into the page, but doesn't create a link.**

The easiest way to create a link using a graphic image is to use the IMG tag inside the <A HREF> </A> container, where you would otherwise put your anchor text. This combination of tags automatically defaults to putting a border around the graphic. The following is an example of this standard HTML code:

```
<A HREF="http://www.ducksinarow.com/process/ ">
<IMG SRC="makingstamps.gif "></A>
```

The result of the above code.

Turning Off Image Borders

Sometimes that pesky blue border around an image is totally wrong for the page it was designed for. If you've gone to a great deal of trouble to make an irregular-shaped image float freely on a background (using techniques described in Chapter 8, "Transparency"), you aren't going to want to ruin the illusion you worked so hard to achieve by having a glaring rectangular shape around your graphic. Here's the code to eliminate the border:

```
<BODY BGCOLOR="#FFFFCC">
<A HREF="http://www.ducksinarow.com/
process/">
  <IMG SRC="makingstamps.gif"
BORDER=0></A>
</BODY>
```

Notice the BORDER=0 attribute in the IMG tag. This attribute tells the browser, "Don't put a border on this image when it's used as a link."

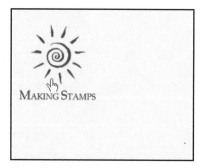

Here's an example of a linked image with no border. The border was turned off within the HTML, but the pointing finger cursor still appears when the mouse rolls over the linked image. The background color of the page matches the background color of the image, making it appear as if the image's shape is free floating. This was achieved by putting the same color yellow as a BGCOLOR attribute inside the BODY tag.

Just as you can make the border disappear, you can also make it appear stronger. This code tells the browser to use a thicker border with the image:

```
<BODY BGCOLOR="#FFFFCC">
<A HREF="http://www.ducksinarow.com/
process/">
  <IMG SRC="makingstamps.gif"
BORDER=25></A>
</BODY>
```

This linked image has been programmed to have a border of 25 pixels.

Sometimes your page has a specific color theme and the standard blue rectangle doesn't fit in. You can also change the color of your borders using the LINK attribute with the BODY tag. This code changes the border color of the images, as well as the color of any text links, on the page:

```
<BODY BGCOLOR="#FFFFCC" LINK="#996600">
<A HREF="http://www.ducksinarow.com/
process/">
  <IMG SRC="makingstamps.gif"
BORDER=25></A>
</BODY>
```

This image has a different color border (still left at the astonshing 25 pixel setting!), programmed with specific hexadecimal color values. Most browsers default to using blue borders unless told otherwise.

Importance of ALT Text

Many people either use browsers that don't support inline images or have their browser set to not automatically show them the images as they surf the web. The reasons for surfing that way include physical disabilities (e.g, Braille or vocal browsers for the blind) or technological limitations (e.g, those darn images take too long to download!). For these situations, the IMG tag includes a special attribute called ALT for specifying text that will be displayed in place of the image if the image is not available for some reason.

Using our example one more time, here's where the ALT attribute would be included:

```
<BODY BGCOLOR="#FFFFCC" LINK="#996600">
<A HREF="http://www.ducksinarow.com/
process/">
<IMG SRC="makingstamps.gif"
ALT="a rubber stamp graphic."></A>
</BODY>
```

It's not necessary to put ALT text on every graphic, but always use it on essential buttons and images. ALT text can be used on static graphics as well as linked graphics.

The ALT **text appears on text-based browsers, or if someone's images are turned off in their browser preferences.**

The Importance of WIDTH and HEIGHT

The first thing a web browser does—in preparation for displaying a web page—is download the HTML code for the page from the server. The browser then interprets the HTML in order to decide what to do next. If there are images on the page, the browser has no way of knowing how to lay out the page before it knows the specific dimensions of the images. How can it find out?

In order to lay out the page, the browser must first know the dimensions of each image. The browser could do this by downloading each image and checking the dimensions in the image file; but this can take time, especially if the image is large. A faster way was provided with an extension to the HTML language, introduced by Netscape with version 2.0 of Netscape Navigator. By using this feature, which has since been adopted by the HTML standards group as part of HTML 3.2 and later, you can specify the WIDTH and HEIGHT of your graphic as attributes to the IMG tag.

When you use WIDTH and HEIGHT with your IMG tags, you provide enough information for the browser to lay out your page without first downloading the associated graphics. When you use these attributes, the page displays with markers in place of the graphics until the graphics are available to display in their respective places. These attributes are supported by the latest versions of most browsers, and using them greatly speeds up the display of your web pages. Your graphics don't load any faster, but text will display before the graphics do, giving the end user the impression of a faster-loading page.

Here's the way to use HEIGHT and WIDTH attributes.

```
<A HREF="http://www.ducksinarow.com/
process/">
<IMG SRC="makingstamps.gif"
WIDTH=110 HEIGHT=115
ALT="rubber stamp graphic.">
</A>
```

The values you assign to the WIDTH and HEIGHT attributes reflect how large the image is, measured in pixels. Most image editing programs have a feature that enables you to identify your image's size by pixel values.

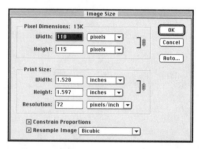

To determine the image's size in Photoshop 4.0, choose Image:Image Size, this will appear with the correct values.

Image	
Width:	110
Height:	115
Bits Per Pixel:	24
Max # of Colors:	16 Million
Source File	
File Name:	
File Type:	OS/2 or Windows Bitmap
Sub Type:	OS/2
Transparent Index:	None
Status	
Has Been Changed?	No
Has a Selection?	No
Has Mask Channel?	No
Memory Used	
Image:	37K
Selection:	0K
Mask:	0K
Undo:	0K
Total:	37K

To see the size of an image in Paint Shop Pro 4.0, choose View:Image Information.

Resizing Using WIDTH and HEIGHT Info

You can even resize an image by using values that are larger or smaller than the image! Basically, the browser uses your information for the image size and reformats the image to fit.

Here's an example of putting values larger than the true values in the `WIDTH` and `HEIGHT` attributes. This process stretches the image and rarely looks very good.

Here's an example of putting values smaller than the true values in the `WIDTH` and `HEIGHT` attributes. This process shrinks the image and rarely looks good. If you want to shrink (or enlarge) your graphic, it will look best if you do so in your imaging program, not in your HTML document.

Aesthetics of Interlaced Graphics

If you've toured the web much, you've encountered interlaced GIFs. They're those images that start out blocky and appear less and less blocky until they come into full focus.

These examples simulate the effect of interlacing on a browser. The image starts chunky and comes into focus over time. This allows the end viewer to decide whether to wait for your graphic to finish or click onward.

Interlacing doesn't affect the overall size or speed of a GIF. In theory, interlacing is supposed to make it possible for your end viewer to get a rough idea of your visuals and to make a decision whether to wait or click onward before the image finishes rendering. Again—in theory—interlacing is supposed to save time. Unfortunately for the end viewer, being forced to wait for the entire image to finish coming into focus in order to read essential information is often a frustrating experience. In other words, interlaced images save time only if you don't have to wait for them to finish.

Lynda: My recommendation is that you do not use interlaced GIFs for important visual information that's critical to your site. An imagemap or navigation icon (more about how to make these in Chapter 14, "Navigation"), for example, must be seen in order to fulfill its function. Although interlaced GIFs serve their purpose on nonessential graphics, in my opinion, they only frustrate end users when used on essential graphics.

▶ note

Caching Images

It's possible to load images before they are visible in order to "cache" them, or pre load them. Some people trick the browser into preloading images by specifying the desired images to appear with small WIDTH and HEIGHT attributes (such as 1 pixel by 1 pixel), so they are barely visible or hidden on a part of the screen where they won't be noticed. A following page might request the image at full-size, and it will load quickly because the computer has cached the image.

If you choose to preload images, it is helpful to put a note on the page explaining that images are being preloaded. Some users may become confused if they notice the excess network activity.

▶ e x e r c i s e

Linking Graphics

We've supplied a file on the <chd> CD-ROM in the chap05 folder called imagelinks.html. In this exercise, you'll experiment with changing the code to try different ideas.

If you open the imagelinks.html **file inside your browser of choice, you'll see it display as depicted here.**

Step 1: Launch a text editor.

Step 2: Change the border color by putting different hexadecimal values into the LINK attribute. Save the file with a new name (be sure to put the .html or .htm extension at the end) and open the changed file in your browser again.

Step 3: Change the weight of the border by putting different values into the BORDER attribute and re-save the HTML document. Preview the change in the browser.

Step 4: Change the WIDTH and HEIGHT attributes and re-save the HTML document. Preview the change in the browser.

Step 5: Change the ALT text message. Change your browser's preferences to turn off image loading, and see if your message appears. Preview the change in the browser. (**Note:** You may need to clear your browser's cache and/or restart your browser after turning off image loading before you can see the ALT text on the page!)

What Are Imagemaps?

At many web sites, you will see a list of underlined text links on a page (often referred to as a hotlist). This is simply a list of multiple URLs assigned to multiple text objects. Instead of using multiple text links, however, the list of URLs could be attached to a single image object. Such an object is called an imagemap, which is a fancy way of presenting a list of links. This takes a little longer to download than a hotlist because of the added time required for the graphic to load. Most of the time, it's worth the wait because imagemaps are a more convenient, visual way to present multiple choices to your audience.

This image works well as an imagemap.

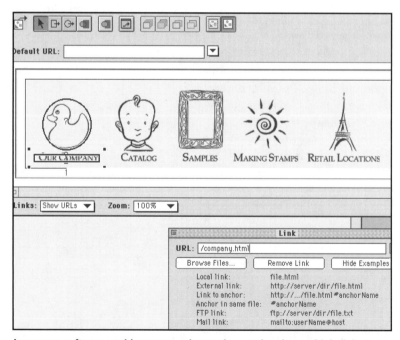

Imagemap software enables you to select regions and assign multiple links to a single image. This example shows the navigation bar graphic loaded into a Claris Home Page for the Macintosh.

Client-Side or Server-Side Imagemap?

An imagemap contains shapes and coordinates for regions within a single image that are hyperlinked to separate URLs. There are two different types of imagemaps: client-side and server-side.

A client-side imagemap contains all the information about the imagemap and is stored within the HTML document. A server-side imagemap has the same information in a slightly different format, is stored in a "map definition file" on the server, and is accessed by the server software, or a separate CGI program.

- **Client-side imagemaps** are interpreted by the browser, so they will only work with browsers that support them. Versions of Netscape Navigator since 2.0 and versions of Microsoft Internet Explorer since 3.0 support client-side imagemaps.

An advantage to client-side imagemaps is the fact that the information is stored within an HTML document instead of on a server. This means the server will not get bogged down by user requests, and the performance of your imagemaps will be more responsive.

- **Server-side imagemaps** work with all browsers, but are more complex to set up. A server-side imagemap is accessed via CGI and requires knowledge of how the server is configured. To install a server-side imagemap, you will need to contact your server administrator (or read the server documentation if you are running your own server) and find out how it is configured.

Another difference between client-side and server-side imagemaps is how they display data with-in the browser. A server-side imagemap shows the coordinates in the status line at the bottom of the screen, whereas a client-side imagemap shows the actual URL, which is much nicer and looks like a hyperlink.

Most users prefer client-side imagemaps over server-side imagemaps; unfortunately, some older browsers don't support this feature. That's why some designers include both types of imagemaps in their documents.

Here's an example of a server-side imagemap display on the status line in Netscape Navigator. It shows the coordinates of the mouse cursor within the imagemap.

Here's an example of a client-side imagemap display on the status line in Netscape Navigator. It shows the URL of the link. Much better!

♦ **e x e r c i s e**

Client-Side Imagemaps in Mapper (Macintosh)

Create a working folder on your hard disk and name it mapex for this exercise. You will save all your files in this folder. These are the steps for creating a client-side imagemap using Mapper on a Macintosh:

Step 1: Open the navbar.gif file from the chap05 folder of the <chd> CD-ROM and copy it into the mapex folder you just created. **Tip:** Any web graphic will work for this purpose as long as it is a GIF (standard, transparent, animated, and inter-laced will all work) or a JPEG.

Step 2: Launch Mapper from the Software/Mac folder of the <chd> CD-ROM.

Step 3: The program prompts you to locate a file. Open navbar.gif from the chap05 folder of the <chd> CD-ROM. The program will load the file and prompt you to:

Open map file. Since you don't have a map file yet, choose **New** to create one.

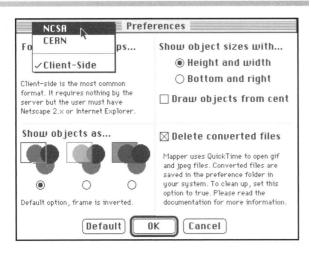

Under **Edit:Preferences**, choose **Client-Side**.

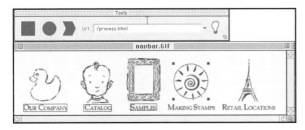

Step 4: Using the drawing tools, drag shapes around the graphics. When you close the shape, it will highlight with four little anchors on each corner, similar to what's shown above on the Making Stamps image. Enter the URL for the link inside the URL entry cell.

Step 5: When you are finished, choose **File:Save As** and name the new file navbar.html. Save it in the mapex folder you created at the start of this exercise. The HTML file will automatically be generated.

Mapper asking for the name of the map.

Mapper will now ask for the name of the map. Name it navbar and save it in the mapex folder you created at the start of this exercise.

▶ continued

The HTML file we created using Mapper looks like:

```
<map name="navbar"><!-- Created with Mapper 1.0, http://www.calles.pp.se -->
<area shape="rect" coords="421,103,528,117" href="/retail.html">
<area shape="polygon"
coords="453,95,462,77,469,55,475,21,475,55,482,81,491,98,487,98,476,86,469,89,461,
99,453,95" href="/retail.html">
<area shape="rect" coords="310,103,411,120" href="/process.html">
<area shape="circle" coords="358,59,34" href="/process.html">
<area shape="rect" coords="235,103,290,117" href="/samples.html">
<area shape="polygon"
coords="243,14,279,16,292,16,296,28,296,76,293,95,280,97,243,96,232,95,228,65,231,
23,232,16,243,14" HREF="/samples.html">
<area shape="rect" coords="141,104,198,119" href="/catalog.html">
<area shape="rect" coords="202,13,202,13" nohref>
<area shape="polygon"
COORDS="157,28,166,22,172,26,174,27,189,31,194,46,190,60,193,59,201,59,195,70,186,
79,178,86,180,90,189,98,189,101,149,100,156,92,157,86,146,78,144,74,134,61,139,58,
144,59,139,41,144,35,157,28" href="/catalog.html">
<area shape="rect" coords="19,103,108,119" href="/company.html">
<area shape="polygon"
coords="62,36,68,47,67,57,65,62,74,61,80,52,84,48,95,59,89,83,73,95,52,96,38,91,
33,81,37,71,46,64,45,61,34,56,33,50,40,48,44,35,62,36" href="/company.html"></map>
```

It's still not a complete HTML file, though. At the top of the document, insert this code:

```
<HTML>
<HEAD>
    <TITLE>navbar sample</TITLE>
</HEAD>
<BODY BGCOLOR="#FFFFCC">
```

After the closing </MAP>, you need to add:

```
<P><CENTER>
    <IMG SRC="navbar.gif" WIDTH=440 HEIGHT=116 BORDER=0 USEMAP="#navbar">
</CENTER>
```

Finally, at the end of the document, close the BODY and HTML tags, like this:

```
</BODY>
</HTML>
```

Open the navbar.html file from the chap05 folder of the <chd> CD-ROM to see the finished file as we intended. If you have any problems, compare your code to ours.

▶ exercise

Client-Side Imagemaps in MapEdit (Windows)

For the Windows (95 or NT) imagemap editor, we chose MapEdit by Tom Boutell (http://www. boutell.com/mapedit/). MapEdit creates client-side image-maps and inserts them directly into an existing HTML document.

Step 1: Create a working folder on your hard disk and name it mapex for this exercise. You will save all your files in this folder. Copy the file navbar-clean.html from the chap05 folder on the <chd> CD-ROM to your mapex directory and rename it navbar.html.

When you open the file, it should look like this:

```
<HTML>
<HEAD>
   <TITLE>navbar sample</TITLE>
</HEAD>
<BODY BGCOLOR="#FFFFCC">
<IMG SRC="navbar.gif"
   WIDTH=440 HEIGHT=116 BORDER=0>
</BODY>
</HTML>
```

When you open the file in your browser, you should see something like this:

Step 2: Now, launch MapEdit (you can install it from the chap05 folder of the <chd> CD-ROM). You will first be presented with the Open/Create Map dialog box. Click on the **Browse** button or type in the path of the HTML file you just created.

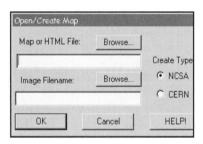

Then you'll get a list of all the images in the file. Select the navbar.gif image.

Step 3: The image will be displayed in the main editing window. Now you can define the hot regions by using the Rectangle, Circle, and Polygon tools.

continued

MapEdit's main editing window.

When you are done with a given region, press the right mouse button. You will get the Object URL dialog box. **Note:** The Alternate Text area is for the link's ALT text attribute within the imagemap. This is not currently used by any browsers that we know of, but it can't hurt to fill it in for future browsers.

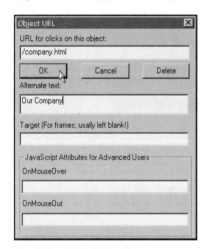

The Object URL dialog box.

Step 4: For each region that you define, you will need to fill in the Object URL dialog box. The only required information is the URL for clicks on this object text box. You can fill in this box with a full URL (e.g., http://www.yahoo.com/) or just the name of a file on the same site as yours (as in our example, "/company.html"). The use of relative and absolute URLs is explained in depth in Chapter 12, "Organization."

The completed imagemap in MapEdit.

Step 5: When you're all done, select **File:Save As** to tell MapEdit where to save the imagemap. To save the client-side imagemap in your HTML file, be sure to select **Client Side Map (HTML)** as the **Save As** Format. Press the **Browse** button, browse to the mapex folder that you created, and name the file navbar.html.

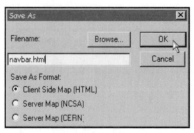

Here is the Save As dialog box with the client-side imagemap format selected.

Your page is now done. MapEdit integrates the imagemap directly into the HTML file so that you don't need to do any cut-and-paste to get the file to work. Here's the HTML from this example, after MapEdit has inserted the imagemap:

```
<HTML>
<HEAD>
   <TITLE>navbar sample</TITLE>
</HEAD>
<BODY BGCOLOR="#FFFFCC">
<IMG SRC="navbar.gif" WIDTH=440 HEIGHT=116 BORDER=0 USEMAP="#navbar">
<map name="navbar">
<area shape="polygon" alt="Our Company"
coords="84,58,83,64,78,72,67,78,59,79,53,79,46,77,39,72,37,67,41,59,44,56,46,54,46,51,
43,50,37,47,35,43,38,43,42,41,46,32,50,30,55,29,58,30,62,34,64,37,63,42,63,46,60,48,63,
52,70,52,73,47,74,43,78,40,83,46,84,52" href="/company.html">
<area shape="polygon" alt="Catalog"
coords="122,67,126,69,129,70,131,74,122,80,122,82,156,82,156,79,147,74,147,71,152,67,
154,64,154,61,158,60,159,55,162,52,162,48,159,48,157,51,158,43,158,33,152,26,140,24,
139,20,135,20,130,26,122,28,117,38,117,47,111,50,111,54,115,57,117,61,120,63"
href="/catalog.html">
<area shape="rect" alt="Samples" coords="187,15,236,79" href="/samples.html">
<area shape="circle" alt="Making Stamps" coords="287,51,28" href="/making.html">
<area shape="polygon" alt="Retail Locations"
coords="390,81,381,61,378,41,377,13,374,13,372,41,367,62,357,81"
href="/locations.html">
<area shape="rect" coords="21,82,98,97" href="/company.html">
<area shape="rect" coords="113,83,166,96" href="/catalog.html">
<area shape="rect" coords="186,81,236,96" href="/samples.html">
<area shape="rect" coords="244,81,325,95" href="/making.html">
<area shape="rect" coords="332,81,419,96" href="/locations.html">
<area shape="default" nohref>
</map>

</BODY>
</HTML>
```

Understanding the Client-Side Imagemap Code

Creating client-side imagemaps is slightly easier than server-side imagemaps because you do not need a CGI program or a separate map definition file (more about
this later in the Server-Side Imagemap sections). Everything within the client-side
imagemap information gets stored within the HTML. Let's analyze what's at work
within the HTML.

```
1.  <map name="navbar">
2.  <area shape="rect"
3.  coords="421,103,528,117"
4.  href="/retail.html">
    <area shape="polygon"
    coords="453,95,462,77,469,55,475,21,475,55,482,81,491,98,487,98,476,
    86,469,89,461,99,453,95" href="/retail.html">
    <area shape="rect" coords="310,103,411,120" href="/process.html">
    <area shape="circle" coords="358,59,34" href="/process.html">
    <area shape="rect" coords="235,103,290,117" href="/samples.html">
    <area shape="polygon"
    coords="243,14,279,16,292,16,296,28,296,76,293,95,280,97,243,96,232,
    95,228,65,231,23,232,16,243,14" href="/samples.html">
    <area shape="rect" coords="141,104,198,119" href="/catalog.html">
    <area shape="rect" coords="202,13,202,13" nohref>
    <area shape="polygon"
    coords="157,28,166,22,172,26,174,27,189,31,194,46,190,60,193,59,201,
    59,195,70,186,79,178,86,180,90,189,98,189,101,149,100,156,92,157,86,
    146,78,144,74,134,61,139,58,144,59,139,41,144,35,157,28"
    HREF="/catalog.html">
    <area shape="rect" coords="19,103,108,119" href="/company.html">
    <area shape="polygon"
    coords="62,36,68,47,67,57,65,62,74,61,80,52,84,48,95,59,89,83,73,95,
    52,96,38,91,33,81,37,71,46,64,45,61,34,56,33,50,40,48,44,35,62,36"
    href="/company.html">
5.  </map>
6.  <IMG SRC="navbar.gif" WIDTH=440 HEIGHT=116
7.  BORDER=0
8.  USEMAP="#navbar" >
```

1. `<map name="navbar">`

The map name is something that you define. It must match what is used in the USEMAP attribute in the associated IMG tag.

2. `<area shape="rect"`

This part of the code defines the shape for this region of the imagemap.

3. `coords="421,103,528,117"`

The coordinates of each defined point in the shape. Each coordinate is a pair of numbers, x,y, where x is the number of pixels from the left side of the image, and y is the number of pixels from the top of the image. A rectangle (rect) has two coordinates (four numbers) one for the upper-left corner and one for the lower-right corner; a circle has two coordinates (four numbers), the center and one point on the perimeter; and a polygon (poly) has one coordinate (one pair of numbers) for each defined point on the polygon.

4. `href="/retail.html">`

The href attribute contains the URL of the destination of this link.

5. `</map>`

The end tag is required to end the client-side imagemap.

6. `<IMG SRC="navbar.gif"`

The source URL for the image.

7. `BORDER=0`

Just like the server-side example shown later in this chapter, the BORDER=0 attribute turns off the default blue border. It's not necessary to turn the border off, but it can ruin the illusion of irregular-shaped regions if you leave it turned on.

8. `USEMAP="#navbar">`

The usemap attribute specifies the name of the client-side imagemap file to use. The # character must always precede the map name.

Creating Server-Side Imagemaps

Server-side imagemaps are more complicated
to explain than client-side imagemaps because
they tend to work differently on different servers.
Fortunately, the simplest implementation is also
the most common. According to the most recent
Netcraft survey (http://www.netcraft.co.uk/Survey/),
the Apache web server (or its derivatives) is running on over 45% of all public Internet domains.

The method described here will work only
on servers running Apache with the imagemap
module (mod_imap) installed. The default
Apache installation includes this module, but
some servers may have it configured differently
or otherwise disabled. Check with your system
administrator if this doesn't work on your server.

For an exhaustive explanation of imagemaps, see *The CGI
Book,* **by Bill Weinman (ISBN 1-56205-571-2).**

Server-Side Imagemaps in MapEdit

This exercise builds on the last exercise. If you did not create a mapex folder, or the preceding client-side imagemap document, we've created an HTML file called navbar.html inside the examples/mapex folder of the chap05 folder of the <chd> CD-ROM.

Step 1: Edit your navbar.html file (in your mapex folder) to use the server-side image map by adding the ISMAP attribute to the IMG tag and adding <A HREF="navbar.map"> before, and </A> after, the image. (The navbar-ncsa.html file inside the examples/mapex folder of the chap05 folder of the <chd> CD-ROM includes these changes.) That part of the file should now resemble this:

```
<A HREF="navbar.map">
  <IMG SRC="navbar.gif" WIDTH=440
HEIGHT=116 BORDER=0
    USEMAP="#navbar" ISMAP></A>
```

Step 2: Using **Steps 2–4** from the client-side imagemaps exercise earlier in this chapter, define the regions for your imagemap. Then, instead of selecting **Client Side Map (HTML)**, as you did in the previous exercise, select the **Server Map (NCSA)** format. Name the file navbar.map.

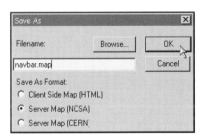

Saving an imagemap in NCSA format with MapEdit.

Step 3: Transfer your new navbar.html and navbar.map to your web server. **Remember:** Server-side imagemaps work only on a web server; they will not work on your local hard disk.

Step 4: Test the server-side imagemap.

Bring up the file in your browser. If your browser supports client-side imagemaps, you will see normal URLs in the status line when you pass your mouse cursor over the navigation bar. In order to test the server-side imagemap, change the USEMAP attribute to X-USEMAP and save the file (and upload it to your server) again. (**Note:** Server-side imagemaps cannot be tested from your hard drive—they must be transferred to the server to function.) This will force your browser to ignore the client-side map so you can test the server-side function. Now your browser should show the coordinates (for example, navbar.map?206,72) as you pass the mouse over the navigation bar. This means that the server-side imagemap is working.

If your server-side imagemap doesn't work at this point, you will need to speak to the system administrator of your server to find out how server-side imagemap support is configured on the server.

Be sure to restore the USEMAP attribute after you have tested the server-side imagemap.

> ## ▶ note

Do You Need an Imagemap?

Carefully analyze whether you really need an imagemap or whether there's some other way to accomplish the same goal. For example, if your image is composed of rectangles, or can be seamed together by using rectangular shapes (or transparent irregular shapes, see Chapter 8, "Transparency"), it might be easier on your end to load multiple single graphics with independent links than to load one graphic with multiple links.

You will see examples of imagemaps used on opening menu screens all over the web. Sometimes an imagemap is used even when the menu bar is composed of rectangular shapes. Some sites do this because one image loads faster than multiple images. This is a valid reason to use an imagemap, but even so, the difficulty of creating and maintaining one might outweigh the performance increase.

> ## ▶ note

Imagemap Resources

Imagemap Tutorial URLs

http://www.ihip.com/http://www.spyglass.com/techspec/tutorial/img_maps.html

Imagemap Software Tools

MapEdit and Unix)
http://www.boutell.com/mapedit/

Glenn Fleishman's Server-Side to Client-Side Online Converter
http://www.popco.com/popco/convertmaps.html

The Importance of ALT Text

Using an imagemap as a navigation tool is a wonderful way to exercise your freedom of design and open the doors to more creativity. Unfortunately, it can also make life a lot more difficult for those who do not use graphical browsers.

Two classes of users will have problems with imagemaps: those who browse with their image loading turned off (for speed, usually); and those who are using a non-graphical browser like Lynx (http://www.slcc.edu/lynx/), which is designed for use on character-terminals.

Here's how our current example looks on Lynx:

Lynx users don't see our imagemap.

This is what the sample page looks like in Netscape Navigator 4.0 with image loading turned off:

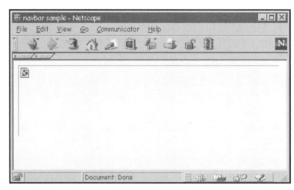

Many users browse with image loading turned off. This is what they would see on this page.

One easy way to make these pages more useful to these users, without sacrificing any design criteria, is to use the ALT attribute in our IMG tags. **Note:** MapEdit adds ALT text to the AREA tags in the client-side imagemap. We have not yet found a browser that will display this text. It would be nice, though. :-)

To add `ALT` text to the imagemap, simply add the `ALT` attribute to the `IMG` tag in the same way you would for any other image:

```
<A HREF="navbar.map">
  <IMG SRC="navbar.gif" WIDTH="440"
HEIGHT="116" BORDER="0"
    USEMAP="#navbar" ISMAP
ALT="Navigation Bar"></A>
```

Now it looks like this:

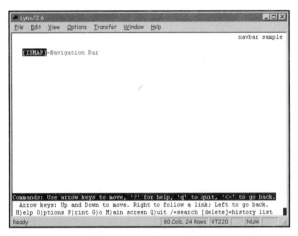

With `ALT` text, it's easier to see what's on the screen in Lynx, but the user is still left wondering what to do about it.

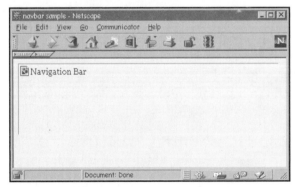

Netscape Navigator with `ALT` text. Now the user may decide to load the image.

Even though we've added `ALT` text, the user will still be left wondering where the links are. Our imagemap is actually active, but without any visual cues it would be impossible (or at least difficult) for most people to use.

That's why it's such a good idea to include a simple text menu, especially on pages where all the navigation is in graphics. You can create this menu in a number of ways (let your imagination be your guide!), but here's one that we have used on our pages with good results. Simply add this HTML right after the imagemap:

```
<P>
[
<A HREF="/company.html">Our Company</A> |
<A HREF="/catalog.html">Catalog</A> |
<A HREF="/samples.html">Samples</A> |
<A HREF="/making.html">Making Stamps</A> |
<A HREF="/locations.html">
Retail Locations</A>
]
```

Your graphically challenged users will see this:

With the text menu, this page is now useable by Lynx users. They will thank you for it!

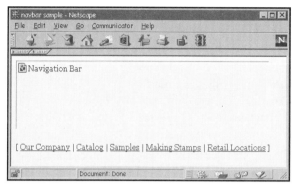

Netscape users with their graphic loading disabled will also see the menu. This may encourage them to look around a little longer. They may even decide to press the little button that loads the images!

Finally, looking at the page with images loaded, we can see that this little menu at the bottom doesn't detract from our design much at all.

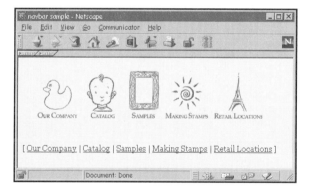

The imagemap with text menu and graphics showing.

In the end, it's really your decision. There may be sites where you will want to trade off the non-graphical audience for a certain design, but it's always a good idea to at least consider the decisions, and try to find a way to accommodate as many potential users as possible, without sacrificing the look of the site.

▶ chapter five summary

One of the coolest things about the web is the fact that you can link viewers anywhere you want from your site. Some of the techniques for creating linked graphics are simple; and some, as in the case of imagemaps, are more complex. This chapter should serve as a useful reference for creating linked graphics and as a springboard to delve into other HTML techniques.

6

"Well, I set my monkey on the log
And ordered him to do the Dog
He wagged his tail and shook his head
And he went and did the Cat instead
He's a weird monkey, very funky!"
—Bob Dylan, I Shall Be Free No. 10, 1964

Tiles

Tiles
filling the source

Making full-screen, wall-to-wall graphics on the web would seem to be an impossible feat given the slow modems and itsy-bitsy phone lines most of us have to squeeze connections through. Not to mention the fact that full-screen graphics can mean one thing to a compact portable computer web user and another to someone with a 21" monitor! You might think it would take way too long to download an image that fills a viewer's browser screen and that it would be irresponsible to prepare images of this size for web graphics.

Repeated, or tiled, graphics are the answer. This chapter covers the BACKGROUND attribute for the BODY tag, which allows a single small image to be repeated endlessly so that it fills an entire web page, regardless of size. Tiled images have the advantage of being small, so they load fast, and they include the capability to repeat over the size of whatever web screen they appear on. Because a small graphic loads faster than a big one, this technique works well to cover a lot of real estate on a web page without incurring a lot of overhead in downloading time.

Tiling Backgrounds

The BODY BACKGROUND="URL" feature tells the browser to repeat a small graphic and turn it into a full-screen graphic. It accomplishes this effect by tiling a single image, creating a repeating image that will fill any size screen regardless of computer platform and browser area. The browser needs to load only a single source file for the pattern, and once it's downloaded, it fills the entire web page. This saves time because the wait time is for a single, small image to download, even though the result is that the entire screen fills with an image. Repeated tiles are a great solution for creating full-screen graphics for low-bandwidth delivery systems such as the web.

Bandwidth limitations aren't the only problem that tiled background patterns solve. In the past, HTML has not allowed images to be layered. If you consider that layering is a main feature of programs such as Photoshop, QuarkXpress, and PageMaker, you'll understand why this feature in HTML is sorely missed. Cascading style sheets is an alternative solution for implementing layered images (see Chapter 13, "Style"), but using tiled background patterns is still a much easier route.

HTML allows text, links, and images to be placed on top of tiled backgrounds, making it an extremely useful and economical design element. The HTML code for this tiling effect is quite simple. The real challenge is making the art look good and controlling whether the edges of each repeated image are obvious or invisible.

The source file for a repeatable tile.   **The repeated tile in a web browser.**

Determining Tiled Pattern Sizes

One of the first questions to consider is how big the tiled image should be? HTML puts no restrictions on the size of a source for a background tile. The image has to be in a square or rectangue, however, because that's the native shape of any computer image.

The size of the image is entirely up to you. You should realize that the size of a tile is going to affect how many times it repeats. If a viewer's monitor is 640×480 pixels and your tile is 320×240, the image will repeat 4 times. If the tile is 20×20 pixels, it will repeat 768 times.

If your tile has images that repeat on each side, it will not show visible seams, and the viewer will not know how many times it repeats. If the image has an obvious border around it, the border will accentuate the fact that the image is being tiled. The size of your tile is up to you and the effect you are striving for.

Be aware, however, that file size restrictions must still be honored. If you create a tile that takes up a lot of space, it will take the same amount of time to load as any other graphic of the same size. If need be, refer back to Chapter 3, "Speedy Graphics" for methods to minimize file sizes.

If you use an image source that has large dimensions, it will not repeat as often. If it is large enough, it will not repeat at all. In that event, the speed advantages of having a small image load once and automatically repeat without incurring any additional downloading time would not exist. On the other hand, if you could make a graphic large in dimensions and not file size, then loading it in as a background image instead of a regular graphic could have its merits. We show examples of large background images later in this chapter.

Large source file.

Results.

Medium file.

Results.

Small file.

Results.

Full-Screen Body Backgrounds?

Why would you use an image with large pixel dimensions as a tiled background, as it seems to defeat the point? Because it could go behind other images and text, making a full-screen backdrop to other images on your page. HTML doesn't easily let you put text or images over regular images. The easiest way around this restriction is to use a background tiled graphic.

Here's full-screen (571×499 pixel) graphic that is only 9k. Because there are very few colors in this image, it compresses well as a GIF file.

Other images are placed over the full-screen background. This is a very effective and economical use of a large background tile.

Here's an example of a 30k JPEG image used as a background image in the "Making Stamps" section of the Ducks In A Row site.

Combined with a transparent GIF of the Making Stamps logo, this page looks rich and layered and is not too large to download.

▶ **warning**

Pitfalls of Full-Screen Backgrounds

Full-screen background tiles are a neat idea, but there is a problem with them. By creating a full-screen background, you have to make an assumption about the browser size of your audience. When viewers with large monitors look at these graphics, the illusion can be quickly broken, and you may cringe at the results.

On large monitors, the illusion of full-screen backgrounds is easily shattered.

There's no true solution to this problem. You have to second guess the target size of your end-viewer's display in order to determine the size of your full-screen tile. There's no foolproof way to do this. We're not saying, "Don't use full-screen backgrounds!" We're simply warning you of the pitfalls to this technique.

File Formats for Patterned Background Tile

GIFs and JPEGs are the standard file formats for the web, and tiled patterns are no exception. Just remember to follow the kilobyte rule: Every kilobyte of file size represents 1 second of download time to your viewer. The full size of the background pattern gets added to the download! If you have a background that's 60k and two images that are 10k each, the total file size of your page will be 80k. You would have just added a minute of download time to your page! Therefore, tiled backgrounds that take up a lot of memory are extra annoying to your audience during download.

Be careful if you are trying to match foreground and background tile images. They must both be the same file format—GIF and GIF or JPEG and JPEG—if you want the colors to match perfectly.

As usual, always save your file names in lowercase and use the extensions .jpg or .gif to let the HTML code know what kind of image it has to load. I usually put the word "pat" somewhere in a pattern file name, just for my own reference. That way, I know what I intended to use the file for when searching for it in a text list, such as my server directory.

Seams or No Seams?

There are two fundamentally different types of repeating tiles that can be used for background images: seamed and seamless. This section takes a look at these two different ways to present your background tiles on your web pages.

Seams

When an image has obvious seams, it looks tiled on purpose. Some web pages look great wallpapered with an obvious border. Andy Warhol shocked the art world in the 1960s and first earned his notoriety by making images of repeating soup cans on a single canvas. Video walls are often built on the power of images repeating in squares. There's nothing wrong with making patterns that have obvious borders and repeats, especially if that's what you had in mind. Making a tiled pattern with an obvious repeating border is fairly simple.

The source file has an obvious edge. This edge will be accentuated once the tile is repeated in a browser.

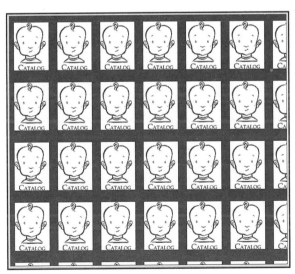

The finished tile is unmistakably repeated, with all the seams proudly showing!

No Seams, the Photoshop Way

When "seamless" patterns are described, it means the border of the pattern tile is impossible to locate. There aren't any pros or cons to using seamless or seamed tiles; it's purely an aesthetic decision. Seamless tiles, however, are much trickier to make.

The source file for a seamless tile.

The seamless tile repeated and displayed in a web browser.

▶ e x e r c i s e

A Seamless File in Photoshop 4.0

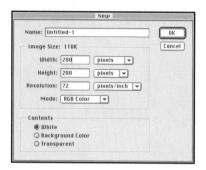

Step 1: Launch Photoshop and Open the smlogo.pct file from the chap08 folder of the <chd> CD-ROM. Under **Edit:New**, create a new document that is 200×200 pixels at 72 dpi in RGB color.

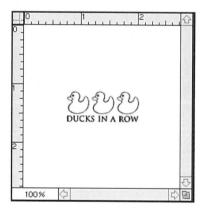

Step 2: Click on the smlogo.pct document to make it active. Choose **Select:Select All**, and then **Edit:Copy**. Click on the untitled document and choose **Edit:Paste**. **Tip:** Whenever you paste an image into a Photoshop document, it is automatically centered. Centering the graphic at this point is key to this exercise.

Step 3: Using the upper arrow on the Layers Palette, choose **Flatten Image**. This merges the layer that was created automatically with the last Paste command so that all the artwork will now reside on the Background layer.

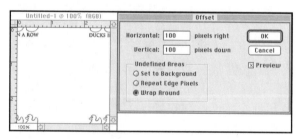

Step 4: Click the Untitled document to ensure that it's active. Under the **Filters** menu, choose **Other:Offset**. Make sure that **Wrap Around** is selected and enter 100 pixels into the **Horizontal** and **Vertical** entry cells. Notice how the Ducks logo just split and repositioned into the four corners of this document? That's exactly the goal of this exercise. The reason for flattening the image in the previous step was so the entire document would wrap around, instead of an individual layer.

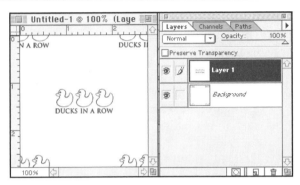

Step 5: Choose **Edit:Paste** again. The file should still be in your clipboard and will paste centered one more time. Voilà! You've just created a symmetrical seamless tile.

Step 6: Under **Image:Mode**, select **Index Color**. You will be prompted to flatten the image, which is necessary in order to create a GIF file. **Tip:** If you want to further reduce the file size of this tile, change the **Palette** from **Exact** to **Adaptive** and type 8 colors into the **Color Depth** entry cell. Save the file as smducksym.gif.

Step 7: Write the following code, and save this HTML as smducksym.html:

```
<HTML>
<HEAD>
  <TITLE>tile test</TITLE>
</HEAD>
<BODY BACKGROUND="smducksym.gif">
</BODY>
</HTML>
```

Step 8: Preview the tile in a browser. Here it is in Netscape Communicator 4.0 on a Mac.

▶ e x e r c i s e

Seamless Tile Exercise 2

Here is a variation on seamless tile creation:

Step 1: Repeat **Steps** 1/2 from previous exercise.

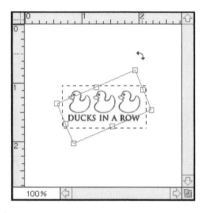

Step 2: Use the Selection Marquee tool to create a rectangular selection around the pasted logo. Choose **Layer:Free Transform**. Position your cursor away from the image until you get the rotation symbol. Drag the image to the left and double-click on it once you're happy with the positioning.

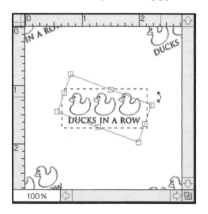

Step 3: Be sure to flatten! Under **Filter:Other**, select **Offset** again. The value 100 should still be in both entry cells. Repeat Step 2's operation, but rotate the pasted image in the other direction.

Step 4: Be sure to flatten again! Under **Filter:Other**, select **Offset**. This time, enter 50 pixels into the **Horizontal** and **Vertical** settings. This creates a different offset than before.

Step 5: Open the smburst.pct file from the chap06 folder of the <chd> CD-ROM. Choose **Select:Select All** and **Edit:Copy**. Click on the untitled tile you've been working on and paste the new image into the new offset position. The new image will paste into the center again, but use the Move tool to reposition it. Paste the image twice and position the images according to this figure. Repeat **Steps 6/7** from the previous exercise, but name this file asym.gif and be sure to change your HTML too.

The code should look like the following.

```
<HTML>
<HEAD>
   <TITLE>tile test</TITLE>
</HEAD>
<BODY BACKGROUND="asym.gif">
</BODY>
</HTML>
```

Step 6: Save the HTML document as asym.html.

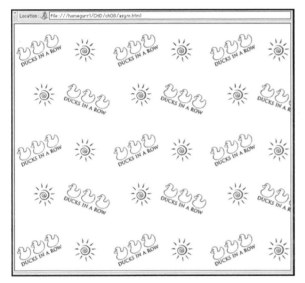

The finished file in a browser!

Special Effects Tiles

There are so many variations on tile making that the possible combinations of effects are unlimited. Here are some sample source files and their finished results in a browser to give you some ideas. Try your own variations. One thing to keep in mind is that the browser will load the tile from left to right or top to bottom. If you make a wide and skinny or narrow and tall tile, the loading process can actually look like a subtle animation of the tile painting itself into place. It should be noted, however, that this subtle animation effect gets tiresome after you've seen the page multiple times.

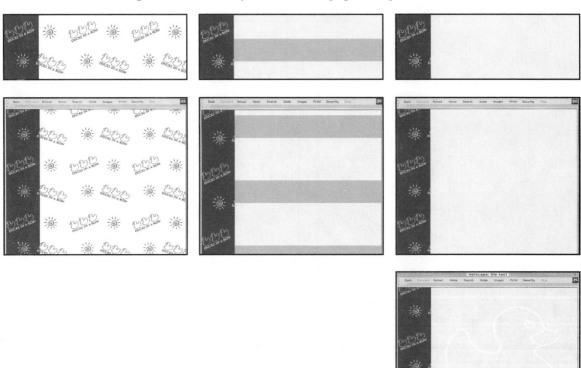

Aesthetics of Backgrounds

Always pay attention to contrast and value (lights and darks) when creating background tiles. If you have a light background, use dark type. If you have a dark background, use light type. If you aren't going to change your browser's default colors for text, links, visited links, and active links, use a light background—about the same value as the default light gray you see as the background color of most browsers. The light background ensures that the default colors of black, blue, and purple text will read against your custom background.

When making art for pattern tiles, try to use either all dark values or all light values. If you have both darks and lights in a background, neither light nor dark type will work consistently against them. This is a basic, simple rule to follow, and your site will thank you as it avoids the pitfalls of poor background tile aesthetics. Using either all dark values or all light values seems like common sense, but tour the web a bit and you'll soon see rainbow colored backgrounds with unreadable black type everywhere.

Make sure your images read. We don't mean your tiles should go to school to learn phonetics or any-thing—instead we're talking about readability of image versus background. The examples we've shown so far have great contrast and "read" as tiled images, but the second you try to put type over them, they will not "read" anymore.

If you create light and faded back-grounds, dark and colored text will read perfectly. Although it might seem obvious, dark and medium value col-ors will read over a light background.

With a dark background, the reverse is true. It's not enough to make a cool looking background tile—always check to make sure your type reads over it as well! If it doesn't read, make the necessary adjustments to the type color or contrast of the background image. See the following exercise, "How to Color Tiles in Photoshop," to study how to do this.

When the background is black and white, nothing reads well on top of it. Eventually, black type will intersect with a dark area of the background, or light text will appear on the white area. No solution can make this page work, except to redo the background tile with a better choice of colors.

▶ note

Specify Text Color Schemes!

Beware if you use a background image but don't specify the color of text! Some people change the text colors and may select a color that doesn't read well against your background!

Our recommendation: If you use a background image (or color), specify the text and link colors too. This ensures that everyone can at least read the text on your page. In fact, you may even want to specify a BGCOLOR so that the text on your page is readable even before the background loads.

▶ warning

Printing Issues

Many people print web pages instead of reading the content on screen. In older browsers, it is impossible to print the background tile. This can create readability problems in printed documents! If you use white text, for example, and the background tile doesn't print, your audience will get white text on white paper, or in other words, "nothing." One solution is to avoid pure white text on pages that you suspect might get printed.

▶ e x e r c i s e

How to Color Tiles in Photoshop

We're going to cover two different recoloring techniques in this section: the first with an anti-aliased example and the second with an aliased example.

Anti-Aliased Example

When working with anti-aliased graphics, it's necessary to worry about clean edges when recoloring artwork. The following exercise uses the Color Range tool in Photoshop 4.0, which is an effective way to select anti-aliased artwork for color editing.

Step 1: Launch Photoshop and Open the anti.pict file from the chap06 folder of the <chd> CD-ROM.

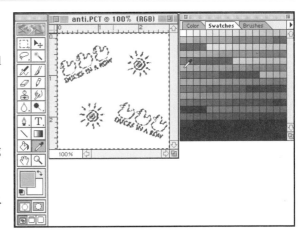

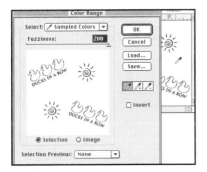

Step 2: Under the **Select** menu, choose **Color Range**. Use the default Eyedropper tool to click outside the Color Range dialog box into the white area of the anti.pict file. Increase Fuzziness to 200, make sure your screen matches this figure, and click **OK**.

Step 3: The Color Range feature in Photoshop just created a mask, and the selection of the mask will be loaded when you return to the anti.pict file. Make sure you've loaded your browser-safe color chart (it's called bclut2.aco and is in the chap06 folder of the <chd> CD-ROM). **Aesthetic Tip:** Pick colors close in value to each other so that you can choose a good contrasting type value. Read more about the importance of value in Chapter 4, "Web Color."

> continued

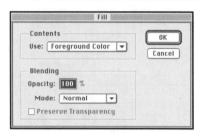

Step 4: Choose Edit:Fill. Make sure the **Use Foreground Color** is selected.

Step 5: You should have filled what used to be white with the new color you selected. To fill the line work, choose **Select:Inverse** to invert the selection. Choose a second color with the Eye-dropper tool, select **Edit:Fill**. Voilà! You should have a nicely recolored tile now.

Aliased Example

Unlike anti-aliased artwork, when working with aliased graphics, there's no need to worry about clean edges. It's much easier to select colors with the Magic Wand tool than the Color Range tool, which was used in the preceding example. The following steps walk you through the stages of re-coloring an aliased graphic:

Step 1: Launch Photoshop and Open the file, aliased. pict from the chap06 folder of the <chd> CD-ROM.

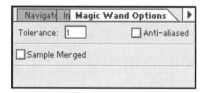

Step 2: Double-click on the Magic Wand tool to define its Option settings. Set the **Tolerance** to 1 and make sure **Anti-aliased** is turned off.

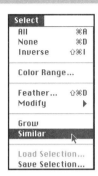

Step 3: Click on the white area of your graphic with the Magic Wand tool. Under the **Select** menu, choose **Select Similar**. This will select the white areas that the Magic Wand didn't capture.

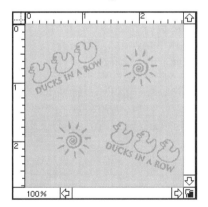

Step 4: Select a color from the browser-safe swatch palette and choose **Edit:Fill**. Under the **Select** menu, choose **Inverse** to invert the selection and choose and fill with a second color. Voilà! You should be finished with a newly colored aliased tile.

▶ chapter six summary

Background tiles are a great asset to most web pages. There are a lot of factors that go into making effective tiles. Here is a list:

• Background tiles are one way to fill a web page with visual content without taking up a lot of memory and downloading time.

• Choosing whether to make tiles that have visible seams is an aesthetic decision that is dependent on the content of your page.

• There is no "right" size for a background tile. The size affects the number of times the graphic repeats.

• Be sure to pay attention to the "value" (lights and darks) of your web pages. Make dark backgrounds with light text or light backgrounds with dark text. Don't use high-contrast source material for background tiles.

• You cannot reliably match colors between different file formats. If you are looking to match color, be sure to use a JPEG background tile with a JPEG foreground image, or a GIF with a GIF.

7

"There isn't any symbolism.
The sea is the sea.
The old man is an old man.
The boy is a boy the fish is a fish."
—Ernest Hemingway

Buttons & Rules
graphics & html conventions

The web environment has unusual limitations that don't exist in other design mediums. Web pages have no set length like printed pages do. The visual techniques and metaphors available to print designers, such as using a block of color behind text or images, changing the text color in an isolated paragraph or sidebar, or using a different screened-back image or picture frame to separate an idea or theme, are not easily replicated on the web.

It's often necessary to accept a more limited aesthetic and work with conventions that are tailored to web constraints. HTML generates limited graphics, such as rules and bullets, and it's also possible to include custom graphics for more variety and originality. This chapter covers the HTML and image editing techniques used to create these small, but necessary, graphics and embellishments.

Buttons & Rules

Horizontal Rules

A horizontal rule that serves as a page divider is something you'll rarely see in print design. These divider lines are commonly observed across web sites the world over, however. Some are embossed, some are thick, some are thin, and some are colored or have different shapes. The web term for these lines is horizontal rule, and they are used for many things:

- Defining a page break

- Completing an idea

- Beginning a list

- Separating one picture from another

If you want to add horizontal rules to your pages, you have some choices. You can use HTML code, or you can insert your own artwork to make custom horizontal rules, and vertical rules, too. When all else fails, you can also use libraries of horizontal rule clip art.

▶ definition

Rules

The term rule is derived from the printing and typesetting fields, where it commonly refers to a straight, unadorned line used to separate objects on a page. The most common rules seen in print are those used to separate the columns of a newspaper.

Horizontal Rules, the HTML Way

The basic HTML horizontal rule tag looks like this: `<HR>`. Here it is in the context of code.

```
Some Text
<HR>
Some More Text
```

Some Text
Some More Text

This tag will put an embossed line horizontally through your page at whatever point you insert it into an HTML document. If you stretch your browser window wider, the horizontal rule will get wider, and vice versa if you narrow your window. Horizontal rules have no set width, except to fill the horizontal distance of your browser screen. Techniques for setting a fixed width rule follow.

Sometimes, you may want to add some breathing room because the horizontal rule will butt up underneath whatever text or image that was in the HTML code before it. The following code adds a row of empty space above and below the rule.

```
<P>Some Text
<P>
<HR>
<P>Some More Text
```

Some Text
Some More Text

If you want to add more breathing room between your text and rules, insert a paragraph break with the P **tag. That effectively puts the rule in its own paragraph.**

Fancier Horizontal Rule Tags

An advanced course in horizontal rule-making would include:

- Changing the rule's width
- Changing the rule's weight (thickness)
- Changing both the rule's width and weight
- Left-aligning the rule
- Eliminating fake emboss shading

Notice that if you define a width, the resulting horizontal rule is automatically centered. Any value you put after the = (equals) sign tells the rule how wide to be in pixels.

Here's the code telling the rule to be 10 pixels wide:

```
<HR WIDTH=10>
```

Using a WIDTH **attribute can adjust the length of the line.**

The following code changes the weight, or thickness, of the line. Notice that this stretches for the length of a page:

```
<HR SIZE=10>
```

By changing the SIZE **attribute, the entire line gets thicker.**

The following code changes the thickness and width at the same time. Here's an example that shows the results of code specifying that the rule be square—equal height and width.

```
<HR SIZE=25 WIDTH=25>
```

By changing the SIZE **and** WIDTH **together, you can make other rectilinear shapes like this square.**

The following code aligns the square left and sizes it at 10 pixels high and 10 pixels wide:

```
<HR ALIGN=LEFT SIZE=10 WIDTH=10>
```

You can use alignment attributes on horizontal rules, too!

Look ma, no fake emboss shading!

```
<HR NOSHADE>
```

The NOSHADE **attribute creates a black line.**

Horizontal Rules the Do-It-Yourself Way

Anything gets old when you see it too often, and horizontal rules are no exception. If you want to be a little more creative, here are some tips to creating custom artwork to design your own rules. When you create your own horizontal rule art, your artwork dictates the length, width, and height. It's a graphic like any other graphic. It can be aliased, anti-aliased, a GIF, a JPEG, interlaced, transparent, blurred, 2D, 3D—you name it. If you know how to make it, it can be a horizontal rule.

To include a graphic as a horizontal rule, the HTML code would be:

```
<IMG SRC="your_horizontal_rule_art_here.gif">
```

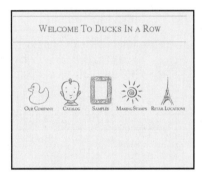

Here's the Ducks In A Row site with two HTML rules.

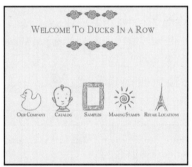

Here's the Ducks In A Row site with a custom rule. Rules don't have to be lines, ya know! We've included the smflowerule.gif file in the chap07 folder of the <chd> CD-ROM, if you'd like to try it out.

Vertical Rules

Vertical rules are not an easy task to take on with web pages. Making the custom artwork is identical to making any other custom artwork and all the Photoshop, Paint Shop Pro, and Illustrator tips shared in this book should be of help. The trick is how to get vertical lines aligned to a web page because there is no easy way to assign vertical columns by using HTML. There's a lesson called Vertical Rules on how to position vertical ruled lines using tables in Chapter 9, "Alignment."

Clip Art Rules, Too

There are many kind, generous souls on the web who lend their wares for free. Other gifted souls may charge for their art so that they can do what they're good at—satisfy you and me—and still feed themselves and their families. Clip art is a wondrous thing in a pinch, and with tools such as Photoshop, Illustrator, and Painter, there's no end to the cool ways you can personalize clip art files. Make sure that the images are royalty-free in the respective licensing agreements if you are going to modify them. Some authors have stipulations that must be honored. Read the readmes!

Here are some clip art collections that we think are cool:

Gifs R Us—Jay Boersma's prolific collection:
http://www.ecn.bgu.edu/users/gas52r0/Jay/home.html

Yahoo search for Clip Art:
http://www.yahoo.com/Computers_and_Internet/
Multimedia/ Pictures/Clip_Art/

Bullets

You'll see plenty of pages with diverse information on the web, but lists of one type or another are universally needed on the majority of sites. List items can appear indented with numbers or preceded by icons known as bullets. Bullets on the web can look standardized, using solid circles in front of text (much like those generated by a word processor), or they can include custom artwork that looks more typical of a CD-ROM or magazine page layout. Creating custom bullets is similar to creating custom horizontal rules. Basically, any artwork that you're capable of creating is a candidate for bullet art.

When designing bulleted lists for the web, you can choose from either HTML bullets or image-based bullets. HTML bullets are created by using tags that identify the type of list you are creating; such bullets appear as basic circles or squares. Image-based bullets are those you generate from clip art or your own artwork, and they can be used to enhance a list or provide added functionality, such as links. This next section shows you how to create both HTML and image-based bullets, including several variations on both themes.

Creating HTML Bulleted Lists

Using HTML-based bullets is certainly less work than creating your own custom artwork. Sometimes, they're more appropriate, as well. Simple and clean design often looks best without a lot of custom artwork on a page. There will be many instances where an HTML-based bullet or indent will do the job more effectively than custom bullet artwork.

To create a list with solid circle bullets, use the UL (Unordered List) tag. Individual lines are designated with the LI (List Item) tag, as shown in the following code:

```
<UL>
<LI> The first thinga-dingy
<LI> The second thinga-dingy
<LI> The third thinga-dingy
</UL>
```

The UL element is a container, and it requires an end tag. The LI element is also a container, but its end tag is optional.

The results of using UL **and** LI.

Lists can be nested by nesting UL elements. The following code uses an additional UL tag to create a bulleted list nested within another bulleted list.

```
<UL>
<LI> The first thinga-dingy
<LI> The second thinga-dingy
<LI> The third thinga-dingy
<UL>
<LI> More types of thinga-dingies
<LI> Yet More types of thinga-dingies
<LI> Even more types of thinga-dingies
</UL>
<LI> Forth thinga-dingy
</UL>
```

You can nest bulleted points by adding multiple UL **tags before the close** /UL **tag.**

You can link items in your list to other pages or sites by using the anchor <A HREF> tag within an ordered list or an unordered list. The following code shows how to use link tags to include links within a bulleted list:

```
<UL>
<LI> <A HREF="http://www.domain.com">
The first thinga-dingy</A>
<LI> <A HREF="http://www.domain.com">
The second thinga-dingy</A>
<LI> <A HREF="http://www.domain.com">
The third thinga-dingy</A>
</UL>
```

The items in your list can be straight text, or hypertext by changing a few tags.

Creating Ordered and Definition Lists

At times, you may not want your lists to be preceded by bullets. When creating a list of steps to be followed in order, for example, using numbers rather than bullets will help get your point across. Such numbered lists are called ordered lists. Likewise, lists such as glossaries can appear with indents rather than bullets or numbers. These lists are known as definition lists.

To make a list that automatically generates numbers in front of its items, use the OL (**o**rdered **l**ist) tag. The following code lines show how to use OL to produce a numbered list:

```
<OL>
<LI> The first thinga-dingy
<LI> The second thinga-dingy
<LI> The third thinga-dingy
</OL>
```

Using the "ordered list" would automatically generate numbers, instead of bullets in front of each "list item":

1. The first thinga-dingy
2. The second thinga-dingy
3. The third thinga-dingy

The OL tag generates ordered (numbered) lists.

If you want to indent items in a list without seeing a bullet shape, you may want to use a DL (**d**efinition **l**ist) tag instead of creating an organized list or unorganized list. You use the DT tag for the flush left items and the DD tag for the indented items, as shown in the following code:

```
<DL>
<DT>
Thingy Dingies
<DD>The first thinga-dingy
<DD>The second thinga-dingy
<DD>The second thinga-dingy
</DL>
```

Thingy Dingies

The first thinga-dingy
The second thinga-dingy
The second thinga-dingy

Using the DL definition list tags creates indented lists.

If you want to change the shape of the automatically generated bullets, you can use the TYPE=circle, TYPE=square, or TYPE=disc attributes, as shown in the following code:

```
<UL>
<LI TYPE=circle>Circle-shaped Bullet
<LI TYPE=square>Square-shaped Bullet
<LI TYPE=disc>Disc-shaped Bullet
</UL>
```

○ Circle-shaped Bullet
□ Square-shaped Bullet
● Disc-shaped Bullet

Using the TYPE attribute can change the shape of HTML generated bullets.

You can also organize your ordered lists by using alphabetic and roman numerals for bullets. You can do this by adding the variations shown in the following table.

Attribute	List Type	Example
TYPE=1	Numbers	1, 2, 3
TYPE=A	Uppercase letters	A, B, C
TYPE=a	Lowercase letters	a, b, c
TYPE=I	Uppercase Roman	I, II, III
TYPE=i	Lowercase Roman	i, ii, iii

The following code shows variations of the TYPE attribute, which produces these results:

```
<OL>
<LI TYPE=1> Thingy One
<LI TYPE=1> Thingy Two
<LI TYPE=1> Thingy Three
<P>
<LI TYPE=A> Thingy One
<LI TYPE=A> Thingy Two
<LI TYPE=A> Thingy Three
<P>
<LI TYPE=a> Thingy One
<LI TYPE=a> Thingy Two
<LI TYPE=a> Thingy Three
<P>
<LI TYPE=I> Thingy One
<LI TYPE=I> Thingy Two
<LI TYPE=I> Thingy Three
<P>
<LI TYPE=i> Thingy One
<LI TYPE=i> Thingy Two
<LI TYPE=i> Thingy Three
</OL>
```

An example of several types of HTML-generated bullets.

Button Clip Art

You'll find clip art for buttons all over the World Wide Web. Clip art buttons follow the same rules for custom bullet art; use the <IMG SRC> tag if you want to use the button for decoration only. Add the anchor <A HREF> tag if you want the artwork to link elsewhere. Clip art typically already exists in GIF or JPEG web file formats, and if not, you can use Photoshop to convert them.

Bullets can be abstract, such as dots and cubes, or an icon that actually means something. Michael Herrick, of http://www.matterform.com, has invented something called QBullets, after cue-bullet, or bullets that cue you to their hint or function. These buttons are part of a proposed interface standard that his site discusses in detail.

Creating Custom-Made Bullets

If you want to use bullets that show more creativity than the basic square or circle, or if you need added linking functionality, you can create your own custom-made bullets. Custom-made bullets can be ornamental, where their sole purpose is to decorate the beginning of a list item. They can also be functional, where they serve as icons that link you to another page or site.

If you plan to make your own artwork or use clip art for buttons, you'll need to use different HTML tags to make the art behave as you want. For visual enhancement only, use the IMG tag to include image-based bullets at the front of a list, as shown in the following code example. You won't use the OL or the UL tags because the image itself is creating both the bullet and the indent. Note that you do have to put a BR tag at the end of each list item to tell the browser to jump to a new line for the next entry in the list. The BR tag wasn't necessary when working with the OL or UL tags because it's a built-in part of the list functionality.

```
<HTML>
<HEAD>
    <TITLE>ducks process</TITLE>
</HEAD>
<BODY BGCOLOR="#FFFF99">
<IMG SRC="process.gif">
<P><IMG SRC="littleduck.GIF">Joan designs
the artwork
<BR>
<IMG SRC="littleduck.GIF">It's sent out to
get made into molds
<BR>
<IMG SRC="littleduck.GIF">The designs are
produced on big sheets of rubber
<BR>
<IMG SRC="littleduck.GIF">
The sheets are cut apart and glued
onto wood
<BR>
<IMG SRC="littleduck.GIF">
The stamp design is printed on the
wood blocks
</BODY>
</HTML>
```

Here is the original graphic. Adding more space to the right of the graphic will push the text to its right in the HTML document.

Here's the result of the HTML code shown on the left. Notice how the ducks are crowded next to the text? You can fix this by changing the source graphic.

Adding more space to the right of the graphic in your paint program will add the space we want between the button graphic and the text.

There's more space between the bullets and the text because the source graphic is wider. This is a big improvement! Be sure to read Chapter 9, "Alignment," to learn other techniques to control text and image alignment.

▶ exercise

Changing Button Size in Photoshop

In this exercise, you will experiment with creating different alignment settings by inserting different sized bullet artwork into your HTML.

Step 1: Open the littleduck.gif file located on the <chd> CD-ROM in the chap07 folder.

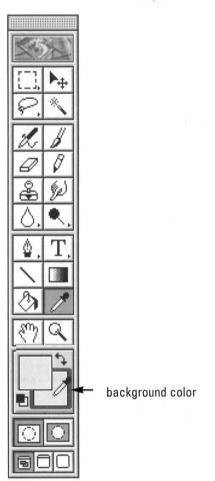

background color

Step 2: Select your Eyedropper tool and click once on the background color of littleduck.gif so you can put the same color into the background color picker of Photoshop. The background color has a red outline for the purposes of this explanation. **Hint:** To use the Eyedropper to fill the background color, **Option-click** (Mac) or **Alt-click** (PC).

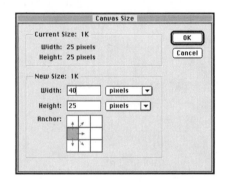

Step 3: Choose **Image:Canvas Size** and enter new dimensions into the settings. You can either expand the image with centering or other alignments by clicking the **Anchor** settings.

Step 4: Re-save the GIF file by choosing **File:Save**.

Step 5: Open the process.html file located on the <chd> CD-ROM in the chap07 folder. Copy it into the same folder as the newly saved GIF file and choose **File:Open** inside the browser of your choice.

Linked Bullets

If you want to use the bullets as icons to link to
another site or page, use the anchor <A HREF>
tag, as shown in the following code example.
Because linked images typically have a blue border around them, you'll want to use the BORDER=0
attribute inside the IMG tag. Note the pointing
hand cursor on the company link in the following
image. Your viewer's cursor will change to this
hand when gliding over a linked image to let the
viewer know the image is a link.

```
<HTML>
<HEAD>
    <TITLE>ducks process</TITLE>
</HEAD>
<BODY TEXT="#333300" BGCOLOR="#FFFF99"
LINK="#330000">
<IMG SRC="siteview.gif">

<P><A HREF="catalog.html">
<IMG SRC="littlecat.GIF"
BORDER=0></A>catalog

<P><A HREF="process.html">
<IMG SRC="littleproc.GIF"
BORDER=0></A>process

<P><A HREF="company.html">
<IMG SRC="smcomp.GIF"
BORDER=0></A>company

<P><A HREF="retail.html">
<IMG SRC="smretail.GIF"
BORDER=0 ></A>retail locations

<P><A HREF="samples.html">
<IMG SRC="smsamp.GIF"
BORDER=0></A>samples
</BODY>
</HTML>
```

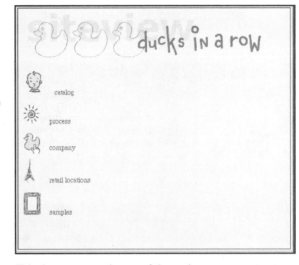

This demonstrates the use of the anchor <A HREF> tag to
link the buttons to URLs. The BORDER=0 attribute was used
to turn off the default borders around the linked graphics,
creating a seamless effect. The only way an end user would
know to click on the buttons would be to pass their cursor
over the illustrations.

▶ chapter seven summary

Working with bullets, buttons, and rules on the web is a
lot less straightforward than in a text or print document.
It requires a mixture of programming and design skills.
The contents of this chapter are summarized here:

• Horizontal rules and bullets can be added using either
  HTML or custom graphics. Graphics take longer to download, but can add a lot more originality to a page design.

• It's helpful if you make your buttons and bullets mean
  something rather than just exist for decoration. You might
  want to refer to Michael Herrick's Matterform page at
  http://www. matterform.com for ideas, or better yet—create
  your own ideas!

> *"The secret of ugliness consists
> not in irregularity,
> but in being uninteresting."*
> —*Ralph Waldo Emerson (1803–82)*

Transparency
look ma, no matte lines

> ▶ **this chapter**
>
> *transparency tricks*
> *matching backgrounds*
> *clean transparency*
> *transparency software*

A technique called "masking" is commonly used in computer graphics to make artwork appear in irregular shapes rather than squares and rectangles. In web design, the term "masking" is often referred to as "transparency" because transparent GIFs are the most prevalent means used to create a masking effect. Creating transparency mostly involves image editing techniques, making it more a web graphics process than a function of HTML.

This chapter will cover transparency techniques in Photoshop and Paint Shop Pro. We'll look at the common pitfalls and solutions to making clean transparent GIFs and examine PNG transparency, a new format that is not yet supported by most browsers, but holds the promise of becoming a superior masking method. We'll also examine graphic processes such as anti-aliasing, aliasing, masking, and alpha channels.

A computer image file by definition is automatically saved in a rectangle. Way too much artwork on the web is in the shape of ectangles—buttons, pictures, splash screens, menu bars—ugh! Mastering transparency is the only escape!

Transparency Tricks

There are two types of transparency—one requires true masking, and the other involves trickery. The trickery method is the easiest, so let's study it first.

Let's say you make a graphic of a circle and want it to look as if it's free-floating. Make the background behind the circle the same color as your web page. When you put the elements together in HTML, there should be no obvious rectangular border. However, there's a snag. Making foreground and background images on the web match in color takes an extra bit of education. This chapter reviews how to set exact background colors (assuming your end viewer has not changed his or her preferences to override color choices) using two HTML-based techniques. One involves using hexadecimal code to set a specific background color, and the other requires setting up the HTML to use a solid pattern tile. Step-by-step examples help you explore these two techniques and show you how to make the irregularly shaped artwork lay on top of colored backgrounds.

result in browser

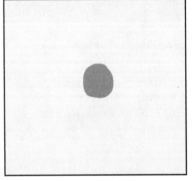

source file

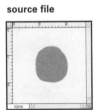

You can easily create the illusion of irregularly shaped images by making the foreground artwork include the same color as the target background on your web page.

▶ warning

Color Preferences in Browsers

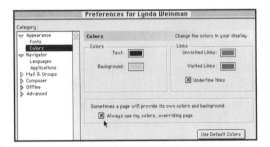

It's kind of scary for web publishers who count on the background colors they pick to achieve an illusion of irregular-shaped images, because end viewers can check **Always use mine**, which overrides the color choices you've specified! If you want to view sites as designers intended them to be seen, make sure **Always use my colors, overriding page** is always checked instead.

▶ warning

JPEG or GIF?

Your images and tiled background patterns may be saved as either a JPEG or GIF. If you are going to use a solid background image and want it to match your solid foreground image, you must use a JPEG background and JPEG foreground, or a GIF background and a GIF foreground between the elements; otherwise, color shifting will occur.

▶ exercise

Creating Background Color the Hex Way

This technique was covered in Chapter 4, "Web Color," but will be reviewed here for the purpose of transparency. This first example demonstrates how to include irregularly shaped artwork using the BGCOLOR attribute. This technique works especially well on images that include anti-aliasing, soft edges, glows, or drop shadows.

Step 1: Launch Photoshop, **Open** the floatduck.gif file from the chap08 folder of the <chd> CD-ROM.

Step 2: Use the Eyedropper to find out the RGB values of the image. **Hint:** If you use the browser-safe color charts in Chapter 4, "Web Color," it will be easy to find the hex and RGB colors.

Step 3: Next, write the HTML in the following column. This code tells the background to be green by using the hexadecimal code #999966 and inserts the floatduck.gif image on the same page.

```
<HTML>
<HEAD>
  <TITLE>transparency trick!</TITLE>
</HEAD>
<BODY BGCOLOR="#999966">
<CENTER>
  <IMG SRC="floatduck.gif">
</CENTER>
</BODY>
</HTML>
```

Step 4: Save the document as floatduck.gif.

Step 5: View the final result in a web browser. With this technique, you do not need transparency software to achieve the illusion of transparency.

Background Color Using Solid Patterns

Another way to color the background of a page is to use a solid color swatch with the BACKGROUND attribute of the BODY tag (BODY BACKGROUND). This tag is more commonly used with artwork that has an image in it, such as those examples demonstrated in Chapter 6, "Tiles." The BACKGROUND attribute takes whatever art you specify in your HTML and repeats it to fill an entire web page.

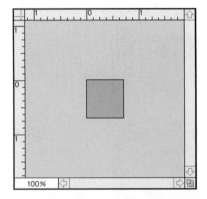

Here's an example of a Photoshop file that is filled with the same solid green used in the last hexadecimal-based example. If this image were requested using the BACKGROUND attribute, the HTML could not be overridden even in the event an end user had changed their browser color defaults.

For instructions on how to make images repeat as tiles, refer to Chapter 6, "Tiles." We are going to use the same HTML technique that Chapter 6 described in detail, but our source image for the pattern tile is made out of a solid color instead of an image. As it is repeated over the page, this tile will produce a solid background identical in appearance to what the hexadecimal method demonstrated in the previous exercise.

You can actually use both the BGCOLOR and BACKGROUND attributes inside the same BODY tag, which ensures the safest results with this technique. Here's an example of the code:

```
<HTML>
<HEAD>
  <TITLE>transparency trick.2</TITLE>
</HEAD>
<BODY BGCOLOR="#999966"
BACKGROUND="green.gif">
<CENTER>
  <IMG SRC="floatduck.gif">
</CENTER>
</BODY>
</HTML>
```

Transparent GIFs

If transparent GIFs are an unfamiliar term to you, don't sweat. We know of no common application for transparent GIFs other than the web, so they're relatively new to everyone. Transparent GIFs are used to create the illusion of irregularly shaped computer files by assigning one color in a graphic to be invisible. This process is also called masking.

Transparency is assigned when the file is saved. A variety of software applications enable you to save and define transparency, and we'll cover several of them in this chapter. When working with transparent GIFs, there are two things to keep in mind: first, how to make art properly for one color masking transparency and second, how to use the programs that let you save the artwork in this file format.

When to Use Transparent Artwork

We recommend using transparent GIFs (and PNGs, but more on this later in the chapter) only on web pages that have pattern background tiles because you can more easily create the masking effect against solid colors by using the trickery technique we just covered. Establishing transparency in a GIF or PNG adds extra steps in production, so there's no reason to do that when there's an easier way.

The reason we recommend transparency with pattern background tiles is because you can't reliably match the position of a foreground image to that of a background tile with only standard HTML. (This problem is described in more detail in Chapter 9, "Alignment.") If you want to put irregularly shaped artwork over patterned backgrounds, you'll have to use transparency.

You can try to align a foreground image with a pattern to the identical background pattern, but they won't line up. And to make matters worse, the alignment is different on a Mac and PC! Note: We used the same artwork in the BACKGROUND and IMG SRC attributes, but intentionally reversed the color in the foreground image to accentuate the offset alignment problem. On a Mac, most browsers introduce an 8-pixel offset on the upper and left sides of the foreground image, and on a PC there is a 10-pixel offset. This makes it impossible to align a foreground to a background in the cross-platform web environment.

Making Clean Transparent GIF Artwork

The key to producing effective transparent GIFs is to ensure that your artwork is produced correctly. We need to begin by first going through a short primer on aliased versus anti-aliased artwork. Anti-aliasing is the process of blending around the edges of a graphic to hide the jagged square pixels it is made of.

Many of the transparent GIFs we see on the web have very ugly residual matte lines, usually in the form of white or black edges. These matte lines can be traced back to the way in which the image was anti-aliased.

Anti-aliasing is the process where one color and shape blends into another in order to hide the jagged square pixel nature of computer-generated graphics.

For web graphics, anti-aliasing is not always the best approach. Creating clean transparent GIFs is one of those exceptions where aliased graphics create the least amount of problems.

The anti-aliased blended edge is precisely what causes matte line or "fringing" problems once the graphic is converted to transparent GIFs. Because transparent GIFs mask only one color out of your image, the remaining colors along the blended edge of anti-aliased artwork remain, even when you really wanted them to disappear.

Glows, Soft-Edges, and Drop Shadows with GIF Transparency

Because of the problems anti-aliasing introduces, artwork with glows, soft-edges, and drop shadows can look awful as transparent GIFs. One popular solution is to build artwork against roughly the same color background that it will be seen against in the web browser. The artwork will look terrible when you make it, but it will look fine once placed against the final background in a web browser.

GIF Transparency Compositing Chart

Aliased

Anti-Aliased

Glow

When the different examples of edges are made into transparent GIFs using 1-color transparency, did you notice how every example except the aliased version picked up the background color they were made against, resulting in an unwanted white rim around the graphic? That's because the images with soft edges picked up parts of the white color they were created against. This created an unsightly problem, which is commonly called a halo, fringe, rim, or matte line in the industry.

Making clean transparent artwork with no fringes around the edges involves setting the background color to the same target color as the pattern it will lay over in HTML. This example shows the anti-aliased ducks against green.

This example shows the ducks with a glow against green. By setting the target color to green, the fringing problem will go away once the artwork is on top the pattern background in the HTML file.

When the transparency is set, the files look pretty terrible. They won't look good until they are laid over their target green background. If the files are prepared this way, you will correct their predisposition to favor any other color.

The end result looks quite acceptable now. Look ma, no matte lines!

▶ note

Transparent GIF URLs

Here are some useful URLs you can use to track down transparency tips:

Online Transparent GIF Creation
http://www.vrl.com/Imaging/filters.html

**Thomas Boutell's WWW FAQ
on Transparency**
http://sunsite.unc.edu/boutell/faq/tinter.htm

**Chipp Walter's Excellent GIF
Transparency Tutorial**
http://www.chipp.com/igor/photosho.htm

HTML for Transparent GIFs

The HTML for transparent GIFs is identical to the HTML for any other type of GIF or JPEG. The IMG SRC tag is all you need. For an unlinked transparent GIF graphic, the HTML code looks like this:

```
<IMG SRC="transgif.gif">
```

For a linked transparent GIF graphic, the HTML would look like this:

```
<A HREF="http://www.destination_domain_
name.com">
<IMG SRC="transgif.gif" BORDER=0></A>
```

Other Transparency Experiments

We've included numerous files in the chap08 folder of the <chd> CD-ROM with which to try your own transparency experiments. The ducks.psd file has different variations of background colors and feathered edges. If you want to change the color background, selectively turn on and off eye icons to make the layers you wish to try visible. Using the coloring techniques and Preserve Transparency features of Photoshop described in Chapter 4, "Web Color," experiment with changing the colors and trying your hand at making transparent GIFs. Be sure to change the HTML file to reflect any new file names you create, and you will be able to see the results of your experiments inside a browser.

Transparent GIF Software

There are lots of popular software packages that support GIF transparency. It's impossible to cover all of them in this book, but we've included instructions for Photoshop and Paint Shop Pro.

Adobe Photoshop GIF89a Export Plug-In

Current versions of Photoshop ship with a Mac or PC compatible GIF89a plug-in that supports transparency. This plug-in is pre-installed in current versions of Photoshop.

Here's a step-by-step tour through Photoshop's GIF89a plug-in features:

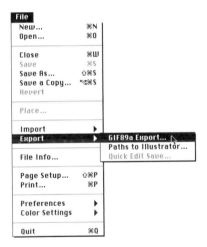

Step 1: Open the aduck.gif file from the chap08 folder of the <chd> CD-ROM. **Note:** This file is already saved in Index Color mode. If you worked with an RGB image, we recommend that you convert it to Indexed Color before you use this filter.

Step 2: Under **File**, select **Export**, **GIF89a**. **Note:** Most Photoshop filters are located under the **Filter** menu. The GIF89a filter is located under the **Export** menu.

Step 3: Use the Eyedropper tool to click on the white background, and it will change to gray, which indicates it will be masked. (**Note:** You can change the default gray color to any other by clicking in the gray box and accessing the color picker.) Make sure your settings match the above image, or you can choose to use **Interlace**.

Step 4: When you click **OK**, you are prompted to save the file. Photoshop automatically inserts the .gif extension, which causes the words .gif to repeat in this example. Delete one of the .gif repeats before saving.

Step 5: Insert the file you just saved in a folder with the files trans.html and smpat.gif from the chap08 folder of the <chd> CD-ROM. Check to see if the transparency worked by choosing **File:Open** and selecting trans.html in a browser of your choice.

▶ e x e r c i s e

Transparency in Paint Shop Pro 4.0

Step 1: Open the aduck.gif file from the chap08 folder of the <chd> CD-ROM.

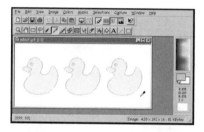

Step 2: Using the Eyedropper tool, find a spot on the area that you want to be transparent and look at the palette display to find out what color index it is. In the palette display, you will see four numbers, R, G, B, and I. The number by the "I" is the index in the palette for that color. Write this number down; you will need it to set your transparency.

Step 3: Under **File**, select **Save As**. In the Save As dialog box, make sure the **Save as type** option is set to GIF-Compuserve, and the **Sub type** option is set to **Version 89a-noninterlaced**. Now select the **Options** button.

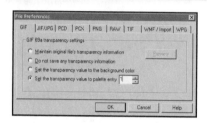

Step 4: In the File Preferences dialog box, select the **Set the transparency** value to palette entry and insert the number that you wrote down earlier. This sets the color you selected from the palette to be transparent in the browser. Press the **OK** button.

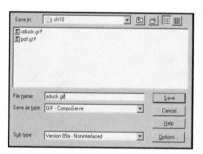

Step 5: Type the name and location to save the file.

Step 6: Insert the file you just saved in a folder with the files trans.html and smpat.gif from the chap08 folder of the <chd> CD-ROM. See if the transparency worked by choosing **File:Open** and selecting trans.html in a browser of your choice.

PNG Transparency

The PNG file format has a sensational masking feature, which unfortunately isn't supported very well yet. It allows you, in an 8-bit image, to create a mask with up to 256 levels of transparency. No other file format has ever allowed this! What it means is that very small 8-bit (and lower) files can be generated with varying levels of translucency, unlike GIF, which only has one level of masking: on or off.

If you want to see PNG transparency in action, you must install a plug-in into your browser first. Unfortunately, at the time this chapter was written no tools for Mac or Windows existed to save a PNG file with 8-bit transparency. An example of PNG transparency is in the Alpha Channel Transparency section of Chapter 3, "Speedy Graphics." Here are some URLs for the plug-in and sites with sample files for viewing:

The Siegel & Gale PNG Live Plug-in Netscape 4
http://codelab.siegelgale.com/solutions/pnglive2.html

Greg Roelofs's PNG Resource
http://www.wco.com/~png/

The PNG Home Page
http://www.wco.com/~png/

The PNG Specification at W3C
http://www.w3.org/TR/REC-png-multi.html

▶ chapter eight summary

This chapter covered the complex decisions of transparency creation. Here's a summary of key points:

- If you create artwork against solid colors and match the same solid color to your web page background, you can fake transparency. This method is just as effective as creating a transparent GIF, but a lot easier! We recommend using transparent GIFs only when you want to put an irregularly shaped image on top of a patterned background tile.

- If you create the transparent artwork with anti-aliased edges, it will be predisposed to work with the colored background it was created against. This often causes unwanted fringing or halos around transparent artwork.

- Creating aliased edges is the key to making transparent artwork look good against any background color or pattern. Create artwork with aliased tools to avoid anti-aliased edges.

- PNG transparency is much better than GIF transparency, but there is currently insufficient browser and tool support to implement it on anything but experimental web pages.

9

"It's not wise to violate rules
until you know how to observe them."
—T. S. Eliot

Alignment
bossing pixels around

If you are used to laying out graphics and text in other media, even other computer-based media, you will find a unique challenge in HTML's alignment capabilities—or its lack thereof.

Because of the web's unique distributed environment, where you have no idea what disparate types of systems your page will be viewed on, HTML was not originally equipped with facilities for aligning the various elements on a page. The original HTML had no facility for text alignment, tables, or even inline images, let alone a method of sizing and aligning them.

Fortunately, that has changed significantly. It's still common to hear web publishers complain about the lack of control they have over the final display properties of a given page; however, the situation is rapidly improving.

As you read this chapter, keep in mind that alignment in HTML is not an easy issue. You are dealing with a lot of variables that you have no control over. Many of your efforts in this area will be more of a compromise than you are probably used to. Absolute control over layout is not possible with pure HTML, but it's more than possible to create pages that will look great on a variety of platforms.

Alignment

Text Alignment Tags

In its simplest form, aligning text is a matter of how a paragraph flows from one line to the next. For example, the paragraphs in this book are aligned on the left sides of each line relative to the margins on the page. This is called left-justified text.

HTML gives us the ability to center or align text against the left or right margins. Beginning with HTML 4.0, justified alignment is also available. The 4.0 versions of Netscape Navigator and MS Internet Explorer support full-justification. HTML supports text content anywhere within a document. In fact, HTML treats most content as text, including inline graphics. However, in order to control the appearance of text, it must be within some sort of container that specifies the desired attributes. The most common container for text is the paragraph element (the P tag).

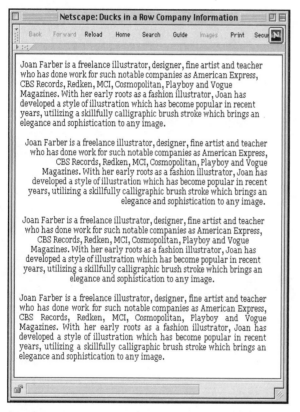

Examples of text justification options: left, right, middle, **and** justified (left **and** right).

Using P to Align Text

The P tag is used to place a block of text within a paragraph. Normally, the purpose for this is to apply vertical spacing between paragraphs as a visual cue. You can also use paragraphs to specify horizontal alignment for your text, using the ALIGN attribute.

For example, to create a paragraph of text you could enclose it in <P> and </P> like this:

```
<P> Ducks In A Row products represent a
unique concept in rubber stamping. Our
original designs created by Joan Farber,
internationally recognized illustrator,
are unlike anything found in the stamp
market today. </P>

<P>Joan Farber is a freelance illustrator,
designer, fine artist, and teacher who
has done work for such notable companies
as American Express, CBS Records, Redken,
MCI, Cosmopolitan, Playboy and Vogue
Magazines. With her early roots as a
fashion illustrator, Joan has developed
a style of illustration which has become
popular in recent years, utilizing a
skillfully calligraphic brush stroke which
brings an elegance and sophistication to
any image. </P>

<P>Because the style of art throughout
the catalog is consistent, any of the
designs may be used together side by side
or superimposed, making the possibilities
for personal expression boundless. </P>
```

In practice, the end tag (/P) is rarely necessary, so you don't see it very often. We use it here only to show that P creates a container with both a beginning and an end. By default, most browsers will display paragraphs of text left-aligned—that is, with a ragged right-margin.

Here's what the code on the left looks like in Netscape Navigator:

> Ducks In A Row products represent a unique concept in rubber stamping. Our original designscreated by Joan Farber, internationally recognized illustrator, are unlike anything found in the stamp market today.
>
> Joan Farber is a freelance illustrator, designer, fine artist, and teacher who has done work for such notable companies as American Express, CBS Records, Redken, MCI, Cosmopolitan, Playboy and Vogue Magazines. With her early roots as a fashion illustrator, Joan has developed a style of illustration which has become popular in recent years, utilizing a skillfully calligraphic brush stroke which brings an elegance and sophistication to any image.

The default left-alignment of text in Netscape Navigator.

If you want different alignment, you must specify it. The P tag may be used with the ALIGN attribute:

```
<P ALIGN=RIGHT>

Ducks In A Row products represent a unique
concept in rubber stamping. Our original
designs created by Joan Farber, interna-
tionally recognized illustrator, are unlike
anything found in the stamp market today.
```

With the ALIGN=RIGHT attribute, the paragraph is displayed with the right side aligned and the left side ragged.

> Ducks In A Row products represent a unique concept in rubber stamping. Our original designscreated by Joan Farber, internationally recognized illustrator, are unlike anything found in the stamp market today.

A paragraph in Netscape with ALIGN=RIGHT.

The ALIGN attribute can also be set to CENTER or JUSTIFY. The CENTER alignment will center each line in a paragraph.

Ducks In A Row products represent a unique concept in rubber stamping. Our original designscreated by Joan Farber, internationally recognized illustrator, are unlike anything found in the stamp market today.

A paragraph in Netscape with `ALIGN=CENTER`.

Finally, the `JUSTIFY` alignment will align both sides to their margins.

Ducks In A Row products represent a unique concept in rubber stamping. Our original designscreated by Joan Farber, internationally recognized illustrator, are unlike anything found in the stamp market today.

A paragraph in Netscape Navigator 4.0 with `ALIGN=JUSTIFY`.

The usefulness of this setting is somewhat reduced by the way it is implemented. In order to justify both margins, spaces are inserted between words, but not between letters. This results in lines of text like the second-to-last line in our example. The spaces between the words are so large as to really detract from the overall value of the technique.

The `ALIGN=JUSTIFY` setting exaggerates a long-time problem with the Netscape browser: The right margin is larger than the left. This is true in all versions of the Netscape browser, but it's much more noticeable with justified text. Using style sheets and/or frames, it is possible to overcome this limitation (more about those techniques in Chapters 13, "Style," and 14, "Navigation"), but with the simple justified paragraph it's pretty obvious that the margins don't match.

Another important point to mention is that these margins are defined by the width of the browser. This means that if someone has their browser window maximized to the width of the screen, the lines of type will be quite long. It's also possible to use the `ALIGN=JUSTIFY` setting with tables to limit the width of text lines. We'll cover this technique later in this chapter.

Using DIV to Align Blocks of Text

More often than not, when you want to apply a specific alignment to a paragraph, you will want to apply that alignment to more than one paragraph at a time. That's what the DIV tag is for.

The DIV tag is a container, and it requires an end tag. By using DIV, you are effectively saying, "Apply this alignment from here to there." Here's an example:

```
<DIV ALIGN=CENTER>

<P> Ducks In A Row products represent a
unique concept in rubber stamping. Our
original designs created by Joan Farber,
internationally recognized illustrator,
are unlike anything found in the stamp
market today.

<P>Joan Farber is a freelance illustrator,
designer, fine artist, and teacher who
has done work for such notable companies
as American Express, CBS Records, Redken,
MCI, Cosmopolitan, Playboy and Vogue
Magazines. With her early roots as a
fashion illustrator, Joan has developed a
style of illustration which has become
popular in recent years, utilizing a
skillfully calligraphic brush stroke which
brings an elegance and sophistication to
any image.

<P>Because the style of art throughout
the catalog is consistent, any of the
designs may be used together side by side
or superimposed, making the possibilities
for personal expression boundless.

</DIV>
```

Ducks In A Row products represent a unique concept in rubber stamping. Our original designscreated by Joan Farber, internationally recognized illustrator, are unlike anything found in the stamp market today.

Joan Farber is a freelance illustrator, designer, fine artist, and teacher who has done work for such notable companies as American Express, CBS Records, Redken, MCI, Cosmopolitan, Playboy and Vogue Magazines. With her early roots as a fashion illustrator, Joan has developed a style of illustration which has become popular in recent years, utilizing a skillfully calligraphic brush stroke which brings an elegance and sophistication to any image.

Use the DIV **tag to align a block of paragraphs.**

The DIV tag can be used with any of the ALIGN values that work with paragraphs—CENTER, LEFT, RIGHT, or JUSTIFY.

CENTER

Netscape first introduced the CENTER tag with version 1.1 of the Navigator browser. (Long before the DIV tag, was invented.) Because Navigator was the browser of choice for the vast majority of web users, the CENTER tag was quickly adopted by others and is now supported by virtually all browsers in common use on the Net. With the introduction of the DIV tag the CENTER tag was supposed to go away, and in fact it's still considered "obsolescent" in the HTML specifications. In technical terms, <CENTER> is just an alias for <DIV ALIGN=CENTER>.

We don't expect CENTER to go away any time soon, so feel free to use it. It's convenient. The browser developers, especially Netscape, appear to have a lot more respect for the needs of the marketplace than they do for the needs of the people who write the specifications. Whether you feel that's a good thing or a bad thing (there are plenty of arguments for each of those opinions), the fact is that CENTER is here to stay.

As you can see from this example, <CENTER, has exactly the same effect as <DIV ALIGN=CENTER>:

```
<CENTER>
<P> Ducks In A Row products represent a
unique concept in rubber stamping. Our
original designs created by Joan Farber,
internationally recognized illustrator, are
unlike anything found in the stamp market
today.

<P>Joan Farber is a freelance illustrator,
designer, fine artist, and teacher who has
done work for such notable companies as
American Express, CBS Records, Redken, MCI,
Cosmopolitan, Playboy and Vogue Magazines.
With her early roots as a fashion illustra-
tor, Joan has developed a style of
illustration which has become popular in
recent years, utilizing a skillfully cal-
ligraphic brush stroke which brings an
elegance and sophistication to any image.

<P>Because the style of art throughout
the catalog is consistent, any of the
designs may be used together side by side
or superimposed, making the possibilities
for personal expression boundless.

</CENTER>
```

Ducks In A Row products represent a unique concept in rubber stamping. Our original designs created by Joan Farber, internationally recognized illustrator, are unlike anything found in the stamp market today.

Joan Farber is a freelance illustrator, designer, fine artist, and teacher who has done work for such notable companies as American Express, CBS Records, Redken, MCI, Cosmopolitan, Playboy and Vogue Magazines. With her early roots as a fashion illustrator, Joan has developed a style of illustration which has become popular in recent years, utilizing a skillfully calligraphic brush stroke which brings an elegance and sophistication to any image.

Use the CENTER tag to center a block of paragraphs.

The text formatting capabilities of HTML are indeed limited. There is no way to adjust leading, character or word spacing, kerning, or even the size of the text. In Chapter 13, "Style," we will discuss how you can overcome some of these shortcomings with CSS style sheets, but even then it's good to remember that the web was not designed as a presentation medium. It will take some more time for the medium itself to catch up with its potential.

Graphic Alignment Tags

When we discuss aligning graphics on the page, it's important to first understand that HTML considers a graphic object (the IMG tag) to be part of the text stream. That's right, as far as HTML is concerned, graphics are part of the text, unless you tell it to do something special. For example, notice how Netscape renders this HTML:

```
<HEAD>
<TITLE> Graphic Alignment </TITLE>
</HEAD>
<BODY BGCOLOR=white>

<P>This paragraph has a small
<IMG SRC="ducky.gif">
graphic in the middle of it.

</BODY>
</HTML>
```

A graphic is considered part of a paragraph.

As you can see, the graphic was inserted directly in the paragraph along with the text. This is what is meant by "inline" graphics. The graphic itself is in line with the stream of text in the paragraph.

Notice also that the bottom of the graphic lines up with the baseline of the text. This is typical for most browsers.

IMG ALIGN Attribute

If you want the inline image to align differently (relative to the line of text it is on) you must supply an `ALIGN` attribute:

ALIGN=BOTTOM   Aligns the bottom of the image with the baseline (default).

ALIGN=MIDDLE   Aligns the middle of the image with the baseline.

ALIGN=TOP   Aligns the top of the image with the top of the tallest object on the line.

Here's what each of the inline image alignment types look like in Netscape Navigator 4.0:

This paragraph has a small graphic in the middle of it.

The `ALIGN=BOTTOM` **attribute.**

```
<HEAD>
<TITLE> Graphic Alignment </TITLE>
</HEAD>
<BODY BGCOLOR=white>

<P>This paragraph has a small
<IMG SRC="ducky.gif" ALIGN=BOTTOM>
graphic in the middle of it.

</BODY>
</HTML>
<HEAD>
```

This paragraph has a small graphic in the middle of it.

The `ALIGN=MIDDLE` **attribute.**

```
<TITLE> Graphic Alignment </TITLE>
</HEAD>
<BODY BGCOLOR=white>

<P>This paragraph has a small
<IMG SRC="ducky.gif" ALIGN=MIDDLE>
graphic the middle of it.

</BODY>
</HTML>
<HEAD>
```

This paragraph has a small graphic in the middle of it.

The `ALIGN=TOP` **attribute.**

```
<TITLE> Graphic Alignment </TITLE>
</HEAD>
<BODY BGCOLOR=white>

<P>This paragraph has a small
<IMG SRC="ducky.gif" ALIGN=TOP>
graphic in the middle of it.

</BODY>
</HTML>
```

Floating Graphics

You can also align a graphic to one side or the other and have text wrap around that graphic. This is done with the floating-type ALIGN values, RIGHT and LEFT. Consider this example:

```
<HTML>
<HEAD>
    <TITLE>Ducks in a Row Company
Information</TITLE>
</HEAD>
<BODY BGCOLOR=WHITE>

<P><IMG SRC="joan.jpg" ALIGN=LEFT>Joan
Farber is a freelance illustrator, design-
er, fine artist and teacher who has done
work for such notable companies as
American Express, CBS Records, Redken,
MCI, Cosmopolitan, Playboy and Vogue
Magazines. With her early roots as a
fashion illustrator, Joan has developed
a style of illustration which has become
popular in recent years, utilizing a
skillfully calligraphic brush stroke which
brings an elegance and sophistication
to any image.

</BODY>
</HTML>
```

Joan Farber is a free-lance illustrator, designer, fine artist and teacher, who has done work for such notable companies as American Express, CBS Records, Redken, MCI, Cosmopolitan, Playboy and Vogue Magazines. With her early roots as a fashion illustrator, Joan has developed a style of illustration which has become popular in recent years, utilizing a skillfully calligraphic brush stroke which brings an elegance and sophistication to any image.

By using ALIGN=LEFT, **the image aligns to the left side of the page, and the text wraps around it.**

In this example, the inline image is a photo of the person we're talking about in the text. So we actually want the text to flow around the image. Here's what it looks like in the browser:

Joan Farber is a free-lance illustrator, designer, fine artist and teacher, who has done work for such notable companies as American Express, CBS Records, Redken, MCI, Cosmopolitan, Playboy and Vogue Magazines. With her early roots as a fashion illustrator, Joan has developed a style of illustration which has become popular in recent years, utilizing a skillfully calligraphic brush stroke which brings an elegance and sophistication to any image.

By using ALIGN=RIGHT, **the image floats to the right.**

In HTML parlance, the LEFT and RIGHT values for the ALIGN attribute tell the browser to "float" the image to the right or left side of the text. This is a distinct behavior from that of the TOP, BOTTOM, and MIDDLE values, which apply to the image as an inline text element.

Now and then you may wonder if you can use ALIGN=RIGHT and ALIGN=MIDDLE for the same image. No, you cannot use the same attribute more than once in the same element. But stay tuned to this chapter for the Tables for Graphics section, and you'll see how you can accomplish the same effect.

Insert a Line Break with BR

You are probably already familiar with the BR tag at this point, but you may not be aware that it has some peculiarities when used with floating images. Let's take a quick look at those peculiarities, so that you know how to break lines when you need to.

First, let's consider this small piece of HTML:

```
<P><IMG SRC="ducky.gif">
Line one
<BR>Line two
<BR>Line three
```

BR **with no attributes.**

Notice that the image is part of the paragraph. This is the normal behavior for an inline image. Notice that the BR tags break the lines of text, but the Line one text is inline with the image. That's because the text and the image are part of the same paragraph. Now, let's see what happens if we add ALIGN=LEFT to the IMG tag:

```
<P><IMG SRC="ducky.gif" ALIGN=LEFT>
Line one
<BR>Line two
<BR>Line three
```

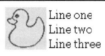

IMG **with** ALIGN=LEFT **makes the image "float" to the left.**

When we add ALIGN=LEFT to an IMG tag, the image floats to the left, leaving the paragraph text to wrap around it. Now the BR tag no longer brings the text out under the image; instead, it breaks the text but leaves it next to the image. This is the behavior with a floating (as opposed to inline) image.

The BR tag has an attribute called CLEAR, which allows you to force the text to clear the floating image. For example, use CLEAR=LEFT to force a text break below an image floating on the left:

```
<P><IMG SRC="ducky.gif" ALIGN=LEFT>
Line one
<BR>Line two
<BR CLEAR=LEFT>Line three
```

BR **with** CLEAR=LEFT.

Use CLEAR=RIGHT to force a text break below an image floating on the right:

```
<P ALIGN=RIGHT>
<IMG SRC="ducky.gif" ALIGN=RIGHT>
Line one
<BR>Line two
<BR CLEAR=RIGHT>Line three
```

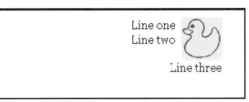

BR **with** CLEAR=RIGHT.

You can also use CLEAR=ALL to force a break below images on both sides:

```
<P ALIGN=CENTER>
<IMG SRC="ducky.gif" ALIGN=RIGHT>
<IMG SRC="ducky.gif" ALIGN=LEFT>
Line one
<BR>Line two
<BR CLEAR=ALL>Line three
```

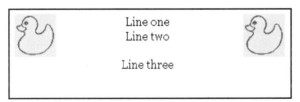

BR **with** CLEAR=ALL.

The BR tag can be a little confusing when you are using it with floating images. As a rule-of-thumb, it can't hurt to just get into the habit of using CLEAR=ALL any time you want the break to go below an image.

Image Gutters

Did you notice that when we wrapped text around the duck image, there was a space between the image and the text? This space is called a gutter. It is controlled with the VSPACE and HSPACE attributes to the IMG tag.

```
<P><IMG SRC="ducky.gif" ALIGN=LEFT
HSPACE=0>
Line one
<BR>Line two
<BR>Line three
```

Notice that by setting the HSPACE to zero, we have eliminated all the space between the image and the text.

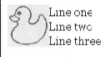

IMG **with** HSPACE=0.

On the other hand, it is also possible to create extra space by increasing the value of HSPACE (the default value is 3 for most browsers).

```
<P><IMG SRC="ducky.gif" ALIGN=LEFT
HSPACE=25>
Line one
<BR>Line two
<BR>Line three
```

In this case, we have increased the horizontal gutter to 25 pixels.

IMG **with** HSPACE=25.

Notice that 25 pixels have been added to both sides of the image! In many cases, this may not be what you want. If you want to add 25 pixels of space to only one side, see the following trick.

The Single-Pixel GIF Trick—Part I

Let's say, for design purposes, you wanted 25 pixels of gutter only on the right side of the duck. You can't do that with the normal HSPACE attribute; instead, we have to get creative.

First, some background: When you supply WIDTH and HEIGHT attributes to the IMG tag, the browser will display the graphic at the specified height and width, regardless of the original size of the image. If the image was that size in the first place, that's fine. This will actually speed up the display of the page (see Chapter 3, "Speedy Graphics"). On the other hand, if the graphic is not those dimensions, the browser will stretch (and/or shrink) the graphic to fit the dimensions specified by HEIGHT and WIDTH. Why would you want to do that?

The trick is to use a 1 pixel by 1 pixel GIF file, with the color of the pixel set to transparent. Then you can stretch that GIF to whatever size you want for the explicit purpose of creating space! Using a transparent GIF, you can use this trick to create horizontal space or vertical space. This example uses the blank.gif file from the chap09/images folder

of the <chd> CD-ROM to create the one-sided gutter for us:

```
<P><IMG SRC="ducky.gif" WIDTH=50 HEIGHT=50
HSPACE=0 ALIGN=LEFT>
  <IMG SRC="blank.gif" WIDTH=25 HEIGHT=50
HSPACE=0 ALIGN=LEFT>
Line one
<BR>Line two
<BR>Line three
```

Creating a gutter with a single-pixel transparent GIF.

We have provided a number of single-pixel GIFs in assorted colors in the chap09/images folder on the <chd> CD-ROM. Among these is the blank.gif file, which is transparent and can be used for spacing.

Look out for the Single-Pixel GIF Trick—Part II later in this chapter.

HTML Tables

Unless you are dealing with a strictly textual site, you will likely want somewhat more freedom to express your design than what is available with the HTML we have discussed so far. Fortunately, most current browsers support HTML tables.

Using tables, it is possible to display tabular data, create columns of text, precisely position various elements of your design, and solve many other design problems with HTML.

The HTML Tables specification has been around in various forms since early 1995. In that time, it has undergone many changes and transformations and continues to change as we move toward the HTML 4.0 specification. This chapter documents those features of tables that work with the widest variety of browsers. What is documented here, unless otherwise specified, works in Netscape Navigator versions 2.0 and later, as well as all the browsers that are designed to be compatible with it. That includes at least 85% of the browsers that will visit your site.

Table Basics

In its simplest form, a table is useful for organizing data into rows (horizontal) and columns (vertical). For example:

```
<TABLE>
   <TR>
     <TD> Ducks In A Row products repre-
sent a unique concept in rubber stamping.

     <TD> Our original designs created by
Joan Farber, internationally recognized
illustrator, are unlike anything found
in the stamp market today.

     <TD> Joan Farber is a freelance
illustrator, designer, fine artist,
and teacher who has done work for such
notable companies as American Express,
CBS Records, . . .
</TABLE>
```

The TABLE element is a container, so it requires both the start tag and the end tag. Everything in between is part of the table. The TR tag (also a container, but the end tag is optional) designates the beginning of a row (horizontal), and each of the TD tags (also containers with optional end tags) mark the beginning of a column (vertical). Because there are one TR and three TD tags, there are one row and three columns in this table.

Ducks In A Row products represent a unique concept in rubber stamping.	Our original designs created by Joan Farber, internationally recognized illustrator, are unlike anything found in the stamp market today.	Joan Farber is a freelance illustrator, designer, fine artist, and teacher who has done work for such notable companies as American Express, CBS Records, . . .

A simple table example.

The table itself becomes the size of all the elements within it. If the elements within the table are not fixed-size, the table gravitates to the size of the window it is displayed in—and gives equal space to—each of the elements in the table. It's easier to see what the table is doing if you turn on the border with the BORDER attribute in the TABLE tag:

```
<TABLE BORDER>
  <TR>
    <TD> Ducks In A Row products represent
a unique concept in rubber stamping.

    <TD> Our original designs created by
Joan Farber, internationally recognized
illustrator, are unlike anything found
in the stamp market today.

    <TD> Joan Farber is a freelance
illustrator, designer, fine artist,
and teacher who has done work for such
notable companies as American Express,
CBS Records, . . .
</TABLE>
```

Ducks In A Row products represent a unique concept in rubber stamping.	Our original designs created by Joan Farber, internationally recognized illustrator, are unlike anything found in the stamp market today.	Joan Farber is a freelance illustrator, designer, fine artist, and teacher who has done work for such notable companies as American Express, CBS Records, . . .

A table with the BORDER **attribute.**

You may have noticed that the columns do not line up at the top. That's because the default behavior is for each column to vertically align to the middle. This can be controlled with the VALIGN attribute for either the TR (to apply it to a whole row) or TD (for column-only) tags. Here's the same table with VALIGN in both the TR and TD elements:

```
<TABLE BORDER>
  <TR VALIGN=TOP>
    <TD> Ducks In A Row products represent
a unique concept in rubber stamping.
    <TD VALIGN=BOTTOM>
           Our original designs created by
Joan Farber, internationally recognized
illustrator, are unlike anything found
in the stamp market today.

    <TD> Joan Farber is a freelance
illustrator, designer, fine artist,
and teacher who has done work for such
notable companies as American Express,
CBS Records, . . .
</TABLE>
```

We used VALIGN=TOP in the TR element to align all the cells in the row to the top. We also used VALIGN=BOTTOM in the second TD to align only that cell to the bottom. So, the first and third columns are top-aligned, and the second column is bottom-aligned.

Ducks In A Row products represent a unique concept in rubber stamping.	Our original designs created by Joan Farber, internationally recognized illustrator, are unlike anything found in the stamp market today.	Joan Farber is a freelance illustrator, designer, fine artist, and teacher who has done work for such notable companies as American Express, CBS Records, . . .

Using VALIGN **to vertically align table cells.**

Sometimes, you may want headings for your different columns. You can do this with the TH element. TH works just like TD, except it displays the cell in a bold heading-style.

Parnership	Design	Bio
Ducks In A Row products represent a unique concept in rubber stamping.	Our original designs created by Joan Farber, internationally recognized illustrator, are unlike anything found in the stamp market today.	Joan Farber is a freelance illustrator, designer, fine artist, and teacher who has done work for such notable companies as American Express, CBS Records, . . .

A table with TH cells for headings.

Finally, a caption for the entire table can sometimes help to identify it on the page.

```
<TABLE BORDER>
  <CAPTION> <BIG> About The Company
</BIG> </CAPTION>
  <TR>
    <TH> Parnership
    <TH> Design
    <TH> Bio
  <TR VALIGN=TOP>
    <TD> Ducks In A Row products repre-
sent a unique concept in rubber stamping.

    <TD> Our original designs created by
Joan Farber, internationally recognized
illustrator, are unlike anything found in
the stamp market today.

    <TD> Joan Farber is a freelance
illustrator, designer, fine artist, and
teacher who has done work for such
notable companies as American Express,
CBS Records, . . .
</TABLE>
```

The CAPTION element works a lot like TITLE, but for a table. The text in the CAPTION is displayed above the table by default, and uses the default font for text. Here we used BIG to make it larger.

About The Company		
Parnership	**Design**	**Bio**
Ducks In A Row products represent a unique concept in rubber stamping.	Our original designs created by Joan Farber, internationally recognized illustrator, are unlike anything found in the stamp market today.	Joan Farber is a freelance illustrator, designer, fine artist, and teacher who has done work for such notable companies as American Express, CBS Records, . . .

The table with a caption.

If you prefer that the caption display at the bottom of the table, you may use ALIGN=BOTTOM in the CAPTION element, like this:

```
<CAPTION ALIGN=BOTTOM> <BIG> About The
Company </BIG> </CAPTION>
```

Parnership	**Design**	**Bio**
Ducks In A Row products represent a unique concept in rubber stamping.	Our original designs created by Joan Farber, internationally recognized illustrator, are unlike anything found in the stamp market today.	Joan Farber is a freelance illustrator, designer, fine artist, and teacher who has done work for such notable companies as American Express, CBS Records, . . .
About The Company		

The caption with ALIGN=BOTTOM.

Coloring and Spacing in Tables

Let's remove the border from the table and experiment with color for identifying the different cells in the table. To start with, we'll use the BGCOLOR attribute for the whole table to see what happens:

```
<TABLE BGCOLOR="#FFFFCC">
<TR>
    <TH> Parnership
    <TH> Design
    <TH> Bio
  <TR VALIGN=TOP>
    <TD> Ducks In A Row products repre-
sent a unique concept in rubber stamping.

    <TD> Our original designs created by
Joan Farber, internationally recognized
illustrator, are unlike anything found in
the stamp market today.

    <TD> Joan Farber is a freelance
illustrator, designer, fine artist, and
teacher who has done work for such
notable companies as American Express,
CBS Records, . . .
</TABLE>
```

Here, we took out the BORDER attribute and put in a BGCOLOR attribute instead. The BGCOLOR attribute works exactly the same way as the BGCOLOR attribute to the BODY tag, which we have used quite a bit already.

Parnership	Design	Bio
Ducks In A Row products represent a unique concept in rubber stamping.	Our original designs created by Joan Farber, internationally recognized illustrator, are unlike anything found in the stamp market today.	Joan Farber is a freelance illustrator, designer, fine artist, and teacher who has done work for such notable companies as American Express, CBS Records, . . .

The table with the BGCOLOR attribute.

When used with the TABLE element, the BGCOLOR attribute sets a default background color for the entire table.

You have probably noticed that the space between the cells is not colored. We'll show you how to control—or remove—spaces a bit later.

We can also use the BGCOLOR attribute with the TR element to set the background color of a row, and with the TD element to set the background color for an individual cell.

```
<TABLE BGCOLOR="#FFFFCC">
  <TR BGCOLOR="#CCCCFF">
    <TH> Parnership
    <TH> Design
    <TH> Bio
  <TR VALIGN=TOP>
    <TD> Ducks In A Row products repre-
sent a unique concept in rubber stamping.

    <TD BGCOLOR="#CCFFFF">
        Our original designs created by
Joan Farber, internationally recognized
illustrator, are unlike anything found in
the stamp market today.

    <TD> Joan Farber is a freelance
illustrator, designer, fine artist, and
teacher who has done work for such
notable companies as American Express,
CBS Records, . . .
</TABLE>
```

Here we set the color for an entire row (the row with the headings in it) and for an individual cell (the middle one in the second row). All the other cells are the default color, set in the TABLE tag.

Parnership	Design	Bio
Ducks In A Row products represent a unique concept in rubber stamping.	Our original designs created by Joan Farber, internationally recognized illustrator, are unlike anything found in the stamp market today.	Joan Farber is a free-lance illustrator, designer, fine artist, and teacher, who has done work for such notable companies as American Express, CBS Records, . . .

The BGCOLOR attribute in rows and cells.

Space Between Table Cells

The space between the table cells is controlled by the CELLSPACING attribute in the TABLE tag. By setting CELLSPACING to zero, you can remove all the space between the cells of your table.

Let's start by setting CELLSPACING and BORDER to zero for our example (the rest of the code remains the same):

```
<TABLE BGCOLOR="#FFFFCC" BORDER=0
CELLSPACING=0>
```

This removes all the space between the cells of our table.

Parnership	Design	Bio
Ducks In A Row products represent a unique concept in rubber stamping.	Our original designs created by Joan Farber, internationally recognized illustrator, are unlike anything found in the stamp market today.	Joan Farber is a free-lance illustrator, designer, fine artist, and teacher, who has done work for such notable companies as American Express, CBS Records, . . .

Our example with CELLSPACING=**0.**

Notice that this example leaves all the text jammed up against the edges of the cells. You can adjust the space inside of the cell borders with the CELLPADDING attribute.

```
<TABLE BGCOLOR="#FFFFCC" BORDER=0
CELLSPACING=0 CELLPADDING=5>
```

Parnership	Design	Bio
Ducks In A Row products represent a unique concept in rubber stamping.	Our original designs created by Joan Farber, internationally recognized illustrator, are unlike anything found in the stamp market today.	Joan Farber is a free-lance illustrator, designer, fine artist, and teacher, who has done work for such notable companies as American Express, CBS Records, . . .

The table with CELLSPACING=0 **and** CELLPADDING=5.

This gives a little breathing room for the text inside the cells.

This technique can be nicely applied to columnar-type data, giving you some design flexibility that would otherwise be difficult without using large graphics files:

```
<TABLE BGCOLOR="#FFFFCC" BORDER=0
CELLSPACING=0 CELLPADDING=6>
   <TR><TD>
     You will find designs in our catalog
which cover a vast array of categories:
   <TR><TD BGCOLOR="#CCCC99">
floral images
   <TR><TD> humor
   <TR><TD BGCOLOR="#CCCC99"> holiday stamps
   <TR><TD> border designs
   <TR><TD BGCOLOR="#CCCC99">
decorative imagery
</TABLE>
```

In this decorative table, we use a separate row for each element of the list. Remember: You need both a TR and a TD to create a row. In this example, we used a BGCOLOR in the TABLE tag as a default and then changed the color in every other row.

You will find designs in our catalog which cover a vast array of categories:

floral images

humor

holiday stamps

border designs

decorative imagery

A decorative table for listing options.

There are many other interesting designs you can create by using tables. Hopefully, we've given you enough tools to be able to experiment on your own, and use your creativity.

▶ **warning**

The BORDER Attribute in Netscape

There is a bug in the Netscape implementation of tables, which goes all the way back to the first version of Netscape that supported tables (Navigator version 1.1). According to the specification, a table that has CELLSPACING set to 0 should have no space between the cells. In the Netscape browser, there is still space if you have not explicitly set BORDER=0.

The default value of the BORDER attribute should be zero, but it's not in Netscape Navigator. Even though the border is not rendered, it still takes up space unless you set it to zero. Other browsers may emulate this behavior.

Tables for Spacing

Another common use for tables is to create accurate spacing. By using HEIGHT and WIDTH attributes in the TABLE and TR tags, it is possible to precisely position text and graphics on the page.

note

Margins in HTML

It is possible to precisely position elements on the page relative to each other. It is not always possible to position objects accurately relative to the edge of the screen. Most browsers (including Netscape's and Microsoft's) have various margins on the page, which differ from version to version and platform to platform. The only way around this limitation is to use frames (which can be set to have zero margins), but that solution prevents those members of your audience without frames-capable browsers from viewing your site. (For instructions on how to align text and images using frames, check out Chapter 14, "Navigation.")

For these reasons, we recommend that you accept the variable margins in your design, if possible, and instead use tables to precisely align objects relative to each other. This approach has worked well for many web sites.

The HEIGHT and WIDTH attributes can be used in the TABLE tag to fix the minimum height and width of the entire table. Keep in mind that if you use any elements that are larger than these minimums, your table will expand accordingly.

```
<TABLE BORDER=0 CELLSPACING=0
BGCOLOR="#00CCCC"
  WIDTH=200 HEIGHT=50>
  <TR><TD ALIGN=CENTER> 200 X 200 Table
</TABLE>
```

In this table, we have specified a width of 200 pixels and a height of 200 pixels. The table has only one cell, and that cell has the sentence "200 X 200 Table" in it. To help us see the size of the table visually, we have given it a cyan background color. We set the BORDER and CELLSPACING attributes to 0 so that the cell itself will fill all the space of the table.

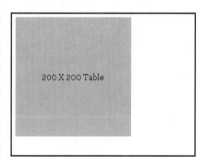

A 200 X 200 table.

Spacing Text with Tables

Tables are commonly used to create space so that text doesn't flow all the way across the page.

```
<TABLE BORDER=1 CELLSPACING=0
CELLPADDING=8 WIDTH=350>
  <TR>
    <TD HEIGHT=50><BR>
    <TD>
  <TR>
    <TD WIDTH=50>
    <TD WIDTH=300 BGCOLOR=#FFFF99>
      <P> Joan Farber is a freelance
illustrator, designer, fine artist, and
teacher who has done work for such notable
companies as American Express, CBS Records,
Redken, MCI, Cosmopolitan, Playboy and
Vogue Magazines.
</TABLE>
```

This table has two rows. The first row exists only to create a 50-pixel high margin to keep the text away from the top of the window. The BR tag is there to give the cell content; otherwise, it won't take up any space. The second row sets the spacing of the table: the first column is 50 pixels wide to provide space to the left of the text. The second column contains the text itself, on a nice duck-yellow background, and it will be 50 pixels down and 50 pixels across from the left margin. The text is in a cell that is 300 pixels wide, no matter how wide the window is opened. This keeps the text from becoming one long line across somebody's huge screen.

We left the border on so you could see the table layout. Normally you would turn it off with BORDER=0.

Joan Farber is a free-lance illustrator, designer, fine artist and teacher, who has done work for such notable companies as American Express, CBS Records, Redken, MCI, Cosmopolitan, Playboy and Vogue Magazines.

A table used to create space for text.

You could easily use this same table to create another space for an image to accompany the text.

```
<TABLE BORDER=0 CELLSPACING=0
CELLPADDING=8 WIDTH=500>
  <TR>
    <TD HEIGHT=50><BR>
    <TD>
  <TR>
    <TD WIDTH=50>
    <TD WIDTH=300 BGCOLOR=#FFFF99>
      <P> Joan Farber is a freelance
illustrator, designer, fine artist, and
teacher who has done work for such notable
companies as American Express, CBS Records,
Redken, MCI, Cosmopolitan, Playboy and
Vogue Magazines.
    <TD WIDTH=150><IMG SRC="joan2.jpg"
WIDTH=118 HEIGHT=127>
</TABLE>
```

We have added the image to the table in its own cell. Be careful that the width of the table is equal to the sum of all the cells.

Joan Farber is a free-lance illustrator, designer, fine artist and teacher, who has done work for such notable companies as American Express, CBS Records, Redken, MCI, Cosmopolitan, Playboy and Vogue Magazines.

The table can be used to align different types of objects, including text and graphics.

In the advanced tables department, you may sometimes want to have a table with cells that span more than one row or column. If this seems strange to you, feel free to skip the next section. Otherwise, screw on your thinking cap and join the fun!

Tables with Odd Numbers of Cells

The cells in HTML tables can, for many reasons, span more than one column or row at a time. In this section, we will briefly consider such tables, showing you how to construct them. If you take your time with each of these examples—and experiment with them freely—you may find them good for hours of fascinating fun!

```
<TABLE BORDER=0 CELLSPACING=0
BGCOLOR="#00CCCC"
      WIDTH=200 HEIGHT=200>
   <TR>
      <TD WIDTH=50 HEIGHT=50
BGCOLOR="#CCCC00" ALIGN=CENTER>
         50 X 50
      <TD WIDTH=150 HEIGHT=50
BGCOLOR="#999900" ALIGN=CENTER>
         150 X 50
   <TR>
      <TD WIDTH=200 HEIGHT=150 COLSPAN=2
ALIGN=CENTER>
         200 X 150 <BR> COLSPAN=2
</TABLE>
```

In this example, the table itself is set to 200×200, and there are three cells. The first row has two cells, and the second row has one. In the first row, the first cell has a width of 50 pixels and a height of 50 pixels. The second cell is 150 pixels wide and 50 pixels high. They each have a different background color, so we can see what's going on.

But the second row has something new. Notice the COLSPAN=2 attribute. This tells the browser that the cell takes up two columns. This is important: In HTML tables, every row must take up the same number of columns, and every column must take up the same number of rows. If your first row has two columns, but the second row has only one, the browser will definitely do something unpredictable! So, if you want a cell to span more than one column, you need to tell the browser which cell it's going to be! You do this with the COLSPAN attribute.

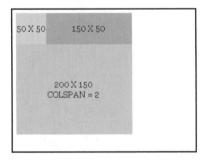

A three-celled table with COLSPAN.

Likewise, you can have a cell span more than one row. You do this with the ROWSPAN attribute.

```
<TABLE BORDER=0 CELLSPACING=0
WIDTH=200 HEIGHT=200>
   <TR>
      <TD WIDTH=100 HEIGHT=200 ROWSPAN=2
BGCOLOR="#CCCC00" ALIGN=CENTER>
         100 X 200 <BR> ROWSPAN=2
      <TD WIDTH=100 HEIGHT=50
BGCOLOR="#00CCCC" ALIGN=CENTER>
         100 X 50
   <TR>
      <TD WIDTH=100 HEIGHT=150
BGCOLOR="#999900" ALIGN=CENTER>
         100 X 150
</TABLE>
```

In the table to your below, we have a cell that spans two rows. The first row has two columns, a 100×200 cell and a 100×50 cell. Notice that the first cell has ROWSPAN=2 in it. This means that the cell will also be part of the next row! So the second row has only one cell in it (100×150), and that cell is positioned in the second column because the first column is occupied by a cell from the previous row.

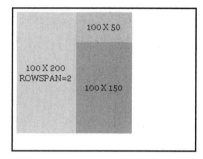

A three-celled table with ROWSPAN.

We know that this aspect of tables can be confusing. It requires that you think over your design carefully, and usually draw a map first. The tables shown with the numeric markings in them represent the sorts of drawings Bill makes when he plans complex tables. This makes it a lot easier to code the tables when it's time for that.

Tables For Graphics

Another very common usage for tables is to break apart a graphic and reassemble it. There are many good reasons to do this:

- Some parts of the graphic may compress better than others.

- Perhaps you want to animate part of the graphic (animating a large file takes up a lot more space than animating a small file).

- You can speed up downloading time because some of the images will load before others, rather than waiting for a huge image to download.

- It can produce an interesting effect when multiple images appear at different intervals.

▶ e x e r c i s e

Cutting Up an Image in Photoshop 4.0

Step 1: Open the cutapart.psd file in the chap19 folder of the <chd> CD-ROM.

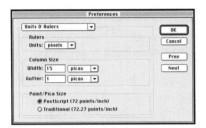

Step 2: Set your preferences to use pixels by choosing **Edit:Preferences:Units&Rulers** and changing Units to pixels.

Step 3: After your Units and Rulers preferences are set, make sure that you've specified **Snap To Guides** under the **View** menu.

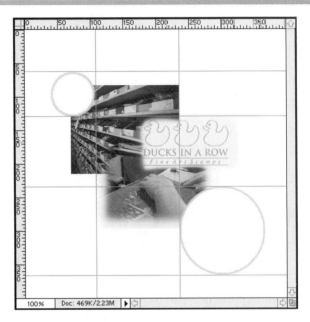

Step 4: To access the rulers, go to **View:Show Rulers**. Place your cursor inside the ruler and drag each guide to where you want to cut apart the image. Since **Snap To Guides** was checked in Step 3, your cursor ought to easily "snap" to each region.

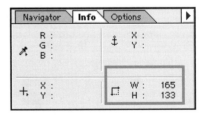

Step 5: If you choose **Window:Show Info**, you can get the width and height measurements to use for your HTML tables.

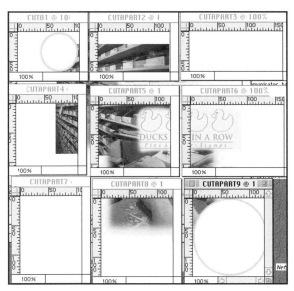

Here's an example of making separate files out of each grid's rectangle.

41k	4k	1k
2k	7k	3k
1k	2k	48k

Each piece of the "cutapart" image has a different file size. The upper-left and lower-right graphics are actually animated GIFs (more on this technique in Chapter 17, "Animation & Sound"), so they are quite a bit larger than the other images. This is precisely the reason why this technique is

so valuable—you don't have to make one giant animation when only a small part of your image is animating. Breaking the graphic up into many small pieces will help speed up the wait time once this is viewed from a web page.

Step 6: Select each region within the grid. **Copy** and **Paste** into nine new documents. Save each file as a separate GIF file using the web palette and **Diffusion Dither**.

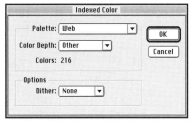

The next section will describe how to write the code to put this image back together using tables. You can use our naming scheme or create your own and modify the HTML to work with your names.

Piecing the Artwork Back Together

Using the techniques you've already learned in
this chapter, it's relatively easy to create the table
to display this compound graphic. There are three
rows and three columns, so piecing it back together is just a matter of building the table, right?

First, let's look at the wrong way to do this:

```
<TABLE BORDER=0 CELLSPACING=0
CELLPADDING=0>
   <TR>
     <TD><IMG SRC="cutapart1.gif">
     <TD><IMG SRC="cutapart2.gif">
     <TD><IMG SRC="cutapart3.gif">
   <TR>
     <TD><IMG SRC="cutapart4.gif">
     <TD><IMG SRC="cutapart5.gif">
     <TD><IMG SRC="cutapart6.gif">
   <TR>
     <TD><IMG SRC="cutapart7.gif">
     <TD><IMG SRC="cutapart8.gif">
     <TD><IMG SRC="cutapart9.gif">
</TABLE>
```

Earlier, you learned that the TD and TR elements
had optional end tags, and this is true. However,
when an end tag is optional in HTML, it only
means that the browser is able to guess where the
end of the element should be. In most cases, that
guess is good enough, but in some cases it may
not be. This is one of those cases where guessing
won't work.

In the case of the TD element, unless told otherwise, the browser will terminate the table cell at
the beginning of the next cell, or at the end of the
current row or table. In this case, since the next TD
or TR is on the next line, the browser may insert a
space after each part of the image!

A table with non-terminated TDs.

Now, let's look at the right way to piece the image
back together:

```
<TABLE BORDER=1 CELLSPACING=0
CELLPADDING=0>
   <TR>
     <TD><IMG SRC="cutapart1.gif"></TD>
     <TD><IMG SRC="cutapart2.gif"></TD>
     <TD><IMG SRC="cutapart3.gif"></TD>
   <TR>
     <TD><IMG SRC="cutapart4.gif"></TD>
     <TD><IMG SRC="cutapart5.gif"></TD>
     <TD><IMG SRC="cutapart6.gif"></TD>
   <TR>
     <TD><IMG SRC="cutapart7.gif"></TD>
     <TD><IMG SRC="cutapart8.gif"></TD>
     <TD><IMG SRC="cutapart9.gif"></TD>
</TABLE>
```

In the HTML to the right, we told the browser to terminate the cell immediately after the image with no space between the image and the end of the cell. The result is a perfectly clean rendering of the image with no seams and no spaces.

A table with terminated TDs. **This file is called** cutapart.html **and is available in the** chap09 **folder of the <chd> CD-ROM.**

Piecing together an image can leave you a lot of room to create dynamic content. You can have different words over parts of an image for different pages, animate parts of an image, or change it in any number of ways. Understanding how tables work will help you design these pages more freely as a part of your web design repertoire.

Table Tricks and Tips

Tables don't have to be large and complex to be useful. In fact, once you understand the basics of tables, you will find them useful for a number of little things.

The Single-Pixel GIF Trick—Part II

Ever wanted to add a little vertical space to a page? Maybe add a little air before a graphic? One way to do it is with the single-pixel GIF. We showed you earlier how to use it to add horizontal space, but it can also be used to add vertical space.

```
<IMG SRC=blank.gif WIDTH=1 HEIGHT=50><BR>
This is 50 pixels down.
```

The disadvantage of using a GIF for adding space is that, while the GIF itself is small, it requires a whole new connection to download it, and that can slow your page down. And, if for some reason that download fails, you could get a broken-image icon on the page instead of the pretty little blank space you wanted.

As an alternative, here's a little table that works just as well:

```
<TABLE><TR><TD HEIGHT=50></TABLE>
This is 50 pixels down.
```

This is 50 pixels down.

The table-spacer at work!

Just change the 50 to something else for a different amount of space. A lower number will create less space, and a higher number will yield more.

Bulleted List

Do you sometimes get tired of the UL tag? Want some new bullets? Create your own! Here's a small table to do it with:

```
<TABLE>
  <TR><TD><IMG SRC="bull1.gif">
      <TD> Each item in the list can be
either very, very long; meandering with
interminably circumlocutory ruminations,
  <TR><TD><IMG SRC="bull1.gif">
      <TD> Or they can be short.
  <TR><TD><IMG SRC="bull1.gif">
      <TD> To the point.
  <TR><TD><IMG SRC="bull1.gif">
      <TD> Succinct.
</TABLE>
```

Each item in the list can be either very, very long; meandering with interminably circumlocutory ruminations.

Or they can be short.

To the point.

Succinct.

Bullets: not just for breakfast any more!

Center an Object on the Page

Here's a simple table for centering an object both vertically and horizontally on the page. This technique is really useful for a splash screen ("entrance tunnel" in web-speak).

```
<TABLE WIDTH=100% HEIGHT=100%>
  <TR VALIGN=MIDDLE ALIGN=CENTER><TD>
    <A HREF="home.html">
<IMG SRC="ducky.gif" BORDER=0></A>
</TABLE>
```

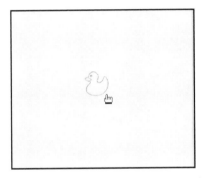

Keep your hands and arms inside the vehicle...

Vertical Rules

Here's a technique for making vertical rules by using a table. The advantage of this technique is that the line will automatically extend to the height of the text. There are other methods for creating vertical rules using the HR tag or a single-pixel GIF, but those techniques do not automatically fill the space. The table method has the additional advantage over the GIF method of not requiring an extra file to download.

```
<BODY BGCOLOR=FFFFCC>

<TABLE CELLSPACING=10 CELLPADDING=0
BORDER=0>
  <TR VALIGN=TOP><TD>

    <P>
    We have seen several ways to make
vertical rules, all of which must use a
table, and most of which also use another
element -- like a single-pixel GIF --
that adds bandwidth and is prone to prob-
lems.

    <!-- this cell is the vertical rule -->
    <TD BGCOLOR="Black" WIDTH=1><BR>
    <TD>

    <P>
    This technique uses a one-pixel-wide
table cell, with a dark background color
for the rule itself. It's low in calories
and Good-Webkeeping&reg; Approved!

</TABLE>
```

> We have seen several ways to make vertical rules, all of which must use a table, and most of which also use another element -- like a single-pixel GIF -- that adds bandwidth and is prone to problems.
>
> This technique uses a one-pixel-wide table cell, with a dark background color for the rule itself. It's low in calories and Good-Webkeeping® Approved!

A simple, elegant, vertical rule made from recycled electrons.

This technique uses a single-pixel-wide table cell, with a dark background, for the rule itself. As a side-effect of it being a table cell, the rule will automatically grow or shrink to the size of the table no matter how the user's browser is configured, which ensures that it will always extend to the height of the tallest column.

▶ chapter nine summary

HTML does make it more difficult to align your work than you may be used to with print or other multimedia work. But it is possible to make great-looking web pages, if you understand the tools at your disposal.

In this chapter, you learned a lot of techniques for aligning your text and graphics, but even more valuable, you learned about the tools at your disposal. Let your imagination guide you a little, and you will find a lot of opportunity buried in the limitations of HTML.

In the next chapter, we'll talk more about text and type, and what options you have for controlling typography on the web.

10

"It isn't writing at all, it's typing."
—Truman Capote, 1959

Typography
overcoming the limits

Typography is an incredibly powerful visual design medium, but good typography requires much more control than HTML easily affords. HTML is about display flexibility and cross-platform distribution of information. Typography is about precise control and variety. This chapter will clue you in to the many techniques available to trick and coerce HTML into generating pages with typographic control.

There's a lot of change afoot in the web type world. We'll examine some of the different web typography options—from HTML tags and attributes, to using images that contain bitmapped type treatments, to new font embedding proposals.

Typography

Limited Choices

Until now, most web publishers and designers have lived in a chocolate-and-vanilla typographical world. Web browsers have defaulted to using two basic typefaces: a proportional-spaced serif font for standard text and a monospaced (or fixed-space) font for code.

A serif is the small stroke (sometimes called the fiddly bit) at the end of the main strokes of letterforms.

Sans serif fonts have no serifs (sans means "without" in French).

Monospaced fonts are typefaces in which each character takes the same amount of width. Standard typefaces have varying widths.

This example depicts the default serif font display in Netscape Navigator 4.0 on a Macintosh.

This example depicts a monospaced font—also typical of the generic web.

Generic type on web pages is the easiest form of typography to program and view, so we will first focus on HTML defaults for creating typographic effects on the web.

HTML Type Versus Graphical Type

There are basically two kinds of typographical elements on the web (or the printed page, for that matter): body type and headline type. Body type, often referred to as body copy, composes the bulk of the written text. Body type is typically smaller and contains the majority of the written content of a web page. Headline type is typically larger and is used to quickly draw the viewer's eye, help define a page break, and, or organize multiple ideas.

This example demonstrates the difference between body and headline type.

You can make body and headline type a couple of different ways on the web. The first way we'll examine involves using HTML's specialized font tags and attributes.

HTML-Based Typography

The advantages of using HTML for most body-type needs are obvious. First of all, the memory and download time required for using native text is much lower than that used for graphics. Many sites are text-intensive, and using HTML-based type is the only choice to present large quantities of written information in a timely and efficient manner.

The following demonstrates how to use type tags.

Headings

```
<H3>Welcome to Ducks in a Row!</H3>
<H4>Welcome to Ducks in a Row!</H4>
<H5>Welcome to Ducks in a Row!</H5>
```

> **Welcome to Ducks in a Row!**
>
> **Welcome to Ducks in a Row!**
>
> **Welcome to Ducks in a Row!**

Bold

Here are a couple of ways to make type bold.

```
<P> Rubber <B>STAMPS</B>
<P> Rubber <STRONG>STAMPS</STRONG>
```

> Rubber **STAMPS**
>
> Rubber **STAMPS**

Italics

Here are a couple of ways to italicize type.

```
<P> Rubber<I>STAMPS</I>
<P> Rubber<EM>STAMPS</EM>
```

> Rubber *STAMPS*
>
> Rubber *STAMPS*

▶ note

<B> and <I>

Are you wondering why there are two tags that do the same thing for bold and italic? Although they may appear to be the same tag disguised with different names, they do not actually do the same thing. Here is the difference…

The B tag tells the browser to display the text in a bold face, and the I tag tells it to display the text in an italicized face.

<STRONG> and <EM>

The STRONG tag tells the browser that this text should be read in a strong voice. For visual browsers, that usually means to use a boldfaced type. For an audio browser (perhaps for the blind), it tells the browser to speak the text in a stronger voice, louder, deeper, and more forcefully. Likewise, the EM tag tells the browser to emphasize that part of the text, perhaps with a raised pitch in the voice. EM text is normally rendered in italics on a visual browser.

We recommend that you use STRONG and EM tags where possible, so your pages are more accessible to the visually impaired.

Preformatting

Preformatted text usually shows up in Courier or monospaced type, unless the end user's font preferences have been changed (more on this later.) When you use the PRE tag, the formatting appears exactly as you type it. Here's the code.

```
<PRE>     Rubber STAmPs are

c    o    o    l.

check

out                 [!]

.

our

.

.

.

selection..............</PRE>
```

```
    Rubber STAmPs are
c   o   o   l.
check
out                 [!]
.
our
.
.
.
selection. . . . . . . . . . . .
```

Blinking Text

Use with caution! Many end viewers find this tag to be very annoying.

```
<BLINK> flash news!</BLINK>
```

Note: The blinking tag cannot be viewed in a book since it is a dynamic effect. To check out this example: Open the blink.html file from the chap10 folder of the <chd> CD-ROM. For a refreshingly artistic use of this tag, check out http://www.jodi.org.

Changing Font Sizes

Font sizes can be changed by using the two tags, <FONT SIZE> and </FONT>. To see a list of the different sizes and how they will appear in your browser, visit:

http://ncdesign.kyushu-id.ac.jp/html/Normal/font.html

Here's how it works:

```
Do you <FONT SIZE=5>like</FONT> your
rubber stamps?
```

Do you **like** your rubber stamps?

Caps and Small Caps

Here's the code for creating caps and small caps.

```
<FONT SIZE=4>C</FONT>APS
<FONT SIZE=4>F</FONT>UN
```

CAPS FUN

Small Caps

Use the following whenever you want small caps.

```
<FONT SIZE=1>SMALL CAPS </FONT>
<BR>REGULAR CAPS
```

Centering Text

Text can be centered by using the CENTER tag. Use the following code.

```
<CENTER>
I'm in the middle...
</CENTER>
```

> I'm in the middle...

HTML Font Choices

Chances are, the person looking at your web page is using the default settings for whatever browser he or she is viewing the page from. Most browsers default to using a Times Roman font. We've seen sites that include instructions to the viewer to change their default font to some other typeface. We wish them luck! We know very few web navigators who would take the time to change their settings to see an individual page. If you want your HTML type to be something other than Times Roman, don't count on asking your viewer to change his or her web browser settings as a fool-proof method. In fact, we would imagine an extremely low percentage of viewers would actually act on the suggestion. As an alternative, try the FONT FACE tag described next.

▶ **note**

Experiment with Type

Open the ducks.txt file from the chap10 folder of the <chd> CD-ROM. Here's an example of some different type treatments based on what's been covered so far. Try your hand at creating a variation on this theme, incorporating some of the tags and attributes we've just reviewed.

Font Face Attribute

If you want your audience to see your body copy in a font other than their default font settings, you can use a relatively new attribute to the FONT tag, which is written as FONT FACE.

The FONT FACE element enables you to specify which font your text will be displayed in. The catch is that your end user must have the font you specify installed in their system. There is no danger in using this tag, however, because if they don't have the requested font, the browser will use their default font settings. They are no worse off than if you hadn't used <FONT FACE> in the first place!

Here is some sample code which demonstrates how to use FONT FACE.

```
<FONT FACE="helvetica, arial"> TESTING,
</FONT> one, two, three.
```

TESTING, one, two, three.

Notice that two fonts were specified in the above example. This simply tells the browser to try Helvetica first, and if that's not found, try Arial. You can list as many alternatives as you want here. If it can't find any of them, it will just use the default font.

To add size variation, add the size attribute:

```
<FONT FACE="helvetica, arial" SIZE=5>
TESTING, </FONT> one, two, three.
```

TESTING, one, two, three.

To change the color, add the color attribute:

```
<FONT FACE="helvetica, arial" SIZE=5
color="CC3366"> TESTING,
</FONT> one, two, three.
```

TESTING, one, two, three.

Which Fonts?

If you choose to use FONT FACE in your HTML, you might be curious to know which native fonts ship on Macs and PCs.

PC	Mac
Arial	Helvetica
Courier New	Courier
Times New Roman	Times

Newer versions of Windows 95 ship with two other very special and wonderful fonts called Verdana and Georgia (see the section on these font families later in this chapter).

Microsoft has made a huge effort to increase the number of font styles by offering a free web fonts package for Mac and PC owners to download:

http://www.microsoft.com/typography/fontpack/default.htm

Even though Microsoft offers the free web fonts package to Mac and PC users, the odds are most of your web audience won't know about the offer or take the time to install fonts that don't ship on their system. For that reason, it's safest to go with the basic fonts that ship with every Mac and PC. Still, there's no harm in requesting a font that your end user doesn't have, because the worst penalty is they'll see your text in their default font setting.

[NEW]

Download Webdings for Windows 95 & Windows NT [webdin32.exe: 178KB, self installing file] or Windows 3.1 & Windows 3.11 [webdings.exe: 95KB, self extracting archive]. For more information about Webdings see our Webdings info page.

Trebuchet MS, **Trebuchet MS Bold**, *Trebuchet MS Italic*, ***Bold Italic***

Download Trebuchet for Windows 95 & Windows NT [trebuc32.exe: 217KB, self installing file] or Windows 3.1 & Windows 3.11 [trebuc.exe: 173KB, self extracting archive] or Apple Macintosh [TrebMS.sit.hqx: 220KB, BinHex]. For more information about Trebuchet see our Trebuchet info page.

Georgia, **Georgia Bold**, *Georgia Italic*, ***Georgia Bold Italic***

Download Georgia for Windows 95 & Windows NT [georgi32.exe: 238KB, self installing file] or Windows 3.1 & Windows 3.11 [georgia.exe: 196KB, self extracting archive] or Apple Macintosh [Georgia.sit.hqx: 248KB, BinHex].

[WGL4] Verdana, **Verdana Bold**, *Verdana Italic*, ***Bold Italic***

Download Verdana for Windows 95 & Windows NT [verdan32.exe: 321KB, self installing file] or Windows 3.1 & Windows 3.11 [verdana.exe: 152KB, self extracting archive] or Apple Macintosh [Verdana.sit.hqx: 208KB, BinHex]. For more information about Verdana see our Channel Verdana page.

Comic Sans, **Comic Sans Bold**

Download Comic Sans MS for Windows 95 & Windows NT [comic32.exe: 178KB, self installing file] or Windows 3.1 & Windows 3.11 [comic.exe: 102KB, self extracting archive] or Apple Macintosh [ComicSansMS.sit.hqx: 152KB, BinHex]. For more information about Comic Sans MS visit our Comic Sans Café.

[WGL4] **Arial Black**

Download Arial Black for Windows 95 & Windows NT [ariblk32.exe: 150KB, self installing file] or Windows 3.1 & Windows 3.11 [ariblk.exe: 81KB, self extracting archive] or Apple Macintosh [ArialBlack.sit.hqx: 64KB, BinHex].

[WGL4] **Impact**

Download Impact for Windows 95 & Windows NT [impact32.exe: 167KB, self installing file] or Windows 3.1 & Windows 3.11 [impact.exe: 92KB, self extracting archive] or Apple Macintosh [Impact.sit.hqx: 76KB, BinHex].

[PACK] All of the above fonts except Webdings are included in one file for Windows 95 & Windows NT [newfnt32.exe: 760KB, self installing file] or Windows 3.1 & Windows 3.11 [newfonts.exe: 712KB, self extracting archive] or Apple Macintosh [newfonts.sit.hqx: 880KB, BinHex].

[WGL4] Arial, **Arial Bold**, *Italic*, ***Bold Italic***

Download Arial for Windows 95 & Windows NT [arial32.exe: 410KB, self installing file] or Apple Macintosh [Arial.sit.hqx: 348KB, BinHex].

[WGL4] Times New Roman, **Times New Roman Bold**, *Italic*, ***Bold Italic***

Download Times New Roman for Windows 95 & Windows NT [times32.exe: 495KB, self installing file] or Apple Macintosh [TimesNewRoman.sit.hqx: 420KB, BinHex].

[WGL4] Courier New, **Courier New Bold**, *Italic*, ***Bold Italic***

Download Courier New for Windows 95 & Windows NT [courn32.exe: 474KB, self installing file] or Apple Macintosh [CourierNew.sit.hqx: 408KB, BinHex].

[PACK] Arial, Courier New and Times New Roman are included in one file for Windows 95 & Windows NT [fontn32.exe: 1.12MB, self extracting archive] or Apple Macintosh [corfonts.sit.hqx: 872KB, BinHex].

Web Type Blues

Although we often think of the web as a graphical medium, most of the information we see is in text. In fact, most of the information available throughout human history is text. The ability to read and write is probably right up there with the domestication of the cat as one of the top ten hallmarks of civilization.

In the past few hundred years, the art of typography has made tremendous strides. The pioneering work of typographic artists such as Johann Gutenberg, Claude Garamond, William Caslon, Eric Gill, and Jan Tschichold have contributed to the advance of civilization by making our text more readable and more enjoyable to read. Yet all that progress is in danger of being rendered worthless as the information age finally fulfills its promise of delivering the combined knowledge of humanity to our collective desktop in a poorly rasterized version of Times Roman.

One problem with type on the web is that the typefaces available were designed for print, not screen delivery. To look good on the screen, fonts should be hinted (extra information about how to display them at lower resolutions), have enough space between the letters, and have enough of an x-height (the height of a lowercase "x" relative to a capital "X") to be readable at the smaller sizes. These criteria are often very different from the criteria used in designing fonts for print.

Digital type is generally not well hinted for the screen. Letters often touch each other, making them hard to read, especially in very small sizes (9 pt. and below). Serifs help readability when printed at high resolution, but actually interfere with readability on the screen. Italics are even more problematic and are almost illegible in many sizes and on many platforms.

If we are going to get a wider range of choices for type on the web, it's not just a matter of being able to display different fonts—it's a matter of creating fonts from the ground up that are designed for the screen. Microsoft has taken a leadership role in this endeavor by hiring renowned type designer Matthew Carter (ITC Galliard, Snell Roundhand, Charter, and Bell Centennial, the font used in phone books) to develop two screen-based font families for web use.

Verdana and Georgia

Matthew Carter's first two fonts for Microsoft, Verdana and Georgia, are part of a larger web font library that Microsoft distributes for free (http://www.microsoft.com/typography/web/fonts/). Looking at the differences between these font families and the default font families, offers a primer on which features work better for screen-based typography. Georgia and Verdana were designed with a larger x-height (the height of the lowercase letter "x"). Letter combinations such as "fi," "fl," and "ff" were designed clearly so they do not touch; uppercase characters are a pixel taller than their lowercase counterparts at key screen sizes to add extra readability. The spacing between characters is much looser, making it easier to scan quickly.

Compare Georgia to Times New Roman. Georgia reads beautifully, even at small sizes.

Compare Verdana to MS Sans. Verdana reads beautifully, even at small sizes.

It took Matthew Carter two years to create these typefaces, for which he was probably paid handsomely. By giving these fonts away, Microsoft is doing both a service and a disservice to the web community. On one hand, the community gets immediate use of these sorely-needed fonts (and an excellent example of how to design fonts for screen-use). On the other hand, by giving away the fonts, they are making it much more difficult—perhaps impossible—for other font designers who don't have the resources of a multi-billion dollar corporation to practice their craft and sell their fonts to this lucrative market.

Arial

Ducks in a Row

From the inspired partnership of Laurel Dekker and Joan Farber, comes a unique concept in rubber stamping. Our original designs created by Joan Farber, an internationally recognized illustrator, are unlike anything found in the stamp market today.

Joan Farber is a free-lance illustrator, designer, fine artist and teacher, who has done work for such notable companies as American Express, CBS Records, Redken, MCI, Cosmopolitan, Playboy and Vogue Magazines. With her early roots as a fashion illustrator, Joan has developed a style of illustration which has become popular in recent years, utilizing a skillfully calligraphic brush stroke which brings an elegance and sophistication to any image.

Because the style of art throughout the catalog is consistent, any of the designs may be used together side by side or superimposed, making the possibilities for personal expression boundless.

You will find designs in our catalog which cover a a vast array of categories, from floral images to humor, holiday stamps, border designs and decorative imagery for all around use.. You, as the stamping artist will be the one to create original art works from these designs, and nothing pleasures us more than to see the beautiful and original ways in which our designs are being used.

Throughout the catalog you will find some helpful hints on some of the usages and techniques to enjoy your stamps, but we're sure that you as the stamping artist can teach us a thing or two! One thing for certain, the possibilities are endless!

Verdana

Ducks in a Row

From the inspired partnership of Laurel Dekker and Joan Farber, comes a unique concept in rubber stamping. Our original designs created by Joan Farber; an internationally recognized illustrator, are unlike anything found in the stamp market today.

Joan Farber is a free-lance illustrator, designer, fine artist and teacher, who has done work for such notable companies as American Express, CBS Records, Redken, MCI, Cosmopolitan, Playboy and Vogue Magazines. With her early roots as a fashion illustrator, Joan has developed a style of illustration which has become popular in recent years, utilizing a skillfully calligraphic brush stroke which brings an elegance and sophistication to any image.

Because the style of art throughout the catalog is consistent, any of the designs may be used together side by side or superimposed, making the possibilities for personal expression boundless.

You will find designs in our catalog which cover a a vast array of categories, from floral images to humor, holiday stamps, border designs and decorative imagery for all around use.. You, as the stamping artist will be the one to create original art works from these designs, and nothing pleasures us more than to see the beautiful and original ways in which our designs are being used.

Throughout the catalog you will find some

Times

Ducks in a Row

From the inspired partnership of Laurel Dekker and Joan Farber, comes a unique concept in rubber stamping. Our original designs created by Joan Farber; an internationally recognized illustrator, are unlike anything found in the stamp market today.

Joan Farber is a free-lance illustrator, designer, fine artist and teacher, who has done work for such notable companies as American Express, CBS Records, Redken, MCI, Cosmopolitan, Playboy and Vogue Magazines. With her early roots as a fashion illustrator, Joan has developed a style of illustration which has become popular in recent years, utilizing a skillfully calligraphic brush stroke which brings an elegance and sophistication to any image.

Because the style of art throughout the catalog is consistent, any of the designs may be used together side by side or superimposed, making the possibilities for personal expression boundless.

You will find designs in our catalog which cover a a vast array of categories, from floral images to humor, holiday stamps, border designs and decorative imagery for all around use.. You, as the stamping artist will be the one to create original art works from these designs, and nothing pleasures us more than to see the beautiful and original ways in which our designs are being used.

Throughout the catalog you will find some helpful hints on some of the usages and techniques to enjoy your stamps, but we're sure that you as the stamping artist can teach us a thing or two! One thing for certain, the possibilities are endless!

Georgia

Ducks in a Row

From the inspired partnership of Laurel Dekker and Joan Farber, comes a unique concept in rubber stamping. Our original designs created by Joan Farber; an internationally recognized illustrator, are unlike anything found in the stamp market today.

Joan Farber is a free-lance illustrator, designer, fine artist and teacher, who has done work for such notable companies as American Express, CBS Records, Redken, MCI, Cosmopolitan, Playboy and Vogue Magazines. With her early roots as a fashion illustrator, Joan has developed a style of illustration which has become popular in recent years, utilizing a skillfully calligraphic brush stroke which brings an elegance and sophistication to any image.

Because the style of art throughout the catalog is consistent, any of the designs may be used together side by side or superimposed, making the possibilities for personal expression boundless.

You will find designs in our catalog which cover a a vast array of categories, from floral images to humor, holiday stamps, border designs and decorative imagery for all around use.. You, as the stamping artist will be the one to create original art works from these designs, and nothing pleasures us more than to see the beautiful and original ways in which our designs are being used.

Throughout the catalog you will find some helpful hints on some of the usages and techniques to enjoy your stamps, but we're sure that you as the stamping artist can teach us a thing or two! One thing for certain, the possibilities are endless!

Compare Arial to Verdana and Times to Georgia, and we think you'll agree that the Matthew Carter's fonts are superior. His fonts print nicely as well.

Embedding Options

Wouldn't it be cool if you could specify a certain font and have it automatically download *and* apply itself to your page without the end user needing to install anything? Netscape and Microsoft are both offering "font embedding" in version 4.0 of their browser software releases.

Unfortunately for us, Netscape and Microsoft are duking it out in the type arena and are each offering different embedded font technologies. It makes a web designer's job very difficult to have to make decisions between which specification to support.

TrueDoc

Netscape is supporting TrueDoc font files, which were developed by Bitstream, a major supplier of digital type (http://www.bitstream.com). The idea is that fonts will be downloaded along with an HTML page, the same way as GIF and JPEG images are. A browser that can display TrueDoc font files will render the fonts on the screen (or on a printer). Browsers that cannot display TrueDoc fonts will use alternative fonts on the user's system.

If you are creating web pages and want to use TrueDoc dynamic fonts, you will need a TrueDoc-enabled authoring tool that will generate a PFR (**P**ortable **F**ont **R**esource) file that the browser can link to using FONT FACE or Cascading Style Sheets. TrueDoc requires that fonts are generated with a CSR (**C**haracter **S**hape **R**ecorder) and rendered with a CSP (**C**haracter **S**hape **P**layer). Many manufacturers of authoring tools are licensing this technology, including Macromedia, Corel, Sausage, SoftQuad, and InfoAccess.

TrueType Embedding and OpenType

Microsoft was originally pushing TrueType Embedding (http://www.microsoft.com/
truetype/embed/embed.htm) for its Explorer browser, then switched gears and publicized
a newly formed alliance with former type competitor Adobe, and started promoting
a new format jointly developed called OpenType (http://www.adobe.com/aboutadobe/
publicrelations/HTML/9704/970423.admictyp.html). Since OpenType isn't available yet,
Microsoft was only able to offer TrueType embedding when this chapter was written.

TrueType Embedding does not support Type1 fonts, the more popular format among
graphic designers, which utilizes PostScript. Unfortunately, tools that support authoring TrueType Embedding are Windows-only, making Mac developers (still the highest
population of web designers) unable to author this type of content.

> ▶ **definitions**
>
> ### Type Standards
>
> Your eyes might be glazing over just about now with all these
> standards and document types. Here's a handy definition list:
>
> **OpenType:** A standard for font embedding established by
> Microsoft and Adobe.
>
> **TrueDoc:** A standard for font embedding established
> by Bitstream.
>
> **TrueType:** A type format developed by Apple as an alter-
> native to PostScript for computer displays.
>
> **Type1:** A type format developed by Adobe for print usage.
>
> **Postscript:** A page description language developed for
> printing type and graphics.

A Peek into Font Embedding

When this chapter was written, Microsoft only had beta releases of Internet Explorer 4.0, and their font embedding tools were unreleased. Netscape beat Internet Explorer to the punch by providing a working font embedding solution. Unfortunately, this technique works only on Netscape, so in our opinion we still classify font embedding features as "not ready for prime time."

Here's a peek into the procedure for using font embedding with Netscape Navigator 4.0. First, we visited the site of HexMac, the only existing tool today for type embedding, located at:

http://www.hexmac.com/

If you look at this site using Netscape 4.0, you can watch font embedding in action. The page loads first in standard HTML default fonts, then once the embedded fonts download, you'll see the page load again with embedded typography. It doesn't cause any delay in the page load speed because the HTML default fonts load first and then transform to the embedded font as soon as the embedded font has finished loading.

This is what the screen looked like before the embedded fonts downloaded.

This is what the screen looked like with embedded fonts.

> ▶ **note**
>
> ## TrueDoc Anti-Aliasing Defaults
>
> We find it difficult to read anti-aliased fonts at small sizes, and this appears to be a built-in feature of the TrueDoc font embedding technology. Good hinting for raster displays will help alleviate this problem. We look forward to more type-faces becoming available with good hinting for computer displays. It's also rumored that future versions of TrueDoc will allow anti-aliasing to be disabled by the end user view-ing a web page. You can find more information about font aliasing in the section "Aliasing Versus Anti-Aliasing," which appears later in this chapter.

The HexMac tool allows you to create PFR (**P**ortable **F**ont **R**esource) files. Once they are created, you can embed them using the LINK tag in the HEAD element of your HTML like this:

```
<HTML><HEAD>
<LINK REL="fontdef" HXBURNED SRC="dynamoe.pfr">
<LINK REL="fontdef" HXBURNED SRC="dolores.pfr">
<LINK REL="fontdef" HXBURNED SRC="karton.pfr">
<LINK REL="fontdef" SRC="../../../../../pfr/eyeballs.pfr">
<TITLE>HexWeb Typograph Gallery</TITLE>
```

Then, just like for a normal resident font, you can use FONT FACE to request the PFR fonts in your HTML document. **NOTE:** REL stands for relationship. The REL attribute is described in the HTML 4.0 Reference at the end of this book.

Graphics-Based Typography

Using graphics instead of HTML for text is where you get the chance to flash your type design aesthetic for the world to see. You'll be able to use any font your heart desires and add special effects to it, such as drop shadows, glows, and blurs. A great advantage to using this technique is that your end users will not have to own the font you used or have it installed on their system. Because it's a graphic, it shows up like any other graphic, regardless of what system your site is viewed on.

Earlier chapters demonstrated some techniques we recommend you use with your text-based graphics. Using transparency and solid colors that match the background color of your page are two processes in particular that can be employed in combination to achieve some of the effects described here.

Some of our favorite books on type include:

Digital Type Design Guide: The Page Designer's Guide to Working with Type
Authors: Sean Cavanaugh and Ken Oyer
Publisher: Hayden Books
ISBN: 1568301901

Photoshop 4 Type Magic 1
Authors: David Lai and Greg Simsic
Publisher: Hayden Books
ISBN: 1568303807

Stop Stealing Sheep & Find Out How Type Works
Authors: Erik Spiekermann and E.M. Ginger
Publisher: Hayden Books
ISBN: 0672485435

Aliasing Versus Anti-Aliasing

Most digital artists prefer the way anti-aliasing looks, but anti-aliasing is not always the best technique for screen-based typography.

Very small type actually looks worse and quite mushy if it's anti-aliased. If you look at other examples of very small type that is displayed on computer screens (HTML type, the type on your computer desktop, and the type in a word processor), you will see that none are anti-aliased. This is because very small type sizes (12 pt. and below) do not look good anti-aliased.

Anti-aliasing at small point sizes tends to look mushy and is hard to read.

This anti-aliased small type looks bad.

Type at small point sizes (12 pt and below) looks better without anti-aliasing.

This aliased HTML type looks much better.

Writing the HTML to Place Your Text Graphics

Placing graphics on a web page is addressed in depth in Chapter 7, "Buttons & Rules," and "Navigation" in Chapter 14. The basic way to insert a graphic on a page is to use the IMG tag. Here's how to put the drop shadow artwork, created earlier, on a page.

```
<HTML>
<IMG SRC="dropshad.jpeg">
</HTML>
```

If you want to link the drop shadow image to another source, add an anchor tag to the above image like this:

```
<HTML>
<A HREF="http://www.domain.com">
<IMG SRC="dropshad.jpeg"></A>
</HTML>
```

See Chapter 5, "Clickable," for more about combining links with graphics.

> ▶ **note**
>
> ### Type Facts
>
> **Upper and Lowercase:** Originally, lead type was kept in wooden "type cases." The capital letters were typically kept in the "upper case" because they were used less frequently, and the "lower case" was used for the more common small letters.
>
> **Leading:** Indicates the amount of vertical space between lines of text. This spacing was created by inserting lead bars in between lines of type. The term remains with us, even though lead type is hardly used anymore.
>
> **Cold Type:** A photographic process of typesetting, developed before electronic typesetting.
>
> **Hot Type:** Original lead-type presses referred to setting "hot" type. The metal had to be hot at the time of press to physically imprint the tiny details of typeface designs into the paper.
>
> **Electronic Typesetting:** Setting type with computers and typesetting machines that render the type via software instead of photographic or physical methods.

Leading Techniques

Leading is the term used to describe the space between lines of type. In professional typesetting circles, programs like PageMaker and QuarkXPress allow you to easily specify leading settings. Raw HTML doesn't have any leading control. Ah, but there are tricks, and we shall share them with you!

Trick 1: Use the paragraph tag (see leadingp.html inside the chap10 folder of the <chd> CD-ROM):

```
<HTML>
<HEAD>
  <TITLE>Paragraph Leading</TITLE>
</HEAD>
<BODY BGCOLOR="#ffffff">
<CENTER>
<IMG SRC="logo.jpg" WIDTH="419"
HEIGHT="108">
<P><FONT FACE=GEORGIA SIZE=+1>Ducks
In A Row products represents a unique
concept in
<P> rubber stamping.
Our original designs, created by
<P> internationally recognized
illustrator Joan Farber,  are
<P>unlike anything found in the
stamp market
today.</FONT></CENTER>
</BODY>
</HTML>
```

Trick 2: You can use the single-pixel GIF trick.

- Create a document in Photoshop that is 1 pixel by 1 pixel. Make it transparent or color it the same as your background page. Alternatively, you can use the white.gif file from the chap10 folder of the <chd> CD-ROM.

- Using the VSPACE attribute, specify your leading with pixels. **Note:** You can experiment with changing the VSPACE attribute in the singlep.html file from the chap10 folder on the <chd> CD-ROM.

```
<HTML>
<HEAD>
  <TITLE>Paragraph Leading</TITLE>
</HEAD>
<BODY BGCOLOR="#ffffff">
<CENTER>
<IMG SRC="logo.jpg" WIDTH="419"
HEIGHT="108"><P><FONT FACE=GEORGIA
SIZE=+1>Ducks In A Row products represent
a unique,<BR><IMG SRC="white.gif"
VSPACE=10>
concept in rubber stamping. Our
original designs, created
<BR><IMG SRC="white.gif" VSPACE=10>
by internationally recognized
illustrator Joan Farber,  are
<BR><IMG SRC="white.gif" VSPACE=10>
unlike anything found in the stamp
market today.</FONT></CENTER>
</BODY>
</HTML>
```

Trick 3: Use the PRE tag for preformatted text. **Note:** The pre.html file is located inside the chap10 folder of the <chd> CD-ROM.

```
<HTML>
<HEAD>
   <TITLE>Paragraph Leading</TITLE>
</HEAD>
<BODY BGCOLOR="#ffffff"><CENTER>
<IMG SRC="logo.jpg" WIDTH="419"
HEIGHT="108"> <PRE><FONT FACE=GEORGIA
SIZE=+1>
Ducks In A Row products represent a
unique concept in rubber stamping. Our
original designs created by Joan Farber,
internationally recognized illustrator,
are unlike anything found in the stamp
market today.

</FONT></CENTER>
</BODY>
</HTML>
```

Trick 4: Use a graphic and set the leading in a program like Photoshop. The following HTML file is called pshop.html and is located inside the chap10 folder of the <chd> CD-ROM.

```
<HTML>
<HEAD>
   <TITLE>Photoshop Leading</TITLE>
</HEAD>
<BODY BGCOLOR=white>
<CENTER>
<IMG SRC="logo.jpg" WIDTH="419"
HEIGHT="108">
<BR><IMG SRC="lead.gif" ALT="Ducks In A
Row represents a uniqueconcept in rubber
stamping. Our original designs created by
Joan Farber, internationally recognized
illustrator, are unlike anything found
in the stamp market today.">
<BR CLEAR=ALL>
</CENTER>
</BODY>
</HTML>
```

There are some basic disadvantages to each of these techniques. The first two, using paragraphs and single-pixel GIFs between lines of text, assume that users have not changed their default font size (some people make it much larger, especially if they have vision problems), and have their browser windows open as wide as yours. If either of those assumptions are not true, your line breaks will be different and you may end up with widows, lines of text with only one word on them.

The example that uses the PRE tag assumes that the browser will allow you to change the font inside the PRE container. Some browsers don't allow that.

Finally, the example that uses a graphic for the text is inefficient. Make sure that your graphic is as small as possible (in terms of file size) so that it will download quickly. Of course, users who use text-only browsers, or have graphic loading turned off, will not see your text at all. Be sure to use ALT text with this one, as we have done in our example pshop.html, located in the chap10 folder of the <chd> CD-ROM.

▶ warning

Unreliable Leading Methods

Bill is probably not the only person who hates HTML leading techniques that introduce space by manually breaking the lines of text. He recommends that you avoid them if at all possible and use CSS instead. (See Chapter 13, "Style," to learn how to lead with CSS.)

When you use the techniques presented here, you will probably go to a lot of trouble to get the lines to break just where you want them to. Then, if all goes well, you will put your masterpiece of faux typesetting up on the web for all to see, and herein lies the problem.

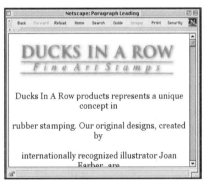

Type on the web is not all the same size. Variations in screen sizes, operating systems, browser settings, and available fonts all conspire to change the actual size of the type displayed on the screen. The end result is that your lines will break in other places, and you will end up with something that looks like this, and never know it!

Indent Techniques

Creating indents in HTML is most often done
with tables. The following file is called indtable.html
and is located inside the chap10 folder of the
<chd> CD-ROM:

```
<HTML>
<HEAD>
   <TITLE>Table Indents</TITLE>
</HEAD>
<BODY BGCOLOR="ffffff">
<IMG SRC="logo.jpg">
<TABLE WIDTH="450" BORDER="0"
HEIGHT="129">
<TR>
<TD WIDTH="124" HEIGHT="105"></TD>
<TD WIDTH="335">Ducks In A Row products
represent a unique concept  in
<P> rubber stamping. Our original
designs, created by
<P> internationally recognized
illustrator Joan Farber,  are
<P>unlike anything found in the
stamp market today.</TD></TR>
</TABLE>
</BODY>
</HTML>
```

You can also create indents by using invisible graphics or single-pixel GIFs and the HSPACE attribute.
The following file is called gifindent.html and is located
inside the chap10 folder of the <chd> CD-ROM:

```
<HTML>
<HEAD>
   <TITLE>Table Indents</TITLE>
</HEAD>
<BODY BGCOLOR="ffffff">
<IMG SRC="logo.jpg">
<P>
<IMG SRC="white.gif" HSPACE=45>Ducks In
A Row products represent a unique
<P><IMG SRC="white.gif" HSPACE=45> concept
in rubber stamping. Our original designs,
<P><IMG SRC="white.gif" HSPACE=45>created
by internationally recognized illustrator
Joan Farber,  are
<P><IMG SRC="white.gif" HSPACE=45>unlike
anything found in the stamp market today.
</BODY>
</HTML>
```

Digital Font Foundries

Today there are tens of thousands of PostScript and TrueType fonts available to personal computer users. It's a great benefit to be able to view and order fonts online, especially during those late nights when you're designing something that's due the next day and you need a specific font you don't yet own. If you're looking for new fonts, check out these URLs:

House Industries: http://www.houseind.com/

Letraset Online: http://www.letraset.com/letraset/

Handwriting Fonts: http://www.execpc.com/~adw/

Fonthead Design: http://www.fonthead.com

Fonts Online: http://www.dol.com/fontsOnline/

Emigre: http://www.emigre.com

Interesting Typography-Based URLs

Razorfish's amazing site, Typographic: Teaches the principles of type using hypertext at its best. Oh, and a little Shockwave, animated GIF action, and an amazing type glossary, too!

http://www.subnetwork.com/typo/
http://www.subnetwork.com/typo/glossary/

Typofile: An online magazine devoted to type techniques and technology. This site has lots of great tutorials and essays about typography.

http://www.will-harris.com/type.htm

David Siegel's Font Summit: Lively commentary on the state of web typography.

http://fonts.verso.com/

Paul Baker Typographic, Inc.: A short presentation on basic typography that includes the use of letter and word spacing, measure, leading, and choosing a typeface, etc.

http://www.pbtweb.com/typostyl/typostyl.htm

Just van Rossum and **Erik van Blokland:** Acclaimed type designers work from their homes in The Hague and the Netherlands. Their goal is to create typefaces that do more than the usual fonts, and they create animations, music, typography, web sites, and some graphic design as well. Be sure to read their rant on embedded fonts.

http://www.letterror.com/LTR_About.html

Type-Centric Bookstore: Educational articles.

http://www.fontsite.com/

Type Glossary: Excellent (and funny).

http://www.microsoft.com/truetype/glossary/content.htm

▶ chapter ten summary

Typography on the web is challenging because controls that typographers want are nonexistent in HTML. This chapter covers a few good tricks that will help you break through the limits of HTML:

• HTML offers limited control over typography. Even so, it's important to know all the tags and learn to combine them for visually interesting type design.

• You can use images of type on web pages, just like images of anything else. This helps break up the predictability of HTML type.

• Using the PRE tag can help to create interesting alignment.

• Visit digital type foundries for a rich selection of fonts and type tips.

11

"Reality leaves a lot to the imagination."
—John Lennon

Planning
ideas and metaphors

It might seem strange to talk about site planning in the middle of this book instead of the beginning. We made the choice to place this chapter later in the book because we thought it was important to teach some of the capabilities of HTML and web design before teaching storyboarding and planning. It's hard to plan something you've never done before.

This chapter walks you through the planning and art direction process for the Ducks In A Row sample site profiled in this book. As with most things, there are many ways to approach the same task. This chapter documents some of the methods we used when planning this and other web sites. There is no one "correct" or "right" way to plan a web site. Each site is different, and different methods and rules will apply on an individual basis. Our goal with this chapter is to help you develop your own site planning techniques by sharing the way we did it.

Looking Ahead

Once you're finished learning what this book has to teach, you will want to plan your own web site before you get started. There are many approaches, some more effective than others. Some people prefer to launch an HTML editor and start making pages without thinking through the site structure beforehand. Others start a small web site, not realizing it might grow into something much bigger in the future. A web site is a different type of enterprise than any other kind of publishing we can think of, and most likely you've never planned for anything like this before.

Organizing Your Site

One of the greatest features of the World Wide Web, indeed the very attractiveness of it, is how easy it is to jump from one train of thought to another. One could say that the *dis*organization of the web is what makes it work!

How do you organize a web? Indeed, how do you organize something that is by its very nature unorganized? In 1974, psychologist and mathematician Tony Buzan (who was the editor of Mensa magazine at the time) invented a method of note-taking called Mind Maps as a means of organizing another inherently unorganized web of information, the human brain.

Mind Maps

In mind mapping, you start your notes in the middle of the page by writing a word or two that represents the overall subject of your notes. Then, radiating outward from the center, you attach brief thoughts—in words and pictures—that represent related concepts and ideas, all the while connecting each thought by a line from the thought that preceded it.

Mind mapping techniques are very valuable in designing and organizing web sites. In fact, there are those who claim that the concept of hypertext was based on the concept of mind mapping. All hyperbole aside, the two concepts are very similar, and the techniques of the former apply well to the latter.

We find the mind mapping techniques useful for generating the first cut of a web site layout. From there, it's easy to refine, expand, and integrate to get the final layout for the site.

Here's the mind map we made when we started to lay out the Ducks In A Row web site:

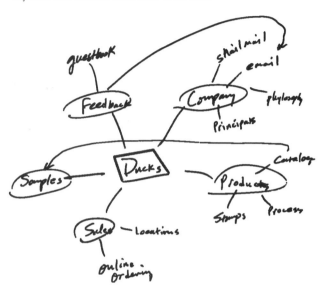

After the site is mapped like this, it becomes easier to organize the site—both logically and physically—on the server.

 note

More On Mind Maps

Pete Russel's description of mind maps:
http://artfolio.com/pete/mindmap.html

The Buzan Centres home page (England):
http://www.gold.net/Buzan/

Ducks In A Row Goals

When we approached the principals at DIAR (**D**ucks **I**n **A R**ow) with the idea of creating a web site for them, we talked about their goals and how a web site might further them. Determining the GOALS of the site is the first stage of web design. Here's what we established from these early conversations:

- A web site could be a great way for Ducks In A Row to achieve better visibility, without the expense of advertising in magazines.

- It could provide a means for potential rubber stamp buyers to locate retail outlets that sell DIAR stamps. We were specifically told not to create an online retail catalog because Ducks In A Row is a wholesaler of rubber stamps; they do not sell their products at a retail level.

- It could be an opportunity to promote the retailers that carry DIAR stamps.

- It could serve as an educational site to show the process of making rubber stamps.

- A gallery could be created to show off how to make great looking designs with DIAR rubber stamps.

Once we knew these goals, we were able to break the site into navigational divisions:

- **Our Company:** An area to profile the company and its principals.

- **Catalog:** An area to show some of the DIAR stamp catalogs.

- **Samples:** A gallery of designs made with DIAR rubber stamps.

- **Process:** An area to profile the rubber stamp creation process.

- **Retail Locations:** An area on the site where people could locate retail outlets that stock DIAR rubber stamps.

Because we didn't want to take up a lot of room with each icon, it was important to settle on one or two word descriptions of each navigational element.

Art Direction

Before starting the project, we looked carefully at the existing catalogs and promotional materials (called collateral in marketing-speak) that the Ducks In A Row company had already created. Their catalogs were printed with one color on colored paper, and they provided more elaborate, handmade color samples to their retail outlets for in-store displays. For the web site design, we chose to borrow and expand on the design direction that the company already set.

We looked first at Ducks In A Row catalogs to get an idea of what their existing design direction was.

We thought the stamps themselves would work well throughout the site as icons and artistic elements. Even though ducks come in a variety of colors, the word "rubber" in rubber stamps and "ducks" from Ducks In A Row made us think of rubber duckies. This triggered the idea to use yellow as a unifying color throughout the site. A bright yellow could be overbearing, so we arrived at a muted yellow color (using the browser-safe color chart, of course!) as the dominant color.

To us, these rubber stamps were sophisticated and classy—a departure from typical rubber stamps that might be kitsch or campy. To emphasize the difference between these stamps and other rubber stamp designs, we chose colors that were muted and subdued rather than bright and saturated.

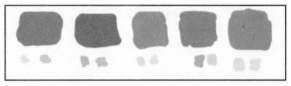

This color chart helped us limit the palette in order to make the site feel unified and consistent. Reddish browns, muted greens, deep blues, and mauves were chosen because they work well against the light yellow theme. We alternated these color themes throughout the site to add variety while maintaining continuity.

We felt that overt drop shadows and 3D effects, such as beveled buttons and specular highlights, were inappropriate for the subject matter of this site. The stamp designs were flat, so there seemed to be no reason to throw dimensional effects into the artwork.

We added headlines to the pages so that our audience would always know where they were on the site. We chose to work with a classical sans serif font (Gill Sans) and offset it with a handwritten font (Chauncy Snowman) to lend a friendlier, more homemade feeling to the site.

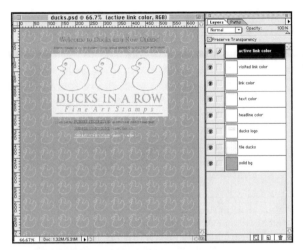

Creating a layered Photoshop document can help you experiment with a design direction and allow you to make multiple versions of a site to show a client.

These decisions were all made in advance of making any artwork. We created a layered Photoshop document that allowed us to try out designs and colors and show them to our client before we went forward with production or went live with the site. This layered document is called ducks.psd and can be found in the chap11 folder of the <chd> CD-ROM.

Metaphors

It's often helpful when planning a site to draw up a list of metaphors. Webster's dictionary defines metaphor as, "a figure of speech in which one thing is spoken of as if it is another" Visual metaphors build on free associations of objects or ideas. Helpful metaphors for web building can relate to sounds, images, or movement. Here's a list of potential metaphors for Ducks In A Row:

Sounds
quack
water
paper folding
splashing

Visual
water splashing
water ripples
rubber ducks
yellow
the actual stamps

Animation
pond ripples
stamps animating on and off
ducks swimming

A list like this can help feed you with ideas while you create your animations, sounds, rollovers, navigation, and images.

Flowcharting

There are many ways to create a flowchart of a site—from scribbles on a napkin or chalkboard, to index cards, to computer software. Margaret Gould Stewart, creative director at http://www.tripod.com, described her storyboarding process at a web design conference. She uses index cards, which allow her to spread the cards out on a table or floor so that they can be easily reorganized. When she is finished, she gives the same cards to other members of her team to see if they come up with a different structure. This process allows her to get valuable input from others and ensures that all the possible navigation choices have been explored.

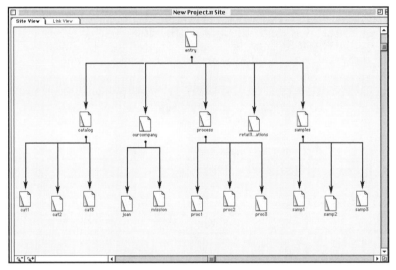

Some HTML editors, such as Go Live (pictured above) and Net Objects Fusion, help you set up the site structure in flowcharting windows. If you use these products, they automatically generate HTML pages that are linked with the proper hierarchy and can be viewed like this, as a map.

11

▶ chapter eleven summary

Planning a site is important to its overall aesthetic continuity and navigational success. This chapter has outlined some of the techniques we use when approaching a new site design.

Here's a handy checklist to follow when planning a site:

• Determine the goals of the site.

• Document the goals and share them with your client and or partners.

• Identify the different sections of the site.

• Determine the art direction of the site—colors, layout, metaphors, and typefaces.

12

*"Man is an over-complicated organism.
If he is doomed to extinction
he will die out for want of simplicity."*
—Ezra Pound (U.S. poet, 1885–1972)

Organization

Organization
absolutely relative

If you are planning a site of any substantial size—with, say, 10 or more different files—it's a good idea to organize it so you can find things when you need to work with them.

It's common to start a web site small, with a couple of `.html` files and a few `.gif` files, and then add some here and tack something else on there. Before long you have hundreds of files all in one folder, and you haven't got a clue what they all are!

Some of the files may no longer be in use; some of them may be older versions of files that are still in use. But you don't know, and it doesn't really matter because everything works just fine.

And then the fateful day comes when you save a new file with the name of an old file and poof!, you've got trouble in River City! You thought that was an old version of something, but it was actually a page that you had spent hours getting just right, and now you're going to have to do it all over again!

Keeping it organized can help a lot.

Simplicity Versus Chaos

Some may argue that it's far simpler to keep everything in one folder, and indeed it is—at least for the person putting it there. But can you also argue that it's easier in the long run? When you come back a year (or even just a week!) from now to update that site with 387 different files in one folder, will that be easy? Expedience belies chaos.

On the other hand, let's say we put all the images in one folder called images, all the files for the company information page in a company folder, and all the files used for the personal biographies in a folder called people, and so on. Now each folder has a dozen or so files, and it's easier to keep them straight!

Not only does this make the maintenance of the site easier, but it becomes easier to share files—images, for instance—between different parts of the site. This process is only difficult if we don't start the site with organization in mind. If we start the site with all the files in one folder, then we will have a much harder time getting it organized later.

What's in a Name?

The location of each object on the World Wide Web can be described with a URL (**U**niform **R**esource **L**ocator). A URL is an address in a specific format that can uniquely identify an individual object on the web.

The purpose of a URL is to describe to a computer precisely how to ask for an object that resides on another computer somewhere on the Net. A URL is like a sophisticated address or phone number, in that it tells your computer exactly where to find that particular object.

The Parts of a URL

A URL has a number of different parts. Referring to the diagram, you can see that a complete URL can have scheme, host, port, path, parameters, query, and fragment parts. In practice, though, a URL almost never uses all of them at once.

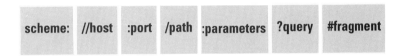

The parts of a URL.

The most common form of a URL looks like this:

- **The first part** (http:) is called the scheme. That's a fancy way of saying that this is the protocol that the browser will use to ask the server for the file it needs. In this case (as in most), we will use the HTTP protocol to retrieve the object.

- **The second part** (www.htmlbook.com) is called the host. This is the name (or it can be the IP address) of the server (host computer) that holds the object we want. Many web browsers will accept just the host part and connect you to that machine using HTTP (the protocol used by web servers). For example, you could access our site by typing http://www.htmlbook.com, or you could type just the host part, www.htmlbook.com, and most browsers would still find our site. If you use the host-only feature, remember that it is a shortcut on the part of the browser and is not a proper URL.

- Finally, **the last part** (/examples/url.html) is the path to the object on that particular server. The path consists of directories (or folders) and the file name itself. In this case, the directory is /examples and the file name is url.html. Directories are separated by slashes (/) by convention, probably because that's how you do it on UNIX, and the web was developed on UNIX.

Absolute and Relative URLs

When you specify a URL, such as http://www.host.com/thatpage.html, you are telling the browser everything it needs to know to find that object on the web, including the protocol to use (http), the host to contact (www.host.com), and the absolute (exact) path to the object on that host (/thatpage.html).

There are times, however when it may be more useful to refer to the location of an object relative to the location of the last object you requested. For example, if a web page needs to refer to a graphic file that will be displayed on the same page, it's useful to use a notation that says "get this other file from the same place (the same server, protocol, folder, etc.) where you got the page that asked for it." That way, when you move the page to another server, or even another folder on the same server, you don't need to update all the URLs in all the HTML files. A relative URL, like newpage.html, is the simplest way to accomplish this goal.

- An absolute URL is a complete URL that specifies the exact location of the object on the web, like this:

  http://www.htmlbook.com/examples/url/url.gif

- A relative URL gives the location of the object relative to the location of the page that contains the URL, like this:

  url.gif

In context, here's an example of a page using an absolute URL:

```
<HTML>
<HEAD>
<TITLE> URL Example </TITLE>
</HEAD>
<BODY BGCOLOR=white>

<H1> The Parts of a URL </H1>
<IMG SRC="http://www.htmlbook.com/
examples/url.gif">
<P> A URL has a number of different
parts. Referring to the diagram,
you can see that a complete URL
can have scheme, host, port, path,
parameters, query, and fragment parts.
In practice, though, a URL almost
never uses all of them at once.

</BODY>
</HTML>
```

1.

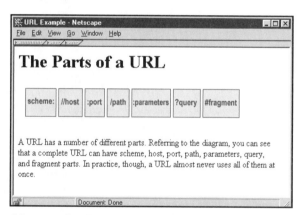

A browser showing the Parts of a URL page.

1. Notice the IMG tag, which specifies an image using an absolute (complete) URL. However, it is much more convenient—and more common—to use a relative (partial) URL like this:
    `<img src="url.gif">`

    By definition, the SRC attribute must always contain a URL, but it can be a relative URL. In this case, when the browser sees url.gif, it knows to look in the same folder, on the same server, as where it got the page that contains the URL.

Paths in Relative URLs

Remember that the part of the URL after the **host** part is called the **path** part. It can include a path of directories that will lead to the specific file that has the object you want.

Paths in a relative URL describe the location of the object on the server in a hierarchical directory structure. Each level of the hierarchy is separated by a slash (/) character in the relative URL. This directory structure is, for all intents and purposes, the same sort of structure as the folders or directories on a Mac, PC, or UNIX system. Though you may be more accustomed to using a colon (:) or a reverse slash (\) to separate levels of folders in your OS, the concepts involved are the same.

When the browser encounters a relative URL in a file, it uses the location of the HTML file that contains the reference as a base URL. The browser builds a full URL by combining the relative URL with the base URL.

By definition, a base URL must be an absolute URL, including the name of the file at the end. (That's just because the URL specification treats the path part, including the file name, as a single unit.) In practice, however, the file name part is discarded, and the relative URL is attached in its place.

For example, let's use the document at http://www.htmlbook.com/ examples/url/ex2.html as a base URL and url.gif as a relative URL:

- **Base URL:** http://www.htmlbook.com/examples/url/ex2.html

- **Relative URL:** url.gif

- **Resulting URL:** http://www.htmlbook.com/examples/url/url.gif

In order to build the resulting URL, the browser first discards the file name part of the base URL, which leaves http://www.htmlbook.com/ examples/url/. For the purposes of this discussion, we'll call this the base URL path (there is no official name for it, as the URL specification doesn't deal with this part separately). Then it appends the relative URL, effectively replacing the file name that was just removed. The resulting URL is effectively the concatenation of the base URL—minus the file name—and the relative URL.

Relative URL Examples

In order to help you visualize what happens when you use relative URLs, we've prepared a few examples using two files, a base file called ex2.html and a graphic file, url.gif.

The following diagrams show where the graphic file will be found, using various relative URLs:

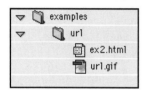

`<IMG SRC="url.gif">` **will find the** url.gif **file in the current** base **folder.**

- **Base URL:**
  http://www.htmlbook.com/examples/url/ex2.html

- **Relative URL:**
  url.gif

- **Resulting URL:**
  http://www.htmlbook.com/examples/url/url.gif

The relative URL is simply pasted onto the base URL path.

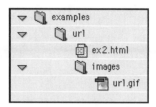

`<IMG SRC="images/url.gif">` **will find the** url.gif **file in the** images **folder, under the** url **folder.**

- **Base URL:**
  http://www.htmlbook.com/examples/url/ex2.html

- **Relative URL:**
  images/url.gif

- **Resulting URL:**
  http://www.htmlbook.com/examples/url/images/url.gif

The relative URL is simply pasted onto the base URL path.

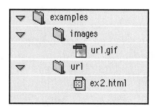

`<IMG SRC="../images/url.gif">` **will find the** url.gif **file in the** images **folder one level above the current folder.**

- **Base URL:**
  http://www.htmlbook.com/examples/url/ex2.html

- **Relative URL:**
  ../images/url.gif

- **Resulting URL:**
  http://www.htmlbook.com/examples/images/url.gif

Two dots together in place of a directory name is a special case, meaning "go up one level." If the path begins with two dots (..), the path will start one directory higher than the current directory.

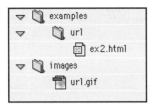

`<IMG SRC="/images/url.gif">` **will find the** url.gif **file in the** images **folder at the root level of the web site.**

- **Base URL:**
  http://www.htmlbook.com/examples/url/ex2.html

- **Relative URL:**
  /images/url.gif

- **Resulting URL:**
  http://www.htmlbook.com/images/url.gif

If the relative URL begins with a slash (/), the entire path part of the base URL is replaced with the relative URL.

From ex2.html, `<IMG SRC="../../ images/url.gif">` **will find the** url.gif **file in the** images **folder two levels above the current folder.**

- **Base URL:**
  http://www.htmlbook.com/examples/url/ex2.html

- **Relative URL:**
  ../../images/url.gif

- **Resulting URL:**
  http://www.htmlbook.com/images/url.gif

Taking the ".." concept one step further, "../../" means "go up two directories."

Convert a Relative URL

If you are still a little confused about how relative URLs work, don't despair! Bill wrote a CGI program that converts relative URLs to absolute URLs so that you can get a better feel for how this all works. To use our converter check out: http://www.htmlbook.com/examples/url/conv-url.cgi.

Here's how it works:

Convert a Relative URL

Because the resulting URL is derived from a base URL and a relative URL, this program requires both:

Base URL: http://www.htmlbook.com/examples/url/ex1.html

Relative URL: url.gif

[Convert]   [Start Over]

© 1997 Lynda and Bill Weinmar.

Just enter the base and relative URLs in the form fields, and press **Convert**.

Result

The base URL was: **http://www.htmlbook.com/examples/url/ex1.html**
The relative URL was: **url.gif**
The resulting URL is: **http://www.htmlbook.com/examples/url/url.gif**

© 1997 Lynda and Bill Weinmar.

The result shows up on the next page. This program should give you more confidence to use relative URLs in your own pages.

Relative URLs as Links

You can also use relative URLS as links. For example, if your page is at http://www.htmlbook.com/examples/url/ex3.html, you could have a relative link to ex4.html without having to type the entire URL.

```
<A HREF="ex4.html">Over Here!</A>
```

The browser would then apply the rules it uses for relative URLs and treat the link as if you had typed http://www.htmlbook.com/examples/url/ex4.html as a complete URL.

Here's an example that uses a few different types of relative URLs. Below the screen shot is a separate screen shot of the status line as the cursor is passed over each link. (The status bar shows the full URL for each of the links.) This page is available as http://www.htmlbook.com/examples/url/ex3.html on the <chd> web site, so you can see it run on your system.

```
<HTML>
<HEAD>
<TITLE> Relative URL Link Example </TITLE>
</HEAD>
<BODY BGCOLOR=white>

<H1> Relative URL Links </H1>

<P> This page is at http://www.htmlbook.com/
examples/url/ex3.html
</P>

<TABLE WIDTH=400><TR><TD>
Run your mouse cursor over the links below,
and see what they look like in your status
bar. Can you see how the browser completes
the URL for you?
```

```
</TABLE>

<UL>
  <LI><A HREF="ex4.html">Over Here!</A>
ex4.html
  <LI><A HREF="company/index.html">
Over there.</a> company/index.html
  <LI><A HREF="bios/">Yonder.</a> bios/
  <LI><A HREF="../">Somewhere . . .
</a>   ../
  <LI><A HREF="images/url.gif">. . .
else.</A> images/url.gif
</UL>

<P>
<HR>
&copy; 1997 Lynda and Bill Weinman

</BODY>
```

By understanding how relative URLs work, you can organize your site more flexibly and make it easier to maintain, as well as easier to navigate. By using relative URLs throughout your site, you can create a site that is well-organized and have it still work when you move the site from one machine to another.

Say, for example, you build your site on your local machine at home or in your office. But when you are ready to put the site up on the Net, you have to move it to another machine. By using relative URLs, you can ensure that the links on your site still work when you move it to your web server.

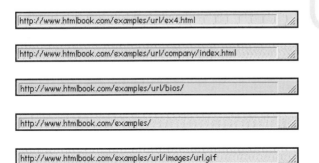

Relative URL Links

This page is at http://www.htmlbook.com/examples/url/ex3.html

Run your mouse cursor over the links below, and see what they look like in your status bar. Can you see how the browser completes the URL for you?

- Over Here! ex4.html
- Over there. company/index.html
- Yonder./ bios/
- Somewhere . . . . ../
- . . . else. images/url.gif

© 1997 Lynda and Bill Weinman

The relative URL links page.

http://www.htmlbook.com/examples/url/ex4.html

http://www.htmlbook.com/examples/url/company/index.html

http://www.htmlbook.com/examples/url/bios/

http://www.htmlbook.com/examples/

http://www.htmlbook.com/examples/url/images/url.gif

The status bar for each of the links on the page.

▶ **note**

Relative URL Resources

Relative URL Specification
http://www.w3.org/Addressing/rfc1808.txt

The URL Specification
(does not include relative URLs)
http://www.w3.org/Addressing/URL/Overview.html
http://www.w3.org/Addressing/rfc1738.txt

The CGI Book, by Bill Weinman
Chapter 4, "Understanding URLs"

Directory Structure

Now that you have a good understanding of how relative URLs work, it will be much easier to organize your site into various directories according to a logical plan. In fact, it will even be easier to change the structure of your site, if you should be so inclined in the future.

The structure of the directories should roughly match the layout of the site. In other words, if you have a section of the site about "Company," you can put that section in a directory called company; you can use a directory called sales for your "Sales" section, and so on.

If one of your sections has other branches, like "Products" in our example, you may want to use other subdirectories under the products directory.

A proposed directory layout for Ducks In A Row:

```
ducks
├── company
├── products
│   ├── catalog
│   ├── samples
│   └── process
├── sales
│   ├── locations
│   └── order
├── feedback
    ├── email
    └── guestbook
```

A sample directory layout for the Ducks In A Row site.

In this case, we chose to put each of the major sections in its own folder, and we further separated sections into subsections, where we felt they were still too complex. This organization allows us to deal with each section's complexity as distinct from the others, while sharing those elements of the site that are in common.

Repeating Elements

In dealing with the commonalties of different parts of the site, you will find yourself using exactly the same HTML in many places. For example, you may have a common menu, or a common BODY tag that you use over and over again. Not only is it inconvenient to have to continually rewrite the same bit of code, but it's prone to error when you eventually need to make changes.

For example, let's say you have a common BODY tag that you want to use throughout your site.

```
<BODY BGCOLOR="#FFFFCC" TEXT="#663333"
LINK="#006699" VLINK="#006699">
```

This creates a nice color scheme with a yellow background, brown lettering, and teal links. But, six months or a year from now, you may find yourself tired of it. But in order to change it, you have to find all the places you used it and replace the code throughout your site!

When you do decide to change it, what are the odds that you'll miss a page here and a page there? Then some visitors who find those less-used pages will see the old color scheme, while the rest of the site uses the new!

One solution to this problem is to consolidate the repeating elements of the site into one place. We can do this with a technique called Server-Side Includes.

Server-Side Includes

The term **S**erver-**S**ide **I**ncludes (SSI) refers to the ability of a web server to merge various files together into one file, while serving an HTML file. The concept of file inclusion is probably not entirely foreign to you because most word processors have similar capabilities.

For example, if your word processor has templates for creating certain types of documents, or if it can merge-print a form letter from a database, these are file includes in the same way that SSI is for web servers.

How SSI Works

On many web servers, in order to use SSI you must name your file with the `.shtml` extension instead of `.html`. Your system may differ, though, so check with your system administrator for the correct requirements. The examples in this book use the `.html` extension because we have configured our server to use SSI with all the pages on our site.

> ### ▶ note

> ### Potential SSI Problems

> Some web servers, especially those with many users on them, have some SSI capabilities turned off—or have disabled SSI entirely—for security reasons. If so, you will have to ask your system administrator to enable it for you.

> Some other servers may use such a radically different paradigm that these examples may not work at all! The problem is that there's no standard for SSI. Most web servers use the SSI specification that was developed for the NCSA server (one of the original web servers, developed at the University of Illinois). The server that we use is called Apache. It's a free server based on the original NCSA code, and it's by far the most popular server on the Internet as of this writing. Most other servers, including Netscape's servers, also use this same SSI model.

> If you find that these examples don't work on your server, ask your system administrator for the proper syntax for including files on your server. It may be one of those servers that just works differently.

◗ note

File and Folder Names

On many systems—especially if you are using an NCSA-derived server, like Apache or Netscape—you can name your files anything that you want to and put them in whatever folder you want to.

On some web servers, you are required to use the `.shtml` extension for any HTML documents that use SSI. On our web server, since we use SSI on all our pages, we chose to configure the server to accept SSI in files with the `.html` extension. So, all of our pages use `.html`.

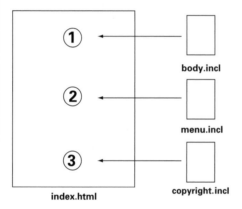

For the included files, you can usually use whatever file name extension that you want to. We end our file names with the `.incl` extension so that we can easily distinguish between full HTML files and included files that aren't otherwise a full page.

We also chose to put all of our included files in a separate folder called incl. That allows us to use a consistent syntax for including the files throughout the site.

SSI has a number of different features. Depending on your server, you can use SSI to include files, run external programs, display server parameters, and more! Most of those features are outside of the scope of this book. For this book, we will concentrate on using SSI to help organize and manage a complex web site. For information on other SSI features, see Chapter 8 of *The CGI Book* or consult your server documentation.

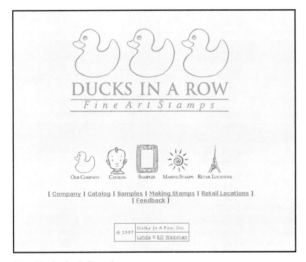

The Ducks In A Row home page.

SSI commands are embedded in HTML comments (`<!-- this is an HTML comment -->`) so that they won't display in the browser if, for some reason, the server fails to intercept them. The format of an SSI command is like this:

```
<!--#include virtual="filename" -->
```

The pound sign (#) introduces the keyword (`include`) so that the server knows to interpret the rest of the comment. The keyword `virtual` tells the server to treat the file name as a relative path instead of an absolute file path. (SSI also allows the keyword `file` instead of `virtual`, but it is far more complicated to use, and we don't recommend it.) The space after the file name is required, and no space is allowed before the pound sign.

For the Ducks In A Row site, we created a separate folder called include for all of our included files. We named the included files with the `.incl` extension so that we could easily distinguish them from complete HTML files. For example, the index.html file from the site looks like this:

```
<HTML>
<HEAD>
    <TITLE>Ducks in a Row
Homepage</TITLE>
</HEAD>
1.  <!--#include virtual="/include/
body.incl" -->

<P ALIGN=CENTER>
<BR CLEAR=ALL>

<!-- Logo -->
<A HREF="sitemap.html">
<IMG SRC="/images/ylogo1.gif"
    ALT="Ducks in a Row Logo"
    BORDER=0    WIDTH=419
HEIGHT=219></A>

<TABLE><TR><TD HEIGHT=20></TABLE>
<!-- for spacing -->
2.  <!--#include virtual="/include/
menu.incl" -->

<TABLE><TR><TD HEIGHT=20></TABLE>
<!-- for spacing -->
3.  <!--#include virtual="/include/
copyright.incl" -->
</BODY>
</HTML>
```

This brings in all the elements from the include directory, and the server sends the fully assembled HTML page to the browser.

1. By using SSI for the BODY tag, our common menus, and the copyright elements, we were able to reduce the size of our HTML files and create a consistent look with a minimum of effort.

    The include file for the BODY tag, /include/body.incl, looks like this:

    ```
    <BODY BGCOLOR="#FFFFCC" TEXT="#663333" LINK="#006699" VLINK="#006699"
    ```

    This allows for a consistent color scheme across the site without having to keep track of different pages.

2. The SSI file for the menu /include/menu.incl looks like this:

    ```
    <!-- menu include -->
    <map name="navbar">
    <area shape ="polygon" alt="Our Company
    coords="84,58,83,64,78,72,67,78,59,79,53,79,46,77,39,72,37,67,41,59,44,56,46,54,46,
    51,43,50,37,47,35,43,38,43,42,41,46,32,50,30,55,29,58,30,62,34,64,37,63,42,63,46,60,
    48,63,52,70,52,73,47,74,43,78,40,83,46,84,52" href="/company/">
    <area shape="polygon" alt="Catalog"
    coords="122,67,126,69,129,70,131,74,122,80,122,82,156,82,156,79,147,74,147,71,152,
    67,154,64,154,61,158,60,159,55,162,52,162,48,159,48,157,51,158,43,158,33,152,26,140,
    24,139,20,135,20,130,26,122,28,117,38,117,47,111,50,111,54,115,57,117,61,120,63"
    href="/products/">
    <area shape="rect" alt="Samples" coords="187,15,236,79" href="/samples/">
    <area shape="circle" alt="Making Stamps" coords="287,51,28" href="/making.html">
    <area shape="polygon" alt="Retail Locations"
    coords="390,81,381,61,378,41,377,13,374,13,372,41,367,62,357,81" href="/sales/">
    <area shape="rect" coords="21,82,98,97" href="/company/">
    <area shape="rect" coords="113,83,166,96" href="/products/">
    <area shape="rect" coords="186,81,236,96" href="/samples/">
    <area shape="rect" coords="244,81,325,95" href="/making.html">
    <area shape="rect" coords="332,81,419,96" href="/sales/">
    <area shape="rect" nohref>
    </map>

    <P ALIGN=CENTER>
    <IMG SRC="/images/navbar.gif"
      WIDTH="440" HEIGHT="116" BORDER="0" USEMAP="#navbar">
    <BR CLEAR=ALL>
    <FONT FACE="verdana,helvetica,arial">
    <SMALL><STRONG>
    [
    <A HREF="/company/">Company</A> |
    <A HREF="/catalog/">Catalog</A> |
    <A HREF="/samples/">Samples</A> |
    <A HREF="/process/">Making Stamps</A> |
    <A HREF="/locations/">Retail Locations</A>
    ]
    <BR>[
    <A HREF="/feedback/">Feedback</A>
    <!--#if expr="\"$DOCUMENT_URI\" != \"/index.html\"" -->
      <A HREF="/">Home</A>
      <!--#if expr="$HTTP_REFERER" -->
        | <A HREF="<!--#echo var="HTTP_REFERER" -->">Back</A>
      <!--#endif -->
    <!--#endif -->
    ]
    </STRONG></SMALL></FONT></P>
    <!-- end menu include -->
    ```

With that menu include, we can use a complex menu, with imagemaps and a text menu, without having to duplicate all that code on each page.

3.   The include file for the copyright notice, /include/copyright.incl, looks like this:

```
<!-- copyright include -->
<CENTER>
<!-- outer table -->
<TABLE BORDER=0 CELLSPACING=0 CELLPADDING=0 BGCOLOR=#663333>
  <TR><TD>

    <!-- inner table -->
    <TABLE BORDER=0 CELLPADDING=4 CELLSPACING=1 WIDTH=100% BGCOLOR="#FFFFCC">
      <TR><TD ALIGN=CENTER ROWSPAN=2>
         <FONT SIZE=-2 COLOR="#006699" FACE="verdana,helvetica,arial">
         &copy 1997</FONT></TD>
      <TD>
         <FONT SIZE=-2 COLOR="#006699" FACE="verdana,helvetica,arial">
         Ducks In A Row, Inc.</FONT></TD>
    <TR><TD>
       <FONT SIZE=-2 COLOR="#006699" FACE="verdana,helvetica,arial">
       <A HREF="http://www.lynda.com/">Lynda</A> &
       <A HREF="http://www.weinman.com/wew/">Bill</A>
       <A HREF="http://www.weinman.com/">Weinman</A></FONT></TD>
      </TR>
    </TABLE>     <!-- end inner table -->

  </TD></TR>
</TABLE>  <!-- end outer table -->
</CENTER>
<!-- end copyright include -->
```

This is a nice-looking nested table with a discreet 1-pixel outline. Again, the use of SSI allows us to use this level of complexity without having to duplicate it across the site.

> **▶ note**
>
> **SSI Resources**
>
> **NCSA SSI Tutorial**
> http://hoohoo.ncsa.uiuc.edu/docs/tutorials/includes.html
>
> **The CGI Book**
> http://www.cgibook.com/
> http://www.cgibook.com/chap08/

▶ chapter twelve summary

Organizing your web site is more than just designing an attractive and functional interface. It means deciding how the site best breaks down and using the tools that HTML provides, such as relative URLs, to keep it all manageable.

In this chapter, you learned how to use relative URLs and Server-Side Includes to keep your site organized and manageable at the same time.

13

*"My spelling is Wobbly.
It's good spelling but it Wobbles,
and the letters get in the wrong places."*
—A. A. Milne (1882–1958)

Style Sheets
control at last

When you've been writing HTML for a while, you'll start wishing that it could do a few more tricks. Wouldn't it be nice, for instance, if you could adjust the spaces between lines? Wouldn't it be nice if you could create shortcuts for some common formatting operations? Wouldn't it be nice if you could position a graphic right up against the upper-left corner of the browser window?

Style sheets are the tooth-fairy for a lot of these wishes.

A style sheet is a collection of templates, or styles, that apply to various parts of your document and describe the way it gets rendered. Style sheets have been available in all the major word processing programs for quite some time.

Early in the development of HTML and the web, designers and programmers started asking for a form of style sheets that could be applied to HTML documents. A number of different proposals were fielded, and one proposal, **C**ascading **S**tyle **S**heet (CSS), was implemented. There are other style sheet specifications, but CSS is the form that has been accepted, and all the major browser vendors are working hard to adopt it.

Style Sheets

Cascading Style Sheets

The **C**ascading **S**tyle **S**heets (CSS) specification is the form of style sheets recommended by the **W**orld **W**ide **W**eb **C**onsortium (W3C) as appropriate for use with HTML. It is also the form that is being deployed by the two major browser manufacturers, Netscape and Microsoft.

Unfortunately for those of us who would like to really use CSS, it is implemented neither completely nor consistently enough in either of the major browsers for us to use CSS with any confidence. With that in mind, the intent of this chapter is to show you how CSS works and what its potential is, so that you will be familiar with it when it eventually becomes ready for prime time.

Therefore, we urge you to read this chapter with this caveat emptor: The details of CSS will almost certainly change somewhat before the dust settles. The basic principles will almost certainly not change. Treat what you learn in this chapter as a preview of things to come, and experiment with it, but don't be surprised if it works differently in later versions of your favorite browser. (We conducted our tests using Netscape Navigator 4.03 and Microsoft Internet Explorer 4 [preview release 2], and we have only included examples that work the same between the two.)

The scope of this chapter is to show you generally what style sheets are going to be able to do. The scope of this chapter is not to show you all the details of CSS because most of it doesn't work today and is subject to a lot of change before it does work. Or spoken more simply, "Your mileage may vary."

How CSS Style Sheets Work

A CSS style sheet is a type of document that is used by a web browser to redefine the properties of the various elements and tags in the HTML.

The style sheet document may be contained within the HTML document, or it may be in a separate file on the server. An internal style sheet is one that's contained within the HTML document. An external style sheet is stored in a separate file on the server, allowing one style sheet to be used for a whole group of HTML documents. In the future, you may also be able to specify a style sheet with your favorite settings in your browser and have it apply to pages without style sheets, or even override some style sheets on some pages.

For our purposes, we will work with **internal style sheets**. (See the sidebar, "External Style Sheets," for a brief description of the other method.) Just keep in mind that there are other ways to do this.

> ▶ **note**
>
> ## External Style Sheets
>
> External style sheets are convenient for situations when you may want to apply a set of styles across a number of different documents. For example, you could create an external style sheet that defines a color scheme for your web site, including a background image, fonts and sizes for headings and paragraphs, etc. Then whenever you want to change the look of your site, you simply update the external style sheet and voilà! Your site is updated! For more details about linking external style sheets, see the W3C's documentation at:
>
> http://www.w3.org/TR/WD-style#intro.

For the first few examples, we use a page from the Ducks In A Row site, which explains how the rubber stamps are used. First, here's what the page looks like in plain old ordinary HTML. If you want to follow along, you can find this page as css1.html in the chap13 folder on the <chd> CD-ROM:

```
<HEAD>
<TITLE>CSS Examples</TITLE>
</HEAD>
<BODY BGCOLOR="#FFFFCC" TEXT="#663300"
LINK="#006699" VLINK="#006699">

<H1>Working with Ducks in a Row Rubber
Stamps</H1>

<P>
Because the style of art throughout the
catalog is consistent, any of the designs
may be used together side by side, or
superimposed, making the possibilities
for personal expression boundless.

<P>
You will find designs in our catalog
which cover a vast array of categories,
from floral images to humor, holiday
stamps, border designs and decorative
imagery, for all around use. You, as the
stamping artist will be the one to create
original art works from these designs,
and nothing pleasures us more than to see
the beautiful and original ways in which
our designs are being used.
```

```
<P>
Throughout the catalog you will find
some helpful hints on some of the uses
and techniques to enjoy your stamps,
but we're sure that you as the stamping
artist can teach us a thing or two!
One thing for certain, the possibilities
are endless!

</BODY>
```

Sample page without CSS.

Adding a Style Sheet

One major concern when using style sheets, especially today when only the very latest browsers
understand them, is making sure that older
browsers can still view pages that use them.

Using our example, we'll add a style sheet to a
page by using the STYLE tag. We can hide the style
sheet from older browsers by putting comment
tags around everything within the STYLE container. Here's what that looks like in the HEAD section of our current example (this file is css2.html
in the chap13 folder on the <chd> CD-ROM):

```
<HEAD>
<TITLE>CSS Examples</TITLE>

<STYLE TYPE="text/css">
<!--

H1 {
   font-family: Verdana
   }

-->
</STYLE>
</HEAD>
```

Because the style sheet itself is enclosed in HTML
comments, browsers that don't understand the
STYLE tag are prevented from displaying the style
sheet in the browser window. Browsers that do
understand the style sheet will ignore the comment tags and apply the style sheet to the page.

Let's pretend we're an older browser, so we can see
why we don't get confused by the style sheet here.
We're merrily reading through the file (top-to-bot-
tom), and we get to the STYLE tag. Since we don't
know what it is, we just ignore it (that's one of the
rules of HTML: Ignore the tags you don't understand). Then we get to the comment beginning
(<!--), and we become blind to everything until
we see the comment ending (-->), so none of the
style sheet syntax is noticed by us at all! Now we
see the end tag for the STYLE element (</STYLE>),
which we ignore, and we can merrily continue as if
nothing happened.

We'll look at the style sheet itself more closely in a
moment, but right now let's see what a new browser and an older browser do with it. First, here's a
screen shot of this page in Netscape Navigator 4,
which understands simple CSS style sheets:

Working with Ducks in a Row Rubber Stamps

Because the style of art throughout the catalog is consistent, any of the designs may be used together side by side, or superimposed, making the possibilities for personal expression boundless.

You will find designs in our catalog which cover a vast array of categories, from floral images to humor, holiday stamps, border designs and decorative imagery, for all around use. You, as the stamping artist will be the one to create original art works from these designs, and nothing pleasures us more than to see the beautiful and original ways in which our designs are being used.

Throughout the catalog you will find some helpful hints on some of the uses and techniques to enjoy your stamps, but we're sure that you as the stamping artist can teach us a thing or two! One thing for certain, the possibilities are endless!

css2.html **in Netscape Navigator 4.**

And here's what it looks like in Netscape Navigator 3, which does not understand style sheets:

Here's what some of your users may see if you don't hide your style sheet with comment tags:

Working with Ducks in a Row Rubber Stamps

Because the style of art throughout the catalog is consistent, any of the designs may be used together side by side, or superimposed, making the possibilities for personal expression boundless.

You will find designs in our catalog which cover a vast array of categories, from floral images to humor, holiday stamps, border designs and decorative imagery, for all around use. You, as the stamping artist will be the one to create original art works from these designs, and nothing pleasures us more than to see the beautiful and original ways in which our designs are being used.

Throughout the catalog you will find some helpful hints on some of the uses and techniques to enjoy your stamps, but we're sure that you as the stamping artist can teach us a thing or two! One thing for certain, the possibilities are endless!

H1 { font-family: Verdana }

Working with Ducks in a Row Rubber Stamps

Because the style of art throughout the catalog is consistent, any of the designs may be used together side by side, or superimposed, making the possibilities for personal expression boundless.

You will find designs in our catalog which cover a vast array of categories, from floral images to humor, holiday stamps, border designs and decorative imagery, for all around use. You, as the stamping artist will be the one to create original art works from these designs, and nothing pleasures us more than to see the beautiful and original ways in which our designs are being used.

Throughout the catalog you will find some helpful hints on some of the uses and techniques to enjoy your stamps, but we're sure that you as the stamping artist can teach us a thing or two! One thing for certain, the possibilities are endless!

As you can see, browsers that don't understand the style sheets ignore them because of the comment tags. When you add a style sheet to an HTML document, it's always a good idea to use the comment tags inside the STYLE element so that older browsers won't display the style sheet.

The Anatomy of a CSS Style Sheet

Now that you know how to add a style sheet to a document, let's take a quick look at the style that we defined in this document.

1.
```
<STYLE TYPE="text/css">
<!--

H1 {
   font-family: Verdana
   }

-->
</STYLE>
```

1. The `STYLE` element is a container that goes in the `HEAD` section of your HTML document. The `TYPE` attribute specifies the type of style sheet being used, which in this case is CSS. The `STYLE` element can contain any number of different styles. This style element contains one style, it applies to the `H1` tag, changing its font to Verdana.

A look at how the style itself is constructed.

The first part of the style is called the selector. The selector specifies where the style should be applied. In this case, the selector is `H1`, indicating that this style should be applied to the text in all `H1` tags in this document.

The curly braces ("`{`"and"`}`") enclose the body of the style. Within the body of the style are lines with properties and values. The word on the left side of the colon is called a property, and the right side is the value assigned to the property. In this example, the font-family property is given the value, Verdana, which effectively tells the browser to use the Verdana font for `H1` elements in this document.

You can specify more than one property in a single style, and they needn't be in any particular order. If you need to specify more than one property in a style, you must end each one with a semicolon (`;`) character. For example,

```
H1 {
   font-family: Verdana;
   font-size: 24px;
   }
```

Working with Ducks in a Row Rubber Stamps

Because the style of art throughout the catalog is consistent, any of the designs may be used together side by side, or superimposed, making the possibilities for personal expression boundless.

You will find designs in our catalog which cover a vast array of categories, from floral images to humor, holiday stamps, border designs and decorative imagery, for all around use. You, as the stamping artist will be the one to create original art works from these designs, and nothing pleases us more than to see the beautiful and original ways in which our designs are being used.

Throughout the catalog you will find some helpful hints on some of the uses and techniques to enjoy your stamps, but we're sure that you as the stamping artist can teach us a thing or two! One thing for certain, the possibilities are endless!

css3.html: **Both font-family and font-size properties.**

You can also specify more than one style in a single style sheet. This style sheet has styles for both H1 and P elements:

```
H1 {
   font-family: Verdana;
   font-size: 24px;
   }

P {
   font-family: Georgia;
   font-size: 18px;
   }
```

Now that you know the basic format for adding a style sheet to a document, instead of showing you the whole STYLE section for each change we make, the rest of our examples will just concentrate on the individual style that we're working on.

Working with Ducks in a Row Rubber Stamps

Because the style of art throughout the catalog is consistent, any of the designs may be used together side by side, or superimposed, making the possibilities for personal expression boundless.

You will find designs in our catalog which cover a vast array of categories, from floral images to humor, holiday stamps, border designs and decorative imagery, for all around use. You, as the stamping artist will be the one to create original art works from these designs, and nothing pleasures us more than to see the beautiful and original ways in which our designs are being used.

Throughout the catalog you will find some helpful hints on some of the uses and techniques to enjoy your stamps, but we're sure that you as the stamping artist can teach us a thing or two! One thing for certain, the possibilities are endless!

css4.html: **Styles for both** H1 **and** P **in the same style sheet.**

Type and Measurements

Before we discuss CSS measurement units for text, it's important to understand the terminology used in measuring type.

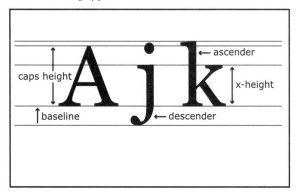

Back in the days when "setting type" meant a physical activity handled by skilled professionals with leaded type and wooden typecases, the body size of a type referred to the actual size of the metal block on which the letter was formed. This is a size somewhat larger than any of the measurable dimensions of the printed letters, though not by any specific ratio. There is no analogous measurement in electronic type, so when we refer to a "twelve-point" typeface, a certain amount of ambiguity cannot be resolved.

Unit Measurements

With that in mind, let's look at some measuring units. The table that follows lists the English name, the CSS name, and a short description for each measurement unit.

English	CSS	Description
Pixel	px	A pixel is the distance from one dot to the next on a computer screen (pixel literally means picture element).
Point	pt	A point is 1/72 inch. How many pixels that is depends on the resolution of your screen, but it is one pixel on 72 dpi systems.
Pica	pc	12 points.
Em	em	The "body size" of the font. That is, if the font size is 12 points, one em is 12 points.
En	en	1/2 em.
x-height	ex	The height of a lower-case "x".
Inch	in	The length of the thumb of King Henry VIII.
Centimeter	cm	1/100 meter.
Millimeter	mm	1/1,000 meter

Let's look at an example. If you wanted to display the word Quack in 3 inch type, you could use this:

```
<HTML>
<HEAD>
<STYLE TYPE="text/css">
P {
   font-size: 3in;
   font-family: Garamond;
   font-style: italic;
   }
</STYLE>
</HEAD>
<BODY BGCOLOR=WHITE>
<P ALIGN=CENTER> Quack
</BODY>
</HTML>
```

quack.html: **Quack in 3-inch letters.**

Because most web-based graphics are a fixed number of pixels wide and a fixed number of pixels high, we recommend that you use pixel measurements most of the time. That way, you can always be sure that your page will look more-or-less uniform relative to the size of the graphics on the page.

As we go through the chapter, you will see more uses for these measurements.

Text-related Properties

CSS defines a number of different properties for working with text. You have already seen the font-family property that we used in our last example. This property lets you specify a particular font family, either by name (like Verdana) or by generic type (like sans-serif).

```
Property: font-family
Values:
        Name of the font family, like Verdana or Georgia
        or one of the following generic names:
                serif
                sans-serif
                cursive
                fantasy
                monospace
```

You can also give a list of values (separated by commas) for font-family. For example,

```
H1 {
    font-family: Verdana, Helvetica,
sans-serif
    }
```

In that case, the system would try to use Verdana, or if that's not available, Helvetica; otherwise, it will use whatever sans-serif font is available.

Another useful text-related property is line-height. This property affects the space between lines, also called leading, after the strips of lead used to provide the spaces between lines of metal type.

```
Property: line-height
Values:
        number
        default
Sets the amount of space between lines of text
```

The line-height is measured from the baseline of one line to the baseline of the next. The special value default will set the line-height to the default of the browser, which is probably about the same as 1.2em.

```
P {
    font-family: Georgia;
    font-size: 12px;
    line-height: 1.5em;
    }
```

This will set the line-height to 1.5em. Remember: 1em is the same as the font-size, so 1.5em is one-and-a-half times the body size of the type.

Working with Ducks in a Row Rubber Stamps

Because the style of art throughout the catalog is consistent, any of the designs may be used together side by side, or superimposed, making the possibilities for personal expression boundless.

You will find designs in our catalog which cover a vast array of categories, from floral images to humor, holiday stamps, border designs and decorative imagery, for all around use. You, as the stamping artist will be the one to create original art works from these designs, and nothing pleasures us more than to see the beautiful and original ways in which our designs are being used.

Throughout the catalog you will find some helpful hints on some of the uses and techniques to enjoy your stamps, but we're sure that you as the stamping artist can teach us a thing or two! One thing for certain, the possibilities are endless!

css5.html: **A line-height of 1.5em.**

Selectors

So far, we've been using the selector to specify what tag the style will apply to, but the selector can do more than that! You can also use the selector to apply to only some instances of a particular tag.

For example, what if you wanted every paragraph except the first to have an indent on the first line.

```
P {
   font-family: Georgia;
   font-size: 12px;
   line-height: 1.5em;
   text-indent: 1.5em;
   }
```

The text-indent property indents just the first line of a paragraph. Our P style now has a 1.5em indent for the first paragraph. Now we add another style with a class selector like this:

```
.first {
   text-indent: 0;
   }
```

A class selector always starts with a dot (.). Now you can use the CLASS attribute in your HTML to apply that style in addition to the existing style on the paragraph tag:

```
<P CLASS="first">
Because the style of art throughout the
catalog is consistent, any of the designs
may be used together side by side, or
superimposed, making the possibilities
for personal expression boundless.
```

The result is like this:

Working with Ducks in a Row Rubber Stamps

Because the style of art throughout the catalog is consistent, any of the designs may be used together side by side, or superimposed, making the possibilities for personal expression boundless.

You will find designs in our catalog which cover a vast array of categories, from floral images to humor, holiday stamps, border designs and decorative imagery, for all around use. You, as the stamping artist will be the one to create original art works from these designs, and nothing pleasures us more than to see the beautiful and original ways in which our designs are being used.

Throughout the catalog you will find some helpful hints on some of the uses and techniques to enjoy your stamps, but we're sure that you as the stamping artist can teach us a thing or two! One thing for certain, the possibilities are endless!

css6.html: **Look Ma! No single-pixel GIFs!**

The potential of this for simplifying web sites and reducing bandwidth is truly exciting! It used to be that you needed to trick HTML into indenting your paragraphs and adding space between the lines by using single-pixel transparent GIFs. Now you can do it with style sheets!

The SPAN Tag

Sometimes you will want to apply a style to some text that doesn't otherwise fit into standard HTML categories, like STRONG or EM. You may even want several different types of emphasis within one paragraph. The new SPAN tag applies formatting that you define to small parts of text, without affecting the way the text is rendered in browsers that don't understand style sheets.

Using the SPAN tag with class selectors, you can create effects that are much more complex than using straight HTML. Suppose you want to be able to highlight certain types of references using a combination of a different font, bold weight, and a different color. Without style sheets, you may decide that it's just too much trouble to put this in each instance:

```
<FONT FACE="Footlight MT Light" SIZE="+1"
    COLOR="#6699CC"><STRONG>
  text
</STRONG></FONT>
```

With a style sheet, you can specify all that stuff just once:

```
.high {
  font-family: Footlight MT Light;
  font-size: large;
  color: #6699CC;
  font-weight: bold;
  }
```

And then, each time you want to use this formatting, you just use the SPAN tag. The SPAN tag doesn't do anything at all by itself. It's only purpose is to apply a style to a span of text. Here's an example:

```
<P CLASS="first">
Because the style of art throughout
the catalog is consistent, any of the
designs may be used together side by
side, or superimposed, making the
possibilities for <SPAN CLASS="high">
personal expression</SPAN> boundless.

<P>
You will find designs in our catalog
which cover a vast array of categories,
from floral images to humor, holiday
<SPAN CLASS="high">stamp</SPAN>s,
border designs and decorative imagery,
for all around use. You, as the
<SPAN CLASS="high">stamp</SPAN>ing
artist will be the one to create
<SPAN CLASS="high">original art</SPAN>
works from these designs, and nothing
pleasures us more than to see the beauti-
ful and original ways in which our
designs are being used.
```

```
<P>
Throughout the catalog you will find some
helpful hints on some of the uses and
techniques to enjoy your
<SPAN CLASS="high">stamp</SPAN>s,
but we're sure that you as the
<SPAN CLASS="high">stamp</SPAN>ing
<SPAN CLASS="high">artist</SPAN>
can teach us a thing or two! One thing for
certain, the possibilities are endless!
```

Working with Ducks in a Row Rubber Stamps

Because the style of art throughout the catalog is consistent, any of the designs may be used together side by side, or superimposed, making the possibilities for **personal expression** boundless.

You will find designs in our catalog which cover a vast array of categories, from floral images to humor, holiday **stamp**s, border designs and decorative imagery, for all around use. You, as the **stamp**ing artist will be the one to create **original art** works from these designs, and nothing pleasures us more than to see the beautiful and original ways in which our designs are being used.

Throughout the catalog you will find some helpful hints on some of the uses and techniques to enjoy your **stamp**s, but we're sure that you as the **stamp**ing **artist** can teach us a thing or two! One thing for certain, the possibilities are endless!

css7.html: **Simple highlighting with** SPAN **and** CLASS.

Absolute Positioning

Graphic designers have long complained that it's not possible to absolutely position a graphic on a page using HTML. CSS has a solution to that problem, too.

First, let's look at one more type of selector—the ID selector—and a few new properties:

```
1.    #smduck1 {
2.        position: absolute;
3.        top: 0px;
4.        left: 0px;
5.        z-index: 1;
          }
```

1. `#smduck1 {`

The ID selector always begins with a hash mark (#) and must be unique within the document. That means that you can only define it once, and can only use it once (see the sidebar, "ID vs. CLASS"). It works almost exactly like the class selector (.), but is usually used for absolute positioning of objects on a page, where only one object will have any single position.

2. `position: absolute;`

The position property can be either absolute or relative. Use absolute for objects that you want to have at a specific position on the page and relative for objects that you want to position relative to wherever they would have otherwise fallen. We used absolute positioning in this example to position the graphic at a specific point on the page. We'll see an example of relative a little later.

3. `top: 0px;`
4. `left: 0px;`

The top and left properties are used to position the object. These measurements are absolute measurements—from the top-left corner of the screen—with no padding. This style will place the graphic in the absolute upper left-hand corner of the screen.

5. `z-index: 1;`

Objects that are put on the screen with absolute positioning can be laid on top of each other. The z-index property tells the browser which objects should be on top of (or under) other objects. Higher-numbered objects will overlay lower-numbered objects.

Here's a page that uses the style we just defined:

```
<HTML>
<HEAD>
<TITLE>Absolute Positioning:
Simple</TITLE>
<STYLE>

#smduck1 { position: absolute; }
top: 0px; left: 0px; }
</STYLE>
<BODY>
```

1.
```
    <DIV ID="smduck1">
<IMG SRC=revgreentile.gif
   WIDTH=50 HEIGHT=50></DIV>

</BODY>
</HTML>
```

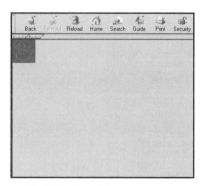

css-abs1.html: **That GIF is right up against the corner!**

1.
```
    <DIV ID="smduck1">
<IMG SRC=revgreentile.gif
   WIDTH=50 HEIGHT=50></DIV>
```

Notice the use of the DIV element that encloses the IMG. The DIV tag has a new attribute called ID, which is used to specify the selector in the style. The DIV element is necessary to make the absolute positioning work.

The little image in this example is 50×50 pixels in size, so we should be able to lay another one right on its lower right-hand corner by positioning it 50 pixels in and down:

```
<HEAD>
<TITLE>Absolute Positioning:
Simple</TITLE>
<STYLE>

#smduck1 { position: absolute; top: 0px;
left: 0px; z-index: 0; }
#smduck2 { position: absolute; top: 50px;
left: 50px; z-index: 0; }

</STYLE>

<BODY BGCOLOR="#999966"
BACKGROUND="greentile.gif">

<DIV ID="smduck1">
<IMG SRC=revgreentile.gif
  WIDTH=50 HEIGHT=50></DIV>
<DIV ID="smduck2">
<IMG SRC=revgreentile.gif
  WIDTH=50 HEIGHT=50></DIV>

</BODY>
```

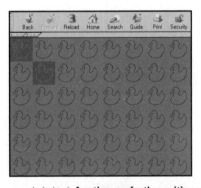

css-abs1a.html: **Another perfectly positioned image.**

In this example, we also added a 50×50 tiled background so that you can better see the perfect alignment of the images against a repeating background.

> ▶ **note**
>
> ### ID vs. CLASS
>
> On the surface, the ID and CLASS selectors seem so similar that it makes us wonder why there are two different methods for the same thing!
>
> As best we can determine, the only difference is that it is considered an error to use the same ID selector more than once. Validation engines—and some future browsers—may flag errors on duplicate ID selectors.

> ▶ **note**
>
> ### DIV and Absolute Positioning
>
> According to the specification, you should be able to forgo the DIV tag and use the ID attribute directly in the IMG tag, but the current crop of browsers will not perform absolute positioning without the DIV tag. This is one of those areas that will likely change in the next generation of browsers.

Layering Text and Images

By extending these same techniques to a mixture of text and graphics, we are able to create a nice effect that requires very little bandwidth. This example is a little complex, but keep in mind that we've already seen all the techniques involved.

Let's first take a look at the result, and then see what it takes to do this.

css-abs2.html: **Overlapping text and a simple graphic make a nice splash page.**

This example is basically just 20 copies of the text "ducks in a row" using the Verdana font and a number of different overlapping browser-safe colors, covered with a black oval cutout duck and one more "ducks in a row" in black.

```
<HTML>
<HEAD>
<TITLE>Absolute Positioning:
Complex</TITLE>

<STYLE TYPE="text/css">
```

```
1.   H1 {
       font-family: verdana;
       font-weight: bold;
       font-size: 52px;
       color: black;
       }
```

```
2.   H2 {
       font-family: verdana;
       font-weight: bold;
       font-size: 32px;
       }
```

```
3.   #words1 {
       position: absolute;
       top: 50px;
       left: 50px;
       z-index: 1;
       }
```

```
4.   #words2 {
       position: absolute;
       top: 60px;
       left: 90px;
       z-index: 2;
       }
```

```
5.   .ovalduck {
       position: absolute;
       top: 35px;
       left: 30px;
       z-index: 3;
       }
```

```
6.   .ducktitle {
       position: absolute;
       top: 130px;
       left: 0px;
       }
```

```
7.   .duck1 { color: #999900; }
     .duck2 { color: #FFCC00; }
     .duck3 { color: #FF9933; }
     .duck4 { color: #FF6633; }
     .duck5 { color: #FF9933; }
```

8.
```
#w00 { position: absolute; top: 112px; left: 52px; }
#w01 { position: absolute; top: 24px; left: 45px; }
#w02 { position: absolute; top: 95px; left: 62px; }
#w03 { position: absolute; top: 142px; left: 138px; }
#w04 { position: absolute; top: 128px; left: 74px; }
#w05 { position: absolute; top: 63px; left: 122px; }
#w06 { position: absolute; top: 79px; left: 36px; }
#w07 { position: absolute; top: 158px; left: 29px; }
#w08 { position: absolute; top: 83px; left: 146px; }
#w09 { position: absolute; top: 42px; left: 12px; }
#w10 { position: absolute; top: 112px; left: 52px; }
#w11 { position: absolute; top: 24px; left: 45px; }
#w12 { position: absolute; top: 95px; left: 62px; }
#w13 { position: absolute; top: 142px; left: 138px; }
#w14 { position: absolute; top: 128px; left: 74px; }
#w15 { position: absolute; top: 63px; left: 122px; }
#w16 { position: absolute; top: 79px; left: 36px; }
#w17 { position: absolute; top: 158px; left: 29px; }
#w18 { position: absolute; top: 83px; left: 146px; }
#w19 { position: absolute; top: 42px; left: 12px; }

</STYLE>

</HEAD>
<BODY BGCOLOR="#FFFFCC" TEXT="#663333" LINK="#006699" VLINK="#006699">
```

9.
```
<DIV ID="words1">
 <H2 CLASS="duck1"><SPAN ID="w00">ducks in a row</SPAN></H2>
 <H2 CLASS="duck2"><SPAN ID="w01">ducks in a row</SPAN></H2>
 <H2 CLASS="duck3"><SPAN ID="w02">ducks in a row</SPAN></H2>
 <H2 CLASS="duck4"><SPAN ID="w03">ducks in a row</SPAN></H2>
 <H2 CLASS="duck5"><SPAN ID="w04">ducks in a row</SPAN></H2>
 <H2 CLASS="duck1"><SPAN ID="w05">ducks in a row</SPAN></H2>
 <H2 CLASS="duck2"><SPAN ID="w06">ducks in a row</SPAN></H2>
 <H2 CLASS="duck3"><SPAN ID="w07">ducks in a row</SPAN></H2>
 <H2 CLASS="duck4"><SPAN ID="w08">ducks in a row</SPAN></H2>
 <H2 CLASS="duck5"><SPAN ID="w09">ducks in a row</SPAN></H2>
</DIV>
```

10.
```
<DIV ID="words2">
 <H2 CLASS="duck5"><SPAN ID="w10">ducks in a row</SPAN></H2>
 <H2 CLASS="duck1"><SPAN ID="w11">ducks in a row</SPAN></H2>
 <H2 CLASS="duck4"><SPAN ID="w12">ducks in a row</SPAN></H2>
 <H2 CLASS="duck2"><SPAN ID="w13">ducks in a row</SPAN></H2>
 <H2 CLASS="duck3"><SPAN ID="w14">ducks in a row</SPAN></H2>
 <H2 CLASS="duck5"><SPAN ID="w15">ducks in a row</SPAN></H2>
 <H2 CLASS="duck1"><SPAN ID="w16">ducks in a row</SPAN></H2>
 <H2 CLASS="duck4"><SPAN ID="w17">ducks in a row</SPAN></H2>
 <H2 CLASS="duck2"><SPAN ID="w18">ducks in a row</SPAN></H2>
 <H2 CLASS="duck3"><SPAN ID="w19">ducks in a row</SPAN></H2>
</DIV>
```

11.
```
<DIV CLASS="ovalduck">
 <IMG SRC="blackoval.gif" width=269 height=136>
 <H1><SPAN CLASS="ducktitle">ducks in a row</SPAN></H1>
</DIV>

</BODY>
</HTML>
```

The HTML file is only 3k and the GIF is only 900 bytes! There are no techniques used here that you haven't already seen in this chapter:

1.
```
H1 {
    font-family: verdana;
    font-weight: bold;
    font-size: 52px;
    color: black;
    }
```

This defines the style for the H1 element, used for the black "ducks in a row" on the top.

2.
```
H2 {
    font-family: verdana;
    font-weight: bold;
    font-size: 32px;
    }
```

This defines the base style that is used for all the overlapping "ducks in a row" strings.

3.
```
#words1 {
    position: absolute;
    top: 50px;
    left: 50px;
    z-index: 1;
    }
```

This defines the ID used for the first layer of words in [9].

4.
```
#words2 {
    position: absolute;
    top: 60px;
    left: 90px;
    z-index: 2;
    }
```

This defines the ID used for the second layer of words in [10].

5.
```
.ovalduck {
    position: absolute;
    top: 35px;
    left: 30px;
    z-index: 3;
    }
```

This defines the position used for the black oval duck image and black type in [11].

6.
```
.ducktitle {
    position: absolute;
    top: 130px;
    left: 0px;
    }
```

This positions the title relative to the image in [11].

7.
```
.duck1 { color: #999900; }
.duck2 { color: #FFCC00; }
.duck3 { color: #FF9933; }
.duck4 { color: #FF6633; }
.duck5 { color: #FF9933; }
```

These classes define colors for the overlapping "ducks in a row" strings.

8.
```
#w00 { position: absolute; top: 112px; left: 52px; }
#w01 { position: absolute; top: 24px; left: 45px; }
#w02 { position: absolute; top: 95px; left: 62px; }
#w03 { position: absolute; top: 142px; left: 138px; }
#w04 { position: absolute; top: 128px; left: 74px; }
#w05 { position: absolute; top: 63px; left: 122px; }
#w06 { position: absolute; top: 79px; left: 36px; }
#w07 { position: absolute; top: 158px; left: 29px; }
#w08 { position: absolute; top: 83px; left: 146px; }
#w09 { position: absolute; top: 42px; left: 12px; }
#w10 { position: absolute; top: 112px; left: 52px; }
#w11 { position: absolute; top: 24px; left: 45px; }
#w12 { position: absolute; top: 95px; left: 62px; }
#w13 { position: absolute; top: 142px; left: 138px; }
#w14 { position: absolute; top: 128px; left: 74px; }
#w15 { position: absolute; top: 63px; left: 122px; }
#w16 { position: absolute; top: 79px; left: 36px; }
#w17 { position: absolute; top: 158px; left: 29px; }
#w18 { position: absolute; top: 83px; left: 146px; }
#w19 { position: absolute; top: 42px; left: 12px; }
```

These are all the positions for the "ducks in a row" strings.

9.
```
<DIV ID="words1">
   <H2 CLASS="duck1"><SPAN ID="w00">ducks in a row</SPAN></H2>
   <H2 CLASS="duck2"><SPAN ID="w01">ducks in a row</SPAN></H2>
   <H2 CLASS="duck3"><SPAN ID="w02">ducks in a row</SPAN></H2>
   <H2 CLASS="duck4"><SPAN ID="w03">ducks in a row</SPAN></H2>
   <H2 CLASS="duck5"><SPAN ID="w04">ducks in a row</SPAN></H2>
   <H2 CLASS="duck1"><SPAN ID="w05">ducks in a row</SPAN></H2>
   <H2 CLASS="duck2"><SPAN ID="w06">ducks in a row</SPAN></H2>
   <H2 CLASS="duck3"><SPAN ID="w07">ducks in a row</SPAN></H2>
   <H2 CLASS="duck4"><SPAN ID="w08">ducks in a row</SPAN></H2>
   <H2 CLASS="duck5"><SPAN ID="w09">ducks in a row</SPAN></H2>
</DIV>
```

There are two layers of overlapping strings, and this is the first one. The DIV element is used to position the block absolutely on the page. Each of the SPAN elements position an individual string within the block. The H2 elements have the font and size for the strings, and the duck1-5 classes have the varying colors.

Since we didn't use the z-index property, the layering occurs in the same order that the text appears in the HTML file. You only need to use z-index when you want to specify a particular order. In this example, we don't really care about the order of the layers, as long as they're layered.

10.
```
<DIV ID="words2">
    <H2 CLASS="duck5"><SPAN ID="w10">ducks in a row</SPAN></H2>
    <H2 CLASS="duck1"><SPAN ID="w11">ducks in a row</SPAN></H2>
    <H2 CLASS="duck4"><SPAN ID="w12">ducks in a row</SPAN></H2>
    <H2 CLASS="duck2"><SPAN ID="w13">ducks in a row</SPAN></H2>
    <H2 CLASS="duck3"><SPAN ID="w14">ducks in a row</SPAN></H2>
    <H2 CLASS="duck5"><SPAN ID="w15">ducks in a row</SPAN></H2>
    <H2 CLASS="duck1"><SPAN ID="w16">ducks in a row</SPAN></H2>
    <H2 CLASS="duck4"><SPAN ID="w17">ducks in a row</SPAN></H2>
    <H2 CLASS="duck2"><SPAN ID="w18">ducks in a row</SPAN></H2>
    <H2 CLASS="duck3"><SPAN ID="w19">ducks in a row</SPAN></H2>
</DIV>
```

This works exactly like [9] and gets overlapped on top of it to provide a more random appearance than just one layer of 10 strings.

11.
```
<DIV CLASS="ovalduck">
    <IMG SRC="blackoval.gif" width=269 height=136>
    <H1><SPAN CLASS="ducktitle">ducks in a row</SPAN></H1>
</DIV>
```

Finally, the oval duck and the black letters are layered on top of the rest, using the classes from [5] and [6] a couple pages back.

As we said, this is a complex example that applies all the elements we have learned in this chapter so far. It's intended to demonstrate the power of style sheets, but it is not really intended for a production web site. There are still too few browsers that understand CSS, and we believe that the specification will change significantly before it is really ready for widespread use.

> ▶ **note**
>
> ## Resources
>
> **typoGRAPHIC**
> http://www.subnetwork.com/typo/
> (A fine glossary of typographic terms)
> http://www.subnetwork.com/typo/glossary/
>
> **Netscape's Dynamic HTML Site**
> http://developer.netscape.com/library/
> documentation/communicator/dynhtml/
> contents.htm
>
> **W3C's CSS Positioning Specification**
> http://www.w3.org/TR/WD-positioning
>
> **Macromedia's Dynamic HTML Zone**
> http://www.dhtmlzone.com/

▶ chapter thirteen summary

CSS style sheets are going to be a very powerful mechanism for enhancing the presentation quality of text on the web. Though not ready for prime time yet, there is good reason to believe that CSS will become a useable feature of mainstream browsers in the not-so-distant future.

Using CSS, you will be able to format your text in manners much closer to that of the printed page, and expect your layouts to work consistently—within certain limits—across platforms, browsers, and differing sizes and resolutions of displays. This has been a major limitation for designers of web sites until now, but the fairy godmother of web standards is finally letting us see the light at the end of the mixed metaphor.

14

Wherever you go,
there you are.
—Buckaroo Banzai

Navigation
take me to your leader

Creating navigation for a web site is one of the most complex undertakings of web publishing. As much as image and HTML editor manufacturers like to tout "easy-to-author-web-pages/ graphics" products, there is no easy way to design or execute navigation. This is one of the uncharted frontiers of web publishing, and you will likely find it the most challenging aspect of creating any new site.

Many decisions face you when creating navigation. For example: Will your audience have current web browsers or do you need to ensure that visitors with older browsers can easily maneuver your site? Do you want to do two versions of your site, such as frames and no-frames? Do you want to rely on graphical icons or text to describe categories? Have you included measures to access the rest of your site from all areas of your site? Do you have "back" buttons on all your pages? Have you given thought to integrating the style of your site with navigational buttons and graphics?

This chapter gives us the opportunity to share the graphics and programming techniques we used for designing the navigation for our Ducks In A Row example .

Navigation

Frames

Netscape introduced the concept of frames with version 2 of the Navigator browser to satisfy designers' needs for more sophisticated navigation. The initial implementation left much to be desired—and in some ways even made navigation harder—but by the time version 3 came along, most of the deficiencies had been addressed, and frames were here to stay. Now frames are part of the HTML 4.0 specification. The basic frames specification works with Netscape Navigator versions 2+ and Microsoft Internet Explorer versions 3+ and is being incorporated into the latest WYSIWYG editors and site-management systems.

Frames are considered by many to be a navigational godsend, and by others, a navigational nightmare. The principle behind frames is that they offer the ability to have regions of a web page change while other regions remain stationary. Before frames, every page of HTML had to be separate. If you had a navigation bar at the bottom of each page on your site, clicking it would cause the entire screen to redraw, loading a completely new page. Frames offer the ability, for example, to have a fixed navigation bar that never refreshes. Clicking a frames-based navigation bar can launch other documents on your screen while the navigation bar itself remains unchanged.

Many people hate frames, with good reason. It's hard to bookmark a page within a framed site because the location that the browser bookmarks is that of the framed site, not of the individual pages. Also, it's confusing to print a page that's nested inside frames. There are workarounds for all these problems, but they require extra effort from your end viewer.

On the other hand, there are times when you have a lot of information to display or simply a lot of different pages on a similar topic in your site, and you want your main navigational elements to remain available to your users. Being able to keep one or more parts of the screen still while the user scrolls through other parts is a technique long available to designers of multimedia but only recently available on the web.

How Frames Work

The basic model of HTML frames revolves around the concept of framesets. A frameset is a container for frames, which are really just windows into other HTML documents. You can think of each frame as almost a separate browser, which shares common buttons and controls with the main window. Let's take a look at a simple example, then we'll get into all the bells and whistles a little later. This document is in the chap14 folder of the <chd> CD-ROM as frames1.html.

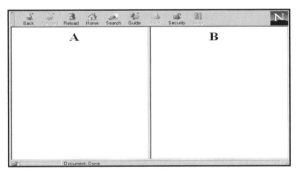

frames1.html: **A simple document with frames.** a.html **is in the left frame, and** b.html **is in the right frame.**

1.
```
<HTML>
<HEAD>
<TITLE> Frames Example </TITLE>
</HEAD>
```
2.
3.
```
<FRAMESET COLS="*,*">
  <FRAME SRC="a.html">
  <FRAME SRC="b.html">
```
4.
```
</FRAMESET>

</HTML>
```

1. The outside container of the document is still the HTML element, just like in any other HTML.

2. The FRAMESET container is an element that goes after the HEAD element and is still inside of the HTML container. The COLS attribute specifies the number of columns (vertical divisions) and the widths of those columns (more about this later). The asterisks (*) mean to evenly divide the space. This value ("*,*") means to use two equally spaced columns. Use ROWS instead of columns to get horizontally divided frames.

3. The actual FRAME tags go within the FRAMESET container. These define the frames themselves. The SRC attribute specifies the HTML document to display inside the frame. In our example, a.html and b.html are the two HTML documents that appear within each frame.

4. The FRAMESET element must be terminated with the z/FRAMESET> tag, or your page won't load.

The file a.html (in the chap14 folder of the <chd> CD-ROM) looks like this:

```
<BODY BGCOLOR=White>
<H1 ALIGN=CENTER> A </H1>
</BODY>
```

And b.html (surprise!) looks like this:

```
<BODY BGCOLOR=White>
<H1 ALIGN=CENTER> B </H1>
</BODY>
```

We will use several files like this as we explain the capabilities of frames in this chapter.

♦ note

Support for Older Browsers

Because there is no BODY in a frames document, and in fact, there is no content at all
outside of the FRAMESET and FRAME tags, a
browser that doesn't understand frames will
see nothing but a blank screen!

The solution to this is to use the special
NOFRAMES element. Any content within
NOFRAMES will not be displayed on frames-
supporting browsers, but will be displayed
on older browsers.

```
<HTML>

<HEAD>
<TITLE> Frames Example </TITLE>
</HEAD>

<FRAMESET COLS="*,*">
   <FRAME SRC="a.html">
   <FRAME SRC="b.html">
</FRAMESET>

<NOFRAMES>
  <P>
  This site uses frames. If you are
  seeing this message, your web
  browser does not support frames.
  You can still see what we have
  to offer, although without the
  navigation advantages of frames,
  by using these links:

  <UL>
    <LI> <A HREF="a.html">Document
A</A>
    <LI> <A HREF="b.html">Document
B</A>
  </UL>

</NOFRAMES>
</HTML>
```

The content within the NOFRAMES element
will be displayed by browsers that don't understand frames, so they will know what to do.
The file to the left is available in the chap14
folder of the <chd> CD-ROM as frames1a.html.

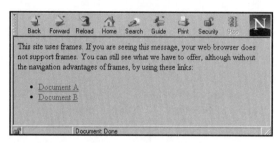

What browsers without frames capability will see.

Of course, you could instead display an entire
web page with alternate content for frames-
challenged browsers.

(…Within Frames (…Within Frames))

"Well now," you may ask, "if a frame is just a window with another HTML document in it, what prevents me from (place wild idea here)?" And we answer, "Absolutely anything you can do with a normal HTML document can be done in a frame." In fact, a frame can even have more frames in it! If we take the previous example and use a frames document in place of b.html, we get more frames in our "B" frame:

frames2.html:

```
<HTML>
<HEAD>
<TITLE> Frames Example </TITLE>
</HEAD>

<FRAMESET COLS="*,*" >
  <FRAME SRC="a.html">
  <FRAME SRC="b2.html">
</FRAMESET>

</HTML>
```

b2.html:

```
<FRAMESET ROWS="*,*">
    <FRAME SRC="c.html">
    <FRAME SRC="d.html">
</FRAMESET>
```

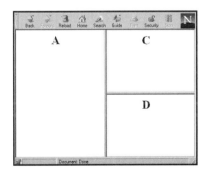

frames2.html: **The right-side document is another frameset.**

There is, however, an easier way to accomplish this same task. You can nest another FRAMESET within your existing FRAMESET. When you nest

frames like this, it's a good idea to put comments in the code so that you can keep track of which frame is which:

frames3.html:

```
<HTML>
<HEAD>
<TITLE> Frames Example </TITLE>
</HEAD>

<!-- cols for vertical divisions -->
<FRAMESET COLS="*,*" >

  <!-- left frame -->
  <FRAME SRC="a.html">

  <!-- right frame is another frameset -->
  <!-- rows for horizontal divisions -->
  <FRAMESET ROWS="*,*">
    <!-- top frame -->
    <FRAME SRC="c.html">
    <!-- bottom frame -->
    <FRAME SRC="d.html">
  </FRAMESET>

</FRAMESET>

</HTML>
```

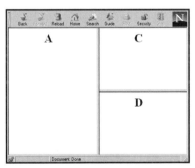

frames3.html: **Looks just like the last one!**

This example accomplishes exactly the same thing as frames2.html, but it does so with one less file. This is the preferred way to nest frames. This version also uses comments to explain what each FRAME and FRAMESET is for. Using comments makes it easier to figure out what you did when you come back and look at your code sometime later.

Adjusting the Size of Frames

As you learned earlier, the ROWS and COLS attributes to the FRAMESET tag take values that define
the size of the frame. So far, we have been using
the default sizes, "*,*".

You can adjust the sizes of the frames by using
values instead of the asterisks, and the values can
be either numbers (for the number of pixels) or
percentages (for a percentage of the remaining
space). In this example, the leftmost frame is 90
pixels wide, and the top right frame is 33% of the
height of the screen. The bottom right frame fills
out the remaining space.

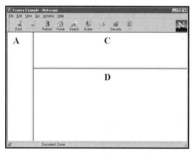

frames4.html: **These frames are specific sizes.**

frames4.html:

```
<HTML>
<HEAD>
<TITLE> Frames Example </TITLE>
</HEAD>

<!-- cols for vertical divisions -->
<FRAMESET COLS="90,*" >

   <!-- left frame -->
   <FRAME SRC="a.html">

   <!-- right frame is another frameset -->
   <!-- rows for horizontal divisions -->
   <FRAMESET ROWS="33%,*">
      <!-- top frame -->
      <FRAME SRC="c.html">
      <!-- bottom frame -->
      <FRAME SRC="d.html">
   </FRAMESET>

</FRAMESET>

</HTML>
```

1. In this first frameset, the COLS attribute specifies
    a number, instead of the default asterisk, for the
    first column. When you use a plain number, this
    indicates pixels. The asterisk for the second col-
    umn means "use the rest of the available space."

2. The inner frameset specifies ROWS, and the first
    number is expressed as a percentage. This means
    "use 33% of the available space."

As you design your site, keep in mind that percentage
values will change as the browser is resized, and pixel
values will not. If you have a frame that holds a single
graphic (like a title bar or an imagemap), you will
probably want to use a specific pixel size for that
frame so that it doesn't change size when the user
changes the size of their browser. If a frame is going to
hold text or other variable-size information, you may
prefer to use a percentage, or even the asterisk. We'll
show examples from DIAR later in this chapter.

Borderless Frames

You can remove the borders from your frames by simply adding the attribute BORDER=0 to your outermost FRAMESET tag.

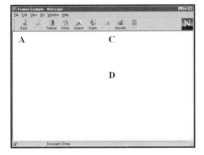

frames5.html: **Borders: Be gone!**

```
   <!-- cols for vertical divisions -->
1. <FRAMESET COLS="90,*" BORDER=0>

   <!-- left frame -->
   <FRAME SRC="a.html">

   <!-- right frame is another frameset
   -->
   <!-- rows for horizontal divisions
   -->
   <FRAMESET ROWS="33%,*">
      <!-- top frame -->
      <FRAME SRC="c.html">
      <!-- bottom frame -->
      <FRAME SRC="b.html">
   </FRAMESET>

</FRAMESET>
```

1. The BORDER=0 attribute is used with the outermost FRAMESET tag to turn off the borders for all the frames on the page. With the borders off and the BGCOLOR of all the frames the same, it becomes impossible to tell where one frame starts and the next frame ends. That can be a nice effect for some purposes, but you may want to have a distinction without the borders.

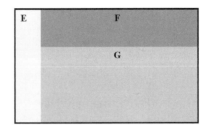

frames6.html: **Different colors for each frame.**

One effective way to distinguish between frames is by having a different BGCOLOR for adjacent frames.

In this example, we have used three different HTML files (*The Cat in the Hat* has nothing on us!). These files have different BGCOLOR values so that we can see the divisions between the frames. This technique often creates a nicer aesthetic than the borders, and it gives you more flexible use of your space.

You can also use a background tile in any of your frames by using the BACKGROUND attribute in the BODY tag of the frame's HTML document. In the next example, we used a background tile for the lower-right frame.

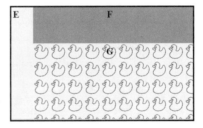

frames7.html: **A tiled background in** g.html **is displayed in the lower-right frame.**

Creative use of this technique could yield many interesting effects. In this case, the color of the left frame and the background color of the tile used in the lower-right frame blend such that the tile appears to run out of ducks on the left!

Navigating Frames

Frames can be a wonderful tool for helping your visitors navigate your site. Using frames, you can put your menus and imagemaps in fixed areas of the screen, keeping them from moving and scrolling as the content of the other frames change.

When using frames for navigation, you need to create links in one frame that cause documents to load in another frame. These are called targeted links.

To create a targeted link, you must first make up a name for your frame and assign that name to the frame, using the NAME attribute in the FRAME tag. This is the name that you will use later to identify the frame in the TARGET attribute of an anchor tag.

frames8.html:

```
<HTML>
<HEAD>
<TITLE> Frames Example </TITLE>
</HEAD>

<!-- cols for vertical divisions -->
<FRAMESET COLS="90,*" BORDER=0>

   <!-- left frame -->
   <FRAME SRC="menu.html" NAME=left>

   <!-- right frame is another frameset -->
   <!-- rows for horizontal divisions -->
   <FRAMESET ROWS="33%,*">
      <!-- top frame -->
   <FRAME SRC="f.html" NAME=upper>
         <!-- bottom frame -->
   <FRAME SRC="g.html" NAME=lower>
   </FRAMESET>

</FRAMESET>

</HTML>
```

1. `<FRAME SRC="menu.html" NAME=left>`

2. `<FRAME SRC="f.html" NAME=upper>`

3. `<FRAME SRC="g.html" NAME=lower>`

1/2/3 Notice the NAME attributes in the FRAME tags. This allows you to assign a name to each of your frames so you can target the frames in your links. The name can be anything you want it to be, but it's best to stick to letters and numbers to avoid compatibility problems with future browsers. To target a particular frame, use the TARGET attribute in the anchor tag when you create your link. For example, this link would load a new page in the frame named "lower":

```
<A HREF="a.html" TARGET="lower">The "A" page</A>
```

As an example, we'll load this page in the left frame:

links1.html:

```
<BODY BGCOLOR="#FFFFCC">
<H1 ALIGN=CENTER> Links </H1>

<A HREF="a.html" TARGET="lower">The "A"
page</A><BR>
<A HREF="b.html" TARGET="lower">The "B"
page</A><BR>
<A HREF="c.html" TARGET="lower">The "C"
page</A><BR>
<A HREF="d.html" TARGET="lower">The "D"
page</A><BR>

</BODY>
```

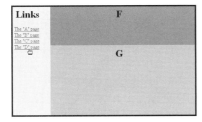

frames8.html **with** links1.html **loaded in the left frame.**

The target frame is the frame named "lower", which is the frame with the g.html file in it. Now, we'll click on a link, and the new file will replace the lower frame:

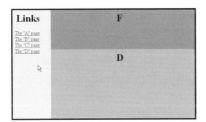

After clicking on the D **link, the** d.html **file will replace the lower frame.**

Scrollbars in Frames

When the content of a frame becomes larger than the size of the frame—either because the content is too long or the users have shrunk their browser window—scrollbars appear to allow the user to access all the content of the frame.

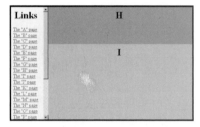

frames9.html **with** links2.html**, a longer list of links loaded in the left-hand frame.**

There may be times when you don't want a scroll-bar to appear, even if the content is too large for the frame. For example, consider this screen:

frames10.html: **The image at the top is too big for its frame.**

In this case we have a title-ish image in the top frame, which extends beyond the bottom of the frame. The image actually looks fine in the frame, but the scrollbar on the right is really unnecessary.

We can get rid of that scrollbar by using the SCROLLING=NO attribute to the FRAME tag:

```
<HTML>
<HEAD>
<TITLE> Frames Example </TITLE>
</HEAD>

<!-- cols for vertical divisions -->
<FRAMESET COLS="130,*" BORDER=0>

<!-- left frame -->
<FRAME SRC="links2.html" NAME=left>

<!-- right frame is another frameset -->
<!-- rows for horizontal divisions -->
<FRAMESET ROWS="75,*">
    <!-- top frame -->
    <FRAME SRC="titlebar.html"
    NAME=titlebar SCROLLING=NO>
        <!-- bottom frame -->
        <FRAME SRC="h.html" NAME=lower>
    </FRAMESET>

</FRAMESET>

</HTML>
```

1. The SCROLLING=NO attribute forces the frame to keep the scrollbar off at all times, even if the content is too big for the frame.

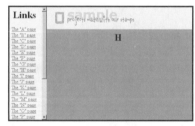

frames10a.html: **Voilà! Zee scrollbar ees vamoose!**

Margins in Frames

Because your frames will sometimes consist of only one graphic, it can be convenient to position the graphic right up against the edge of the frame. Normally, there are both vertical and horizontal margins on the frames. If we temporarily use a contrasting color for the background of the title bar, you can see the margins around the window:

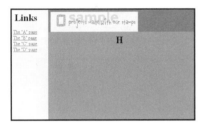

frames11.html **with** titlebar2.html: **There is an unwanted margin around the image.**

You can remove the margins with the MARGIN-HEIGHT and MARGINWIDTH attributes from the FRAME tag:

```
        <HTML>
        <HEAD>
        <TITLE> Frames Example </TITLE>
        </HEAD>

        <!-- cols for vertical divisions -->
        <FRAMESET COLS="130,*" BORDER=0>

          <!-- left frame -->
          <FRAME SRC="links1.html" NAME=left>

          <!-- right frame is another frameset
        -->
          <!-- rows for horizontal divisions
        -->
          <FRAMESET ROWS="67,*">
            <!-- top frame -->
            <FRAME SRC="titlebar2.html"
            NAME=titlebar SCROLLING=NO
1.          MARGINHEIGHT=0 MARGINWIDTH=0>
            <!-- bottom frame -->
            <FRAME SRC="h.html" NAME=lower>
          </FRAMESET>

        </FRAMESET>

        </HTML>
```

The MARGINHEIGHT and MARGINWIDTH attributes adjust the margins in the frame. Setting them to zero should remove the margins entirely, but Netscape Navigator (version 3 and 4) always leaves one pixel.

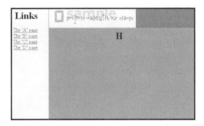

frames11a.html: **With the contrasting background, you can clearly see the one-pixel margin Netscape leaves behind.**

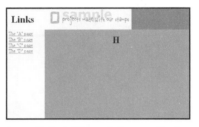

frames11a.html: **Microsoft Internet Explorer 4.0 does not reserve the one-pixel margin.**

Of course, the extra pixel of margin is not critical because your page will still look right when you match the background color.

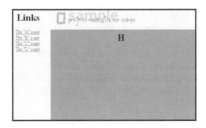

titlebar.html: **The top frame looks great with the matching seamless** BGCOLOR**!**

Aesthetics of Frames

We used frames extensively in the Catalog and
Sample areas the DIAR site because we had a lot
of images to display. Frames worked well as a navigation device to load thumbnail previews that
create a visual directory to our larger image
libraries. (An exercise called "Making Thumbnails"
follows later in this chapter.)

One disadvantages to using frames is that it
divides the real estate on your web page into
smaller pieces. Many web publishers and visitors
are already frustrated by small screen space, so
dividing the screen into smaller sections runs the
risk of being more of an irritant than an enhancement to a site.

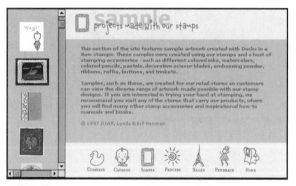

**In order to make our frames feel less confining, we worked
with color relationships that unified the page. Even though
this page is divided into four separate frame regions, it feels
like one page instead of four disjointed parts pieced together. We paid a great deal of attention to visual continuity as
well. The icons and type used inside the frames also
matched the aesthetics of the rest of the site. All of these
factors made our use of frames less annoying than other
examples we see on the web.**

▶ **note**

Do People Scroll?

Lynda recently visited the offices of Hot-
Wired (http://www.hotwired.com) to meet with
her friend Mike Kuniavsky, who heads their
research efforts for interface design.
He had recently set up a video camera to
tape the response of test users who had
never navigated the HotWired site before.
One of the most startling results of his video
taped studies was that the test users almost
never scrolled beyond the initial screen that
appeared, even if the screen contained
essential navigation information lower on
the page. Many respondents didn't even
realize there was more to the page than
what they saw, despite the vertical scrollbars.
Moral of the story? Be careful with key navigational graphics. What we mean by being
careful is don't make the end user work hard
to figure out the navigation to your site.
Make it easy for them to know where they are
and how to get where they want to go, and
make key navigation text and/or graphics
appear within their browser windows without requiring scrolling.

Size Considerations

When you're developing your web site, it's important to think about the size of the browser window and the resulting size relationships of images. The starting point is to establish who your audience is and from what size display you think they will be viewing the web. While many designers have large monitors, most average web visitors have smaller displays. The most common monitor size is 13" or 14". Most people who have average size displays have them set to 640×480.

Netscape Navigator and Microsoft Internet Explorer open in a narrow window on Macintoshes, and fill the screen on PCs. If a web page is bigger than the browser window it appears on, scrollbars automatically appear to signal to the end user that the page is larger than what is visible. Here are some sample browser configurations on a standard 640×480 display.

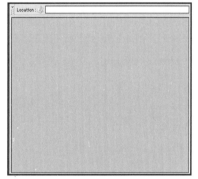

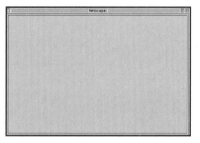

Macintosh Default: In Netscape Navigator 4.0 with large icons turned on, the default size is 382×324 pixels.

Macintosh Maximized: If you turn off the icons in Netscape Navigator 4.0 and maximize the browser window to its fullest, the available space for your web page will be 624×400 pixels.

Macintosh with Small Icons: This is how Lynda typically conforms her Netscape Navigator browser, which yields the available space of 634×324 pixels.

What happens if you make a graphic that is 800 pixels wide? It will require the end user to scroll horizontally to see the graphic. What happens if you make a graphic that is longer than the browser window? Vertical scrollbars will appear.

There are no standard guidelines for the size of navigational graphics, only educated guesses about what is practical and what isn't. We believe it's prudent to create essential navigation elements so they can be seen within 640×480 displays without requiring the end viewer to scroll his or her browser window.

This directive is easier said than done. It's a good idea to set your monitor to 640×480 before you begin creating navigation graphics so that you are working one-to-one to the size relationship from which your artwork will be viewed. In the case of frames, it can be helpful to mock up the navigation artwork in a Photoshop or Paintshop Pro document that matches the size of the browser window. We recommend that you set up your graphic template so it's no wider than 630 and no higher than 320 pixels. We have set up empty templates for you in these two programs, called `browser.psd` and `browser.bmp`, respectively, located in the `chap14` folder of the <chd> CD-ROM. These empty documents should be good starting points for designing navigational graphics, to ensure that your graphics don't end up too big.

Size Considerations Navbars/Frames

Now that you've seen the different size browser windows, let's look at some of the size issues inherent in our Ducks In A Row site design. Lynda uses a 17" monitor on her Macintosh system, which is a fairly typical size setup for many professional designers. Since the majority of the web audience will be on 13" monitors, however, Lynda's setup gave her a false sense of size security that proved wrong when we went live with the DIAR site. Mistakes are best when they're someone else's, so you get to benefit from our hard lessons by understanding where we went awry.

The first navbar we made was constructed while we were writing earlier chapters of this book. It was good enough to show as an example for learning about imagemaps, but the example we made was taken out of context of its true home on our site. Because of this, Lynda made the navbar without thinking about future size constraints.

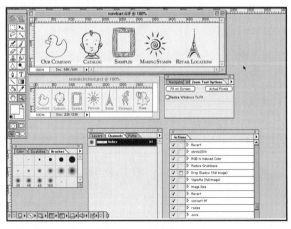

On Lynda's 17" monitor, the navbar.gif shown at the top of this screen seemed like a reasonable size.

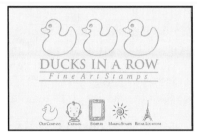

At 640×480 this bottom navbar looks like it's a transplant from the Land of the Giants site.

By switching her monitor to 640×480, it was obvious that the top navbar was way too large. The lower navbar shows the corrected file, and the next screen shot shows it in context of the frames.

After Lynda reduced the bottom navbar, it fit much better in scale to the 640×480 window.

After Lynda got the size of the navbar corrected, it was time to design our framesets for the Sample and Catalog sections of our site. This time, Lynda and Bill readjusted their monitor's resolutions to 640×480 in order to previsualize how the majority of the web audience would view the site.

Moral of the story? Design at the resolution you're planning to publish for. If you want your site to look good at 640×480, switch your monitor's resolution to that resolution while you're designing your graphics for a better reality check.

This example looked great on a 640×480 display.

Once a thumbnail is clicked inside the left scrolling frame, it loads the larger version of the sample into the middle frame of the right frameset. Notice how scrollbars appear on the right that weren't there before?

On a larger monitor, the scrollbars on the right would not appear. Bill created the HTML to ensure that the top, left, and bottom frames were fixed sizes. The right middle frame was set to asterisk (*), which fills the remaining size of the browser window on any size monitor, large or small. You can study the HTML that created this frameset by looking at the files in the diar/catalog folder of the <chd> CD-ROM.

In our Catalog section, we chose a different frames navigation technique. The opening page looks similar to the opening screen of the Sample section.

The difference is that after you click a thumbnail in the left frame, a new window appears with the result rather than loading the artwork into the middle frame, as with the Sample section of the site. This was accomplished in the HTML with TARGET=_top in the anchor tag. You can view the HTML for this technique by viewing the files in the diar/samples folder of the <chd> CD-ROM.

Making Thumbnails and Small Graphics

If you've never heard the term "thumbnail" before, in web-speak it refers to a small graphic that links to a larger graphic. Using thumbnails is common practice on web sites because small graphics (in dimensions and file size) typically load much faster than large graphics (in dimensions and file size). We created thumbnail graphics that link to larger graphics extensively in the Catalog and Sample sections of the DIAR web site.

It's actually a lot trickier to create small graphics than large ones. You'll find that you will resize your artwork over and over in Photoshop or Paint Shop Pro and that quality management will be critical. A good rule of thumb is to save master documents of key graphics, preferably in large sizes, so you can work from copies instead of originals. It will always yield higher quality to shrink a computer image than to enlarge it. The moral of the story? Scan large and reduce—never enlarge raster images such as scans or GIFs or JPEGs.

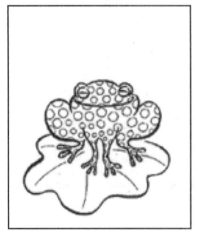

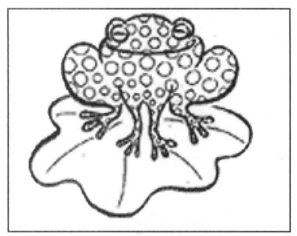

The original scan at 100%. This image looks fine.

The same image reduced 50% and sharpened with the Photoshop Sharpen filter.

The same image enlarged 150%. Even with sharpening filters, this image is soft and lacks good quality.

warning

Reducing Graphics in Photoshop

If you make a GIF and then choose to resize it, be sure to change the mode from Indexed Color to RGB. The reason is that Photoshop disables anti-aliasing in 8-bit mode. Not only that, but your filters in Photoshop won't be available in Indexed Color mode. If you needed to sharpen or blur a scan, for example, those options would be dimmed in Photoshop unless you switched back into 24-bit color. Because GIF is an 8-bit (or lower) file format, you must change the color mode before you reduce the size of graphics.

Change the color mode in Photoshop by selecting **Image**:**Mode**:**RGB**. This enables anti-aliasing, and the resulting graphic will be much higher quality. **Note:** Paint Shop Pro will always reduce-graphics without anti-aliasing regardless of the bit-depth. This is one of the many reasons that Photoshop is a superior graphics authoring tool.

Frames Resources

Netscape's Basic Frames Tutorial:
http://home.netscape.com/assist/net_sites/frames.html

Netscape's Frames Documentation:
http://developer.netscape.com/library/documentation/htmlguid/frames.htm
http://developer.netscape.com/library/examples/html/nested_frames.html

HTML Design Guide: (Network Communication Design, Japan)
http://ncdesign.kyushu-id.ac.jp/html/html_design.html

Bruce Heavin's Portfolio: An good example of frames with background tiles
http://www.stink.com/bruce/

Fragments

One final navigation technique that's effective when you have lots of information on one page is the HTML fragment. An HTML fragment is a separately addressable section of a web page that you access with a special URL part called a fragment.

To create a fragment on a web page, you enclose a section of your page in an anchor element (the A tag) using a NAME attribute to assign a name to it. As an example, we have a text version of the list of retail outlets for the Ducks In A Row rubberstamps at http://ducks.htmlbook.com/sales/locations.html on the DIAR web site. We fragmented the file based on individual states. Here's the entry for Texas:

```
<A NAME="TX">
<H2>TX</H2> [ <A HREF="#top">Top</A> ]

    <P><STRONG>Stamp De Ville</STRONG>
    <BR>1014 S. Broadway Suite 100
    <BR>Carrollton TX
<STRONG>75006</STRONG>

    <P><STRONG>Stamp Asylum</STRONG>
    <BR>201 Coit Rd. #165
    <BR>Plano TX <STRONG>75075</STRONG>

    <P><STRONG>Imprints</STRONG>
    <BR>4912 Camp Boyle Blvd.
    <BR>Fort Worth TX
<STRONG>76107</STRONG>

    <P><STRONG>Iconography</STRONG>
    <BR>P.O. Box 130090
    <BR>Houston TX <STRONG>77219</STRONG>

</A>
```

Now that you have the fragment set aside, you will want a way to link directly to it. For that purpose, you can use a special extension to the URL called the fragment.

A URL with a Fragment

The fragment part of the URL identifies a fragment of a page. So, if you wanted to link to the TX fragment that we just created, you would use the URL http://ducks.htmlbook.com/sales/locations.htlm#TX. The browser will then show the page, starting with the top of the fragment.

The TX **fragment of the** locations.html **file.**

At the top of our locations page, we have a list of states with a link to a fragment of the page for each state.

Links to each of the state fragments.

Just as you can use a relative URL to link to another file on the same web site, you can link to a fragment by itself when it's in the same file. In this case, we used fragment links in the HREF attributes to our anchor tags to link to each U.S. state (or Canadian province) where a customer can find a store that sells DIAR's rubber stamps.

```
<P> [
<A HREF="#AK">AK</A>    |
<A HREF="#AZ">AZ</A>    |
<A HREF="#Alberta">Alberta</A>    |
<A HREF="#CA">CA</A>    |
<A HREF="#CO">CO</A>    |
<A HREF="#CT">CT</A>    |
<A HREF="#FL">FL</A>    |
<A HREF="#GA">GA</A>    |
<A HREF="#IA">IA</A>    |
<A HREF="#IL">IL</A>    |
<A HREF="#KY">KY</A>    |
<A HREF="#MA">MA</A>    |
<A HREF="#MD">MD</A>    |
<A HREF="#MI">MI</A>    |
<A HREF="#MN">MN</A>    |
<A HREF="#MO">MO</A>    |
<A HREF="#NH">NH</A>    |
<A HREF="#NJ">NJ</A>    |
<A HREF="#NM">NM</A>    |
<A HREF="#NV">NV</A>    |
<A HREF="#NY">NY</A>    |
<A HREF="#OH">OH</A>    |
<A HREF="#OK">OK</A>    |
<A HREF="#OR">OR</A>    |
<A HREF="#PA">PA</A>    |
<A HREF="#RI">RI</A>    |
<A HREF="#SC">SC</A>    |
<A HREF="#TN">TN</A>    |
<A HREF="#TX">TX</A>    |
<A HREF="#VA">VA</A>    |
<A HREF="#WA">WA</A>    |
<A HREF="#WI">WI</A>    ]
```

Finally, one important navigational detail: Whenever you have a long page, it's very important to have a link back to the top of the page. This page lists over 130 different retail outlets, so a user could easily get lost in it all.

To accomplish this, we created a fragment at the top of the page, and we called it top:

```
<A NAME="top">
<!-- Logo -->
<IMG SRC="/images/ylogo1.gif"
    ALT="Ducks in a Row Logo"
    BORDER=0
    WIDTH=419 HEIGHT=219>
<H1>List of Retail Stores</H1>
</A>
```

Then, next to every individual state heading, we inserted a link back to #top.

```
<H2>TX</H2> [ <A HREF="#top">Top</A> ]
```

This makes it easy for a user to get back to the top of the page—like a little electronic trail of bread crumbs. Now the users can find their way home!

◗ chapter fourteen summary

In print, no one gives much thought to navigation issues, though they are present there, too. Most people intuitively know how to flip pages, use a Table of Contents, or find a reference in an Index. The web has an unspoken navigation language that is still being defined, and since hyperlinks can transport your end user without them even knowing where they're going, it's a huge challenge to design intuitive navigation for your information.

Frames and fragments are among many navigational devices (including hyperlinks, imagemaps, rollovers, button graphics, and others) that can either enhance or detract from the navigability of your site. Now that you've studied these two new techniques, your navigation design choices are wider. Given how difficult navigation issues are, it's best to understand when and why to use techniques like frames and fragments. We've covered the nuances of both navigation methods and filled you in on the design decisions related to choosing one, the other, or none of the above!

*"Is that a real poncho,
or is that a Sears poncho?"*
—Frank Zappa

▶ this chapter

rollover graphics
javascript rollovers
rollover exercises
dhtml

Rollovers
enhancing navigation

Rollovers were a driving force in multimedia projects long before the web came along. The principle of a rollover is that an icon or text will give a visual cue that it should be clicked, or rolled over. Web browsers have introduced a few preset conventions to indicate that a graphic or text is "hot," such as underlined text, colored borders around images, and the hand cursor. Rollovers allow artists and web publishers to make their own protocols for how a graphic or text looks when the cursor rolls over it, which results in much greater personalization of web site design than standard HTML provides.

When Lynda and Bill were preparing for this chapter, the idea of writing about rollovers excited both of us—but for different reasons. Lynda saw it as an opportunity to write about Photoshop techniques for creating the rollover graphics, and Bill saw the opportunity to write about JavaScript techniques for creating the rollovers.

Since you will need the graphics before you can use the JavaScript, we have put Lynda's section first. If you find that the other order works better for you, feel free to jump ahead.

Rollovers

Creating Rollover Graphics

Photoshop is such a great tool for creating rollovers that you almost wonder if the tool wasn't put on this planet for this purpose. The following exercise will demonstrate some of the possibilities for producing rollovers.

Photoshop Rollover Techniques

In this exercise you'll learn several techniques for manipulating Photoshop graphics for rollovers.

Photoshop Layers for Rollovers

This first exercise will familiarize you with using two layers for a rollover.

Step 1: Open Photoshop and open the rollover.psd file from the chap15 folder of the <chd> CD-ROM.

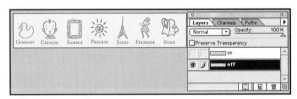

By clicking the eye icons of the on and off layers, you can previsualize how rollovers will react.

Step 2: Click the eye icons to previsualize the rollover effects. By working in a layered document, you can edit the rollovers to make them work they way you want.

Cutting the Rollovers Apart

Step 1: Working with the same rollover.psd file, go to the **View** menu, and choose **Show Guides**. Make sure **Snap to Guides** is set, and Show Rulers are also visible.

Step 2: Using the upper left-hand marquee selection tool, select one of the icons. Notice how your selection snapped to the ruled lines? These grids are very useful in helping you select the same size icon for both the on and off layers.

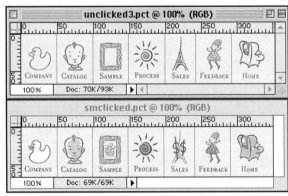

The two versions of icons with Guides turned on for cutting.

Step 3: After you've selected a single icon, **Copy** and **Paste** into a new document. Convert it to a GIF and name it on or off. For example, if you select the Company icon, name it companyon.gif. Be sure to practice the compression and color techniques covered in earlier chapters.

Make Your Own DIAR Icons

You've worked with ours, now it's time for you to make your own. We've provided another file called rollover2.psd in the chap15 folder of the <chd> CD-ROM. It has two layers.

Open rollover2.psd from the chap15 folder of the <chd> CD-ROM to create your own rollover effects.

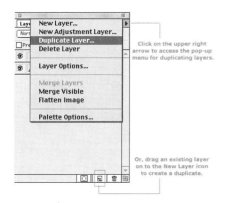

Click on the upper right arrow to access the pop-up menu for duplicating layers.

Or, drag an existing layer on to the New Layer icon to create a duplicate.

Step 1: Duplicate the two layers in this document and modify them to your own liking.

Step 2: Put your own colors into your new background layer by using any of the paint tools. Open the Swatches Palette (**Window:Show Swatches**) and make sure the bclut2.aco file is loaded (it's inside the chap06 folder of the <chd> CD-ROM) so you can paint with browser-safe colors.

Step 3: Recolor the outlines of the icons by checking **Preserve Transparency** in the Layers Palette. After this is checked, you can choose **Edit:Fill** to fill with a new color, or you can even paint the outlines with a brush.

Step 4: Uncheck **Preserve Transparency** to move the icons into new positions. If you don't uncheck **Preserve Transparency**, many of the transformation tools won't work. Experiment with some of the **Layer:Transform** options to rotate, scale, or skew the icons.

Try painting your own icons! Once you get the rollover bug, chances are you'll want to experiment with many new Photoshop techniques.

JavaScript for Rollovers

Now that you've reviewed the graphics creation process for rollovers, it's time to move on to learning how to integrate them into your HTML. This section of the chapter covers JavaScript techniques that will enable rollovers to function on your site.

In working with rollovers on the web for the past year or so, we have encountered three distinct different types of rollovers. We've named them **Pointing**, **Highlighting**, and **Slideshow**. These names are not intended to imply that you must use these types of rollovers for certain purposes; your personal creativity will determine that! These names are only here to distinguish one from the other.

Bill has written a single JavaScript program, called rollover.js, that handles all three of these types of rollovers. In the next few pages, we will show how you can create rollovers using this program by simply modifying a few parts of the example files we have provided on the CD-ROM.

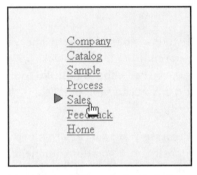

The Highlighting rollover is probably the most common type. As your mouse passes over a set of images, each image is replaced by a "highlighted" version. Of course, you can put whatever you want in the image—there is no law that it must be a highlighted version of the same image.

The Pointing rollover is the kind where there is an image that seems to follow your mouse as you pass it over a set of links. Normally used with a small arrow and a longish list of links, this type of rollover uses one image for the pointer and a blank image for swapping out.

The Slideshow rollover is the least commonly used, but we love the effect (we used a slideshow rollover for the catalog page on the DIAR site). With this type of rollover, as the mouse passes over the links, images are replaced in a single location on the screen (like the word "people" at the top of the image). The effect is somewhat like a slide show.

Pointing Rollover

The Pointing rollover is the easiest type of rollover to implement. All you need is a small pointing image, and a corresponding blank image that is the same size and background color as the pointing.

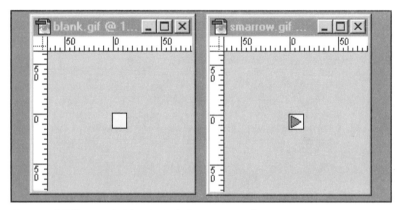

The two GIF files needed for the Pointing rollover effect. The left image is called blank.gif**, and the right image is called** smarrow.gif**. Both files are included in the** chap15/rollover/images **folder of the <chd> CD-ROM.**

This section will explain how you can use Bill's program to include custom images to replace the example images shown above. This will enable you to create your own Pointing rollover effects, without having to learn to write the JavaScript yourself.

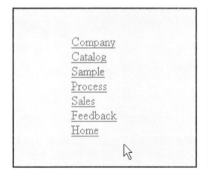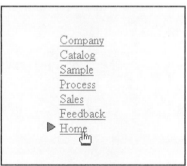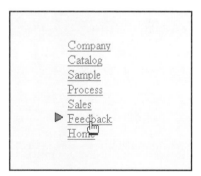

pointing.html: **The pointing rollover in action.**

In this example, we have used a small arrow (14×14 pixels) for the pointer and a flat yellow GIF in the same size for the blank image.

Here's the HTML file that creates the effect on the previous page (pointing.html in the chap15/rollovers folder on the CD-ROM):

```html
<HTML>
<HEAD>
<TITLE> Pointing Rollover Example </TITLE>
```

1.
```
<SCRIPT LANGUAGE="JavaScript1.1">
```
2.
```
<!--
```

3.
```
// initializations section for
// Bill Weinman's Common JavaScript Rollover Engine
// (linked in below)
```

4.
```
// this MUST be the first line of code!
//   ... it prevents the rollovers from trying
//   to run before the code is all initialized.
okay = false;

function var_init()
{
// rollover type: "highlighting", "pointing",
or "slideshow"
```
5.
```
rtype = "pointing";
```

```
// path to the images
// (be sure to include the trailing "/")
```
6.
```
path = "images/";
```

```
// names of images
imagenames = new Array(
```

```
// the name for the image:
```
7.
```
"smarrow"
  );
```

```
// suffixes for mouseover and mouseout
// not used for pointing type rollover.
suffixes = new Array( "", "" );
```

```
// filename extension (".gif", ".jpg", or ".png")
```
8.
```
ext = ".gif";
}

// -->
</SCRIPT>
```

9.
```
<!-- link in Bill Weinman's Common JavaScript
Rollover Engine -->
<SCRIPT LANGUAGE="JavaScript1.1" SRC="rollover.js">
  </SCRIPT>

</HEAD>
```

```
10.  <BODY onLoad="roll_init()" BGCOLOR="#FFFFCC">

     <TABLE><TR><TD HEIGHT=10></TABLE> <!-- spacer -->

     <TABLE><TR><TD WIDTH=40><TD>
11.  <IMG NAME="i1" SRC="images/blank.gif">
12.  <A HREF="" onMouseOver="over('i1')"
     onMouseOut="out('i1')">Company</A><BR>
       <IMG NAME="i2" SRC="images/blank.gif"> <A HREF=""
         onMouseOver="over('i2')"
         onMouseOut="out('i2')">Catalog</A><BR>
       <IMG NAME="i3" SRC="images/blank.gif"> <A HREF=""
         onMouseOver="over('i3')"
         onMouseOut="out('i3')">Sample</A><BR>
       <IMG NAME="i4" SRC="images/blank.gif"> <A HREF=""
         onMouseOver="over('i4')"
         onMouseOut="out('i4')">Process</A><BR>
       <IMG NAME="i5" SRC="images/blank.gif"> <A HREF=""
     onMouseOver="over('i5')"
     onMouseOut="out('i5')">Sales</A><BR>
       <IMG NAME="i6" SRC="images/blank.gif"> <A HREF=""
     onMouseOver="over('i6')"
     onMouseOut="out('i6')">Feedback</A><BR>
       <IMG NAME="i7" SRC="images/blank.gif"> <A HREF=""
     onMouseOver="over('i7')"
     onMouseOut="out('i7')">Home</A><BR>
     </TABLE>

     </BODY>
     </HTML>
```

1. `<SCRIPT LANGUAGE="JavaScript1.1">`

This is where we tell the browser that we are using JavaScript. Some
older browsers don't support enough of the JavaScript specification to
accomplish rollovers, so we specified `"JavaScript1.1"`, so they will
ignore this code.

2. `<!--`

Some browsers don't understand the SCRIPT element at all, and we
want to make sure they don't display the JavaScript (they may think it's
HTML!). We put the content of the SCRIPT element in an HTML com-
ment (between `<!--` and `-->`). Browsers that don't understand
JavaScript will merrily ignore it, and those that do understand the
JavaScript will go ahead and use it.

```
3.    // initializations section for
      // Bill Weinman's Common JavaScript Rollover Engine
```

JavaScript comments are introduced with a pair of slashes (//). Everything following the pair of slashes, to the end of the line, is ignored by the browser.

```
4.    // this MUST be the first line of code!
      //    ... it prevents the rollovers from trying
      //    to run before the code is all initialized.
      okay = false;
```

One of the most common problems with JavaScript programs is that it is extremely difficult to ensure that one part of the program runs before another. The result of this problem is often seen as a page that "works most of the time," but not all of the time.

This line of code cures that problem. It initializes a special variable that instructs the rest of the program to remain idle until it knows that everything is okay. By having this as the very first line of JavaScript in the HTML file, we can ensure that it will be initialized before anything else happens.

```
5.    rtype = "pointing";
```

Here, we select the type of rollovers to use for this file. Since we are using a "pointing" type rollover, we set this to the value, "pointing".

```
6.    path = "images/";
```

This is where we put the path to our images. This is used as the beginning part for all the image file names. It must end with a slash.

```
7.    // the name for the image:
      "smarrow"
```

This is the file name of the image to use for the pointer, without the extension (that is, the ".gif" part).

```
8.    ext = ".gif";
```

This is the extension part of the file name.

9. ```
<!-- link in Bill Weinman's Common JavaScript
Rollover Engine -->
<SCRIPT LANGUAGE="JavaScript1.1"
SRC="rollover.js"></SCRIPT>
```

Here's where we pull in the actual JavaScript program. This part is the same for all the different types of rollovers. We used a relative URL to specify the location of the `rollover.js` program.

10. ```
<BODY onLoad="roll_init()" BGCOLOR="#FFFFCC">
```

The onLoad attribute is used with the BODY tag to run the initialization part of the JavaScript. This is what initializes all the values we entered above and gets the program ready to run.

11. ```
<IMG NAME="i1" SRC="images/blank.gif">
```

Here is where we assign a name to each of the images, using the NAME attribute to the IMG tag.

12. ```
<A HREF="" onMouseOver="over('i1')"
onMouseOut="out('i1')">Company</A><BR>
```

Finally, we use the onMouseOver and onMouseOut attributes (also called events by the object-oriented programming crowd) to make the browser call the JavaScript whenever the mouse is passed over the link.

▶ e x e r c i s e

Make Your Own Pointing Rollover

In this exercise, you will use your own pointing graphic and create a pointing rollover with it.

Step 1: Create a pointing graphic for the rollover.

Step 2: Create a blank graphic filled with the same color as the background of the pointing graphic in the same dimensions.

Step 3: Create a folder called rollover on your local hard disk and place your images into it.

Step 4: Copy the rollover.js and pointing.html files from the chap15/rollovers folder on the <chd> CD-ROM to your local rollover folder.

Step 5: Open your local copy of pointing.html in your favorite text editor.

Step 6: Find the line that says,
```
path = "images/";
```
...and change it to say,
```
path = "";
```
...because your images are in the same folder as your pointing.html file.

Step 7: Find the line that says,
```
"smarrow"
```
...and change it to the file name of your pointer graphic—without the extension. In other words, if your graphic is called pointer.gif, you would use:
```
"pointer"
```

Step 8: Find the line that says,
```
ext = ".gif";
```
...and change it to match the extension of your graphic file, if your file is not a GIF.

Step 9: Confirm that the line,
```
<SCRIPT LANGUAGE="JavaScript1.1"
SRC="rollover.js">
```
...points to the correct location for the rollover.js file. If it's in the same folder as your pointing.html file, you're fine.

Step 10: Now edit the list of links at the end of the pointing.html file. For each link, change the `SRC="images/blank.gif"` to the name of your blank image. For example, if your blank image is called yellow.gif you would use `SRC="yellow.gif"` for your graphic.

Step 11: For each link, place the URL that you want to link to in the quotes of the `HREF=""` attribute.

Step 12: If you need more links, go ahead and add them. Be sure to add the images and the links in equal numbers, and be sure to increment the `IMG NAME` attribute for each link as well. For example, to add one more link, you would add it like this:
```
<IMG NAME="i8" SRC="images/blank.gif">
<A HREF="" onMouseOver="over('i8')"
onMouseOut="out('i8')">Company</A><BR>
```
Notice that the i8 is the next name after i7 and that it goes in three places: in the `IMG NAME` attribute, and in the over and out JavaScript calls. For more links, use i9, i10, i11, etc...

Now, load up pointing.html, and your rollovers should work fine! Go ahead and edit the rest of the file to your liking. Feel free to rename pointing.html to whatever suits its purpose on your site.

Slideshow Rollover

The slideshow rollover is the next level in complexity and is probably the least used (or the least overused?) of the three major types of rollovers. For this type of rollover, you use one image for each link, plus a default image—which doesn't need to be blank—for the state where the mouse is not over any of the links.

For the DIAR catalog page, we wanted to use a vertical navigation bar in a frame along the left side of a page. We chose to use a single shifting image at the top of the bar that changes as the mouse rolls over each icon.

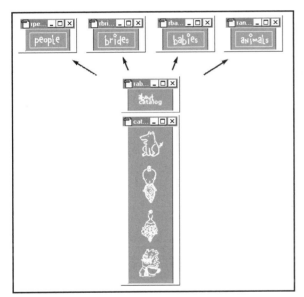

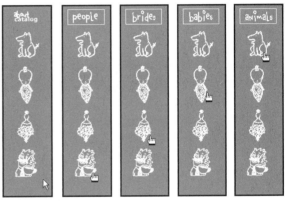

The catalog page navigation bar in action, with the Slideshow rollover at the top.

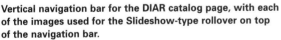

Vertical navigation bar for the DIAR catalog page, with each of the images used for the Slideshow-type rollover on top of the navigation bar.

The HTML for the previous page is on the <chd> CD-ROM as navcatalog.html in the chap15/rollovers folder.

navcatalog.html:

```
    <HTML>
    <HEAD>
    <TITLE> Slideshow Rollover Example  </TITLE>

    <SCRIPT LANGUAGE="JavaScript1.1">
    <!--

    // initializations section for
    // Bill Weinman's Common JavaScript Rollover Engine
    // (linked in below)

    // see rollover.js for instructions

    // this MUST be the first line of code!
    //   ... it prevents the rollovers from trying
    //   to run before the code is all initialized.
    okay = false;

    function var_init()
    {
    // rollover type: "highlighting", "pointing", or "slideshow"
1.  rtype = "slideshow";

    // path to the images
    // (be sure to include the trailing "/")
    path = "images/catalog/";

    // names of images
    imagenames = new Array(

    // these must be in quotes, and separated by commas ...
2.    "rabout", "ranimals", "rbabies", "rbrides", "rpeople"
      );

    // suffixes for mouseover and mouseout
    suffixes = new Array(

    // these are appended to the names above, to get the filename
    itself.
    // this is only used for "highlighting" rollovers
      "", ""
      );

    // filename extension (".gif", ".jpg", or ".png")
3.  ext = ".gif";
    }

    // -->
    </SCRIPT>
```

```
     <!-- include common js functions for rollovers -->
4.   <SCRIPT LANGUAGE="JavaScript1.1" SRC="rollover.js">
     </SCRIPT>

     </HEAD>
     <BODY onLoad="roll_init()" BGCOLOR="#990000" text="WHITE">

5.   <map name="caticons">
6.   <area shape="polygon" alt="Animals"
     coords="22,22,24,25,28,26,27,30,30,32,32,33,26,38,27,45,32,48,27,50,
     27,54,29,55,30,64,38,62,45,63,56,64,51,54,57,50,60,48,60,44,60,40,68,
     34,66,29,62,29,59,34,52,26,51,17,48,8,47,6,44,11,39,5,39,11,21,18"
     href="animals.html"
          onMouseOver="over('ranimals')" onMouseOut="out()">
       <area shape="polygon" alt="Babies"
       coords="39,64,25,63,36,78,27,81,27,85,26,91,28,97,33,104,27,117,28,
       120,31,121,35,133,36,145,52,146,51,130,51,120,57,116,48,106,51,101,
       52,93,54,84,51,77,51,75,56,64"
       href="babies.html"
          onMouseOver="over('rbabies')" onMouseOut="out()">
       <area shape="polygon" alt="Brides"
       coords="43,146,32,145,36,161,37,165,39,170,33,176,30,185,24,186,24,
       189,23,194,27,198,29,202,33,206,32,218,54,218,50,208,52,200,57,200,
       54,194,59,191,53,183,50,175,44,170,50,165,46,158,58,147"
       href="brides.html"
          onMouseOver="over('rbrides')" onMouseOut="out()">
       <area shape="polygon" alt="People"
       coords="37,218,30,218,35,227,27,237,26,243,23,246,25,250,25,258,20,
       267,19,276,52,276,52,273,55,269,60,269,61,262,58,259,57,258,58,255,
       56,254,63,251,56,246,59,243,57,239,61,235,61,231,56,231,59,224,49,
       228,49,218" href="people.html"
          onMouseOver="over('rpeople')" onMouseOut="out()">
       <area shape="default" nohref>
     </map>

     <TABLE BORDER="0" CELLSPACING="0" CELLPADDING="0">
7.     <TR><TD><A HREF="content.html">
     <IMG NAME="rollover"
         SRC="images/catalog/rabout.gif" WIDTH="85" HEIGHT="40"
         BORDER="0"></A></TD>
       <TR><TD><A HREF=""><IMG SRC="images/catalog/caticons.gif"
         WIDTH="85" HEIGHT="290" BORDER="0" usemap="#caticons"></A></TD>
     </TABLE>

     </BODY>
8.   </HTML>
```

1. `rtype = "slideshow";`

We set the type of the rollover to "slideshow".

2. `"rabout", "ranimals", "rbabies", "rbrides", "rpeople"`

This is the list of image file names without the extension.

3. `ext = ".gif";`

And this is the extension for the image file names.

4.
```
<!-- include common js functions for rollovers -->
<SCRIPT LANGUAGE="JavaScript1.1" SRC="rollover.js">
</SCRIPT>
```

Here's where we pull in the actual JavaScript program. This part is the same for all types of rollovers. We used a relative URL to specify the location of the rollover.js program.

5. `<map name="caticons">`

In this example, we have used the rollovers with an imagemap. The concepts are the same as with individual images...

6.
```
<area shape="polygon" alt="Animals"
coords="22,22,24,25,28,26,27,30,30,32,32,33,26,38,27,
45,32,48,27,50,27,54,29,55,30,64,38,62,45,63,56,64,51,
54,57,50,60,48,60,44,60,40,68,34,66,29,62,29,59,34,52,
26,51,17,48,8,47,6,44,11,39,5,39,11,21,18"
href="animals.html"
onMouseOver="over('ranimals')" onMouseOut="out()">
```

In the AREA tag, we use the onMouseOver and onMouseOut attributes to call the JavaScript, just like in an anchor (A) tag.

7.
```
<TR><TD><A HREF="content.html"><IMG NAME="rollover"
SRC="images/catalog/rabout.gif" WIDTH="85" HEIGHT="40"
BORDER="0"></A></TD>
```

Finally, the image location is created with the IMG tag and named with the NAME attribute. The name of the image must always be rollover for a Slideshow-type rollover.

▶ e x e r c i s e

Make Your Own Slideshow Rollover

In this exercise, you will use your own graphics and create a Slideshow rollover with them. For simplicity's sake, we will use text links instead of an imagemap. If you prefer to use images, you certainly can; or, if you want to use an imagemap, the previous example will serve as a guide. We suggest, however, that you do this simplified exercise first to get a feel for how it all works.

Step 1: Create a series of graphics to use for the rollovers. Be sure to make them all the same size.

Step 2: Create a default graphic in the same dimensions as the rollover graphics. The default graphic will be visible until the user rolls over one of the links; then the default graphic will be replaced with the corresponding rollover graphic.

Step 3: Create a folder called rollover on your local hard disk and place your images in folder.

Step 4: Copy the rollover.js and slideshow.html files from the chap15/rollovers folder on the <chd> CD-ROM to your local rollover folder...

Step 5: Open your local copy of slideshow.html in your favorite text editor.

Step 6: Find the line that says,
`path = "images/";`
...and change it to say,
`path = "";`
...because your images are in the same folder as your pointing.html file.

Step 7: Find the line that says,
`"image1", "image2", "image3"`
...and change it to list all the images that you are using for your rollovers—without the extensions. In other words, if you are using graphics named, red.gif, blue.gif, green.gif, orange.gif, and chartreuse.gif, you would list them as: "red", "blue", "green", "orange", "chartreuse"

Step 8: Find the line that says,
`ext = ".gif";`
...and change it to match the extension of your graphic files, if your files are not .gif.

Step 9: Confirm that the line,
`<SCRIPT LANGUAGE="JavaScript1.1" SRC="rollover.js">`
...points to the correct location for the rollover.js file. If it's in the same folder as your slideshow.html file, you're fine.

Step 10: Now edit the list of links at the end of the slideshow.html file. For each link, change the `"over ('image1')"` to use the name of the image you want to appear for that link. Do not include the filename extension here. For example, if the image for a particular link is called red.gif, you would use `"over('red')"` for that link.

Step 11: For each link, place the URL that you want to link to in the quotes of the HREF="".

▶ continued

Step 12: If you need more links, go ahead and add them. Be sure to use the right image name in the `"over('xxx')"` for each link, and be sure that each image is listed in the list in **Step 7**. For example, to add one more link you could add it like this:

```
<A HREF=""
onMouseOver="over('chartreuse')"
onMouseOut="out()">Over There!</A><BR>
```

Step 13: Finally, find the line that says,
```
<IMG NAME="rollover"
SRC="images/blank.gif">
```
...and change the `"images/blank.gif"` to the default graphic you created in **Step 2**. This is the default graphic that will display when the mouse is not over any of the links. Be sure to include the extension (`.gif`) here—this is the one place where you do need it—and be sure to remove the `"images/"`, unless you actually have your graphics files in a folder called images. For example, if your default graphic is named default.gif, you would write your line like this:

```
<IMG NAME="rollover" SRC="default.gif">
```
Now, load up slideshow.html, and your rollovers should work! Go ahead and edit the rest of the file to your liking. Feel free to rename slideshow.html to whatever suits its purpose on your site.

Highlighting Rollover

The Highlighting rollover is the most common of the three, and it's also the most complicated to produce. This is the type of rollover that involves rolling your mouse over a graphic, and having a highlighted version of that graphic appear.

Two pieces of artwork are provided for each position: one normal and one highlighted. As an example, let's use the main menu that we used throughout the DIAR site:

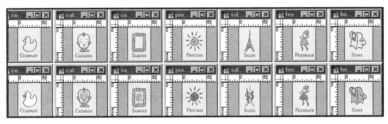

The main menu for the DIAR site required 14 separate pieces of art. Two for each of the seven positions, one normal (top row), and one highlighted (bottom row).

The idea of the Highlighting rollover is to create a highlight over each graphic as the mouse rolls over the position.

The DIAR menu: The Highlighting rollover in action.

Highlighting Rollover File Naming Convention

For use with Bill's JavaScript Rollover Engine, the image files must
be named according to a strict convention. Each file name has
parts: the **name** itself, a **suffix**, and the **extension**. The suffix is used
to distinguish between the normal and the highlighted images.

For example, you have chosen a suffix of -on for your highlighted
images and -off for your normal images; you've named your
images company, catalog, sample, process, sales, feedback, and home;
and your extension is .gif, because you are using GIF images.
Then each of your files would be named like this:

Image Name	Normal File Name	Highlighted File Name
company	company-off.gif	company-on.gif
catalog	catalog-off.gif	catalog-on.gif
sample	sample-off.gif	sample-on.gif
process	process-off.gif	process-on.gif
process	sales-off.gif	sales-on.gif
feedback	feedback-off.gif	feedback-on.gif
home	home-off.gif	home-on.gif

This naming convention is vital to the operation of the highlighting
code in Bill's JavaScript rollover program. The program will not work
if you don't follow this convention. You can use whatever suffixes
make sense to you, but you must use them consistently and specify
them in the proper place in the file. Otherwise, just use the -on and
-off suffixes as we did for this example.

The HTML for the above example is on the <chd> CD-ROM as
highlighting.html in the chap15/rollovers folder.

highlighting.html:

```
<HTML>
<HEAD>
<TITLE> Highlighting Rollover Example </TITLE>

<SCRIPT LANGUAGE="JavaScript1.1">
<!--

// initializations section for
// Bill Weinman's Common JavaScript Rollover Engine
// (linked in below)

// this MUST be the first line of code!
//    ... it prevents the rollovers from trying
//    to run before the code is all initialized.
okay = false;

function var_init()
{
// rollover type: "highlighting", "pointing", or "slideshow"
rtype = "highlighting";

// path to the images
// (be sure to include the trailing "/")
path = "images/";

// names of images
imagenames = new Array(

// base image names, without the "-on", "-off", or ".gif"
   // these must be in quotes, and
separated by commas ...
      "company", "catalog", "sample", "process", "sales",
"feedback", "home"
   );

// suffixes for mouseover and mouseout
suffixes = new Array(

// these are appended to the names above, to get the filename itself.
"-on", "-off"
   );

// filename extension (".gif", ".jpg", or ".png")
ext = ".gif";
}

// -->
</SCRIPT>
```

Labels in margin: **1.** **2.** **3.**

4.
```
<!-- link in Bill Weinman's Common JavaScript Rollover Engine -->
    <SCRIPT LANGUAGE="JavaScript1.1" SRC="rollover.js">
    </SCRIPT>

</HEAD>
<BODY onLoad="roll_init()" BGCOLOR="#FFFFCC">

<TABLE><TR><TD HEIGHT=20></TABLE> <!-- spacer -->

<CENTER>
  <TABLE><TR>
  <!-- List of Links starts here -->
  <TD><A HREF=""
        onMouseOver="over('company')"
        onMouseOut="out('company')">
     <IMG NAME=company SRC="images/company-off.gif"
        BORDER=0></A></TD>
    <TD><A HREF=""
          onMouseOver="over('catalog')"
        onMouseOut="out('catalog')">
     <IMG NAME=catalog SRC="images/catalog-off.gif"
        BORDER=0></A></TD>
    <TD><A HREF=""
        onMouseOver="over('sample')"
        onMouseOut="out('sample')">
     <IMG NAME=sample SRC="images/sample-off.gif"
        BORDER=0></A></TD>
    <TD><A HREF=""
        onMouseOver="over('process')"
        onMouseOut="out('process')">
     <IMG NAME=process SRC="images/process-off.gif"
        BORDER=0></A></TD>
    <TD><A HREF=""
        onMouseOver="over('sales')"
        onMouseOut="out('sales')">
     <IMG NAME=sales SRC="images/sales-off.gif"
        BORDER=0></A></TD>
    <TD><A HREF=""
        onMouseOver="over('feedback')"
        onMouseOut="out('feedback')">
     <IMG NAME=feedback SRC="images/feedback-off.gif"
        BORDER=0></A></TD>
    <TD><A HREF=""
        onMouseOver="over('home')"
        onMouseOut="out('home')">
     <IMG NAME=home SRC="images/home-off.gif"
        BORDER=0></A></TD>
  <!-- List of Links ends here -->
  </TABLE>
</CENTER>

</BODY>
</HTML>
```

The **5.** marker appears at line `<TD><A HREF=""` (first link in the list).

1. `rtype = "highlighting";`

Here, we've set the type of the rollover to `"highlighting"`.

2.  ```
    // base image names, without the "-on", "-off", or ".gif"
    // these must be in quotes, and separated by commas ...
       "company", "catalog", "sample", "process", "sales",
       "feedback", "home"
    ```

This is the major area of difference between the Highlighting and the other types of rollovers. This is the list of names for the images without the suffix or the extension. If this doesn't make sense to you, please go back and read the explanation under the heading, "Highlighting Rollover File Naming Convention," just before the last code listing.

3.  ```
    // these are appended to the names above, to get the
    filename itself.
    "-on", "-off"
    ```

This is the list of suffixes we have chosen to use for this page.

4.  ```
    <!-- link in Bill Weinman's Common JavaScript Rollover Engine -->
       <SCRIPT LANGUAGE="JavaScript1.1" SRC="rollover.js">
       </SCRIPT>
    ```

Here's where we pull in the actual JavaScript program. This part is the same for all the different types of rollovers. We used a relative URL to specify the location of the rollover.js program.

5.  ```
    <A HREF=""
       onMouseOver="over('company')"
       onMouseOut="out('company')">
       <IMG NAME=company SRC="images/company-off.gif"
         BORDER=0></A></TD>
    ```

Each of the links look like this. Notice that the name of the image is used four times, and it must be the same in each case.

▶ e x e r c i s e

Make Your Own Highlighting Rollover

In this exercise, you will use your own graphics and create a Highlighting rollover with them.

Step 1: Create a series of graphics to use for the rollovers. While all the graphics don't need to be the same size, each normal and highlighted pair needs to be precisely the same size as each other. Name the files by using the -on and -off convention described in "Highlighting Rollover File Naming Conventions" earlier in this section.

Step 2: Create a folder called rollover on your local hard disk and place your images in that folder.

Step 3: Copy the rollover.js and highlighting.html files from the chap15/rollovers folder on the <chd> CD-ROM to your local rollover folder.

Step 4: Open your local copy of highlighting.html in your favorite text editor.

Step 5: Find the line that says,
`path = "images/";`
...and change it to say,
`path = "";`
...because your images are in the same folder as your pointing.html file.

Step 6: Find the line that says,
`"company", "catalog", "sample", "process", "sales", "feedback", "home"`
...and change it to list all the images that you are using for your rollovers, without the suffixes or the extensions. In other words, if you are using graphics named, fred-on.gif, fred-off, wilma-on, wilma-off, barney-off, barney-on, betty-off, betty-on, then you would list them here as:
`"fred", "wilma", "barney", "betty"`

Step 7: Find the line that says,
`ext = ".gif";`
...and change it to match the extension of your graphic file, if your file is not .gif.

Step 8: Confirm that the line,
`<SCRIPT LANGUAGE="JavaScript1.1" SRC="rollover.js">`
...points to the correct location for the rollover.js file. If it's in the same folder as your highlighting.html file, you're fine.

Step 9: Important: Pay extra attention to this step, or your rollover will not work!

Edit the list of links at the end of the highlighting.html file. For each link, change the `"over('name')"`, `"out('name')"`, NAME=name, and SRC="name-off.gif" to use the name of the image you are using for that link. Be sure to use the name of your image without the suffix or the extension in the over, out, and NAME parts and to use the full form of the image file name including the non-highlighted suffix and the extension in the SRC part.

Step 10: For each link, place the URL you want to link to in the quotes of the HREF="" attribute.

Step 11: If you need more links, go ahead and add them. Be sure to use the right image name in all the relevant places for each link, and be sure that each image is listed in the list in **Step 6**. For example, to add one more link you could add it like this:

```
<TD><A HREF=""
onMouseOver="over('dino')"
onMouseOut="out('dino')">
<IMG NAME=dino SRC="dino-off.gif"
BORDER=0></A></TD>
```

Now, load up highlighting.html, and your rollovers should work! Go ahead and edit the rest of the file to your liking. Feel free to rename highlighting.html to whatever suits its purpose on your site.

▶ **warning**

Blank Images

Both the Pointing and Slideshow types of rollovers can use a blank image for the default state. Do not use a transparent GIF for your blank image. On some systems (PCs for example), the transparent GIF will replace another image, and on other systems (Macs for example), the transparent GIF will have no effect or may even distort the image instead.

♦ note

JavaScript Uploading Issues

To use the external JavaScript program with your web pages, the program itself, rollover.js, must be uploaded to your server. A proper MIME-type configuration is required by the browser for any program or file to run properly from a web server. Common programs and files like GIFs and JPEGs are usually configured with the correct MIME-type automatically when the server is installed. Unfortunately, most servers are not currently configured to send the correct MIME-type for JavaScript files.

In order to find out if you have this problem, try uploading one of the examples from this chapter, along with the rollover.js file to your server. Then try running that example with Netscape Navigator version 3 (Navigator 4 ignores the MIME-type for JavaScript, which is probably a good thing.) If the browser displays the JavaScript code, instead of running it, you will need to add a MIME-type for JavaScript on your server.

The good news is that it's not hard to configure a MIME-type for JavaScript yourself. On most servers you can update the MIME-type by following these instructions:

Step 1: Create a plain text file (not a word-processor file) called .htaccess and put this one line of text in it:

```
AddType application/x-javascript .js
```

Step 2: Transfer this new .htaccess file to your server and put it in the folder you will use for your JavaScript files.

Important note: If there is already a file named .htaccess in that folder, do not replace it. Just add the above line to it instead.

You will need to quit your browser and restart it in order for it to read the new MIME-type.

If you do this and find that Netscape Navigator version 3 still displays the source code, then you will need to talk to your system administrators and have them add the MIME-type for you. They may have disabled the ability for users to add MIME-types, or they may be running a server that doesn't use .htaccess files.

If all this fails, we have included special versions of these rollover examples that have the entire JavaScript program in the HTML file instead of linking it externally. You will find these special versions on the <chd> CD-ROM in the chap15/rollovers/internal-js folder.

DHTML for Navigation

JavaScript plays an important role in a new type of web multimedia called **D**ynamic **HTML**. DHTML is a loosely defined term that describes enhancements to standard HTML such as animation, sound, rollovers, and better control over typography. These enhancements are achieved through combining various types of existing technologies, such as JavaScript, CSS (**C**ascading **S**tyle **S**heets), and an object model, which allows you to treat ActiveX controls and plug-ins as objects within a document that can be manipulated by CSS and JavaScript.

What this means to the end user is pages created with DHTML will include a new level of dynamic content. With DHTML, it's possible to accurately position artwork and type, animate HTML elements, like GIFs and JPEGs, and create custom navigation more akin to CD-ROMs than the web. Not only could you include rollovers in DHTML, but the artwork for the rollovers could fly together to form, include custom scrollbar graphics, or let the end user move parts of your interface pieces around the screen.

The huge challenge of DHMTL is that same huge challenge that faces any web developer—browser and platform differences. Some JavaScripts work on Netscape and not on Explorer. ActiveX works on PC versions of Explorer, but not Mac versions. If you delve into the nitty gritty, it's horrifying to discover what works where and what doesn't. You could literally spend all your time testing tags and browsers, and forget about ever making any web content at all.

Another drawback of DHTML is that it requires 4.0 browsers in order to be viewed. In our opinion, this makes it available to too narrow an audience to serve many sites' purposes. Also, you may be frustrated by the long download wait time on most DHMTL sites. That's because everything in DHTML works on the client side, so it has to download before anything can be seen. This is both a drawback and a feature. Once the artwork and elements are downloaded, DHTML sites are wicked fast because everything they need to run is on your hard drive.

If you want to see a really exciting example of DHTML in action, visit http://www.dhtmlzone.com/, and click on the Tutorial section. Launch the SuperFly demo, designed by Akimbo Designs (http://www.akimbodesign.com/) and witness the next level of web navigation. Each screen in this demo includes a tutorial, which explains how the page was constructed.

Unfortunately, DHTML knows no standards yet, and so competing methods for creating this type of content abound between the warring browserlords. Netscape and Microsoft have pledged future support for a standard that is currently being decided by the **W**orld **W**ide **W**eb Consortium (W3C), but we've all heard that one before. Meanwhile, life goes on without standards, as usual.

For a visual DHTML design tool, visit http://www. dreamweaver.com/. Dreamweaver is Macromedia's latest web authoring tool, and a free tryout demo is available to Mac and PC web developers. It boasts the ability to write cross-browser compatible DHTML, design CSS layouts without coding by hand, and creating JavaScript animations with a

◗ chapter fifteen summary

Rollovers are a valuable technique for inviting people to press on a link, or for informing them of what they will find on the other end of the link. In this chapter, we covered rollovers from both the design and the programming sides, and by using these techniques, you should be well-equipped to design and implement rollovers on your web sites.

We have identified three major categories of rollovers. The three types we have covered are:

- Pointing rollovers

- Slideshow rollovers

- Highlighting rollovers

Having said that, we must admit that we have seen plenty of rollovers that don't fit all nice and neat in these three categories. But we have not seen any rollovers that we couldn't implement in one of these ways.

"He gains everyone's approval who mixes the pleasant with the useful."
—Horace, Roman Poet ca. 13 BC

Forms
collecting information

The ability to interact with users is one of the most fundamental uses for computers and networks. The ability to ask questions and collect responses is, in turn, one of the most fundamental ways to interact with users.

HTML provides the ability to create forms, text boxes, radio buttons, and other graphical devices for interacting with users and gathering information. If you want to ask for a name and email address, take a survey, run a guestbook, or just get feedback on your web site, you are going to have to use forms.

Forms

The FORM Element

To create a form on your page, you must start with the FORM element. The FORM element is the main container for all your forms. Here's a simple example of the FORM element. This file is form-1.html in the chap16 folder on the <chd> CD-ROM:

```
<HTML>
<HEAD>
<TITLE> Example Form </TITLE>
</HEAD>

<BODY BGCOLOR=white>

<H1> A Sample Form </H1>

<FORM>
Your Name: <INPUT TYPE=text>
</FORM>

</BODY>
</HTML>
```

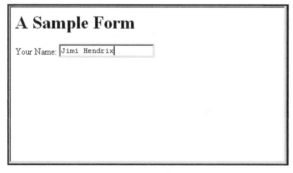

form-1.html: **A simple form.**

This is a simple form that asks for the user's name. It uses the INPUT tag with TYPE=text to create a text box for typing a response.

The FORM element is also where you will tell the form how to transmit the data. We will cover that later in the section, "How Can I Use the Data?"

Widgets

Each of the graphical devices for collecting data are called widgets (some people call them controls, but we think it's more fun to call them widgets). The text box is just one type of widget that you can create in your forms.

There are two basic categories of widgets: those that work with the INPUT tag and those that have their own tags. First, let's look at the INPUT types:

`<INPUT TYPE=text NAME=name>`

The text box is the basic field for typing in a line of text.

`<INPUT TYPE=password NAME=name>`

The password box works exactly like the text box, except it obscures the typing so that people can't watch over the user's shoulder to learn their password.

`<INPUT TYPE=checkbox NAME=name>`

The check box is used for yes/no type of input.

`<INPUT TYPE=radio NAME=name VALUE=value>`

The radio button is used for multiple-choice input. Only one radio button in a set can be on at one time.

`<INPUT TYPE=submit NAME=name>`

The submit button is used to send the form to the server.

```
<INPUT TYPE=reset>
```

The reset button resets the form to its default values.

```
<INPUT TYPE=hidden NAME=name VALUE=value>
```

**The hidden field is used to pass information on to the
server without displaying it on the page. It's mostly used
by programmers for state-management. If that makes no
sense to you, then you don't need this widget.**

```
<INPUT TYPE=image NAME=name SRC=send.gif>
```

**The image type is an alternate to the submit button. It lets
you use an image rather than a button for submitting the
form to the server. It will accept all the same attributes as
the IMG tag.**

```
<INPUT TYPE=button>
```

**The button widget is a button that doesn't do anything.
It's currently only used for JavaScript. When browsers
start supporting the new forms capabilities in HTML 4,
this widget will become very useful.**

```
<SELECT>
  <OPTION> Option 1
  <OPTION> Option 2
  <OPTION> Option 3
  <OPTION> Option 4
  <OPTION> Option 5
</OPTION></SELECT>
```

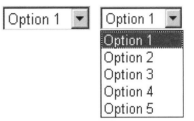

**The select box is another type of multiple-choice input wid-
get. Use it for lists that are too long for radio buttons.**

```
<TEXTAREA>
  Some Default Text
</TEXTAREA>
```

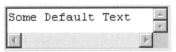

**The text area is for typing long amounts of text, good for
things like guestbooks and email forms.**

Some additional widgets that are part of the
new HTML 4.0 specification can be found in
the Reference section. Unfortunately, we can't
show those to you today because there are no
browsers that support them yet.

Examples

One obvious use for forms on the Ducks In A Row site is for the feedback page. Here's an example of a simple feedback page for the DIAR site:

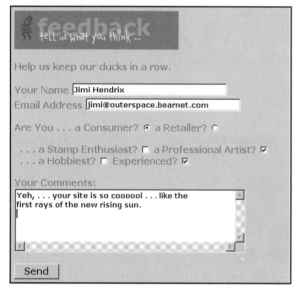

form-2.html: **A simple feedback page.**

```
<HTML>
<HEAD>
<TITLE> Ducks In A Row Info Form
</TITLE>
</HEAD>

<BODY TEXT="#666633" BGCOLOR="#CCCC99"
LINK="#990000" VINK="#990000">
```

1.
```
<FONT FACE="Verdana,Helvetica,Arial">
<B>

<IMG SRC="feedback.gif"
ALT="Feedback">

<P>Help us keep our ducks in a row.
```

2.
```
<FORM>
```

3.
```
Your Name <INPUT TYPE=text
NAME=name><BR>
Email Address <INPUT TYPE=text
NAME=email><BR>

<P>
```

4.
```
Are You . . . a Consumer?
<INPUT TYPE=radio NAME=custtype
VALUE=consumer>
          a Retailer? <INPUT TYPE=radio
NAME=custtype VALUE=consumer><BR>
<P>
```

5.
```
  . . . a Stamp Enthusiast?
<INPUT TYPE=checkbox NAME=enthusiast>
     a Professional Artist?
<INPUT TYPE=checkbox NAME=artist><BR>
  . . . a Hobbiest?
<INPUT TYPE=checkbox NAME=hobbiest>
     Experienced? <INPUT TYPE=checkbox
NAME=hendrixfan>

<P>Your Comments:<BR>
```

6.
```
<TEXTAREA NAME=comments ROWS=5
COLS=30></TEXTAREA>
```

7.
```
<P><INPUT TYPE=submit VALUE="Send">

</FORM>

</B></FONT>

</BODY>
</HTML>
```

1. `<FONT FACE="Verdana,Helvetica,Arial">`
    `<B>`

We used the FONT tag because we like the Verdana typeface for the uniform look of this site. Given the color scheme of this page, using the B tag helps the text be more readable. Notice that even the form fields are affected by the FONT tag.

This is a new behavior for forms in the 4.0 browsers, and it's welcome. Later, in the "Using Tables with Forms" section of this chapter, we'll show you how you can take advantage of this feature to make your forms more pleasant to use.

2. `<FORM>`

The FORM element marks the beginning of the forms. Later in this chapter, we will add the attributes to get it to call the CGI program. It's a good idea to use the FORM tag without any attributes while you're in the process of laying out the page. You can always add the attributes when you're ready to start testing the CGI.

3. `Your Name <INPUT TYPE=text`
    `NAME=name><BR>`
    `Email Address <INPUT TYPE=text`
    `NAME=email><BR>`

We used the INPUT tag with TYPE=text for the text boxes. The NAME attribute identifies an individual widget for the CGI program that will process the form. It's important that you make up a unique name for each widget on a page.

4. `Are You . . . a Consumer?`
    `<INPUT TYPE=radio NAME=custtype`
    `VALUE=consumer>`
    `         a Retailer? <INPUT TYPE=radio`
    `NAME=custtype VALUE=retailer><BR>`

These are radio buttons. Groups of radio buttons are considered one widget, so only one radio button in a group is allowed to be on at one time. All the radio buttons in the group use the same value for their NAME attributes.

That's what puts them in the same group. In the case of the radio button, the VALUE attribute is used to distinguish one button from another, within a group. Both of these radio buttons use the same NAME, so that puts them in the same group. The VALUE attributes are different, so you will be able to tell which one was pushed.

5. `  . . . a Stamp Enthusiast?`
    `<INPUT TYPE=checkbox NAME=enthusiast>`
    `    a Professional Artist?`
    `<INPUT TYPE=checkbox NAME=artist><BR>`
    `  . . . a Hobbiest?`
    `<INPUT TYPE=checkbox NAME=hobbiest>`
    `        Experienced? <INPUT TYPE=checkbox`
    `NAME=hendrixfan>`

Check boxes are not grouped, so each one has its own NAME.

6. `<TEXTAREA NAME=comments ROWS=5`
    `COLS=30></TEXTAREA>`

The TEXTAREA widget provides a space for the user to type comments.

7. `<P><INPUT TYPE=submit VALUE="Send">`

And, finally, the Submit widget is used to make a button that sends the form. The VALUE attribute is used to label the button.

Using Tables with Forms

The next problem with our form is that it's not very nicely aligned. It would be a lot better—even easier to use—if the various elements of the form were lined up better.

To solve this problem, we use HTML tables. We must warn you, however, that putting your forms into tables does limit your audience somewhat. Older browsers, especially early versions of the AOL browser, cannot see forms in tables. We think that's a bug that borders on criminality, but it's true nonetheless.

This is one area where we suggest to go ahead and do it anyway, because there are few things that can benefit more from the use of a table than a form. And for the record, the amount of your audience today that won't be able to use the form is probably a small fraction. But do be aware of the problem, and if your form is for a truly mass audience, make sure you have an alternative non-table form available.

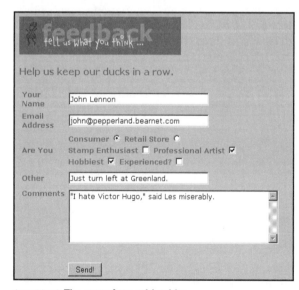

form-3.html: **The same form with tables.**

There is a new behavior for forms in the 4.0 browsers that we really like. Now you can change the font of the characters inside the form widgets! This gives you, the designer, another layer of control over the way your pages look and feel. Unfortunately, combined with the use of tables, it can make the page much more complex.

The reason is that the TABLE element is not valid content for the FONT element. That means that you cannot put a table within a FONT container and expect the contents of the table to use that font. If you do, you will find that all the text in the table is just in the default font. Why did they design it that way? Only God and a few braniacs on the HTML committee know for sure, but it gives us pains in the lower lumbar area.

Fortunately, there's an elegant solution.

Because only the 4.0 browsers use the FONT tags for formatting form fields, it seems that this is one place we can get away with using a style sheet. Here's a version of the above table that uses a style sheet to format the table (this is form-4.html in the chap16 folder on the <chd> CD-ROM):

```
<HTML>
<HEAD>
<TITLE> Ducks In A Row Info Form </TITLE>

<STYLE TYPE="text/css">
<!--

P,TD,SPAN {
  font-family: Verdana,Helvetica,Arial;
  font-size: 14px;
  }

.text {
  font-weight: bold;
  font-size: 16px;
  }

.label { font-weight: bold }
.form { font-weight: normal }

-->
```

```
</STYLE>
</HEAD>

<BODY TEXT="#666633" BGCOLOR="#CCCC99"
LINK="#990000" VINK="#990000">

<IMG SRC="feedback.gif" ALT="Feedback">
<P CLASS=text>Help us keep our ducks
in a row.

<FORM>
<TABLE>
  <TR>
    <TD CLASS=label>
      Your Name
    <TD CLASS=form>
      <INPUT NAME=Name TYPE=TEXT>

  <TR>
    <TD CLASS=label>
      Email Address
    <TD CLASS=form>
      <INPUT NAME=Email TYPE=TEXT>

  <TR>
    <TD CLASS=label>
      Are You
    <TD CLASS=label>
      <SPAN CLASS=label>
      Consumer <INPUT TYPE=RADIO
NAME=Retail VALUE="Consumer" CHECKED>
      Retail Store <INPUT TYPE=RADIO
NAME=Retail VALUE="Store">
        <BR>
      Stamp Enthusiast
<INPUT TYPE=CHECKBOX NAME="Enthusiast">
      Professional Artist
<INPUT TYPE=CHECKBOX NAME="ProArtist"><BR>
      Hobbiest <INPUT TYPE=CHECKBOX
NAME="Hobbiest">
      Experienced? <INPUT TYPE=CHECKBOX
NAME="HendrixFan">
      </SPAN>
<TR>
    <TD CLASS=label>
      Other
      </FONT></B>
    <TD CLASS=form>
      <INPUT NAME=Other TYPE=TEXT>

  <TR VALIGN=TOP>
    <TD CLASS=label>
      Comments
    <TD><SPAN CLASS=form>
      <TEXTAREA COLS=30 ROWS=5
      NAME=message WRAP=HARD></TEXTAREA>
      </SPAN>
  <TR><TD HEIGHT=20>
```

```
  <TR><TD>
    <TD CLASS=label><INPUT TYPE=submit
VALUE=" Send! ">

</TABLE>

</FORM>

</BODY>
</HTML>
```

There were a few places where the form field didn't
pick up the formatting of the style, but we were
able to solve those by using the SPAN tag. This
will probably work a lot better in the 5.0 browsers,
but for now using the SPAN tag in a few spots is
far better than the plethora of FONT tags of the previous version. If this code is confusing to you, turn
to Chapter 13, "Style Sheets," where SPAN and CSS
are thoroughly explained.

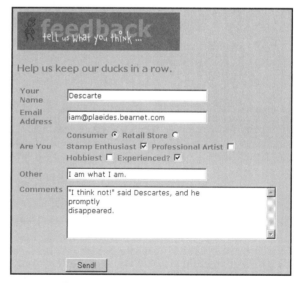

form-4.html: **Tables with a style sheet—looks great, less filling!**

The IMAGE Type

Our form is almost finished, but we need to fix one more aesthetic problem. That "send" button is all wrong. Let's use an image instead, shall we?

The image conforms much more to the look of the page. This is accomplished by replacing the line,

```
<TD CLASS=label><INPUT TYPE=submit
VALUE=" Send! ">
```

with this line:

```
<TD><INPUT TYPE=image NAME=submit
SRC="send.gif" BORDER=0>
```

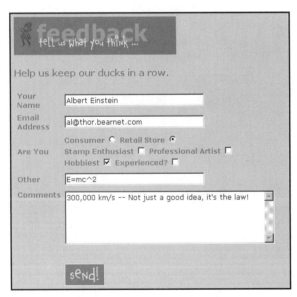

form-5.html: **Using an image for the submit button.**

Be aware that when you use an image for a submit button, the cursor does not change to a pointing finger as it does with an image hyperlink. So your graphic must be compelling. It must say "push me!" in the clearest of visual cues. For this image, we chose a subtle border to go along with the word "send!" Whatever you decide on, you may want to test it on a naïve user to make sure that it communicates the "push me" message clearly.

How Can I Use the Data?

Now that you have a form, you are probably wondering: When someone types information into my form, how does it get to me? The answer to this question goes beyond the realm of HTML because it requires CGI programs written in any number of programming languages.

HTML forms require the cooperation of several different systems in order to work. Forms use HTTP (the **H**yper**T**ext **T**ransport **P**rotocol, used by web servers to communicate with web browsers) to carry information to the server; and forms require the use of a CGI (the **C**ommon **G**ateway **I**nterface) program to process the information on the server and interact with the user.

It is possible to use forms without a CGI program, but all the available ways to do it require certain browsers, which must be configured a certain way in order to work. You can use JavaScript, but that eliminates all but the most current browsers, and it still doesn't allow you to actually collect data from the user. You can use mailto URLs, but that also eliminates all but the latest versions of browsers. Both of these alternatives require that the end user's browser is configured to send email, which many are not.

In order to make this information more useful for you, Bill has written a generic CGI program called mailform.cgi found in the chap19/mailform folder of the <chd> CD-ROM, which you can upload to your server and use with your forms. It requires a UNIX-based server with Perl (version 5 or better) installed and the sendmail program (or one of the many sendmail equivalents). It will simply email the information from the form to an address that you provide. If you want to do something more specific, we recommend picking up a copy of Bill's *The CGI Book*, or hiring a qualified programmer.

Using mailform.cgi

In order to use Bill's CGI program, you will need to edit the Perl source to set your email address, the default subject line for the messages, and the location of the sendmail program on your server. Then you must get the program onto your server, make sure it's executable, and make sure it follows whatever conventions your server uses for running CGI. Finally, you will have to get the correct URL into the ACTION attribute of your FORM tag.

This is not a trivial process, and it requires that you understand something about how your server works. You will have to talk to your system administrator to get this information. If we tell you how this works on our server, it will do you no good. It almost certainly works differently on your server. If you are not technically inclined, we strongly recommend that you hire a professional to help you.

After you have the program configured and running on your server, you will need to fill in the METHOD and ACTION attributes on the form tag. Here's what we used for our server:

```
<FORM METHOD=POST ACTION="/cgi-bin/
mailform.cgi">
```

The METHOD attribute is either GET or POST. The GET method sends the data to the server as part of the URL, and the POST method sends it as a separate message to the server, which is not visible to the user. We like to use the POST method unless there is a reason to bookmark the data itself, so we used POST here.

The ACTION attribute is the URL for the CGI program that will handle the data. Don't just copy this value, it may well be very different on your server.

After the program is installed, and you press the Send button, it will send you an email message with the results. The message will look similar to this one:

```
Date: Tue, 30 Sep 1997 01:37:54 -0500
From: billw@sirius
X-Mailer: mailform.cgi 1.0 (by Bill
Weinman <wew@bearnet.com>)
To: billw@sirius
Subject: Ducks In A Row Feedback Form

Ducks In A Row Feedback Form:

Email : wew@bearnet.com
Name : Bill Weinman
Enthusiast : on
HendrixFan : on
Other : Web Programmer
Retail : Consumer
message : I would like to know more about
your stamps!
submit.x : 45
submit.y : 20


---
  Sent by mailform.cgi 1.0 (by Bill
Weinman <wew@bearnet.com>)
```

This includes all the information on your form. In fact, this same program will work with any form, and will work with both the POST and GET methods. On the other hand, you may need something better formatted, in which case you are welcome to modify the program or hire someone else to do that for you.

◗ chapter sixteen summary

Using HTML forms is an excellent tool for gathering all sorts
of data from your customers. There are many, many programs
available on the web for all sorts of different purposes, from
online ordering, to banner exchange programs, to surveys,
and even games.

A couple of our favorite locations for free CGI programs are:

Matt's Script Archives:
http://www.worldwidemart.com/scripts/

Selena Sol's Digital Soul:
http://selena.mcp.com/

Both of these sites use scripts that allow the designer to
rework the HTML, using the techniques you have learned
here, to make your pages look as good as they work.

"It's kind of fun to do the impossible."
—Walt Disney

Animation & Sound
hype vs. truth

If you're considering adding animation and/or sound to your website design, there are lots of choices and possibilities. Even experienced digital animators and musicians who want to publish to the web will discover new rules, standards, terminology, and tools. This chapter focuses on helping you sort out the various decisions—from how to make the content, to what tools to use, to what delivery methods and file formats to choose from.

In addition to our focus on how to create animation and sound, we also share our opinions about aesthetic considerations. The hype of the web is that the more bells and whistles you add to your site, the more it will attract visitors. In many cases, nothing could be further from the truth.

Animation Process

Animation is one of the biggest digital design challenges around because it relies on many types of design and computer knowledge. This is the animation decision-making process in order of importance:

Concept: You must start with a strong concept. The concept can be formed from a variety of considerations, such as what you are trying to communicate, whether the animation tool you are using has certain strengths or limits, and the overall aesthetic of your site.

Storyboard: A storyboard can be simple or complex. It can be scribbled on a napkin or a beautifully rendered Photoshop file. It depends on what you are trying to accomplish with your storyboard. If you are using your storyboard to work out the "idea" of your animation, scribbled napkins are fine! If you are using your storyboard to convince a client to buy your animation idea, then you might need to go with much fancier presentation methods.

Preparation: Preparing your artwork is a huge key in the success of making an animation. You will need to prepare your artwork differently for different animation tools. We will show the preparation process for some of the animations we created for Ducks In A Row later in this chapter.

Execution: Use the animation tool to realize your idea.

Coding: Put the finished results into a web page and watch it work!

Ducks In A Row Animation Case Study

Phase 1: *Concept*

We already covered some of the brainstorming methods in the Metaphors section of Chapter 11, "Planning." We chose to produce simple animations on the DIAR site that mimicked stamping with rubber stamps and other simple effects. We created all our banner graphics to start with a simple graphic and, over time, "stamp" out the rest of the graphic elements. These concepts were built around the artwork style of the rubber stamps. There's no reason to make 3D rubber stamps rotating in a starfield being zapped by laser beams. Sometimes the clichés in computer animation don't fit the subject matter at hand.

Phase 2: *Storyboard*

It's always helpful to create a storyboard for animations, even if it's just a scribbled note to yourself. This example walks you through a sample animation that Lynda created for the DIAR site.

Lynda's "crude" storyboard, which served to simply map out her animation idea.

She planned to start with the words Ducks In A Row, with the tag line: Fine Art Rubber Stamps. Next, each duck would fade up in a row. When the last duck has faded in, the words Ducks In A Row would glow for a moment.

Phase 3: *Production*

Production techniques for producing animation vary dramatically depending on the animation concept and delivery. Making artwork for an animated feature film, for example, would be quite different than making artwork for the web. We've already covered a lot of the distinctive characteristics of web graphics (low resolution, browser-safe colors, optimizing graphics, etc.) so there's no need to repeat them all here. Instead, we'll look at a real case-study created by Lynda, which gives only a single example of production methodology in context of a real animation project.

This scan is called `duckscan.pct` and is found in the `chap17` folder of the <chd> CD-ROM.

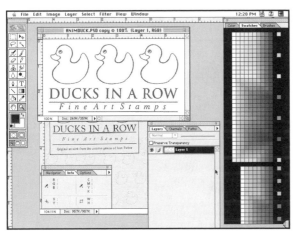

I started with a black and white scan of the logo and reduced it to web size and resolution.

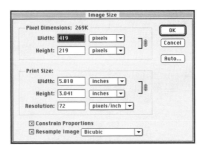

I wanted the width to fit well within most end user's screen sizes (the average monitor is 640×480), and the resolution for web images is always 72 dpi.

Setting Up an Alpha Channel

I wanted to put the logo into browser-safe colors. This type of artwork (flat-style illustration) will always suffer from unwanted dithering if browser-safe colors are not used. The challenge was that this artwork was anti-aliased to white, making it impossible to select colors easily. I decided to use an alpha channel technique that uses the image itself for the mask.

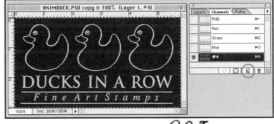

I selected the entire image (**Select:Select All**) and copied it. I clicked on my Channels palette and created a new channel by clicking on the new channel icon (circled). I pasted in the image and inverted it (**Select:Inverse**).

I clicked on the ~~RGB~~ *Black* channel inside the Channels palette and then switched over to the Layers palette. From there, I requested a new layer by clicking on the new layers icon (circled).

Under the **Select** menu, I chose **Load Selection**, and the dialog box appeared. I chose **Channel #4.**

This resulted in a selection of my logo being loaded. I'm loading it onto the new layer so that I can fill it with a color for recoloring later.

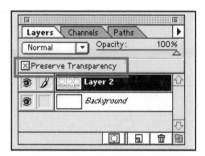

Notice that Preserve Transparency is checked? This allows me to fill the logo with any color of my choosing. I used the bclut2.aco file (inside the chap06 folder of the <chd> CD-ROM) to fill the different areas of the artwork.

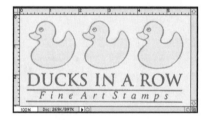

You can open the ducksanim.psd file to check the results of my browser-safe coloring efforts. I named the layers line art and background, respectively.

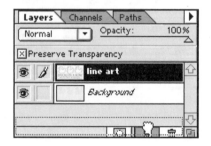

I next wanted to duplicate the line art layer so that I could make my glow art. I took the line art layer and dragged it on to the new layer icon. This made a copy of the layer.

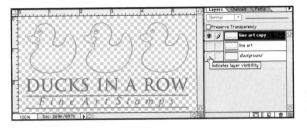

By turning off the eye icons, I can isolate the copy.

I erased everything except the words "Ducks In A Row" (make sure **Preserve Transparency** is unchecked so that you can use the eraser effectively) and then ran the Gaussian Blur filter to make the lettering "glow." I duplicated and merged my glow layer to make it stronger in intensity. Then, I positioned the glow layer underneath the line art. Here's the final. At this point, be sure to **Save**! I always keep this file as a master (in this case, it is called ducks.psd) before I commence animation production.

The next stage is to prepare the separate frames of the animation. I will need to produce six frames:

#1 Only the logo appears (no ducks)

#2 First duck appears (one duck)

#3 Second duck appears next to first duck (two ducks)

#4 Third duck appears (three ducks)

#5 Glow layer with all three ducks

#6 No glow with all three ducks

Before I do that, let me alert you to a palette issue unique to animated GIFs. Even though you can have unlimited frames of artwork, they must all share a common palette. If they don't, you run the risk of the browser not displaying your artwork correctly and flashing your palette to unwanted psychadelic colors. I kid you not. This means that I'd better work out my palette problems now.

I'm going to make a master palette in Photoshop that contains every possible color within my animation frames. To do this, I'll take the layered document I've been working on and index it. You must flatten the layers to do this. Don't worry, since you've saved the .PSD file, you can always revert!

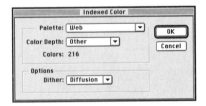

I wanted to use web-safe colors, so I chose **Image: Mode:Indexed Color:Web**. There's only one big problem now. My image has 216 colors assigned to it, many of which are not used or necessary. This will make my file sizes bigger, so it's my job to further reduce the colors. I switched back to **Image: Mode:RGB** and then—without changing a thing—chose **Image: Mode:Indexed Color:Web**. This time, an Exact Palette setting appeared, and as you can see, this image only really used 16 colors!

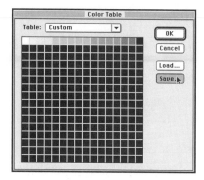

Next, I have to save the palette so that I can load it to all the frames of animation. I called it ducks.aco (.aco is the file extension Photoshop uses for color tables). We'll cover the process of loading the ducks.aco palette soon, but first, let's make all the animation frames.

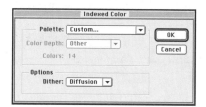

To convert each frame to this palette, choose **Image:Mode:Indexed Color:Custom**.

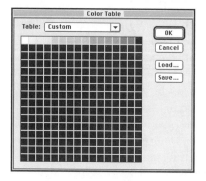

The Custom setting will automatically bring forth the Color Table window where you can load the .aco file.

Through a combination of turning layers off and on using the eraser tools and the paint brush, here are my finished six screens. **WARNING:** Throw away the alpha channel in each document. There's a bug in Photoshop 4.0 that automatically determines transparency based on your alpha, even when you don't want it to!

We're now ready to enter a GIF animation program, armed with artwork that was made properly for the task!

Phase 4: *Execution*

GifBuilder 5.0 for the Macintosh

GifBuilder for the Mac, written by Yves Piguet, can be downloaded from http://iawww.epfl.ch/Staff/Yves.Piguet/clip2gif-home/GifBuilder.html. It's freeware (!), which is pretty suave considering what a sweet program this is.

To load the animation frames into GifBuilder, I could choose to use **File:Open**, or I could drag and drop my images into the GifBuilder Frames window.

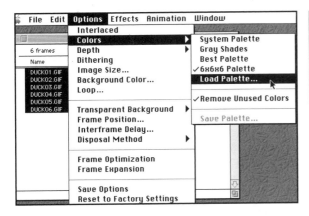

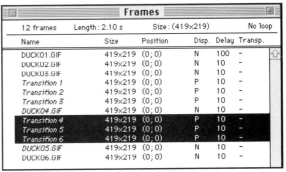

You have to pick the number of steps between each dissolve effect.

After all the frames are loaded, it's time to load the color palette we made back in Photoshop. Under the **Options** menu, choose **Colors:Load Palette**. GifBuilder will recognize the .aco file.

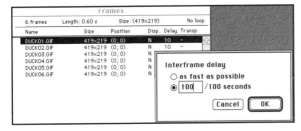

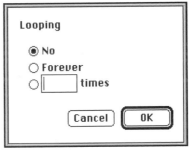

This inserts frames into your animation.

Next, you can set frame delays. This sets the timing for each frame. Here, I want to hold on the first frame. Units of measurement are 100=1 second.

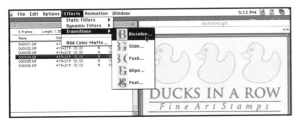

GifBuilder supports transitions between frames, meaning they provide some preset wipes and dissolves that can be automatically added to your animation. In this case, I want my animation to dissolve from frame 4>5>6.

I chose not to loop this animation. In most circumstances, looping animation can be very annoying.

Saving the animated GIF is as easy as **File:Save As**. The GifBuilder program automatically assembles the frames and makes the file!

Photo Impact's GIF Animator (PC)

GIF Animator isn't freeware, but it is my favorite PC-based GIF animation program. You can find out more by checking out ULEAD (PC) at

http://www.ulead.com/products/ga_main.htm

You load each frame by selecting **Layer:Add Images**. This puts all the frames into a frame list, shown above. To set frame delays for individual frames, highlight the frame and change the **Delay** setting (outlined above.)

GIF Animator can load custom palettes generated by Paint Shop Pro (.pal files). Unfortunately, it does not recognize Photoshop palettes.

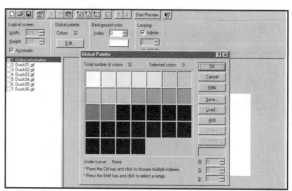

If you double-click on the file Global Palette, however, you'll see that the program pulled the palette that each file was mapped to earlier in Photoshop.

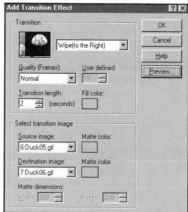

The program doesn't have a "dissolve" effect like GIFBuilder, but it has wipes. I chose to use a **Wipe to the Right** to introduce the glow, and a **Wipe to the Left** to remove it.

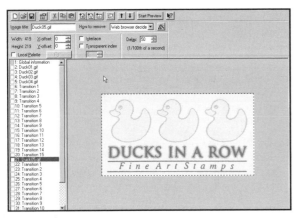

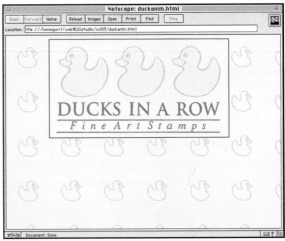

This inserted transition frames into the image list, just like GIFBuilder did.

Once I got all the settings how I wanted, a **File:Save** was all it took to generate an animated GIF. This one was named gaduck.gif if you want to check it out in the chap17 folder of the <chd> CD-ROM.

Phase 5: *Coding*

To insert this file into an HTML page, I also chose to include a background tile similar to the original catalog sample. The file measures 100×100 pixels at 72 dpi and is named tile.gif.

Here's the final result! Open the duckanim.html file from the chap17 folder of the <chd> CD-ROM inside your browser to watch the animated GIF move.

Here's the HTML:

```
<HTML>
<HEAD><TITLE>Animation in Action!</TITLE>
</HEAD>
<BODY LINK="#663333" BACKGROUND="tile.gif">
<P><CENTER>
<A HREF="http://ducks.htmlbook.com">
<IMG SRC="duckanimation.gif" WIDTH=419
  HEIGHT=219 ALIGN=bottom></A>
</CENTER>
</BODY>
</HTML>
```

LOWSRC Animation Trick

In addition to the many different web animation file formats, there are also several HTML tricks for achieving limited animation effects. The LOWSRC attribute to the IMG tag enables a single image separate from the final image to load first, creating a two-frame animation.

To see this effect in action, open lowsrc1.html from the chap17 folder of the <chd> CD-ROM. Here's the HTML deconstructed:

```
    <HTML>
    <HEAD><TITLE>LOW SRC TEST!</TITLE>
    </HEAD>
    <BODY BGCOLOR="#FFFFFF">
1.  <IMG SRC="catalog2.gif"
    LOWSRC="lowcat.gif">
    </BODY>
    </HTML>
```

1. The LOWSRC image loads first in the browser, but is listed second in the tag.

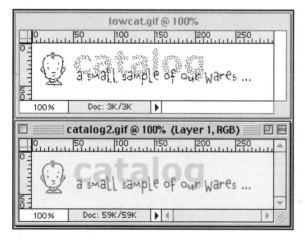

The two image sources used in the lowsrc.html file.

This effect is typically used with a small black-and-white graphic for the LOWSRC image, but it's possible to build variations of this effect.

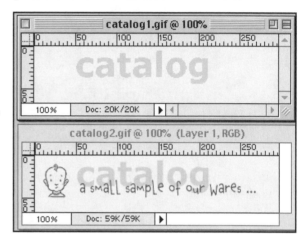

By choosing two color images with different versions of the same artwork, you can create two-frame animation effects that cause the graphics to look like they're "building" on screen. This example, lowsrc2.html, is also inside the chap17 folder of the <chd> CD-ROM.

Client Pull for Slideshows

Client pull relies on the client (your web browser) to request (pull) the next page after a specified delay. This creates a slideshow effect. Because it's client-sided, client pull can be viewed locally from a hard drive or from within an intranet, without the need to post the source images or HTML to a live server. If you post the client pull HTML files to your server, it can also be viewed from the web.

Client pull involves the META tag, which can be programmed to display a series of HTML pages. The META tag includes a REFRESH attribute, which can be set using the CONTENT element with delays. A delay of 1 would theoretically program a 1 second delay for loading the next page, though time measures vary depending on server speed and file sizes.

The pull1.html through pull3.html files are located inside the chap17 folder of the <chd> CD-ROM. The META tag always goes inside the HEAD tag. Besides the TITLE tag, this is the only other tag that belongs inside the HEAD in HTML standards.

Here's the code for pull1.html:

```
<HTML>
<HEAD><TITLE>Client Pull Test</TITLE>
<META HTTP-EQUIV=Refresh
CONTENT="5; URL=pull2.html">
</HEAD>
<BODY BGCOLOR="#FFFFFF">
<IMG SRC="lowcat.gif">
</BODY>
</HTML>
```

Here's the code for pull2.html:

```
<HTML>
<HEAD><TITLE>Client Pull Test 2</TITLE>
<META HTTP-EQUIV=Refresh
CONTENT="5; URL=pull2.html">
</HEAD>
<BODY BGCOLOR="#FFFFFF">
```

```
<IMG SRC="catalog.gif">
</BODY>
</HTML>
```

Here's the code for pull3.html:

```
<HTML>
<HEAD><TITLE>Client Pull Test 3</TITLE>
</HEAD>
<BODY BGCOLOR="#FFFFFF">
<IMG SRC="catalog2.gif">
</BODY>
</HTML>
```

The CONTENT attribute is what instructs the browser to display and wait before loading the next HTML page. In our example, the CONTENT attribute is set for five seconds (this is dependent on many factors, so it's somewhat inaccurate). You can insert any value inside the CONTENT attribute.

Because client pull has to load each file as a separate page, this effect is much more like a slideshow than fluid animation. This technique is great to use with JPEGs and PNGs, which cannot animate like GIFs.

> ### ▶ **warning**
>
> ### Client Pull Disadvantages
>
> If you implement client pull on your web site, keep in mind that your viewers might get annoyed that they've lost control of their browsers. Each page your client pull requested is stacked up in your end viewer's cache, meaning that if they want to click backwards to the page they started from, they might have a long, cumbersome path of clicking backward arrows in their way.

The Aesthetics of Animation

Before we get into the what, where, how, and why of animation, we'd like to stop a moment and consider the broader issue—the aesthetics of animation. With the exception of multimedia, the web is the first medium to combine animation and body text on a single page. For this reason, it's totally understandable that many people struggle to use animation effectively.

Here are some general, personal guidelines we would like to share:

- In most instances, animation that cycles or loops endlessly will eventually become annoying.

- If you use more than one animation on a single page, the effect may be overwhelming to the end viewer instead of impressive.

- Animation calls attention to itself much more than static images on a page. Make sure that the content of your animation is, in fact, the thing you want to receive the most attention on your page. If it isn't, the animation will effectively detract from what you're trying to communicate.

- Using animation for a button is a great idea because the animation will invite the end user to click it more than a static button.

- Make sure your animation loads quickly. If you make your audience wait too long for the animation or plug-in to load, they'll move on before ever seeing it.

Web Animation Technology Overview

In many instances, it's necessary to pick an animation technology before you create the animation. While there are many translation programs that convert one animation file format to another, it's good to have an overview of the technologies first before you commit to an animation delivery method. A brief synopsis of different animation delivery choices follows:

Animated GIFs

Animated GIFs, or for the more technically-inclined, GIF89a's, have been in existence since the late 1980s. The great news is that all the major web browsers currently support the animated GIF spec, making it possible to include these files on web pages without worrying about excluding any potential end viewers.

The GIF89a file format allows for multiple images to be stored inside a single GIF document. When displayed within browser software that recognizes the multiple images, the artwork streams in to the web page in a predetermined sequence, creating a slideshow style animation. Animated GIFs support looping (the capability to repeat multiple images indefinitely) and timing delays between frames of artwork. Animated GIFs also support limited masking, meaning that animations can use the same type of transparency supported by static GIF images.

Animated GIFs do not require plug-ins or programming and don't even require a live web connection, making them perfect for intranets and testing locally on your machine. Animated GIFs are simple to make, easy to include in HTML, and effortless for your web-viewing audience to see. They are one of the most elegant solutions to web animation and lack only in that they cannot include interactivity or sound. For an animated logo or button, however, animated GIFs are a pretty smart option.

To include animated GIFs in web pages, you'll use the standard `IMG` tag. A simple example of the code would look like this:

```
<IMG SRC="my_animation.gif">
```

Specific tools and exercises to create animated GIFs are discussed later in this chapter. Here are some recommended resources for learning how to create and code animated GIFs:

For a good tutorial on animated GIF options, visit **Royale Frazier's amazing animated GIF resource**:

http://member.aol.com/royalef/gifanim.htm.

Another great tutorial exists at (author of GIFBuilder) **Yves Piguet's site**:

http://iawww.epfl.ch/Staff/Yves.Piguet/
clip2gif-home/GifBuilder.html

Plug-Ins

Many enhanced animation options are possible through plug-ins, such as Shockwave, Flash, QuickTime, and more obscure formats. Plug-ins need to be installed by the end viewer, which can be a cumbersome process. Your audience must first download the plug-in, install it in their browser plug-in folder, and restart their browser. Plug-ins do not exactly support effortless web surfing, and the truth is many people will choose to click off a page that requires a plug-in rather than endure the bothersome interruption or time-consuming installation process.

If you do decide to choose an animation format that requires a plug-in, you should keep in mind that your choice to do so probably excludes a portion of your potential audience. You might consider including a link so that your visitors can download the plug-in before viewing the screen that requires it. Notifying your audience that you're using a plug-in is a courtesy, and creating alternate pages for those who won't bother with the plug-in installation process is a recommended practice. An exercise that walks you through some of these processes, titled "Plugging-In," follows later in this chapter.

If your end user doesn't have the plug-in installed, they'll get a broken plug-in icon. Typically, whenever you include content that requires a plug-in, you should consider providing alternate content for your users who don't have the plug-in. In the past, Internet Explorer required the OBJECT tag, and Netscape the EMBED tag when specifying plug-in content.

If you are using the OBJECT tag, you can put your alternate inside the OBJECT container. For example:

```
<OBJECT CODETYPE="application/
x-coolanimation"
  CLASSID="my_suave_animation.foo"
WIDTH=100 HEIGHT=100>

    <IMG SRC="other_animation.gif"
WIDTH=100 HEIGHT=100
      ALT="Your browser doesn't
support CoolAnim!">

</OBJECT>
```

If you are using the EMBED tag, you use the NOEMBED element inside the EMBED container:

```
<EMBED SRC="myanimation.xxx"
WIDTH=400 HEIGHT=200>
  <NOEMBED>
    Your browser doesn't support the Really
Cool plug-in!
  </NOEMBED>
</EMBED>
```

The OBJECT tag is part of the HTML 4.0 standard and is the preferred way to implement all plug-ins today, but it may not be understood by all browsers. Older Netscape browsers—before Navigator 3.0—use the EMBED tag for plug-ins and do not understand the OBJECT tag at all. It's up to you to decide which one to use. We tend to lean toward using OBJECT when we can. Just make sure you test your code on all the browsers you wish to support.

> ♦ **note**
>
> ### HEIGHT and WIDTH
>
> Whenever you use an EMBED or OBJECT tag in your HTML, you must always use the HEIGHT and WIDTH attributes to define the size for any plug-in-based content.

Java

Java has quickly become one of the most re-nowned programming languages of our time. People who would have never before considered learning a programming language are clamoring around Java's allure in unprecedented numbers. What's all the hype about, and is Java a good ani-mation delivery medium?

Java's potential benefits are almost as revolution-ary as the web itself. Java creates mini-executable programs (called applets) that are platform inde-pendent, compact enough to travel over phone wires, and able to expand on anyone's system regardless of OS, make, or model. Another great thing about Java is the two most popular browsers, Netscape and Explorer, support Java without requiring a plug-in. (At the time we wrote this chapter, Microsoft had just announced that it would discontinue support of Java. This could alter Java's appeal significantly, so stay tuned for more rocky roads in the ever changing web landscape.)

In theory, Java wins high marks for accessibility and compatibility. The reality is that we know many people who complain that their browsers still choke on Java, so our suspicion is that we'll be waiting a little longer before the Java hype matches reality. Regardless, a lot of people and companies are investing heavily in Java, which would suggest that the bugs will eventually get ironed out.

Because Java creates custom programs, it has the potential to create computational animation as opposed to sprite-based animation. This means that a Java applet could calculate a changing curve shape on-the-fly, react differently to changeable conditions, or build motion based on external input. Clearly, for the right purposes, Java as an animation delivery medium holds great promise. For simple things, such as moving buttons or animated logos, Java is overkill.

It's possible to combine Java and other animation technologies. One thing that some Java authors are doing is including plug-ins inside a Java applet that's sole purpose is to install the plug-in automatically. For this reason, Java doesn't have to be mutually exclusive from other animation delivery methods that involve plug-ins or proprietary viewing software.

In the past, Java generally used an APPLET tag to be included in HTML pages. A sample line of code that included Java-based content might look like this:

```
<APPLET="my_first_java_programming_
triumph.xxx"
HEIGHT="200" WIDTH="200">
  <IMG SRC="alternatecontent.gif"
WIDTH=200 HEIGHT=200>
</APPLET>
```

Current (HTML 4.0) standards require that you use OBJECT for Java as well. Just as with plug-ins, you will run into a lot of browsers that don't understand OBJECT for Java, so be careful to test your code on the browsers you want to support. Using the OBJECT tag, the code would look like this:

```
<OBJECT CODETYPE="application/octet-stream"
  CLASSID="my_first_java_applet.class"
  WIDTH=100 HEIGHT=100>
    <IMG SRC="alternatecontent.gif"
WIDTH=200 HEIGHT=200
      ALT="Your browser doesn't support
Java!">
</OBJECT>
```

A good starting point for learning about Java is at **Sun's site**:

http://www.sun.com/java/

JavaScript

JavaScript actually has nothing at all to do with full-fledged Java. Initially the Netscape-originated scripting product was slated to be named Live-Script. With the success of Java, Netscape decided to license the Java name from Sun so its custom scripting language could bear the same name. The similarities between Java and JavaScript end there!

Java needs to be compiled, meaning that the code is written and then goes through a post-processing routine that finalizes the code and completes the programming process. Compiled code is invisible to the end user. Any type of software on your computer is an example of compiled code—from your word processor to your imaging programs to your browser applications.

JavaScript gets compiled on your end user's machine, which means that the raw code sits inside HTML documents. This is a great boon to those interested in learning to write JavaScript because, just like HTML, you can "view the source" of any web page that contains JavaScript and then copy, paste, and personalize to your heart's content. If you plan to do this, however, it is proper netiquette to credit the original author of the JavaScript within your pages that have "borrowed" it.

JavaScript-based animation is used for many things, such as scrolling text at the bottom of a web page, rollover effects within linked artwork, or moving artwork around on a page. DHTML, covered in Chapter 14, "Navigation," supports combining Javascript with Cascading Style Sheets for creating simple animation effects.

Good JavaScript Resources:

For a great site that supplies JavaScript Tips of the Week:

http://webreference.com/javascript/960527/animation.html

Excellent tutorials:

http://www.webconn.com/java/javascript/intro/

Animated GIFs in Detail

In our opinion, working with animated GIFs is one of the most sensible choices of web animation formats to choose from. Animated GIFs include the following features:

- The capability to set looping, or number of repeats

- The capability to set delays between individual frames

- The capability to optimize the graphics by using different disposal methods

- Palettes

- Transparency

- Interlacing

Looping: As stated earlier, be careful of unlimited looping animations as they can be annoying to your audience.

Frame delays: Frame delays can be used to alter the timing of animations. The unit of measurement is 100=1 second. If you want your first frame to last 5 seconds, your next three to last 1 second each, and the last frame to last 15 seconds, your frame delays would look something like this:

```
Frame 01=500
Frame 02=100
Frame 03=100
Frame 04=100
Frame 05=1500
```

Download Speeds: The initial download time of the animated GIF will depend on your end user's connection speed, but after the animation has fully downloaded, it will depend on the processor speed of his computer. This can make for wildly different frame delay timings on different systems, regardless of what frame delays you program. Almost all GIF animation software packages support frame delays.

Optimization: Animated GIFs can be optimized, just like regular GIFs. The same rules that applied to file size savings for regular web files apply here. Like other GIFs, you want to make sure that you use as few colors as needed and try to avoid dithering or noise in your image.

Transparency and disposal methods: Disposal methods are a scary sounding term for how the animation is displayed in terms of its transparency. With a single image, this is a nonissue. A transparent image shows through to its background, and that's the end of the story.

With a multiple-frame GIF, however, this presents a bigger issue. Let's say you've animated a ball that's bouncing. If you make the ball transparent, and the image before it has already loaded, the transparency might show part or all of the frame before. Instead of the illusion of motion, the result would be the nonillusion of each frame of the ball animation visible at once.

The disposal method is what instructs the GIF animation how to display preceding frames of the animation. Disposal methods are set within whatever GIF animation software package you're using. These are the terms used by GIFBuilder to describe disposal methods. The names for these disposal methods will vary depending on which GIF animation tool you're using.

Unspecified: Use this disposal method when you aren't using transparency. It will simply present each frame in its entirety and will not yield any added optimization to the file. If I had an animation that changed images every single frame, I would use this disposal method.

Do Not Dispose: This disposal method would reveal each preceding frame of an animation. Let's say I wanted to create an animation of my name writing itself on the screen. If I left the L to draw itself only once and then used the subsequent frame to draw the Y, I would be creating a smaller file size. Use this method when you want the prior frames to show through, and you want to enjoy some file savings with no penalty to image quality.

Restore to Background: Instead of displaying the previous frame, the animation is set to show the background color or tile image of your web page.

Restore to Previous: This function is almost the same as Do Not Dispose except the first frame always stays visible underneath the rest of the animation. As of writing this book, Netscape did not properly support this function.

Palettes: Most GIF animation software allows you to create bit-depth settings. Lower bit-depth settings will result in smaller, faster animated GIFs. One problem that animated GIFs suffer from is that often the software or browser defaults to accepting a different palette for each frame, which will cause palette flashing (a psychedelic feast for the eyes, to be sure)—most likely not the effect you were wishing to see.

The best way to avoid GIF animation palette problems is to map each frame of your animation to a common palette. DeBabelizer (demos included on the <chd> CD-ROM in the Software folder) includes a feature for generating a "super palette" that creates a common GIF animation palette.

Interlacing: Adding the interlace feature to a single or multiple GIF image will cause it to look blocky until it comes into focus. We personally dislike the effect, and especially dislike the effect in the context of animation. It sort of breaks the illusion of motion to see each individual frame come into full focus, don't you think?

Richard Koman has written a short and sweet full-color title about GIF animation, with examples on a CD-ROM that should help anyone wanting to delve further into the GIF animation creation process:

GIF Animation Studio
Full Color book w/CD
Author: Richard Koman
Publisher: O'Reilly
Price: $39.95

Sound on the Web

Sound options on the web are as diverse as animation options. It's possible to program your site to provide background ambient noise, animations with sound, real-time audio on-demand, or sound that can be downloaded and played on external sound players. The following sections examine these options and other issues related to sound.

Shockwave Case Study

We created a sample synchronized sound and animation file using Macromedia Director 6.0 and saving the results as a Shockwave file. This enabled us to combine the GIF animation exercise shown earlier with synchronized and unsynchronized sound.

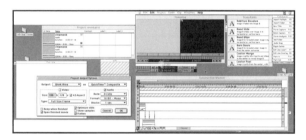

We mixed the sound in Adobe Premiere. It included a recording of Lynda's 8-year old daughter, Jamie, and some generic quack sounds, which were both stored in the AIFF file format. We figured out the timing for the quacks based on appearance of each duck in the GIF animation.

We imported each frame of the GIF animation into Macromedia Director 6.0. It enables you to combine images and sound. We saved the project as a Shockwave file with the .dcr file extension.

In order to view this file, your end user would need to install the Shockwave plug-in in their browser. It's helpful to include instructions on a page that includes a plug-in, and a link to help guide your end user to the plug-in source in the event they don't have it pre-installed.

```
<HTML>
<HEAD><TITLE>Ducks Shockwave</TITLE></HEAD>
<BODY>
<EMBED SRC="ducks.dcr" WIDTH="419"
HEIGHT="219">
</BODY>
</HTML>
```

Shockwave is much more robust than standard HTML; it enables you to include synchronized sound, rollovers with different artwork for mouse over, mouse down and mouse click, and animations that are triggered by events (needed for creating web-based games). The learning curve is high, although the results are worth it to many. One problem with Shockwave, besides the plug-in barrier, is file size. The GIF animation was only 24k. The Shockwave file was 165k. Is the sound worth it? For some purposes yes, and others no. You'll have to be the judge on your own projects!

Sound Aesthetics

Just because you can add sound to your site doesn't mean you should. Keep in mind that people have very strong musical tastes, and while you might love Balinese gamelan music as much as I do, your end viewer might prefer Martin Denny.

Our suggestion is that you are careful about looping sounds, in the event that your end viewer can't stand your choice of music or sound effect, and you are effectively driving them away. Netscape has an interesting technology demo on their site that enables the end viewer to turn on or off looping sound and/or change the type of music entirely.

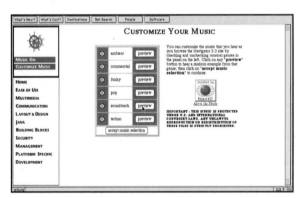

Visit http://search.netscape.com/comprod/products/navigator/
version_3.0/multimedia/audio/index.html **to view the source of
this page and other interesting sound technology demos.**

Our point is, sound can be a wonderful thing to one person, and an annoyance to another. Embedding ambient sound on a web page is discussed later in this chapter, along with techniques to enable your end user to access audio controls to turn sound on and off for your site. You might think you are adding an enhancement to your site by including automatic sound, but it's our job to tell you that others might not agree.

Getting Sound Files into Your Computer

Just like images have to be scanned or created directly in the computer, sounds have to be scanned or digitized or created from scratch as well. This is a complex or easy undertaking, depending on whether you're attempting to achieve professional-level sound or are willing to accept a few snap, crackle, and pops. Here are some ideas for obtaining sound file sources:

Capture Sound from CDs

Most sound-capture software enables you to capture sound from audio CDs. Tips for capturing from CD sources are listed later in this chapter. Be careful about copyrights and other rights—it is not legal to take sound from your favorite band and stick it on your web site or otherwise use it. For more information about copyright laws and music, check out:

http://home.earthlink.net/~ivanlove/music.html

If you're on the other end and want to create a licensing agreement for sound or music you've created, you'll find some boiler plate legal contracts in this book:

Web Developer's Guide to Sound and Music
Publisher: Coriolis Group Books
Price: $39.95
ISBN: 1-883577-95-0

Purchase Royalty Free Sound Libraries

There are zillions of web sites and CD-ROMs that include royalty-free music and sound effects. Check with your favorite search engine to find sources that you like.

Use the microphone that ships with many Macs and PCs to record your voice for narration, greetings, or sound effects

Macs and PCs often ship with microphones and simple sound editing software. This is a great way to add a personal greeting to your site. Lynda has wonderful sound bytes of her daughter singing songs and saying silly things as she was growing up that were all captured this way. Be aware, however, that professional sound designers would cringe at this recommendation! If you are planning to do professional-quality sound, use a professional! They have all kinds of equipment you won't begin to understand that do things like normalize, equalize, remove noise, mixing, dithering, resampling, and more…

Use Sound Editing Software

You can use sound editing software to produce computer generated sounds. There are dedicated sound editing packages, just like there are dedicated image editing software packages. Sound editing software can cut together disparate clips of sound, create transitions like fades and dissolves, and process the sound with effects like echo, reverb, and playing in reverse.

You might try reading the computer and sound trades to find hardware and software that fits your needs and budget. Or visit your favorite search engines to locate some online.

> ## ▶ definition

Digital Audio Terminology

Sample rates: Sample rates are measured in kilohertz (KHz). Sound editing software is where the initial sample rate settings are established. Standard sample rates range from 11.025 KHz, 22.050 KHz, 44.10 KHz, to 48 KHz. The higher the sample rate, the better the quality. The sample rate affects the "range" of digitized sound, which describes its highs and lows.

Bit-depth or sampling resolution: Sampling resolution affects quality, just like dpi resolution affects the quality of images. Standard sampling resolutions are 8-bit mono, 8-bit stereo, 16-bit mono, and 16-bit stereo.

To Stream or Not to Stream?

Streaming is the process whereby sound is downloading as it is playing. This enables your end user to hear the sound as it's downloading. Streaming is a good thing, but not always appropriate. There are times when you'll prefer to set up music archives on a site for downloading. This is especially true if you want to distribute high-quality sound that is too large in file size for smooth streaming. Streaming is appropriate for some things, and not for others. While streaming is much more convenient than downloading, your sound and music will take a quality hit in the process. Since both streaming and non-streaming audio standards still exist, this chapter will cover both topics.

If you are going to prepare audio files for downloading off your site, you'll need to know a few new tricks. We'll look at the HTML tags required to do this, how to make your movies and sounds small, and decide which types of helper applications you and your audience will need.

Making Small Audio Files

Audio on the web has most of the same limitations as images—many files are too large to hear as inline components of a page. In this event, your audience will be required to download audio files in order to listen to them, and it's your job to choose a file format and compression rate. You will base these decisions on what platform you're authoring sounds from, and how to make the files as small as possible while still sounding as good as possible.

Here's a look at the various audio standards and ways to reduce the size of audio files.

Rates and Bits

There are two components of an audio file that make it sound good (and take up space): the sampling rate and the bit depth, which is referred to as the sample resolution.

Sample rates are measured in kilohertz. The sample rate affects the range of a digitized sound, which defines its highs and lows. Higher sample rates result in larger file sizes. The sampling rate is set when the sound is digitized (captured) into the computer. Sound editing software is where the initial sample rate settings are established, and it should be set according to the type of sound being sampled. Some types of sounds can deal with lower sampling rates better. Narration, for example, doesn't depend on high and low ranges to sound good. Here are some typical sampling rates:

    8 KHz
    11 KHz
    22.05 KHz
    44.1 KHz
    48 KHz

Sampling resolution dictates how much range the sound has in highs and lows. Higher kilohertz settings results in a bigger file size. The sampling resolution is also set when the sound is digitized (captured) into the computer. Sound editing software allows users to dictate which sample resolution the sound is captured at. Because noise is introduced at lower sample rates, it's necessary to evaluate individual sound elements to see how far down the sampling resolution can be set without introducing unacceptable noise. You can create digital sound at the following resolutions:

    8-bit mono
    8-bit stereo
    16-bit mono
    16-bit stereo

Generally, when you first digitally record or "sample" a sound, you want to record it at 16-bit resolution at the 44.1 KHz sampling rate. Later, after processing the sound to your satisfaction with digital audio editing applications, you would resample the final file down to 8-bit, 22.05 KHz.

Audio File Formats

Many types of audio files are used and found on the web. Choosing which one to use is often determined by what kind of computer system and software you're authoring sounds from. Here's a breakdown of the various formats:

μ-law

μ-law used to be the only file format you'd find on the web, as it is generated by UNIX platforms. Now that Macs and PCs are the predominant platform, μ-law files are not seen as much. The sound quality is generally considered much lower than the other sound formats described here. It is used much less often now, as a result. If you are going to author μ-law files, they should be saved with an `.au` extension.

AIFF

AIFF was developed by Apple and is used on Macintoshes and SGIs. It stands for **A**udio **I**nterchange **F**ile Format. It can store digital audio at all the sample rates and resolutions possible. You'll also hear about MACE (**M**acintosh **A**udio **C**ompression/**E**xpansion), which is the built-in compression standard for AIFF files. Just like in video, the compression method you use is invisible to the end listener. It does dictate the size and quality of your end result, however. If you are going to author AIFF files, they should be saved with an `.aif` extension.

WAVE

Wave was developed by Microsoft and IBM and is the native sound file format to Windows platforms. Like AIFF, it can store digital audio at all the sample rates and resolutions possible. Basically, WAVE and AIFF files are considered equals in terms of quality and compression, and are easier to use depending on which platform you are authoring from. If you are going to author WAVE files, they should be saved with a `.wav` extension.

MPEG

MPEG audio is well respected as a high-quality, excellent audio compression file format. The only problem is that encoding MPEG requires extra hardware that is out of reach of many audio content creators. Because MPEG files aren't native to any specific platform, your audience will need to download a helper application to hear them. If you are going to author MPEG sound files, they should be saved with the `.mpg` extension.

RealAudio

RealAudio was the first example of streaming audio on the web. Streamed audio files come over the phone lines in small chunks, so the entire file doesn't have to be downloaded before it can be heard. The file can be up to one hour long because the data is coming in as you're hearing it—not downloading fully first to your hard drive. The sound quality is often compared to that of an AM radio station. Because of quality limits, it's best used for narration and not for music or other sounds. You must have the RealAudio player installed on your system to hear sounds play as soon as you click on a link that supplies real audio source material. You can author RealAudio content by using the RealAudio encoder, which can be obtained at http://www.real.com/. You won't be able to offer RealAudio files from your web site unless your provider has installed the Real server. Recently, Progressive Networks, the owners of RealAudio, have started distributing its servers for free. Contact their site for more information.

Tips for Making Web-Based Sound Files

Several free or shareware applications can convert from or to μ-law, AIFF, WAV, and MPEG files, so chances are your audience will be able to access your sounds regardless of which file format you choose to support. Typically, Mac authors will choose AIFF, PC authors will choose WAV or MPEG, and UNIX authors will pick μ-law because those are the file formats supported natively by their systems.

To properly prepare the files, however, you might want to use a sound editing program that offers features like peak level limiting, normalizing, down sampling, and dithering from 16-bit to 8-bit. Premiere is a great entry level video and sound editor, though professional videographers and sound engineers will typically own higher-end dedicated editing programs.

Here are some tips for making web-based sound files:

- Digitize at the standard audio CD sample rate and resolution (44 KHz and 16-bit). Down sample the file to the preferred sample size of 22 KHz or 11 KHz. Typically, the lower the sample rate, the less high end or duller the sound will be. For dialogue or sounds where high end doesn't matter, lowering the sample rate creates smaller files that will be of acceptable quality.

- Halving the sample rate will half the file size. Additionally, changing the file from stereo to mono cuts the file size in half. Use the Mix feature of most audio software packages to create a mono version of a stereo file.

- If the 16-bit file is still too large, you can use dithering algorithms on audio (just like on images) to take the files down to 8-bit. Dithering will add noise in the form of hiss (and in the worse case, electronic buzzing and chattering). Dithering will be most noticeable in files with silences between sounds.

- Because of the electronic noise, dithering should be avoided on dialogue. Dithering works great for rich, full music files such as hard rock and industrial. Another alternative is to re-digitize the 16-bit audio file at 8-bit by playing back and recording a prerecorded 16-bit, 44.1 KHz sound into your digitizer. Often, this creates cleaner 8-bit samples with more "punch."

- When naming audio files, as with all files being prepped for Internet distribution, they must be named with no spaces. Unlike inline images, these files are going to be downloaded by your audience. Therefore, names should be under eight characters long with room for a three-letter file extension, or Windows platform users won't get to hear them!

- Make sure you've done all your sound editing (such as mixing from stereo to mono, filtering, peak level limiting, normalizing, or down sampling) before you convert to 8-bit. If you edit an 8-bit sound and then resave it, you will add electronic noise to your file. Always start with higher bit depth, and do your editing in that file before you save or dither it to 8-bit.

HTML for Downloading Sound Files

A sound file gets the `<A HREF></A>` tag, just like its video and image-based counterparts. Unlike video, where there might be an associated thumbnail image, sounds are usually indicated by a sound icon, or hypertext. Here are a few variations, with the code you would use.

Here's the code to link your audience to a sound and let them know what file size and format it is:

```
<A HREF="snd1.aif>
<FONT SIZE=5>Click here to download this
sound!</A></FONT>
<p>
Excerpt from CD:<BR>
WebaWorld<P>
Cut: Spider<P>
AIFF Sound<BR>
:30<BR>
567k
or, if you want to add an icon, too:
<A HREF="snd1.aif>
<FONT SIZE=5><IMG SRC="ear.gif">Click here
to download this sound!</A></FONT>
<P>
Excerpt from CD:<BR>
WebaWorld<P>
Cut: Spider<P>
AIFF Sound<BR>
:30<BR>
567k
```

MSIE Audio Tags

The `BGSOUND` element is an MS Internet Explorer 2.0 enhancement. `SRC` specifies the URL of the audio file to be played. To view Microsoft's tutorial page on these tags and attributes, check out:

http://www.microsoft.com/kb/articles/q156/1/54.htm

Netscape Audio Tags

Netscape's sound tags work with their LiveAudio plug-in, which comes pre-installed in current versions of Netscape. This means that the tags all revolve around the `EMBED` tag, which is standard for all plug-in based HTML.

LiveAudio plays audio files in WAV, AIFF, AU, and MIDI formats. Audio controls appear according to the size specified in the `WIDTH` and `HEIGHT` parameters in the `EMBED` tag. To view the spec on Netscape's built-in sound options, visit:

http://home.netscape.com/comprod/products/
navigator/version_3.0/multimedia/audio/how.html

> ### ▶ note
>
> ### Cross-Browser Compatibility
>
> Now that you've reviewed the tags for each of the browsers, suppose you want to make a site that works for both?
>
> Try this:
>
> ```
> <EMBED SRC="sound.wav"
> autostart=TRUE hidden=TRUE>
> <NOEMBED><BGSOUND="sound.wav">
> </NOEMBED>
> </EMBED>
> ```

Other Sound Options

Sound is a huge subject worthy of entire books! There are many other sound options available to you for web delivery. Here is a brief synopsis of a few noteworthy ones:

QuickTime: QuickTime movies can be hidden from view, or can include control consoles. This makes their Midi-compatible file format ideal for streaming audio. Check out the specs for QuickTime sound options at:

http://www.quicktime.apple.com

Macromedia Director/Streaming Audio:
Director is one of the oldest authoring tools around for multimedia. Shockwave, a plug-in for web browsers, enables Director content to be viewed on web pages. Streaming audio is now a feature supported by the Shockwave plug-in. To develop streaming audio content, you need to learn to use Director and program interactivity with a proprietary language called Lingo. For more about Director, Shockwave, and Lingo, visit Macromedia's site:

http://www.macromedia.com/support/shockwave/

RealAudio: RealAudio is the oldest streaming and most well-known audio technology on the web. It has three components:

- The RealAudio Player plays files encoded in the RealAudio format

- The RealAudio Encoder encodes files into the RealAudio format

- The RealAudio Server delivers RealAudio over the Internet or your company network

In order to hear RealAudio files, you must have the plug-in. In order to author RealAudio files, you need to convert your sound files so they work in the RealAudio format. To download the encoder:

http://www.real.com/products/encoder.html

The RealAudio Server is the only piece of the puzzle that costs money. It enables you to distribute real audio content from your site. (Late breaking news: Progressive Networks, the owners of RealAudio, are now offering a 60-stream server for free. See http://www.real.com for more information.)

▶ chapter seventeen summary

The web promises to be a place of change, with animation and sound options getting better and easier as the medium matures. Whichever animation or sound technology path you choose to travel, always keep your site's goals and audience in mind. Although animation can add a lot to your site's appeal, it can also create exclusionary walls that only the elite few with fast speed, loads of RAM, and high-end computers can break through. Make sure your medium fits your message, use animation wisely and sparingly, and the web will be a much more inviting place.

18

Get Listed

"If you build it, they will come."
—Field of Dreams, "The Voice"

Get Listed
increasing visibility

As you've probably noticed by now, building web sites is a lot of work. The amount of time you personally devote to making your web site may shock you by the time you finish. What would be an even worse shock, however, would be if no one could find your (and/or your company's) site once your efforts were complete.

We waited until the end of the book to discuss techniques for getting listed because listing methods involve writing HTML. Now that you've studied HTML for the past 17 chapters, our recommendation to learn some new code shouldn't be too surprising or intimidating.

This chapter covers the steps required to list your site with search engines, how to ensure that "keywords" exist on your site so that it can be easily found by search engines, and how advertising banners can play a role in leading your audience to your web site.

Using Search Engines and Directories

Using a search engine or directory is a great way to find things you need to know about web design (or anything else in the universe, for that matter). If you're looking for advice, tutorials, reviews, or new software or hardware, look to the web first! It's the greatest encyclopedia ever created.

Before discussing the use of search engines and directories, it's important to learn the distinction between the two.

A **search engine** is actually a software robot (sometimes called a spider or a crawler) that constantly visits web sites, following their links and maintaining a database of where the search engine has recently visited. Because it is constantly surfing the web, a search engine is likely to have many more sites than a directory.

A **directory** is really just a large catalog built and maintained by humans. People submit their web sites to the directory, and the staff places the listings in the appropriate categories. Because all the listings in a directory are placed there intentionally, the listings in a directory are often more reliable than those found by a search engine. Knowing which type of search engine to use can help yield better search results. For example, if I wanted to help my daughter get information about barn swallows for her bird report, I would choose a spider-based search engine. It would show me all the instances of the words "barn swallow" on the web. Some subjects are too big for a global search. For example, if I wanted to find out about the GIF file format, I might choose to use a directory. This would better enable me to home in on the category file format instead of searching for the word GIF, which is so ubiquitous on the web, I doubt most search engines could even count the number of responses!

▶ **note**

The Trusting Web?

Because the web is such an easy and inexpensive place to publish, many searches will reveal large numbers of sites. Keep in mind that not all of them will be as accurate as, say, the Encyclopedia Britannica. Consider the source: Does the site appear well-researched? Are references available to where the data came from? It's anarchy out there folks! Don't believe everything you read on the web!

Search Engines:

• Digital's AltaVista:
http://www.altavista.digital.com

This search engine is probably the fastest and largest of the search engines. If you can't find it here, it's probably not on the Net.

• Wired's HotBot: http://www.hotbot.com

The newest search engine, HotBot is closely tied to its parent, *Wired* magazine. This search engine is built on a distributed-computing model that holds promise of scaling well as the web grows, which means that it is more likely to keep up with the explosive growth that the web is experiencing.

• Excite: http://www.excite.com

Excite is not the oldest and not the fastest, but it may be approaching the rank of largest. Excite recently purchased two other major search engines, and if it finds a way to combine them, it may find itself with the largest engine on the Net. Excite also licenses its search engine to smaller web sites for local searches.

• Lycos: http://www.lycos.com

The oldest search engine on the Net is still very effective. Many people use this one exclusively just because it works and they haven't bothered to try the newer engines.

Directories:

• Yahoo!: http://www.yahoo.com

Yahoo! is the defacto directory on the Net. It's the oldest and the largest, and its reputation as the best is well-deserved. Like AltaVista's search engine, if it's not listed on Yahoo!, it's not listed anywhere.

For an excellent comparison of search engines and directories, see the **Search Engine Watch Site:** http://www.searchenginewatch.com.

As well as knowing which search engines to use, it's very important to know how to use a search engine. Most of the search engines have help-based tutorials that can make all the difference. The goal of a search is to come up with the exact matches you want. Most engines fail to find the correct response or correct number of responses because the search is too broad.

Using http://www.altavista.digital.com, for example, I typed in Lynda Weinman. The search engine reported 2,487 occurrences of the name Weinman and 20,685 occurrences of the name Lynda. But when I put my name in quotes, as "Lynda Weinman", the search engine knew to report only occurrences of that exact combination of words and yielded the more accurate result of 600.

For a tutorial on using search engines:

• http://searchenginewatch.com/powersearch.htm

• http://www.webreference.com/content/search/

For a list of search engine tutorials, visit:

• http://www.searchenginewatch.com/tutorials.htm

List Your Site with Search Engines

Most search engines have easy procedures for accepting web site listings. This is usually a free but time-consuming process. Most search engines require that you summarize your site in 20 words or less. It can help to assemble a list of "keywords" before you visit these sites so that you can easily fill out their submittal forms. Here are some URLs to contact:

- http://www.yahoo.com
- http://altavista.digital.com
- http://www.excite.com
- http://www.lycos.com
- http://guide.infoseek.com
- http://www.mckinley.com
- http://www.webcrawler.com
- http://www.opentext.com
- http://www.hotbot.com
- http://www.infomarket.ibm.com
- http://www.nln.com
- http://www.shareware.com

If you don't want to do the work of contacting multiple search engines yourself, there are several online services that will submit your site listing to many different search engines. The charge for this service varies, so it's best to contact the listing agencies yourself. We're sure there are more, but here are some listing services we're aware of:

- http://www.submit-it.com/
- http://www.position-it.com/
- http://www.webpromote.com

META Tag for Search Engines

Many search engines use automatic processes called "robots" or "spiders" that constantly troll the web looking for sites to list. The processes automatically determine which categories to list the sites under by scanning your HTML to figure out what content exists on your site. (See "Using Search Engines and Directories" in Chapter 2.)

Using the META tag, you can create special headers for your web pages that will help the automated services list your site more accurately. Use the NAME and CONTENT attributes to form the correct headers, like this:

```
    <HEAD><TITLE>Sample Meta Page</TITLE>
1.  <META NAME="description"
    CONTENT="Ducks In A Row is a
    wholesaler to retail stores of
    custom rubber stamps designed by
    renowned illustrator Joan Farber.">
2.  <META NAME="keywords"
    CONTENT="rubber stamps, greeting
    cards, illustration, hobby, design,
    crafts, birth announcements, wedding
    announcements, creativity">
3.  </HEAD>
```

1. The "description" header is where you enter a one or two sentence description of your site. You can write a longer description, but most search engines limit their scans to 20 or so words.

2. The "keywords" header is for the keywords that best describe your site. You can include more keywords, but most search engines limit their scans to 20 or so words.

3. The META tag must always go inside the HEAD element.

If you'd like to see this HTML in full, open the meta.html file from the chap18 folder of the <chd> CD-ROM.

If you'd like to visit a free online service that will automatically create META tags for search engine purposes, visit:

http://vancouver-webpages.com/VWbot/mk-metas.html

Here's a thorough index of all the different headers you can set with META:

http://vancouver-webpages.com/META/

Ad Banners: From Heaven or Hell?

Ad banners are really nothing more than buttons that link to other sites. Making an ad banner is not the hard part—understanding the dynamics of creating a successful ad banner campaign is. Just like TV commercials, ad banners can be either incredibly annoying or incredibly entertaining.

The purpose of an ad banner is to direct the end user to click on it. The success of an ad banner is usually judged by its number of "click-through hits" (how many people clicked on it). Ad banners are a form of commercialism, and commercialism is usually annoying unless it fulfills another function besides selling. If an ad banner provides entertainment or education, it is normally more accepted than if its sole purpose is to sell.

There are no standard specs for ad banners. You might be asked to design a variety of sizes for a variety of purposes; it is up to the site in which your ad banner is placed to dictate the size standard. Most ad banners are accepted in GIF or JPEG format. Animated GIFs (see Chapter 17, "Animation & Sound") are a great file format for ad banners.

There are numerous markets for ad banners. If you are a professional web designer, you may have clients request that you design an ad for them. Strangely enough, many web design firms make more money creating ad banners than entire web sites! If you are responsible for your own site's promotion, you may want to place your ad banners on other sites. There are no set advertising rates.

Many traditional advertising agencies set up web-based ad programs for their clients, and the methods for where to place these ads is as diverse as the web itself. If you want to place an ad banner on someone's site, the best method is to contact the webmaster to get information about their rates, formats, and size requirements.

To educate yourself on how much it costs to place ad banners, and what some of the major issues are, pay a visit to http://www.doubleclick.net, a web advertising placement service.

If you want some inspiration, or want to read the opinion of a dedicated ad banner critic, check out Microscope/Best Ads on the Web Weekly Ad Review: http://www.pscentral.com/index2.html. This site has ratings, reviews, and archives for ad banners that demonstrate creative excellence.

▶ note

Exchanging Links for Links

There are several banner-exchange programs on the Net that provide free banner advertising for your site. In exchange for your banner appearing in the program, you agree to run the program's banners on your site. Typically, the more times the program banner is viewed on your site, the more times your banner will appear on other sites.

One of the first programs of this type is Trade Banners, run by Resource Marketing: http://resource-marketing.com/banner.html. (The founder of Trade Banners says he got the idea from reading Bill Weinman's *The CGI Book*, New Riders Publishing, 1996.)

Trade Banners' Guidelines

- Using the instructions at http://resource-marketing.com/banner.html, you create a banner of the right dimensions.

- Use their form to generate a user name and password for yourself.

- Upload the banner with their available automatic uploader.

- Trade Banners will then give you a snippet of HTML you must place on a web page somewhere, to display the program's banners. This is important because the program will reward you with more displays of your banners as theirs are displayed on your site.

There are many other banner exchange services; you can find an exhaustive list by entering "banner exchanges" in the search form at **Yahoo!:** http://www.yahoo.com. Visit the **LinkExchange Digest:** http://www.ledigest.com/ for a moderated discussion list with the goal to provide helpful information to those engaged in building traffic to their web sites. Discussions center on the topic of web site promotion on the Internet and World Wide Web, which includes banner advertising.

Click Here

Click Here, written by Raymond Pirouz and developed with Lynda Weinman, is the best resource available for understanding how to increase your site's appeal and increase your click-throughs and hits. This book has so much great advice that it's a must-read for anyone interested in marketing their site effectively. Raymond is responsible for some of the coolest ad banners on the web, and knows of what he speaks!

Click Here includes advice on how to:

- Make sure that banner advertisements do not cause your audience to leave your site

- Evaluate your audience effectively

- Create imaginative copy

- Integrate animation

- Make small and fast loading ad banners

Click Here, by Raymond Pirouz and published by New Riders Publishing (ISBN 1-56205-792-8), is a definitive book about creating effective web banner campaigns.

▶ chapter eighteen summary

Sadly, it isn't enough to master HTML and web design. Unless you understand some of the methods available to promote your site, you run the risk of creating something wonderful that no one will see.

This chapter covered the use of the META tag and its description and keywords headers. We touched on the advantages and pitfalls of ad banners, and made suggestions that should get you going on the path to better visibility. Be sure to visit the links listed in this chapter to learn more about this important aspect of web publishing.

*"You can't fake quality
any more than you can fake a good meal."*
—William Burroughs (1914-1997)

Good HTML
making it work right

The purpose of a web page is the message. The message of the page is sometimes in the words, sometimes in the images, and sometimes in other elements of the page, but the message is rarely in the code itself. So why bother writing good HTML?

The way the message is delivered can have impact on how it is received. HTML is one link in the chain of media that carries your web-based message. Ask a painter why they choose one type of canvas over another, or ask a musician why they choose a type of string or reed or bow for their instrument. You may not be able to discern what type of strings are on a guitar by listening to a recording (although Bill says he can), but it does affect the overall quality of the experience.

Good HTML

Why Write Good HTML?

There are both subjective and objective reasons for writing good HTML. Subjectively, it may or may not be important to you that you do as good a job as possible on every level of every project that you take on. We feel that doing something well is its own reward, but we recognize that it's not always practical.

On the other hand, there are some very pragmatic reasons to at least make sure that your HTML is correct, in spite of the fact that it may already work. As a practical illustration, here's a page that works fine in browsers that are based on the original NCSA Mosaic (including Microsoft Internet Explorer and older Netscape browsers), but does not work in the current Netscape:

```
<HTML>
<HEAD>
<TITLE> Bad Table </TITLE>
</HEAD>
<BODY BGCOLOR=WHITE>

<TABLE>
<TR><TD>

<H1>This entire page is in a table. </H1>

</BODY>
</HTML>
```

Notice that there is no end tag for the TABLE element (/TABLE). This works just fine in Microsoft Internet Explorer.

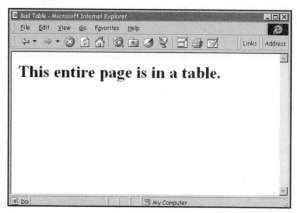

bad-table.html **in Microsoft Internet Explorer 4.**

The end tag is required for the TABLE element— according to both the table specification and the HTML 4 specification. Netscape Navigator (beginning with version 3) won't display a table without an end tag.

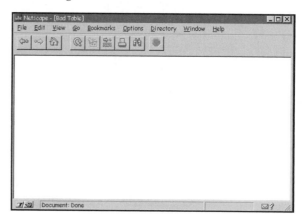

bad-table.html **in Netscape Navigator 3.**

In the case of the missing table end tags, there were a number of web sites that virtually "disappeared" when Netscape 3 was released. A similar problem happened with body backgrounds with the release of Netscape 4 (see the example later in this chapter).

HTML Terminology

Probably the single most important thing you can learn about HTML is the distinction between tags, attributes, containers, and elements. Once you understand these terms, it will be much easier for you to tell when your code is correct. Here's what they mean:

Tag: A tag is an HTML instruction enclosed in angle-brackets (e.g., `<P>`). Some tags may also have end tags that begin with a slash (e.g, `</P>`). The tag without the slash is sometimes called a begin tag or a start tag.

Attribute: An attribute is a property that works with a tag. Attributes go after the name of the tag, and before the right angle-bracket. For example, if you want a horizontal rule without the shading effect, you can use the `NOSHADE` attribute (e.g., `<HR NOSHADE>`). Some attributes have values like the `ALIGN` attribute (e.g., `<P ALIGN=CENTER>`), or the `HREF` attribute for the destination of a link (e.g., `<A HREF="http://www.htmlbook.com">`). The part to the right of the equal sign is called the **value** of the attribute.

Container: A container is a tag that has both a beginning and an end, and generally has content that is placed in between. The beginning of a container is marked by a begin tag, and the end is marked by an end tag. For example, `TITLE` is a container because it has a distinct beginning and end. The content of a `TITLE` is in between the tags, (e.g., `<TITLE> content </TITLE>`). In contrast, `BR` is not a container because it has no end tag; everything it needs is between the brackets of the `BR` tag.

Some containers, like `P` for instance, do not require end tags if the end can be accurately determined by context. But they are still containers because they have content and a limited scope of operation. In the absence of an end tag, the effects of a `P` tag end when the next `P`, or some other tag that is not valid content for `P`, is encountered. This is true of many containers with optional end tags.

Element: Element is a general term for a chunk of HTML that can be treated as a distinct unit in some context. A container, along with all its content, can be considered an element (e.g., `<STRONG> This is a STRONG element </STRONG>`). A stand-alone tag, like `IMG`, can also be considered an element (e.g, `<IMG SRC="element.gif">`). This term is used as a convenience of nomenclature whenever we need to discuss some distinct part of a document or code.

What You See AIN'T What You Get

WYSIWYG editors are a wonderful invention, and we encourage you to use them for prototyping your web sites. The use of a WYSIWYG editor can greatly reduce the amount of time it takes you to layout, view, and re-layout your site while you are in the process of designing it.

But for production work, we implore you to be careful. An excellent example is the "disappearing background" problem that happened with the release of Netscape 4.

The HTML specification allows for one BODY element per page. Both the begin and end tags are optional (that is, the body of the document can be implied if the default properties are acceptable), but you are not allowed to have more than one BODY element in a single document.

However, there are evidently some WYSIWYG editors that don't follow this rule. We have seen a number of sites with two or more BODY tags, and this has created problems with some browsers.

The early release versions of Netscape Navigator 4 would ignore the additional BODY tags and only use the attributes of the first one. For example, consider this HTML:

```
<HTML>
<HEAD>
<TITLE> Bad Body </TITLE>
</HEAD>
<BODY>
<BODY background=white.gif>

<H1>This document has two BODY tags.
</H1>

</BODY>
</HTML>
```

This document has two BODY tags.

bad-body.html **in an early release of Navigator 4.**

Later releases of Navigator 4 (beginning with 4.03) accumulate attributes from BODY tags. But you really can't count on a browser guessing what your HTML means when it's not correct. For instance, Mosaic 3.0 (the last version) also shows a gray background for this error.

The best defense is good HTML.

Cleaning Up After a WYSIWYG Editor

As an example of the sorts of things you need to watch out for with your WYSIWYG editors, I have created a little page using Alaire's Home Site. Here's a screenshot of the page in the editor:

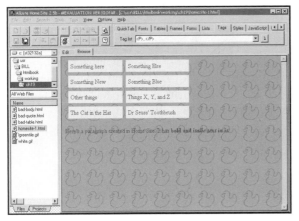

homesite-1.html **in Home Site's viewer.**

Now here's what it looks like in Netscape Navigator:

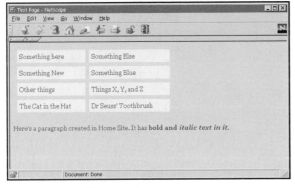

homesite-1.html **in Netscape Navigator.**

Notice anything different?

Let's look at the code and see if we can fix it up.

```
<!-- This document was created with
HomeSite 2.5 -->
<!DOCTYPE HTML PUBLIC "-//W3C//DTD
HTML 3.2 Final//EN">

<HTML>
<HEAD>
       <TITLE>Test Page</TITLE>
</HEAD>

<BODY BACKGROUND="/usr/BILL/htmlbook/
working/ch19/lgreentile.gif" TEXT="Navy"
LINK="Olive" VLINK="#999933"
ALINK="Silver">

<TABLE BORDER=0 CELLSPACING=8
CELLPADDING=5 VALIGN="TOP"
BGCOLOR="#CCFF99" WIDTH=350>
<TR>
       <TD>Something here</TD>
       <TD>Something Else</TD>
</TR>
<TR>
       <TD>Something New</TD>
       <TD>Something Blue</TD>
</TR>
<TR>
       <TD>Other things</TD>
       <TD>Things X, Y, and Z</TD>
</TR>
<TR>
       <TD>The Cat in the Hat</TD>
       <TD>Dr Seuss' Toothbrush</TD>
</TR>
</TABLE>

<P> Here's a paragraph created in Home
Site. It has <B>bold and <I>italic text
in it.</I></B></P>

</BODY>
</HTML>
```

The most glaring problem in the HTML on the previous page is that the background image didn't show up in the browser (even though it was fine in the editor's preview screen). Notice that the URL for the BACKGROUND attribute is not a proper relative URL. This is easy to fix, but it shows a flaw in the editor.

The point here is for you to expect flaws in the code that the editor puts out. Always expect to have to fix the code that an automated tool generates. Some people say that the tools will get better, and that's probably true. But the fact remains that after 20 years of trying, there are still no automated tools for any programming language that do as good a job as a careful human. The promise of artificial intelligence that can better a human's creative efforts is yet to be realized. We don't expect that overall situation to change any time soon.

We also noticed that the tool doesn't break its lines to fit an 80-column screen (this is important for those of us who use multiple platforms to work on the same files), and the use of tabs for indenting is also not portable. Again, these are easy problems to fix, but they require effort. Alway prepare for more complicated pages to have more complicated problems.

As a rule, we feel that the WYSIWYG editors are excellent tools for prototyping, but not for production use. If you must create and maintain a large and complex web site with constantly updated information (like a large news or periodical site), we recommend that you either create custom tools for that particular site (as most of the large major sites do) or retain the services of a programmer to do that for you. For large one-time sites that won't change much over time, you can prototype with your WYSIWYG editor and then modify or rewrite the code by hand to make it correct.

Common HTML Gotchas

There are many common HTML "gotchas" that we see a lot on the web. Of course, each of us has our own peculiar predilection for error, and as such, our problems will not always fit nicely into a pre-ordained list. But we've compiled a short list that you may want to watch out for anyway. These are some of the most frequent HTML problems we see on public web pages.

What's in a Quote?

Quotation marks (either double " or single ') are used in HTML to contain the values of some attributes. When do you need to use quotes? If all the characters in the value are either letters (a–z), numbers (0–9), periods (.), or hyphens (-), you don't need to use quotes. If you have any characters besides those mentioned, you need to use quotes. When in doubt, use the quotes. They can't hurt.

The most common type of value that requires quotes, and often doesn't have them, is the URL (for example, `<A HREF=http://www.htmlbook.com/>Creative HTML Book Site</A>` is not legal HTML because it is missing the quotes around `"http://www.htmlbook.com/"`). Most URLs have slashes, colons, and other characters that must be quoted to be correct. We are not looking forward to the day Netscape starts requiring quotes around attributes that really need them. A lot of the web will need to be fixed!

Hanging Quotes

On the other hand, you have to use your quotes in matching pairs! For example, this doesn't work well:

```
<HTML>
<HEAD>
<TITLE> Bad Quotes </TITLE>
</HEAD>
<BODY BGCOLOR=white>

<P>This is a <a href="link.html">link</a>
with a missing quote.

<P>You won't see any of this text until
<a href="link.html">after</a>
this other link.

</BODY>
</HTML>
```

Notice the missing quote in the first link. You don't see it? Look here then:

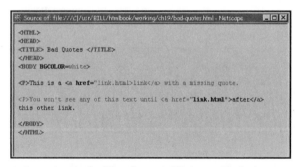

bad-quote.html **in the View:Source of Netscape Navigator.**

The folks at Netscape gave us this handy-dandy missing quote finder in their **View**:**Source** menu, starting with version 3. When you view the source of a document with a missing quote, all the text that's affected will be highlighted and blinking. Try this for yourself: find the bad-quote.html file in the chap19 folder of the <chd> CD-ROM and look at it in Netscape Navigator. Be sure to select **View**:**Source**. See it blink? Tell a friend.

Straddling Containers

Considering the fact that a container—along with all of its content—is a single distinct element, it is reasonable that one container can have other containers as part of its content. That's why you can write something like this:

```
<P> This paragraph has <EM> emphasized
and <STRONG> strong </STRONG> text </EM>
inside it. </P>
```

In this perfectly legal example, the P element contains the EM element, which in turn contains the STRONG element.

Now consider this example:

```
<P> This paragraph has <EM> emphasized
and <STRONG> strong </EM> text </STRONG>
inside it. </P>
```

Here we decided to end the EM element before the end of the STRONG element. What's wrong with this picture? Notice that EM no longer contains STRONG (nor does STRONG contain EM). The elements are straddling each other.

It is perfectly legal to have one element contain another element, as long as the inner element is valid content for the outer element. But it is not legal to have two elements straddle each other. As with many common HTML errors, this may work in some browsers today, and it may not work in later versions of those same browsers.

Line-endings

Unless you are actually trying to make your HTML unreadable (some people actually want to make it a little tougher to "steal" their code), you should keep your lines to under 80 characters wide (75 is a good rule of thumb). That makes it easier to view your source code in the browser and to work on it on the widest possible variety of platforms.

You should also set your editor to use UNIX line-endings, especially if your server runs under UNIX.

There are three different types of line endings:

Carriage Return—used by Macs

Carriage Return + Line Feed—used by PCs

Line Feed only—used by UNIX

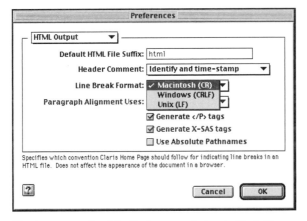

Here's an example of the Preference window in Claris Home Page for the Macintosh. Its default was Macintosh, but you can and should change it to UNIX.

The line-endings are invisible to you, but visible to your web server and many HTML editors. You will probably find the setting for Unix line endings in the Preferences menu of your HTML editor or word processor.

▶ note

A Brief History of Line Endings

Now that your lines are less than 80 characters wide, you may be surprised to find that users of different operating systems may still see your code as one long line of text. The reason for this? The operating system has to know where the end of the line is, and different operating systems tend to represent the end of a line of text differently.

Internally, text—like everything else on a computer—is represented as a string of bytes. In order to display distinct lines of text on a screen or a printer, the computer must know where one line ends and the next one begins. It does this with a special character called a line ending, which tells the computer, "this line is over now," kind of like the return key on your keyboard.

Originally, before video displays existed, computers used mechanical printers that looked like massive typewriters to display text. The printer used a rubberized platen (also called a carriage) to position the paper on the printer. A special character called carriage-return (CR) would move the paper to the left margin, and another special character called line-feed (LF) would advance the paper to the next line. Because of this, lines of text were traditionally ended with a CR-LF sequence.

By the time UNIX became popular, video displays were more prevalent, and UNIX systems began using LF alone to represent line-endings (like many features of UNIX, this was designed to save space).

In contrast, the designers of the Macintosh OS opted to use CR alone to represent line-endings. PCs, because their operating system is based on DOS, which was based on CP/M, which was based on older DEC operating systems that go back to the days of line-printers, use the full CR-LF sequence.

Line Ending	System
UNIX	LF-only
MacOS	CR-only
DOS/Windows	CR-LF sequence

The bottom line is simple. If you want your code to be truly portable, use UNIX line endings wherever possible.

Entities vs. Numbers vs. Embedded Characters

HTML uses something called "entities" for characters outside of the normal English alpha-numeric character set (there's a nice list of them here: http://luna.bearnet.com/ iso8859-1.html). Named entities (e.g., © for the © symbol) are preferable to the numbered entities (e.g., © also for the © symbol), because the names will work on multiple platforms. The numbered entities will not work on all platforms, nor will characters embedded from your word processor. (Some WYSIWYG editors use numbered entities by default.)

Color Names not Browser Safe

Remember that the named colors (e.g., "teal") are not all browser safe. Most of them will dither in 256-color systems. Use the hexadecimal colors instead (e.g., "#669999"). (Some WYSIWYG editors use color names by default.) In-depth information about browser-safe colors is in Chapter 4, "Web Color."

Empty ALT Attributes

The ALT attribute for the IMG tag is an important tool for making your pages work on non-graphical systems, but an empty ALT attribute (e.g., ALT="") can be annoying. In non-graphical systems, it will take up space without saying anything; and in many graphical systems, it will show an empty little tool-help (usually a little yellow square) when the mouse is passed over the graphic. If you don't have content for your ALT attributes, don't include them at all. (Some WYSIWYG editors insert these by default.)

Case-Sensitive File Names

Most web servers run under UNIX, which uses case-sensitive file names. Most web authors use Mac or PC platforms, which do not use case-sensitive file names. That means that if you have a file named Image.gif and you refer to it as IMAGE.GIF, it may work on your system at home, but not on the web. We recommend that you use all lowercase file names, just to avoid problems. They're easier to type anyway.

Relative vs. Absolute Links

Always use relative links when possible. (See Chapter 12, "Organization.") Absolute links will become a major headache for you when you eventually have to move your site to another machine, or even just another folder on the same machine. (Some WYSIWYG editors use absolute links by default.)

▶ chapter nineteen summary

Writing good HTML is not required. No one is going to force you to do it, and most people won't even notice if you don't. But it's a discipline that will serve you well in the long run. It will make life easier on you when new tools and browsers are released and whenever you need to make substantial changes to your site (which will likely be more often than you plan for).

In this chapter, you have seen some of the common problems with incorrect HTML, and how to correct them when they are encountered.

We encourage you to use the HTML Reference in the back of this book as an authoritative source.

Reference
HTML 4.0

The purpose of this reference is to document the HTML 4.0 language, as thoroughly and accurately as possible. By providing this reference, we hope to give you a place to turn when you need to know the details of a particular tag or attribute. This reference grew out of our own personal need to have all the elements of HTML documented in one place, clearly and concisely.

The HTML DTDs (**D**ocument **T**ype **D**efinition) distributed by the W3C (**W**orld **W**ide **W**eb **C**onsortium) are neither convenient nor concise. The DTDs document the exact syntax of the language—if you can figure out how to read them—but their descriptions of the purposes of the various elements and attributes are either lacking in detail, or missing entirely. This reference is designed to fill that need by clearly and succinctly stating the purpose and usage of every HTML element and attribute.

HTML 4.0 Reference

▶ reference (table of contents)

Section 1: *Introduction*

What Version of HTML Is This?

The information in this reference is based on the "Transitional" version of the HTML 4.0 DTD, as of 17 August 1997. We recognize that this is a "work in progress," and as such it may change before (and if) it is eventually finalized. On the other hand, it is our experience that definitions are rarely finalized in the rapidly-changing world of the current web, nor are the browser vendors likely to implement any particular HTML specification completely or accurately.

We chose not to use the "strict" version of the DTD because it omitted many elements that are in common use today, such as FONT and CENTER, and many more attributes commonly used for formatting and decoration, such as BACKGROUND and BGCOLOR. We don't think the W3C (**W**orld **W**ide **W**eb **C**onsortium) intended for people to stop using these features—on the contrary, we believe that they are trying to encourage the software makers to implement full support for the more powerful and flexible formatting capabilities of HTML style sheets. Until that happens, however, designers and programmers will continue to use the features that are supported by the largest numbers of users, and that is what we have documented here.

Are They Tags or Elements?

There is some measure of controversy regarding the proper terminology for referring to the parts of an HTML document. Some HTML purists actually take offense when the term "Tag" is applied more broadly than they feel is correct. The current HTML specification includes this comment:

> "**Elements are not tags.** Some people refer incorrectly to elements as tags (e.g., "the P tag"). Remember that the element is one thing, and the tag (be it start or end tag) is another. For instance, the HEAD element is always present, even though both start and end HEAD tags may be missing in the markup."

If you can understand what they mean by that, then more power to you! We find it confusing. We have chosen to use the word "Tag" more loosely than some would like, for several reasons:

• The word "Tag" is small and neat, and fits nicely in the headings of our tables.

• The word "Element" can be ambiguous. Logically, the P element includes all the content of the container, whereas the P tag does not.

• Our goal is to have our readers understand how to write good HTML. We feel this can be better accomplished by using familiar terminology.

With that in mind, here's our definitions:

Tag: Everything between the "<" and ">" characters. For example, `<P>` is a P tag; `<IMG SRC="foo.gif">` is an IMG tag. `</P>` is an end tag for the P element.

Element: A unit of markup. For example, this is a P element:

```
<P> Here's a small paragraph. </P>
```

We recognize that this seems persnickety, but when you get as much email as we do, you do what you can to answer it in advance.

The Concept of Content

When you are deciding what tags to use, and where to use them, it is useful to understand what it means to put content into an HTML element. In order to understand that, let's take a look at the concept of content.

The content of an HTML element is all the stuff between the start tag and the end tag. Some HTML elements are simply tags. They don't have an end tag, and so they cannot have any content. The tag itself, along with its attributes, is the element. For example, this IMG tag is the whole element:

```
<IMG SRC="foo.gif">
```

Other elements have content. These elements are called *containers*. The content is what goes inside the container, that is, between the start and end tags. For example, consider this P container:

```
<P> This is the content of a paragraph element. </P>
```

The content of the P container is the sentence of text. There are some things that are allowed inside a P container, and some other things that are not.

If everything inside the container is allowed, then the browser will generally do what you expect. On the other hand, if you try to put something inside that is not allowed, the element will automatically end just before the disallowed content.

For example, consider this code:

```
<P> Text here <H1> Heading </H1> Other text here. </P>
```

In this example, the paragraph ends just after "Text here," because the H1 element is not allowed inside a paragraph. The "Other text here" part is not in a paragraph at all, and the </P> end tag is superfluous (and ignored).

With an element like P, that doesn't require an end tag, the browser automatically ends the element when it encounters disallowed content. So it's common, and perfectly legal, to write our previous example like this:

```
<P> Text here
<H1> Heading </H1>
<P> Other text here.
```

The first paragraph ends where the heading begins, and the next paragraph starts right after the heading.

General Content Models

What is, and what is not, allowed inside a given element is called the *Content model* for that element. Some elements allow just a few certain elements as content, while others are far more generalized.

There are two general content models which are shared by a large number of elements. Because so many elements use these same models, we use a shorthand notation to refer to them.

The *Text* content model includes written text, and all the elements that can be included in a paragraph. You will notice that most of these elements can be rendered *inline* with text. These are the tags that are part of the *Text* content model:

Text Content Model

```
A/ACRONYM/APPLET/B/BASEFONT/BDO/BIG/BR/CITE/CODE/DFN/EM/FONT/I
IFRAME/IMG/KBD/MAP/OBJECT/Q/S/SAMP/SCRIPT/SMALL/SPAN/STRIKE/STRONG
SUB/SUP/TT/U/VAR
```

The *Block* content model includes mostly tags that are not rendered inline, or are used to enclose other *Text* content. It does not include written text. The *Block* content model includes all the following tags:

Block Content Model

```
ADDRESS/BLOCKQUOTE/CENTER/DIR/DIV/DL/FIELDSET/FORM/H1/H2/H3/H4/H5/H6
HR/ISINDEX/MENU/NOFRAMES/NOSCRIPT/OL/P/PRE/TABLE/UL
```

For example, consider the P element. According to the specification the allowable content for a P element is *Text*. So, anything in the *Text* content model is allowed in a P element, and other stuff is not. So if we try to put, say an H1 element inside a P element, the P element will simply end, and the H1 element will begin:

```
<P> Text here
<H1> Heading </H1>
<P> Other text here.
```

In this example, the H1 tag will create an automatic end to the P element because H1 is not part of the *Text* content model. The text, "Other text here" is in a separate paragraph.

Reference Layout

The HTML reference itself is organized in tables of Tags and Attributes. The tables are designed to quickly tell you what you need to know, in order to use the elements described.

The **Tag** tables have the following structure:

Tag	End Tag	Content	Attributes	Description / Notes
TAG	*Req or Opt*	Content-model	ATTRIBUTE ATTRIBUTE ATTRIBUTE	A description of what the tag is for, with special notes where necessary.

Tag: The name of the tag. The name of the tag is always the part immediately following the left angle-bracket (`<TAG>`).

End tag: *Req* if the end tag is required, *Opt* if the end tag is optional. Optional end tags can be omitted if the end of the element is otherwise obvious. Usually, that means that the element will end at the first occurrence of any content that is not allowed within the element.

Content: What content (if any) is allowed within this element. This may be the name of one or more of the general content models (*Text or Block*), or it could be a list of tags. Sometimes it will be a combination of content models and tags.

Attributes: A list of the attributes that can be used with this tag.

Description/Notes: A description of the tag and its usage, sometimes with additional notes about the tag.

The **Attribute** tables have the following structure:

Attribute	Required	Value(s)	Parent Tag	Description / Notes
ATTRIBUTE	*Req or Opt*	Value	TAG TAG TAG	A description of what the attribute is for, and how to use it.

Attribute: The name of the attribute. Attributes always go after the name of the tag, but still between the angle-brackets: For example, in `<P ALIGN=RIGHT>`, the name of the tag is `P`, the name of the attribute is `ALIGN`, and `RIGHT` is the value of the `ALIGN` attribute. Tags can have more than one attribute, e.g., `<IMG SRC="foo.gif" ALIGN=RIGHT BORDER=0>`.

Required: *Req* if the attribute is required, *Opt* if the attribute is optional.

Value(s): The allowed value(s), if any, for this attribute.

Parent Tag: The tag(s) that this attribute may be used with. One attribute name may be listed more than once, if it is used differently for different parent tags. For example, the `SRC` attribute is used for `HR` (the thickness of the rule), `FONT` (the size of the font), and `INPUT` (the number of characters wide to render the text box).

Description/Notes: A description of the attribute, its values, and how to use them.

In the **Categorized Reference** section, tags are listed in a logical order, with the most significant tags at the top of the table. Sometimes those are the most commonly used tags; other times they are the tags which contain other tags in that category.

Attributes in the Categorized Reference section are organized alphabetically by *Parent Tag*, and then by *Attribute* within *Parent Tag*. Hopefully this will allow you to quickly find related tags and attributes.

In the **Alphabetical Reference** section, all 89 tags are listed alphabetically, followed by an alphabetical listing of all associated attributes.

GLOBAL ATTRIBUTE GROUPS

There are 89 different tags, and 117 different attributes (176, counting different uses of the same attribute for different tags) in the HTML 4.0 specification. Some of the attributes can be used by nearly all of the tags, so it made sense to group them here, rather than redundantly list them in every category. We call these the *Global Attribute Groups*.

The global attributes are further broken down into three groups, as they are generally applicable in these groups. The groups are Core, Internationalization, and Event.

Core Attributes

The core attributes are those that apply to style sheets and advisory titles. These are the most globally applicable attributes. In the reference tables, we refer to this group as *Core*.

The *Core* attributes may be used with all tags except the following:

BASE/BASEFONT/FRAME/FRAMESET/HEAD/HTML/IFRAME/META/PARAM/SCRIPT/STYLE/TITLE

For example, to apply a style class to a paragraph, you would use the CLASS attribute like this:

`<P CLASS="classname"> This paragraph has class. </P>`

The *Core* attributes are CLASS, ID, STYLE, and TITLE:

Attribute	Required	Value(s)	Parent Tag	Description / Notes
CLASS	*Opt*	List of Class names	*All tags except:* BASE/BASEFONT FRAME/FRAME-SET/HEAD/HTML IFRAME/META PARAM/SCRIPT STYLE/TITLE	Specifies a class (or list of classes) for applying style-sheet properties to the element.
ID	*Opt*	#Unique-ID	"	Unique ID for an individual instance of an element. The "#" character must be used before the value.
STYLE	*Opt*	Style	"	Style information to associate with the element.
TITLE	*Opt*	Text	"	An advisory title. May display as a *tool-tip* or be spoken or rendered some other way for non-visual browsers.

Internationalization Attributes

The internationalization attributes are used to apply language-specific formatting to elements of text. In the reference tables, we refer to this group as *Int'l*.

The *Int'l* attributes may be used with all tags except the following:

`APPLET/BASE/BASEFONT/BDO/BR/FONT/FRAME/FRAMESET/HR/IFRAME/PARAM/SCRIPT`

For example, if you want a paragraph to read right-to-left, you can use the `DIR` attribute:

`<P> Paul McCartney's voice: <Q DIR=RTL> I'm dead! </Q>`

Which would look like this, in a browser that supports the `DIR` attribute:

Paul McCartney's voice: "!daed m'I"

The *Internationalization* attributes are `DIR` and `LANG`:

Attribute	Required	Value(s)	Parent Tag	Description / Notes
DIR	*Opt*	LTR or RTL	*All tags except:* APPLET/BASE BASEFONT/BDO BR/FONT/FRAME FRAMESET/HR IFRAME/PARAM SCRIPT	Direction of text. LTR = Left to Right RTL = Right to Left
LANG	*Opt*	Lang-ID	"	Language identifier, as specified in RFC1766.

Event-Related Attributes

The event-related attributes are for linking various visual elements with events, for use with scripting languages such as JavaScript (ECMA-Script). In the reference tables, we refer to this group as *Event*.

The *Event* attributes may be used with all tags *except* the following:

APPLET/BASE/BASEFONT/BDO/BR/FONT/FRAME/FRAMESET/HEAD/HTML/IFRAME/ISINDEX/META/PARAM
SCRIPT/STYLE/TITLE

For example, if you want a JavaScript routine to run whenever the mouse passes over a link, you can use the ONMOUSEOVER attribute like this:

<A HREF="overthere.html" ONMOUSEOVER="doit(overthere)">

The *Event* attributes are ONCLICK, ONDBLCLICK, ONKEYDOWN, ONKEYPRESS, ONKEYUP, ONMOUSEDOWN, ONMOUSEMOVE, ONMOUSEOUT, ONMOUSEOVER, and ONMOUSEUP:

Attribute	Required	Value(s)	Parent Tag	Description / Notes
ONCLICK	*Opt*	Script	*All tags except:* APPLET/BASE BASEFONT/BDO BR/FONT/FRAME FRAMESET/HEAD HTML/IFRAME ISINDEX/META PARAM/SCRIPT STYLE/TITLE	When the mouse is clicked on the element.
ONDBLCLICK	*Opt*	Script	"	When the mouse is double-clicked on the element.
ONKEYDOWN	*Opt*	Script	"	When a key is pressed down within the element.
ONKEYPRESS	*Opt*	Script	"	When a key is pressed *and* released within the element.
ONKEYUP	*Opt*	Script	"	When a key is released in the element.
ONMOUSEDOWN	*Opt*	Script	"	When a mouse button is depressed on the element.
ONMOUSEMOVE	*Opt*	Script	"	When the mouse cursor moves out of the element's display space.
ONMOUSEOVER	*Opt*	Script	"	When the mouse cursor moves into the element's display space.
ONMOUSEUP	*Opt*	Script	"	When a mouse button is released over the element.

Section 2: *Categorized Reference*

Document Structure Elements

These elements are used to set up the structure of an HTML document.

Tag	End Tag	Content	Attributes	Description / Notes
HTML	*Opt*[1]	HEAD/BODY PLAINTEXT	*Int'l* VERSION	Outer container for an HTML document.
HEAD	*Opt*[1]	TITLE/ISINDEX BASE/META/LINK SCRIPT/STYLE	*Int'l* PROFILE	Container for document header.
BASE	*None*	None	HREF/TARGET	Base URL for dereferencing relative URLs. Valid only within HEAD.
BODY	*Opt*[1]	All	*Core Int'l Event* BACKGROUND BGCOLOR/TEXT LINK/VLINK ALINK/ONLOAD UNLOAD	Container for document body.
LINK	*None*	None	*Core Int'l Event* CHARSET/HREF REL/REV/TYPE MEDIA/TARGET	Defines relationships with other documents.
META	*None*	None	*Int'l* HTTP-EQUIV NAME/CONTENT SCHEME	Meta-information describing properties of the document. Generates HTTP header when used with HTTP-EQUIV. Valid only within HEAD.
STYLE	*Req*	Style Sheet	*Int'l* TYPE MEDIA/TITLE	Container for style-sheet definitions.
TITLE[2]	*Req*	Document title	*Int'l*	Provides a title for the document.

1 Both start- and end-tags are optional for HTML, HEAD, and BODY.
2 Exactly one TITLE tag (more than one is an error) is required in every HTML document.

Attributes (Document Structure Elements)

Attribute	Required	Value(s)	Parent Tag	Description / Notes
HREF	*Req*	URL	BASE	URL for the document base
TARGET	*Opt*	Window name	BASE/LINK	The target window or frame for BASE and LINK. The following magic target names are also supported: _blank a new blank window _self the same window as the link _parent the parent frameset _top the full body of the window
ALINK	*Opt*	Color	BODY	Color of active links (e.g. while the mouse button is pressed on the link).
BACKGROUND	*Opt*	URL	BODY	URL for the background graphic.
BGCOLOR	*Opt*	Color	BODY	Background color of the document page.
LINK	*Opt*	Color	BODY	Color of unvisited links.
ONLOAD	*Opt*	Script	BODY	When the document is finished loading.
ONUNLOAD	*Opt*	Script	BODY	When the document is unloaded (e.g., another document has been called for).
TEXT	*Opt*	Color	BODY	Color of the document text.
VLINK	*Opt*	Color	BODY	Color of visited links.
PROFILE	*Opt*	URL	HEAD	A meta-data profile.
VERSION	*Opt*	URL	HTML	Link to the DTD for this document. Redundant with use of DOCTYPE.
CHARSET	*Opt*	*Name of Character Set*	LINK	Character encoding of the destination link.

Attributes (Document Structure Elements) *continued ...*

Attribute	Required	Value(s)	Parent Tag	Description / Notes
HREF	*Opt*	URL	LINK	URL for the linked resource.
REL	*Opt*	Rel	LINK	The forward relationship for a LINK element.
REV	*Opt*	Rel	LINK	The reverse relationship for a LINK element.
CONTENT	*Req*	Text	META	Content of meta information.
HTTP-EQUIV	*Opt*	Text	META	Name for HTTP header.
NAME	*Opt*	Text	META	Name for meta information.
SCHEME	*Opt*	Text	META	The scheme to be used in interpreting the content. Depends on context.
TITLE	*Opt*	Text	STYLE	Title for the style.
MEDIA	*Opt*	Text	STYLE/LINK	Destination media for style. Defaults to ALL.

Font Markup Elements

The font markup elements are used to change the appearance of the characters on the screen, for parts of text. All of these elements may use the Core, Int'l, and Event attributes.

Tag	End Tag	Content	Attributes	Description / Notes
B	*Req*	Text	*Core Int'l Event*	Bold text.
BIG	*Req*	Text	*Core Int'l Event*	Larger size.
I	*Req*	Text	*Core Int'l Event*	Italic.
S	*Req*	Text	*Core Int'l Event*	Strike-through (e.g. strike-through) (synonym for STRIKE).
SMALL	*Req*	Text	*Core Int'l Event*	Smaller size.
STRIKE	*Req*	Text	*Core Int'l Event*	Strike-through (e.g. strike-through) (synonym for S).
TT	*Req*	Text	*Core Int'l Event*	Teletype (fixed width).
U	*Req*	Text	*Core Int'l Event*	Underline.

Phrase Markup

The phrase markup elements are used to indicate certain common parts of speech. All of these elements may use the *Core*, *Int'l*, and *Event* attributes. These elements may render a certain way on visual browsers, but may also have an effect with non-visual applications, such as Braille browsers or speech synthesizers.

Use these instead of the font markup elements, where possible, to make your site more accessible to the visually impaired.

Tag	End Tag	Content	Attributes	Description / Notes
ACRONYM	*Req*	Text	*Core Int'l Event*	Acronym (e.g., HTML, WWW, etc.). Useful for spelling checkers, speech synthesizers, and other tools. May be rendered in SMALL-CAPS.
CITE	*Req*	Text	*Core Int'l Event*	Citation.
CODE	*Req*	Text	*Core Int'l Event*	Fixed width (for rendering code).
DFN	*Req*	Text	*Core Int'l Event*	Defining instance of a term.
EM	*Req*	Text	*Core Int'l Event*	Emphasis (usually *italic*).
KBD	*Req*	Text	*Core Int'l Event*	Keyboard—text to be typed by a user.
Q	*Req*	Text	*Core Int'l Event*	Inline Quotation (may be rendered with quotation marks).
SAMP	*Req*	Text	*Core Int'l Event*	Sample output from a program.
STRONG	*Req*	Text	*Core Int'l Event*	Strong emphasis (usually **bold**).
VAR	*Req*	Text	*Core Int'l Event*	Variable or argument in a program.

List Elements

These are the elements for making lists. Ordered lists are automatically rendered with numbers (ordinal or roman); Unordered lists are generally rendered with bullets; and Definition lists are for lists of terms with associated definitions. Menu and Directory lists are generally rendered like Unordered lists, although they may be rendered differently on some browsers.

Tag	End Tag	Content	Attributes	Description / Notes
OL	*Req*	LI	*Core Int'l Event* TYPE/START COMPACT	Ordered list.
UL	*Req*	LI	*Core Int'l Event* TYPE/COMPACT	Unordered List.
DL	*Req*	DT DD	*Core Int'l Event* COMPACT	Definition list.
MENU	*Req*	LI –(Block)	*Core Int'l Event* COMPACT	Menu.
DIR	*Req*	LI –(Block)	*Core Int'l Event* COMPACT	Directory list.
DD	*Opt*	Text Block	*Core Int'l Event*	The definition of a term.
DT	*Opt*	Text	*Core Int'l Event*	A term being defined.
LI	*Opt*	Text Block[1]	*Core Int'l Event* TYPE/VALUE	List item.

1 The LI element within DIR or MENU can only contain Text content.

Attributes (List Elements)

Attribute	Required	Value(s)	Parent Tag	Description / Notes
COMPACT	*Opt*	None	DIR/DL/OL MENU/UL	Render the list more compactly. Depreciated.
VALUE	*Opt*	Number	LI	Reset number sequence to the value given.
TYPE	*Opt*	Bullet style	LI/OL/UL	Style of bullet or numbering style. For OL lists: 1 — 1, 2, 3, 4, . . . a — a, b, c, d, . . . A — A, B, C, D, . . . i — i, ii, iii, iv, . . . I — I, II, III, IV, . . . For UL lists: disc — ● square — ■ circle — ○
START	*Opt*	Number	OL	Starting sequence number.

Block Elements

Block elements are generally containers for text. They are used for applying formatting or designating purpose to a block of text at a time.

Tag	End Tag	Content	Attributes	Description / Notes
DIV	Req	Block	Core Int'l Event ALIGN	Null container for applying style and common attributes to block-level content.
P	Opt	Text	Core Int'l Event ALIGN	Paragraph.
CENTER[1]	Req	Block	Core Int'l Event	For centering (alias for <DIV ALIGN=CENTER>).
ADDRESS	Req	Text + P	Core Int'l Event	Logical markup for addresses.
BLOCKQUOTE	Req	Block	Core Int'l Event CITE	For quoted passages (usually indented).
H1 H2 H3 H4 H5 H6	Req	Text	Core Int'l Event ALIGN	Six different levels of headings.
PRE	Req	Text – (APPLET BASEFONT/BIG FONT/IMG OBJECT/SMALL SUB/SUP)	Core Int'l Event WIDTH	Preformatted text.

[1] CENTER was introduced in Netscape Navigator in version 1.1, before DIV was conceived. It is so widely deployed by Netscape and other browser vendors that it has been included in the HTML specification since version 3.2. CENTER is implemented as a synonym for <DIV ALIGN=CENTER>.

Attributes (Block Elements)

Attribute	Required	Value(s)	Parent Tag	Description / Notes
ALIGN	Opt	LEFT/CENTER RIGHT/JUSTIFY	DIV/H1/H2/H3 H4/H5/H6/P	Alignment of the block of text. Defaults to LEFT.
CITE	Opt	URL	BLOCKQUOTE/Q	Source document or message with information about the quotation.
WIDTH	Opt	Number	PRE	Number of characters wide for the display of fixed-width data.

Special Text-Level Elements

These are miscellaneous elements that are valid content as part of a block of text, but are not actually rendered as text.

Tag	End Tag	Content	Attributes	Description / Notes
A	*Req*	Text –(A)[1]	*Core Int'l Events* ACCESSKEY CHARSET/COORDS[2] HREF/NAME ONFOCUS/ONBLUR REL/REV/SHAPE TABINDEX TARGET/TITLE	Anchor for a hypertext link or a named target for hypertext links.
APPLET	*Req*	Text +(PARAM)	CODEBASE/CODE NAME/ALT/ALIGN HEIGHT/WIDTH HSPACE/VSPACE	Embed Java applet.
AREA	*None*	None	*Core Int'l Events* SHAPE/COORDS HREF/NOHREF ALT/TARGET TABINDEX ACCESSKEY	Hotzones for client-side image map.
BASEFONT	*None*	None	ID/SIZE COLOR/FACE	Sets the default size of text.
BDO	*Req*	Text	*Core* LANG/DIR	Override direction of text.
BR	*None*	None	*Core Int'l Event* CLEAR	Force a line break. Moves point of text to the beginning of the next available line.
FONT	*Req*	Text	*Core Int'l Event* SIZE/COLOR/FACE	Sets the appearance of text.
IMG	*None*	None	*Core Int'l Event* SRC/ALT/ISMAP LONGDESC/ALIGN HEIGHT/WIDTH BORDER/HSPACE VSPACE/USEMAP	An embedded image.
MAP	*Req*	AREA	*Core Int'l Event* NAME	Client-side image map.

1 Nested A elements are disallowed.
2 The SHAPE and COORDS attributes are only valid for A within an OBJECT element.

Special Text-Level Elements *continued ...*

Tag	End Tag	Content	Attributes	Description / Notes
OBJECT	*Req*	Text Block PARAM	*Core Int'l Event* DECLARE/CLASSID CODEBASE/DATA TYPE/CODETYPE ARCHIVE/STANDBY ALIGN/HEIGHT WIDTH/BORDER HSPACE/VSPACE USEMAP/SHAPES NAME/TABINDEX	Generic mechanism for including objects.
PARAM	*None*	None	ID/NAME/VALUE VALUETYPE/TYPE	Named parameters that can be read with Java's getParameter() method.
SPAN	*Req*	Text	*Core Int'l Event*	Null-container for applying styles to inline text-level content.
SUB	*Req*	Text	*Core Int'l Event*	Subscript.
SUP	*Req*	Text	*Core Int'l Event*	Superscript.

Attributes (Special Text-Level Elements)

Attribute	Required	Value(s)	Parent Tag	Description / Notes
CHARSET	*Opt*	Name of Character Set	A	Character encoding of the destination link.
HREF	*Opt*	URL	A	The target URL of a hyperlink.
ONBLUR	*Opt*	Script	A	When focus is removed from the element.
ONFOCUS	*Opt*	Script	A	When the element receives the focus.
REL	*Opt*	Rel	A	The forward relationship for the linked resource.
REV	*Opt*	Rel	A	The reverse relationship for the linked resource.
TITLE	*Opt*	Title	A	A title string for the hyperlink.

Attributes (Special Text-Level Elements) *continued ...*

Attribute	Required	Value(s)	Parent Tag	Description / Notes
COORDS	*Opt*	Coordinates	A[3]/AREA	List of coordinates, in pixel units, according to the given shape, e.g.: shape = default shape = rect coords = "*left-x, top-y, right-x, bottom-y*" shape = circle coords = "*center-x, center-y, radius*" shape = poly coords = "$x_1,y_1, x_2,y_2, x_3,y_3, ...$"
SHAPE	*Opt*	RECT/CIRCLE POLY/DEFAULT	A/AREA	Declares the shape of the area. DEFAULT indicates the entire image (use DEFAULT first to overlay the other shapes on top of it). May be used with the A element only within OBJECT.
TABINDEX	*Opt*	Number	A/AREA	Tabbing sequence for keyboard use.
TARGET	*Opt*	Window name	A/AREA	The target window or frame for hyperlinks. The following magic target names are also supported: _blank a new blank window _self the same window as the link _parent the parent frameset _top the full body of the window
ACCESSKEY	*Opt*	Text (single character)	A/AREA BUTTON/INPUT LABEL/LEGEND	Assigns an access (shortcut) key to the associated element. Pressing this key will assign focus to the associated element.
NAME	*Req*	Anchor name	A/MAP	The name of an anchor or client-side image map, for use with a fragment identifier (#) in a hyperlink.
ALT	*Opt*	Alternate text	APPLET	Alternate text for display in circumstances where the applet or graphic control cannot be rendered.
CODE	*Req*	Applet File	APPLET	The name of the file that contains the applet's compiled subclass. This file is relative to the CODEBASE location, if specified (otherwise it is relative to the URL of the document). It cannot be an absolute URL
CODEBASE	*Opt*	URL	APPLET	Base URL for resolving relative URLs for this applet. Specifically used for resolving the CODE URL.

3 COORDS can be used with the A element only within an OBJECT element.

Attributes (Special Text-Level Elements) *continued ...*

Attribute	Required	Value(s)	Parent Tag	Description / Notes
HEIGHT	*Req*	Pixels	APPLET	The height of the applet's display space on the screen. Used to reserve space for the applet on the page so that the page can be laid out before applet is executed.
NAME	*Opt*	Name	APPLET	A name for the applet instance. This allows multiple applets on the same page to communicate with each other.
WIDTH	*Req*	Pixels	APPLET	The width of the applet's display space on the screen. Used to reserve space for the applet on the page so that the page can be laid out before applet is executed.
ALIGN	*Opt*	TOP/MIDDLE BOTTOM/LEFT RIGHT	APPLET/IMG INPUT/OBJECT	Alignment of the element relative to surrounding text.
HSPACE	*Opt*	Pixels	APPLET/IMG OBJECT	The size of the horizontal gutter space around the image. Set this to zero to suppress the horizontal gutter.
VSPACE	*Opt*	Pixels	APPLET/IMG OBJECT	The size of the vertical gutter space around the image. Set this to zero to suppress the vertical gutter.
HREF	*Opt*	URL	AREA	The destination of the hypertext link.
NOHREF	*Req*	*None*	AREA	Declares the area of a client-side imagemap to be a dead zone.
ALT	*Req*[4]	Alternate text	AREA/IMG	Text associated with the image or area for use by text-only browsers and non-visual user agents that cannot display images.
DIR	*Opt*	LTR or RTL	BDO	Direction for overridden text.
CLEAR	*Opt*	LEFT/RIGHT/ALL	BR	Move down past floating images. LEFT clears to the left margin; RIGHT clears to the right margin; ALL clears to both margins.
COLOR	*Opt*	Color	FONT	Sets the color of text.
FACE	*Opt*	*Text*	FONT	Comma-separated list of font names.

4 Yes, that's right, the ALT attribute is required for IMG and AREA in this iteration of the HTML 4.0 specification. We expect this item to generate some more debate before it's finalized. We see this as another example of the HTML committee working in a vacuum—we don't expect people to start including ALT text for their single-pixel spacing GIFs anytime soon.

Attributes (Special Text-Level Elements) *continued ...*

Attribute	Required	Value(s)	Parent Tag	Description / Notes
SIZE	*Opt*	Number	FONT	A number in the range 1–7 that specifies the size of displayed text. As an attribute to the FONT element, SIZE may be a relative number in the form +*n* or -*n*, where the resulting size will be relative to the default size or BASEFONT size.
BORDER	*Opt*	Pixels	IMG	The size of the border when the image is used as a hypertext link. Set this to zero to suppress the border.
HEIGHT	*Opt*	Pixels	IMG	The width of the image. Some browsers use this to reserve space for an image so that the page can be laid out before images are downloaded.
ISMAP	*Opt*	None	IMG	Indicates that this image is a server-side image map. Only valid when the image is within an A (anchor) element with an HREF attribute.
LONGDESC	*Opt*	URL	IMG	Link to a long description.
SRC	*Req*	URL	IMG	Location of the image.
WIDTH	*Opt*	Pixels	IMG	The height of the image. Some browsers use this to reserve space for an image so that the page can be laid out before images are downloaded.
USEMAP	*Opt*	URL	IMG/OBJECT	URL fragment identifier that points to a MAP element for a client-side image map.
ARCHIVE	*Opt*	List of URLs	OBJECT	Preload resources for OBJECT or APPLET. Note: List is comma-separated for APPLET, and space-separated for OBJECT.
BORDER	*Opt*	Pixels or Percentage	OBJECT	The size of the border when the object is used as a hypertext link. Set this to zero to suppress the border.
CLASSID	*Opt*	URL	OBJECT	URL for specific implementation.
CODEBASE	*Opt*	URL	OBJECT	Base URL for resolving relative URLs for this object. Specifically used for the CLASSID URL.

Attributes (Special Text-Level Elements) *continued ...*

Attribute	Required	Value(s)	Parent Tag	Description / Notes
CODETYPE	*Opt*	MIME	OBJECT	MIME-type for the object specified by CLASSID. Defaults to the value of the TYPE attribute.
DATA	*Opt*	URL	OBJECT	Location for the object's data.
DECLARE	*Opt*	None	OBJECT	Declare OBJECT only.
HEIGHT	*Opt*[5]	Pixels	OBJECT	The height of the object's display space on the screen.
SHAPES	*Opt*	None	OBJECT	Object has shapes for a client-side imagemap.
STANDBY	*Opt*	Text	OBJECT	Message to display while loading the object.
WIDTH	*Opt*[5]	Pixels	OBJECT / PARAM	The width of the object's display space on the screen.
TYPE	*Opt*	MIME	PARAM	MIME type.
NAME	*Opt*	Parameter Name	PARAM	Name of parameter.
VALUE	*Req*	Parameter Value	PARAM	Value of the parameter.
VALUETYPE	*Opt*	DATA/REF/OBJECT	PARAM	How to interpret VALUE. Defaults to DATA.

5 Technically, the HEIGHT and WIDTH attributes are not required for OBJECT, but in practice many browsers will not display the object if HEIGHT and WIDTH are omitted.

Forms Elements

The elements for creating forms and widgets.

Tag	End Tag	Content	Attributes	Description / Notes
FORM	*Req*	All	*Core Int'l Event* ACTION/METHOD ENCTYPE ONSUBMIT ONRESET/TARGET ACCEPT-CHARSET	Outer container for all form fields.
INPUT	*None*	None	*Core Int'l Event* TYPE/NAME VALUE/CHECKED DISABLED READONLY/SIZE MAXLENGTH/SRC ALT/USEMAP ALIGN/TABINDEX ACCESSKEY ONFOCUS/ONBLUR ONSELECT ONCHANGE ACCEPT	Generalized tag for all non-container input fields.
SELECT	*Req*	OPTION	*Core Int'l Event* NAME/SIZE MULTIPLE DISABLED TABINDEX ONFOCUS/ONBLUR ONCHANGE	Container for OPTION list.
OPTION	*Opt*	Alphanumeric content	*Core Int'l Event* SELECTED DISABLED/VALUE	Container for individual options.
TEXTAREA	*Req*	Alphanumeric content	*Core Int'l Event* NAME/ROWS COLS/DISABLED READONLY TABINDEX ONFOCUS/ONBLUR ONSELECT ONCHANGE	Container for multi-line text input field.

Forms Elements *continued ...*

Tag	End Tag	Content	Attributes	Description / Notes
BUTTON	*Req*	Text + Block – Forms – (A)	*Core Int'l Event* NAME/VALUE TYPE/DISABLED TABINDEX ACCESSKEY ONFOCUS/ONBLUR	A button for use with forms. Richer presentation possibilities than INPUT type buttons.
FIELDSET	*Req*	Text Block LEGEND	*Core Int'l Event*	Grouping form controls.
LABEL	*Req*	Text –(LABEL)	*Core Int'l Event* FOR/DISABLED ACCESSKEY ONFOCUS/ONBLUR	For attaching labels to form control elements.
LEGEND	*Req*	Text	*Core Int'l Event* ALIGN ACCESSKEY	Assigns a caption (legend) to a FIELDSET.

Attributes (Forms Elements)

Attribute	Required	Value(s)	Parent Tag	Description / Notes
ACCESSKEY	*Opt*	Text (single character)	A/AREA/BUTTON INPUT/LABEL LEGEND	Assigns an access (shortcut) key to the associated element. Pressing this key will assign focus to the associated element.
TABINDEX	*Opt*	Number	A/AREA/BUTTON INPUT/OBJECT SELECT TEXTAREA	Tabbing sequence for keyboard use.
ONBLUR	*Opt*	Script	A/BUTTON/INPUT LABEL/SELECT TEXTAREA	When focus is removed from the element.
ONFOCUS	*Opt*	Script	A/BUTTON/INPUT LABEL/SELECT TEXTAREA	When the element receives the focus.
DISABLED[1]	*Opt*	None	BUTTON/INPUT LABEL/OPTION SELECT TEXTAREA	Make the control unavailable. May be "grayed out" in some browsers.
ACCEPT	*Opt*	MIME	FORM	List of MIME-types allowed by the server processing this form. Used for FILE type form elements.

1 Some browsers may allow you to enable and disable widgets with a script, like JavaScript (ECMAScript).

Attributes (Forms Elements) *continued ...*

Attribute	Required	Value(s)	Parent Tag	Description / Notes
ACCEPT-CHARSET	*Opt*	List	FORM	List of acceptable character encodings for the server processing this form.
ACTION	*Opt*	URL	FORM	Location of CGI program for handling form input.
ENCTYPE	*Opt*	Content-type	FORM	Defaults to "application/x-www-form-urlencoded".
METHOD	*Opt*	POST/GET	FORM	Method of submitting data to HTTP server. Defaults to GET.
ONRESET	*Opt*	Script	FORM	When the form is reset.
ONSUBMIT	*Opt*	Script	FORM	When the form is submitted.
TARGET	*Opt*	Window name	FORM	The target window or frame for hyperlinks. The following magic target names are also supported: _blank a new blank window _self the same window as the link _parent the parent frameset _top the full body of the window
ROWS	Req	List	FRAMESET	Comma separated list of heights for the rows of frames. The number of rows in this list will be used to determine the number of frames in the document.
ALIGN	*Opt*	TOP/MIDDLE BOTTOM/LEFT RIGHT	INPUT	Alignment of the element relative to surrounding text.
ALT	*Opt*	Alternate text	INPUT	Alternate text for display in circumstances where the applet or graphic control cannot be rendered.
CHECKED	*Opt*	None	INPUT	Valid only for RADIO and CHECKBOX widgets. If specified, the default state will be true.
MAXLENGTH	*Opt*	Number	INPUT	The maximum number of characters that can be typed into a TEXT or PASSWORD input field.
SIZE	*Opt*	Number	INPUT	The amount of space assigned for this input field. Valid only for types TEXT and PASSWORD.
SRC	*Opt*	URL	INPUT	The location of the image for an IMAGE type widget.

Attributes (Forms Elements) *continued ...*

Attribute	Required	Value(s)	Parent Tag	Description / Notes
TYPE	*Opt*	TEXT/PASSWORD CHECKBOX/RADIO SUBMIT/RESET FILE/HIDDEN IMAGE	INPUT	Type of widget to use for form element. Defaults to TEXT.
USEMAP	*Opt*	URL	INPUT	URL fragment identifier that points to a MAP element for a client-side image map.
VALUE	*Opt[2]*	Value	INPUT/BUTTON	A default value for this widget.
NAME	*Req[3]*	Widget name	INPUT/OBJECT SELECT/TEXTAREA	The name used to identify data from this widget.
ONCHANGE	*Opt*	Script	INPUT/SELECT TEXTAREA	When the value of the element changes.
ONSELECT	*Opt*	Script	INPUT/TEXTAREA	When text is selected within the widget.
FOR	*Opt*	ID-value	LABEL	Explicitly associate a label with a control.
ALIGN	*Opt*	TOP/BOTTOM LEFT/RIGHT	LEGEND	Alignment of the legend relative to the group of form controls.
SELECTED	*Opt*	None	OPTION	Indicates that this option is selected by default.
VALUE	*Opt*	Alphanumeric	OPTION	The value of the option when selected. Defaults to the content of the OPTION container.
MULTIPLE	*Opt*	None	SELECT	Indicates that multiple items may be selected at a time.
COLS	*Req*	Number	TEXTAREA	The number of visible columns in the text area.
READONLY	*Opt*	None	TEXTAREA/INPUT	Data can be selected, but not modified.

3 The NAME attribute is required for all input types except SUBMIT and RESET.

Table Elements

These are the elements for creating tables. Tables can be used for displaying tabular information, or for relative positioning of visual content.

Tag	End Tag	Content	Attributes	Description / Notes
TABLE	*Req*	CAPTION/COL COLGROUP/THEAD TFOOT/TBODY	*Core Int'l Event* ALIGN/BGCOLOR BORDER/WIDTH CELLSPACING CELLPADDING COLS/FRAME RULES/SUMMARY	Outer container for table.
CAPTION	*Req*	Text	*Core Int'l Event* ALIGN	Captions and figures within tables.
COL	*None*	None	*Core Int'l Event* SPAN/WIDTH ALIGN/CHAR CHAROFF/VALIGN	For sharing attributes among table columns.
COLGROUP	*Opt*	COL	*Core Int'l Event* SPAN/WIDTH ALIGN/CHAR CHAROFF/VALIGN	Groups of table columns, for sharing attributes.
THEAD	*Opt*	TR	*Core Int'l Event* ALIGN/CHAR CHAROFF/VALIGN	For grouping table content. May allow browsers to independently scroll the body of a table.
TFOOT	*Opt*	TR	*Core Int'l Event* ALIGN/CHAR CHAROFF/VALIGN	For grouping table content. May allow browsers to independently scroll the body of a table.
TBODY[1]	*Opt*	TR	*Core Int'l Event* ALIGN/CHAR CHAROFF/VALIGN	For grouping table content. May allow browsers to independently scroll the body of a table.

1 Both the begin- and end-tags of the TBODY element are optional. The TBODY element will exist by default, if a TR element is included directly within a TABLE element.

Table Elements *continued* ...

Tag	End Tag	Content	Attributes	Description / Notes
TR	*Opt*	TD/TH	*Core Int'l Event* BGCOLOR/ALIGN CHAR/CHAROFF VALIGN	Defines rows. At least one TR is required for each table.
TH	*Opt*	Block (including nested tables)	*Core Int'l Event* ABBR/AXIS/AXES NOWRAP/BGCOLOR ROWSPAN/COLSPAN WIDTH/HEIGHT ALIGN/CHAR CHAROFF/VALIGN	Table heading cell.
TD	*Opt*	Block (including nested tables)	*Core Int'l Event* ABBR/AXIS/AXES NOWRAP/BGCOLOR ROWSPAN/COLSPAN WIDTH/HEIGHT ALIGN/CHAR CHAROFF/VALIGN	Table data cell.

Attributes (Table Elements)

Attribute	Required	Value(s)	Parent Tag	Description / Notes
ALIGN	*Opt*	TOP/BOTTOM	CAPTION	Positions the caption at the top or bottom of the table. More than one CAPTION tag per table is an error.
SPAN	*Opt*	Number	COL	Number of columns spanned by group.
WIDTH	*Opt*	Pixels	COL/COLGROUP	Width of the column or default width of the COLGROUP.
ALIGN	*Opt*	LEFT/CENTER RIGHT/JUSTIFY CHAR	COL/COLGROUP TBODY/TD/TFOOT TH/THEAD/TR	Alignment of content within the cell(s). Defaults to LEFT.
CHAR	*Opt*	Character	COL/COLGROUP TBODY/TD/TFOOT TH/THEAD/TR	Alignment character for use with ALIGN=CHAR. Defaults to decimal point character for current language.
CHAROFF[2]	*Opt*	*Unknown*	COL/COLGROUP TBODY/TD/TFOOT TH/THEAD/TR	Offset to first occurrence of alignment character.
VALIGN	*Opt*	TOP/MIDDLE BOTTOM/BASELINE	COL/COLGROUP TBODY/TFOOT THEAD/TR	Sets the vertical alignment of content within the cells of the table row. Defaults to MIDDLE.

2 It is not currently clear how the CHAROFF attribute will be used. As of this writing, there are not any browsers supporting the ALIGN=CHAR feature.

Attributes (Table Elements) *continued ...*

Attribute	Required	Value(s)	Parent Tag	Description / Notes
SPAN	*Opt*	Number	COLGROUP	Default number of columns in group.
ALIGN	*Opt*	TOP/BOTTOM LEFT/RIGHT	LEGEND	Alignment of the legend relative to the group of form controls.
ALIGN	*Opt*	LEFT/CENTER RIGHT	TABLE	Alignment of data within the table.
BGCOLOR	*Opt*	Color	TABLE	Sets the background color for a table.
BORDER	*Opt*	Pixels	TABLE	Number of pixels for the size of the table's border. Defaults to no border if the attribute is not used, or one pixel if the attribute is used without a value.
CELLPADDING	*Opt*	Pixels	TABLE	Sets the space between the border and the content of cells.
CELLSPACING	*Opt*	Pixels	TABLE	Sets the spacing between cells in the table (and consequently, the thickness of the borders between cells).
COLS	*Opt*	Number	TABLE	Number of columns in the table. Used by some browsers to speed up table rendering.[3]
FRAME	*Opt*	VOID/ABOVE BELOW/HSIDES LHS/RHS/VSIDES BOX/BORDER	TABLE	Which parts of the table frame to include.
RULES	*Opt*	NONE/GROUPS ROWS/COLS/ALL	TABLE	Specifies which rules to display between table cells. Defaults to NONE. Depreciated.
SUMMARY	*Opt*	Text	TABLE	Summary statement for non-visual browsers.
WIDTH	*Opt*	Pixels or Percentage	TABLE	Sets the overall width of the table, in pixels or a percentage of the width of the page (as *n*%).
ABBR	*Opt*	Text	TD/TH	Abbreviated name for table cell.
AXES	*Opt*	List of ID values	TD/TH	Used with ID attribute to relate table cells for hierarchical tables.
AXIS	*Opt*	Text	TD/TH	Relates a group of header cells for hierarchical tables structures.

3 Netscape Navigator 4.x also uses the COLS attribute to specify that the table should be rendered with the newer, more accurate, table rendering engine. The table will render more precisely according to the HTML 4 table model, but it will not render the same way on older versions of Navigator. In other words, if you use COLS, and you care how your table looks in different versions of Navigator, be sure to test your table on Navigator 3 and 4.

Attributes (Table Elements) *continued ...*

Attribute	Required	Value(s)	Parent Tag	Description / Notes
BGCOLOR	*Opt*	Color	TD/TH	Sets the background color for a table cell.
COLSPAN	*Opt*	Number	TD/TH	Causes the cell to span a number of columns.
HEIGHT	*Opt*	Pixels	TD/TH	Sets the height of the cell in pixels.
NOWRAP	*Opt*	None	TD/TH	Prevents word-wrapping within the cell.
ROWSPAN	*Opt*	Number	TD/TH	Causes the cell to span a number of rows.
VALIGN	*Opt*	TOP/MIDDLE BOTTOM/BASELINE	TD/TH	Sets the vertical alignment of content within the cell. Defaults to MIDDLE.
WIDTH	*Opt*	Pixels	TD/TH	Sets the width of the cell in pixels.

Frames Elements

Frames are distinct sub-windows within a visual browser. Each sub-window is effectively a separate browser environment.

Tag	End Tag	Content	Attributes	Description / Notes
FRAMESET[1]	*Req*	FRAME/FRAMESET NOFRAMES	TITLE/ROWS COLS/ONLOAD ONUNLOAD	Outer container for the frames.
FRAME	*None*	None	TITLE/SRC MARGINWIDTH MARGINHEIGHT SCROLLING NORESIZE/NAME FRAMEBORDER	Tag describing an individual frame.
NOFRAMES	*Req*	Non-frames document	*Core Int'l Event*	Container for a document that will be seen by non-frames-aware browsers.
IFRAME	*Req*	Block	TITLE/NAME FRAMEBORDER MARGINWIDTH MARGINHEIGHT SCROLLING ALIGN/HEIGHT WIDTH/SRC	Inline frame (sub-window).

1 A frame document has no BODY. If any allowable content for a BODY element appears before a FRAMESET element, a BODY will be implied and the FRAMESET will be ignored.

Attributes (Frames Elements)

Attribute	Required	Value(s)	Parent Tag	Description / Notes
FRAMEBORDER[2]	*Opt*	YES/NO	FRAME	Whether or not the borders for a particular frame are displayed with bevels.[3] Defaults to Yes.
MARGINHEIGHT	*Opt*	Value	FRAME	Height of the top and bottom margins for the frame.
MARGINWIDTH	*Opt*	Value	FRAME	Width of the left and right margins for the frame.
NORESIZE	*Opt*	None	FRAME	If present, does not allow resizing of the frame.
TITLE	*Opt*	Text	FRAME/FRAMESET IFRAME	An advisory title, as for anchors.

2 The current HTML 4 specification is inconsistent in its description of the BORDER and FRAMEBORDER attributes for the FRAME element. What we have documented here is the working behavior of the current browsers which support frames.

3 Because borders are shared between frames, a border will be plain only if all adjacent frames have set FRAMEBORDER=NO.

Attributes (Frames Elements) *continued...*

Attribute	Required	Value(s)	Parent Tag	Description / Notes
NAME	*Opt*	Window name	FRAME/IFRAME	Name of the frame (for use with the TARGET attribute).
SCROLLING	*Opt*	YES/NO/AUTO	FRAME/IFRAME	Controls the display of scrollbars. YES: Always display scrollbars; NO: Never display scrollbars; AUTO: Display scrollbars if warranted. Defaults to AUTO.
SRC	*Req*	URL	FRAME/IFRAME	The URL of the document to be displayed in this frame.
COLS	*Req*	List[4]	FRAMESET	Comma separated list of widths for the columns of frames. The number of columns in this list will be used to determine the number of frames in the document.
ROWS	*Req*	List[4]	FRAMESET	Comma separated list of heights for the rows of frames. The number of rows in this list will be used to determine the number of frames in the document.
ONLOAD	*Opt*	Script	FRAMESET	When all the frames are finished loading.
ONUNLOAD	*Opt*	Script	FRAMESET	When the document is unloaded (e.g., another document has been called for).
ALIGN	*Opt*	TOP/MIDDLE BOTTOM/LEFT RIGHT	IFRAME	Alignment of the element relative to surrounding text.
HEIGHT	*Opt*	Pixels	IFRAME	The height of the object's display space on the screen.
WIDTH	*Opt*	Pixels	IFRAME	The width of the frame's display space on the screen.

4 The numbers in the list are assumed to be in pixels, unless followed by % or *. Numbers followed by % represent a percentage of remaining space. A single * character designates a relative-sized frame and gives the frame all the remaining space. If there are multiple relative-sized frames, the remaining space is divided evenly among them. If there is a value in front of the *, that frame gets proportionally more relative space (e.g., "2*,*" gives 2/3 of the space to the first frame, and 1/3 to the second).

Miscellaneous Elements

Elements that didn't fit nicely in any of the other categories.

Tag	End Tag	Content	Attributes	Description / Notes
DEL	*Req*	Text	*Core Int'l Event* CITE/DATETIME	Deleted text.
INS	*Req*	Text	*Core Int'l Event* CITE/DATETIME	Inserted Text.
ISINDEX	*None*	None	*Core Int'l* PROMPT	Instructs the browser to provide an index search field.
NOSCRIPT	*Req*	Block	*Core Int'l Event*	Alternative content for browsers which don't understand SCRIPT.
SCRIPT	*Req*	*Script*	LANGUAGE/SRC TYPE	Container for in-line scripts.

Attributes (Miscellaneous Elements)

Attribute	Required	Value(s)	Parent Tag	Description / Notes
CITE	*Opt*	URL	DEL/INS	Information on reason for change.

DATETIME	*Opt*	ISO-date	DEL/INS	When the change was made. ISO date format is: YYYY-MM-DDThh:mm:ssTZD
				YYYY = four-digit year
				MM = two-digit month
				DD = two-digit day of month
				T = Literal character "T"
				hh = two-digit hour (00–24)
				mm = two-digit minute
				ss = two-digit second
				TZD = time zone (Z or offset)
				  Z = UTC (Universal Coordinated Time); offset is + or – from UTC
				Examples (both are equivalent to 1 January 1998, 9:49pm, US Eastern Standard Time):
				`1998-01-01T21:49:00-05:00`
				`1998-01-02T02:49:00Z`

PROMPT	*Opt*	Text	ISINDEX	An optional prompt for ISINDEX.
LANGUAGE	*Opt*	Script language	SCRIPT	Language the script is written in.
SRC	*Opt*	URL	SCRIPT	Optional URL for the script.
TYPE	*Opt*	MIME	SCRIPT	MIME type for the script URL.

Section 3: *Alphabetical Reference*

Alphabetical List of All HTML 4.0 Tags

Tag	End Tag	Content	Attributes	Description / Notes
A	*Req*	Text –(A)[1]	*Core Int'l Event* ACCESSKEY CHARSET COORDS[2]/HREF NAM/ONFOCUS ONBLUR/REL/REV SHAPE/TABINDEX TARGET/TITLE	Anchor for a hypertext link or a named target for hypertext links.
ACRONYM	*Req*	Text	*Core Int'l Event*	Acronym (e.g., HTML, WWW, etc.). Useful for spelling checkers, speech synthesizers, and other tools. May be rendered in small-caps.
ADDRESS	*Req*	Text + P	*Core Int'l Event*	Logical markup for addresses.
APPLET	*Req*	Text +(PARAM)	CODEBASE/CODE NAME/ALT/ALIGN HEIGHT/WIDTH HSPACE/VSPACE	Embed Java applet.
AREA	*None*	None	*Core Int'l Event* SHAPE/COORDS HREF/NOHREF ALT/TARGET TABINDEX ACCESSKEY	Hotzones for client-side image map.
B	*Req*	Text	*Core Int'l Event*	Bold text.
BASE	*None*	None	HREF/TARGET	Base URL for dereferencing relative URLs. Valid only within HEAD.
BASEFONT	*None*	None	ID/SIZE COLOR/FACE	Sets the default size of text.
BDO	*Req*	Text	*Core* LANG/DIR	Override direction of text.
BIG	*Req*	Text	*Core Int'l Event*	Larger size.
BLOCKQUOTE	*Req*	Block	*Core Int'l Event* CITE	For quoted passages (usually indented).

1 Nested A elements are disallowed.
2 The SHAPE and COORDS attributes are only valid for A within an OBJECT element.

Alphabetical List of All HTML 4.0 Tags *continued ...*

Tag	End Tag	Content	Attributes	Description / Notes
BODY	*Opt[3]*	All	*Core Int'l Event* BACKGROUND BGCOLOR/TEXT LINK/VLINK ALINK/ONLOAD UNLOAD	Container for document body.
BR	*None*	None	*Core Int'l Event* CLEAR	Force a line break. Moves point of text to the beginning of the next available line.
BUTTON	*Req*	Text + Block – Forms – (A)	*Core Int'l Event* NAME/VALUE TYPE/DISABLED TABINDEX ACCESSKEY ONFOCUS/ONBLUR	A button for use with forms. Richer presentation possibilities than INPUT type buttons.
CAPTION	*Req*	Text	*Core Int'l Event* ALIGN	Captions and figures within tables.
CENTER[4]	*Req*	All	*Core Int'l Event*	For centering (alias for <DIV ALIGN=CENTER>).
CITE	*Req*	Text	*Core Int'l Event*	Citation
CODE	*Req*	Text	*Core Int'l Event*	Fixed width (for rendering code).
COL	*None*	None	*Core Int'l Event* SPAN/WIDTH ALIGN/CHAR CHAROFF/VALIGN	For sharing attributes among table columns.
COLGROUP	*Opt*	COL	*Core Int'l Event* SPAN/WIDTH ALIGN/CHAR CHAROFF/VALIGN	Groups of table columns, for sharing attributes.
DD	*Opt*	Text Block	*Core Int'l Event*	The definition of a term.
DEL	*Req*	Text	*Core Int'l Event* SITE/DATETIME	Deleted text.
DFN	*Req*	Text	*Core Int'l Event*	Defining instance of a term.
DIR	*Req*	LI –(Block)	*Core Int'l Event* COMPACT	Directory list.

3 Both start- and end-tags are optional for HTML, HEAD, and BODY.

4 CENTER was introduced in Netscape Navigator in version 1.1, before DIV was conceived. It is so widely deployed by Netscape and other browser vendors that it has been included in the HTML specification since version 3.2. CENTER is implemented as a synonym for <DIV ALIGN=CENTER>.

Alphabetical List of All HTML 4.0 Tags *continued ...*

Tag	End Tag	Content	Attributes	Description / Notes
DIV	*Req*	Block	*Core Int'l Event* ALIGN	Null container for applying style and common attributes to block-level content.
DL	*Req*	DT/DD	*Core Int'l Event* COMPACT	Definition list.
DT	*Opt*	Text	*Core Int'l Event*	A term being defined.
EM	*Req*	Text	*Core Int'l Event*	Emphasis (usually italic).
FIELDSET	*Req*	Text Block LEGEND	*Core Int'l Event*	Grouping form controls.
FORM	*Req*	All	*Core Int'l Event* ACTION/METHOD ENCTYPE ONSUBMIT ONRESET/TARGE ACCEPT-CHARSET	Outer container for all form fields.
FONT	*Req*	Text	*Core Int'l Event* SIZE/COLOR FACE	Sets the appearance of text.
FRAME	*None*	None	ID/TITLE SRC/NAME MARGINWIDTH MARGINHEIGHT SCROLLING NORESIZE FRAMEBORDER	Tag describing each frame.
FRAMESET[5]	*Req*	FRAME/FRAMESET NOFRAMES	ID/TITL ROWS/COLS ONLOAD/UNLOAD	Outer container for the frames.
H1/H2/H3 H4/H5/H6	*Req*	Text	*Core Int'l Event* ALIGN	Six different levels of headings.
HEAD	*Opt*[3]	TITLE/ISINDEX BASE/META/LINK SCRIPT/STYLE	*Int'l* PROFILE	Container for document header.
HR	*None*	None	ALIGN/NOSHADE SIZE/WIDTH	Horizontal rule (line).
HTML	*Opt*[3]	Plain Text HEAD/BODY	*Int'l* VERSION	Outer container for an HTML document.

5 A frame document has no BODY. If any allowable content for a BODY element appears before a FRAMESET element, a BODY will be implied and the FRAMESET will be ignored.

Alphabetical List of All HTML 4.0 Tags *continued ...*

Tag	End Tag	Content	Attributes	Description / Notes
I	*Req*	Text	*Core Int'l Event*	Italic.
IFRAME	*Req*	Block	ID/TITLE NAME/SRC FRAMEBORDER MARGINWIDTH MARGINHEIGHT SCROLLING ALIGN/HEIGHT WIDTH	Inline frame (subwindow).
IMG	*None*	None	*Core Int'l Event* SRC/ALT LONGDESC/ALIGN HEIGHT/WIDTH BORDER/HSPACE VSPACE/USEMAP ISMAP	An embedded image.
INPUT	*None*	None	*Core Int'l Event* TYPE/NAME VALUE/CHECKED DISABLED READONLY/SIZE MAXLENGTH/SRC ALT/USEMAP ALIGN/TABINDEX ACCESSKEY ONFOCUS/ONBLUR ONSELECT ONCHANGE/ACCEPT	Generalized tag for all non-container input fields.
INS	*Req*	Text	*Core Int'l Event* SITE/DATETIME	Inserted Text.
ISINDEX	*None*	None	*Core Int'l* PROMPT	Instructs the browser to provide an index search field.
KBD	*Req*	Text	*Core Int'l Event*	Keyboard—text to be typed by a user.
LABEL	*Req*	Text –(LABEL)	*Core Int'l Event* FOR DISABLED ACCESSKEY ONFOCUS/ONBLUR	For attaching labels to form control elements.
LEGEND	*Req*	Text	*Core Int'l Event* ALIGN/ACCESSKEY	Assigns a caption (legend) to a FIELDSET.
LI	*Opt*	Text Block[6]	*Core Int'l Event* TYPE/VALUE	List item.

6 The LI element within DIR or MENU can only contain Text content.

Alphabetical List of All HTML 4.0 Tags *continued ...*

Tag	End Tag	Content	Attributes	Description / Notes
LINK	*None*	None	*Core Int'l Event* CHARSET/HREF REL/REV/TYPE MEDIA/TARGET	Defines relationships with other documents. Valid only within HEAD.
MAP	*Req*	AREA	*Core Int'l Event* NAME	Client-side image map.
MENU	*Req*	LI –(Block)	*Core Int'l Event* COMPACT	Menu.
META	*None*	None	*Int'l* HTTP-EQUIV NAME/CONTENT SCHEME	Meta-information describing properties of the document. Generates HTTP header when used with HTTP-EQUIV. Valid only within HEAD.
NOFRAMES	*Req*	Non-frames document	*Core Int'l Event*	Container for a document that will be seen by non-frames-aware browsers.
NOSCRIPT	*Req*	Block	*Core Int'l Event*	Alternative content for browsers which don't understand SCRIPT.
OBJECT	*Req*	Text Block PARAM	*Core Int'l Event* DECLARE/CLASSID CODEBASE/DATA TYPE/CODETYPE ARCHIVESTANDBY ALIGN/HEIGHT WIDTH/BORDER HSPACE/VSPACE USEMAP/SHAPES NAME/TABINDEX	Generic mechanism for including objects.
OL	*Req*	LI	*Core Int'l Event* TYPE/START COMPACT	Ordered list.
OPTION	*Opt*	Alphanumeric content	*Core Int'l Event* SELECTED DISABLED/VALUE	Container for individual options.
P	*Opt*	Text	*Core Int'l Event* ALIGN	Paragraph.
PARAM	*None*	None	ID/NAME/VALUE VALUETYPE/TYPE	Named parameters that can be read with Java's getParameter () method.

Alphabetical List of All HTML 4.0 Tags *continued ...*

Tag	End Tag	Content	Attributes	Description / Notes
PRE	*Req*	Text – (APPLET BASEFONT BIG/FONT/IMG OBJECT/SMALL SUB/SUP)	*Core Int'l Event* CHARSET/HREF REL/REV/TYPE MEDIA/TARGET	Defines relationships with other documents. Valid only within HEAD.
Q	*Req*	Text	*Core Int'l* Event CITE	Inline Quotation (may be rendered with quotation marks).
S	*Req*	Text	*Core Int'l Event*	Strike-through (e.g. ~~strike-through~~) (synonym for STRIKE).
SAMP	*Req*	Text	*Core Int'l Event*	Sample output from a program.
SCRIPT	*Req*	*Script*	LANGUAGE/SRC TYPE	Container for in-line scripts.
SELECT	*Req*	OPTION	*Core Int'l Event* NAME/SIZE MULTIPLE DISABLED TABINDEX ONFOCUS/ONBLUR ONCHANGE	Container for OPTION list.
SMALL	*Req*	Text	*Core Int'l Event*	Smaller size text.
SPAN	*Req*	Text	*Core Int'l Event*	Null-container for applying styles to inline text-level content.
STRIKE	*Req*	Text	*Core Int'l Event*	Strike-through (e.g. ~~strike-through~~) (synonym for S).
STRONG	*Req*	Text	*Core Int'l Event*	Strong emphasis (usually **bold**).
STYLE	*Req*	Style-sheet	*Int'l* TYPE MEDIA/TITLE	Container for style-sheet definitions.
SUB	*Req*	Text	*Core Int'l Event*	Subscript.
SUP	*Req*	Text	*Core Int'l Event*	Superscript.
TABLE	*Req*	CAPTION/COL COLGROUP/THEAD TFOOT/TBODY	*Core Int'l Event* ALIGN/WIDTH BGCOLOR/BORDER CELLSPACING CELLPADDING COLS/FRAME RULES/SUMMARY	Outer container for table.

Alphabetical List of All HTML 4.0 Tags *continued …*

Tag	End Tag	Content	Attributes	Description / Notes
TBODY[7]	*Opt*	TR	*Core Int'l Event* ALIGN/CHAR CHAROFF/VALIGN	For grouping table content. May allow browsers to independently scroll the body of a table.
TD	*Opt*	Block (including nested tables)	*Core Int'l Event* ABBR/AXIS/AXES NOWRAP/BGCOLOR ROWSPAN/COLSPAN WIDTH/HEIGHT ALIGN/CHAR CHAROFF/VALIGN	Table Data cell.
TEXTAREA	*Req*	Alphanumeric content	*Core Int'l Event* NAME/ROWS COLS/DISABLED READONLY TABINDEX ONFOCUS/ONBLUR ONSELECT ONCHANGE	Container for multiline text input field.
TFOOT	*Opt*	TR	*Core Int'l Event* ALIGN/CHAR CHAROFF/VALIGN	For grouping table content. May allow browsers to independently scroll the body of a table.
TH	*Opt*	Block (including nested tables)	*Core Int'l Event* ABBR/AXIS/AXES NOWRAP/BGCOLOR ROWSPAN/COLSPAN WIDTH/HEIGHT ALIGN/CHAR CHAROFF/VALIGN	Table heading cell.
THEAD	*Opt*	TR	*Core Int'l Event* ALIGN/CHAR CHAROFF/VALIGN	For grouping table content. May allow browsers to independently scroll the body of a table.

7 Both the begin- and end-tags of the TBODY element are optional. The TBODY element will exist by default, if a TR element is included directly within a TABLE element.

Alphabetical List of All HTML 4.0 Tags *continued ...*

Tag	End Tag	Content	Attributes	Description / Notes
TITLE[8]	*Req*	Document title	*Int'l*	Provides a title for the document.
TR	*Opt*	TD/TH	*Core Int'l Event* BGCOLOR/ALIGN CHAR/CHAROFF VALIGN	Defines rows. At least one TR is required for each table.
TT	*Req*	Text	*Core Int'l Event*	Teletype (fixed width).
U	*Req*	Text	*Core Int'l Event*	Underline.
UL	*Req*	LI	*Core Int'l Event* TYPE/COMPACT	Unordered List.
VAR	*Req*	Text	*Core Int'l Event*	Variable or argument in a program.

8 Exactly one TITLE tag (more than one is an error) is required in every HTML document.

Alphabetical List of All HTML 4.0 Attributes

Attribute	Required	Value(s)	Parent Tag	Description / Notes
ABBR	*Opt*	Text	TD/TH	Abbreviated name for table cell.
ACCEPT-CHARSET	*Opt*	List	FORM	List of acceptable character encodings for the server processing this form.
ACCEPT	*Opt*	MIME	FORM	List of MIME-types allowed by the server processing this form. Used for FILE type form elements.
ACCESSKEY	*Opt*	Text (single character)	A/AREA BUTTON/INPUT LABEL/LEGEND	Assigns an access (shortcut) key to the associated element. Pressing this key will assign focus to the associated element.
ACTION	*Opt*	URL	FORM	Location of CGI program for handling form input.
ALIGN	*Opt*	TOP/MIDDLE BOTTOM/LEFT RIGHT	APPLET/IFRAME IMG/INPUT OBJECT	Alignment of the element relative to surrounding text.
ALIGN	*Opt*	TOP/BOTTOM	CAPTION	Positions the caption at the top or bottom of the table. More than one CAPTION tag per table is an error.
ALIGN	*Opt*	LEFT/CENTER RIGHT/JUSTIFY	CHAR/COL COLGROUP/TBODY TD/TFOOT/TH THEAD/TR	Alignment of content within the cell(s). Defaults to LEFT.

Alphabetical List of All HTML 4.0 Attributes *continued ...*

Attribute	Required	Value(s)	Parent Tag	Description / Notes
ALIGN	*Opt*	LEFT/CENTER RIGHT/JUSTIFY	DIV/H1/H2/H3 H4/H5/H6/P	Alignment of the block of text. Defaults to LEFT.
ALIGN	*Opt*	LEFT/RIGHT CENTER	HR	Alignment of the horizontal rule.
ALIGN	*Opt*	TOP/BOTTOM LEFT/RIGHT	LEGEND	Alignment of the legend relative to the group of form controls.
ALIGN	*Opt*	LEFT/CENTER RIGHT	TABLE	Alignment of data within the table.
ALINK	*Opt*	Color	BODY	Color of active links (e.g. while the mouse button is pressed on the link).
ALT	*Req*[1]	Alternate text	AREA/IMG	Text associated with the image or area for use by text-only browsers and non-visual user agents that cannot display images.
ALT	*Opt*	Alternate text	APPLET/INPUT	Alternate text for display in circumstances where the applet or graphic control cannot be rendered.
ARCHIVE	*Opt*	List of URLs	OBJECT	Preload resources for OBJECT or APPLET. **Note:** List is comma-separated for APPLET, and space-separated for OBJECT.
AXES	*Opt*	List of ID values	TD/TH	Used with ID attribute to relate table cells for hierarchical tables.
AXIS	*Opt*	Text	TD/TH	Relates a group of header cells for hierarchical tables structures.
BACKGROUND	*Opt*	URL	BODY	URL for the background graphic.
BGCOLOR	*Opt*	Color	BODY	Background color of the document page.
BGCOLOR	*Opt*	Color	TABLE	Sets the background color for a table.
BGCOLOR	*Opt*	Color	TD/TH	Sets the background color for a table cell.
BORDER	*Opt*	Number	FRAMESET	The thickness of all the frame borders in the frame set. Use 0 to get no borders at all.

1 Yes, that's right, the ALT attribute is required for IMG and AREA in this iteration of the HTML 4.0 specification. We expect this item to generate some more debate before it's finalized. We see this as another example of the HTML committee working in a vacuum—we don't expect people to start including ALT text for their single-pixel spacing GIFs anytime soon.

Alphabetical List of All HTML 4.0 Attributes *continued ...*

Attribute	Required	Value(s)	Parent Tag	Description / Notes
BORDER[2]	*Opt*	Pixels	IMG	The size of the border when the image is used as a hypertext link. Set this to zero to suppress the border.
BORDER	*Opt*	Pixels or Percentage	OBJECT	The size of the border when the object is used as a hypertext link. Set this to zero to suppress the border.
BORDER	*Opt*	Pixels	TABLE	Number of pixels for the size of the table's border. Defaults to no border if the attribute is not used, or one pixel if the attribute is used without a value.
BORDERCOLOR	*Opt*	Color	FRAMESET/FRAME	Sets the color of the border.
CELLPADDING	*Opt*	Pixels	TABLE	Sets the space between the border and the content of cells.
CELLSPACING	*Opt*	Pixels	TABLE	Sets the spacing between cells in the table (and consequently, the thickness of the borders between cells).
CHAR	*Opt*	*Character*	COL/COLGROUP TBODY/TD/TFOOT TH/THEAD/TR	Alignment character for use with ALIGN=CHAR. Defaults to decimal point character for current language.
CHAROFF[3]	*Opt*		COL/COLGROUP TBODY/TD/TFOOT TH/THEAD/TR	Offset to first occurrence of alignment character.
CHARSET	*Opt*	*Name of Character Set*	A/LINK	Character encoding of the destination link.
CHECKED	*Opt*	None	INPUT	Valid only for RADIO and CHECKBOX widgets. If specified, the default state will be true.
CITE	*Opt*	URL	BLOCKQUOTE/Q	Source document or message with information about the quotation.
CITE	*Opt*	URL	DEL/INS	Information on reason for change.
CLASS	*Opt*	*List of Class names*	All Elements Except: BASE/BASEFONT FRAME/FRAMESET HEAD/HTML IFRAME/META PARAM/SCRIPT STYLE/TITLE	Specifies a class (or list of classes) for applying style-sheet properties to the element.

2 The definition of the BORDER attribute for the FRAMESET element defines the current behavior of Netscape Navigator. This attribute is not defined in the current HTML 4 specification.
3 It is not currently clear how the CHAROFF attribute will be used. As of this writing, there are not any browsers supporting the ALIGN=CHAR feature.

Alphabetical List of All HTML 4.0 Attributes *continued ...*

Attribute	Required	Value(s)	Parent Tag	Description / Notes
CLASSID	*Opt*	URL	OBJECT	URL for specific implementation.
CLEAR	*Opt*	LEFT/RIGHT ALL	BR	Move down past floating images. LEFT clears to the left margin; RIGHT clears to the right margin; ALL clears to both margins.
CODE	*Req*	Applet File	APPLET	The name of the file that contains the applet's compiled subclass. This file is relative to the CODEBASE location, if specified (otherwise it is relative to the URL of the document). It cannot be an absolute URL.
CODEBASE	*Opt*	URL	APPLET	Base URL for resolving relative URLs for this applet. Specifically used for resolving the CODE URL.
CODEBASE	*Opt*	URL	OBJECT	Base URL for resolving relative URLs for this object. Specifically used for the CLASSID URL.
CODETYPE	*Opt*	MIME	OBJECT	MIME-type for the object specified by CLASSID. Defaults to the value of the TYPE attribute.
COLOR	*Opt*	Color	FONT	Sets the color of text.
COLS	*Req*	List[4]	FRAMESET	Comma separated list of widths for the columns of frames. The number of columns in this list will be used to determine the number of frames in the document.
COLS	*Opt*	Number	TABLE	Number of columns in the table. Used by some browsers to speed up table rendering.[5]
COLS	*Req*	Number	TEXTAREA	The number of visible columns in the text area.
COLSPAN	*Opt*	Number	TD/TH	Causes the cell to span a number of columns.
COMPACT	*Opt*	None	DIR/DL/OL MENU/UL	Render the list more compactly. Depreciated.
CONTENT	*Req*	Text	META	Content of meta information.

4 The numbers in the list are assumed to be in pixels, unless followed by % or *. Numbers followed by % represent a percentage of remaining space. A single * character designates a relative-sized frame and gives the frame all the remaining space. If there are multiple relative-sized frames, the remaining space is divided evenly among them. If there is a value in front of the *, that frame gets proportionally more relative space (e.g., "2*,*" gives 2/3 of the space to the first frame, and 1/3 to the second).

5 Netscape Navigator 4.x also uses the ROWS and COLS attributes to specify that the table should be rendered with the newer, more accurate, table rendering engine. The table will render more precisely according to the HTML 4 table model, but it will not render the same way on older versions of Navigator. In other words, if you care how your table looks in different versions of Navigator, and you use COLS and/or ROWS, be sure to test your table on Navigator 3 and 4.

Alphabetical List of All HTML 4.0 Attributes *continued ...*

Attribute	Required	Value(s)	Parent Tag	Description / Notes
COORDS	*Opt*	Coordinates	A[6]/AREA	List of coordinates, in pixel units, according to the given shape, e.g.: shape = default shape = rect coords = *"left-x, top-y, right-x, bottom-y"* shape = circle coords = *"center-x, center-y, radius"* shape = poly coords = *"x1,y1, x2,y2, x3,y3, ..."*
DATA	*Opt*	URL	OBJECT	Location for the object's data.

DATETIME	*Opt*	ISO-date	DEL/INS	When the change was made. ISO date format is: YYYY-MM-DDThh:mm:ssTZD
				YYYY = four-digit year
				MM = two-digit month
				DD = two-digit day of month
				T = Literal character "T"
				hh = two-digit hour (00–24)
				mm = two-digit minute
				ss = two-digit second
				TZD = time zone (Z or offset)
				  Z = UTC (Universal Coordinated Time); offset is + or − from UTC
				Examples (both are equivalent to 1 January 1998, 9:49pm, US Eastern Standard Time):
				`1998-01-01T21:49:00-05:00`
				`1998-01-02T02:49:00Z`

DECLARE	*Opt*	None	OBJECT	Declare OBJECT only.
DIR	*Opt*	LTR *or* RTL	*All elements except:* APPLET/BASE BASEFONT/BDO BR/FONT/FRAME FRAMESET/HR IFRAME/PARAM SCRIPT	Direction of text. LTR = Left to Right RTL = Right to Left
DIR	*Req*	LTR *or* RTL	BDO	Direction for overridden text.
DISABLED[7]	*Opt*	None	BUTTON/INPUT LABEL/OPTION SELECT/TEXTAREA	Make the control unavailable. May be "grayed out" in some browsers.
ENCTYPE	*Opt*	Content-type	FORM	Defaults to "application/x-www-form-urlencoded".

6 COORDS can be used with the A element only within an OBJECT element.
7 Some browsers may allow you to enable and disable widgets with a script, like JavaScript (ECMAScript).

Alphabetical List of All HTML 4.0 Attributes *continued* ...

Attribute	Required	Value(s)	Parent Tag	Description / Notes
FACE	*Opt*	*Text*	BASEFONT/FONT	Comma-separated list of font names.
FOR	*Opt*	ID-value	LABEL	Explicitly associate a label with a control.
FRAME	*Opt*	VOID/ABOVE BELOW/HSIDES LHS/RHS/VSIDES BOX/BORDER	TABLE	Which parts of the table frame to include.
FRAMEBORDER[8]	*Opt*	YES/NO	FRAME	Whether or not the borders for a particular frame are displayed with bevels.[9] Defaults to Yes.
HEIGHT	*Opt*[10]	Pixels	IFRAME/OBJECT	The height of the object's display space on the screen.
HEIGHT	*Req*	Pixels	APPLET	The height of the applet's display space on the screen. Used to reserve space for the applet on the page so that the page can be laid out before applet is executed.
HEIGHT	*Opt*	Pixels	IMG	The width of the image. Some browsers use this to reserve space for an image to that the page can be laid out before images are downloaded.
HEIGHT	*Opt*	Pixels	TD/TH	Sets the height of the cell in pixels.
HREF	*Opt*	URL	A	The target URL of a hyperlink.
HREF		URL	AREA	The destination of the hypertext link.
HREF	*Req*	URL	BASE	URL for the document base.
HREF	*Opt*	URL	LINK	URL for the linked resource.
HSPACE	*Opt*	Pixels	APPLET/IMG OBJECT	The size of the horizontal gutter space around the image. Set this to zero to suppress the horizontal gutter.
HTTP-EQUIV	*Opt*	Text	META	Name for HTTP header.
ID	*Opt*	#*Unique-ID*	*All Elements Except:* BASE/HEAD/HTML META/SCRIPT STYLE/TITLE	Unique ID for an individual instance of an element.

8 The current HTML 4 specification is inconsistent in its description of the BORDER and FRAMEBORDER attributes for the FRAME element. What we have documented here is the working behavior of the current browsers which support frames.

9 Because borders are shared between frames, a border will be plain only if all adjacent frames have set FRAMEBORDER=NO.

10 Technically, the HEIGHT and WIDTH attributes are not required for OBJECT, but in practice many browsers will not display the object if HEIGHT and WIDTH are omitted.

Alphabetical List of All HTML 4.0 Attributes *continued ...*

Attribute	Required	Value(s)	Parent Tag	Description / Notes
ISMAP	*Opt*	*None*	IMG	Indicates that this image is a server-side image map. Only valid when the image is within an A (anchor) element with an HREF attribute.
LANG	*Opt*	Lang-ID	*All elements except:* APPLET/BASE BASEFONT/BR FONT/FRAME FRAMESET/HR IFRAME/PARAM SCRIPT	Language identifier, as specified in RFC-1766.
LANGUAGE	*Opt*	Script Language	SCRIPT	Language the script is written in.
LINK	*Opt*	Color	BODY	Color of unvisited links.
LONGDESC	*Opt*	URL	IMG	Link to a long description.
MARGINHEIGHT	*Opt*	Number	FRAME	Height of the top and bottom margins for the frame.
MARGINWIDTH	*Opt*	Number	FRAME	Width of the left and right margins for the frame.
MAXLENGTH	*Opt*	Number	INPUT	The maximum number of characters that can be typed into a TEXT or PASSWORD input field.
MEDIA	*Opt*	Text	STYLE/LINK	Destination media for style. Defaults to ALL.
METHOD	*Opt*	POST/GET	FORM	Method of submitting data to HTTP server. Defaults to GET.
MULTIPLE	*Opt*	*None*	SELECT	Indicates that multiple items may be selected at a time.
NAME	*Opt*	Anchor name	A MAP	The name of an anchor or client-side image map, for use with a fragment identifier (#) in a hyperlink.
NAME	*Opt*	Name	APPLET	A name for the applet instance. This allows multiple applets on the same page to communicate with each other.
NAME	*Opt*	Text	META	Name for meta information.
NAME	*Opt*	Window name	FRAME/IFRAME	Name of the frame (for use with the TARGET attribute).

Alphabetical List of All HTML 4.0 Attributes *continued ...*

Attribute	Required	Value(s)	Parent Tag	Description / Notes
NAME	*Req*[11]	Widget name	INPUT/OBJECT SELECT/TEXTAREA	The name used to identify data from this widget.
NAME	*Opt*	Parameter Name	PARAM	Name of parameter.
NOHREF	*Opt*	*None*	AREA	Declares the area of a client-side imagemap to be a dead zone.
NORESIZE	*Opt*	*None*	FRAME	If present, do not allow resizing of the frame.
NOSHADE	*Opt*	*None*	HR	Sets the horizontal rule to display as a solid rule, instead of the traditional embossed groove.
NOWRAP	*Opt*	*None*	TD/TH	Prevents word-wrapping within the cell.
OBJECT	*Opt*	Resource Name	APPLET	Serialized representation of an applet.
ONBLUR	*Opt*	Script	A/BUTTON/INPUT LABEL/SELECT TEXTAREA	When focus is removed from the element.
ONCHANGE	*Opt*	Script	INPUT/SELECT TEXTAREA	When the value of the element changes.
ONCLICK	*Opt*	Script	*All elements except:* APPLET/BASE BASEFONT/BDO BR/FONT/FRAME FRAMESET/HEAD HTML/IFRAME ISINDEX/META PARAM/SCRIPT STYLE/TITLE	When the mouse is clicked on the element.
ONDBLCLICK	*Opt*	Script	*All elements except:* APPLET/BASE BASEFONT/BDO BR/FONT/FRAME FRAMESET/HEAD HTML/IFRAME ISINDEX/META PARAM/SCRIPT STYLE/TITLE	When the mouse is double-clicked on the element.
ONFOCUS	*Opt*	Script	A/BUTTON INPUT/LABEL SELECT TEXTAREA	When the element receives the focus.

11 The NAME attribute is required for all input types except SUBMIT and RESET.

Alphabetical List of All HTML 4.0 Attributes *continued ...*

Attribute	Required	Value(s)	Parent Tag	Description / Notes
ONKEYDOWN	*Opt*	Script	*All elements except:* APPLET/BASE BASEFONT/BDO BR/FONT/FRAME FRAMESET/HEAD HTML/IFRAME ISINDEX/META PARAM/SCRIPT STYLE/TITLE	When a key is pressed down within the element.
ONKEYPRESS	*Opt*	Script	*All elements except:* APPLET/BASE BASEFONT/BDO BR/FONT/FRAME FRAMESET/HEAD HTML/IFRAME ISINDEX/META PARAM/SCRIPT STYLE/TITLE	When a key is pressed and released within the element.
ONKEYUP	*Opt*	Script	*All elements except:* APPLET/BASE BASEFONT/BDO BR/FONT/FRAME FRAMESET/HEAD HTML/IFRAME ISINDEX/META PARAM/SCRIPT STYLE/TITLE	When a key is released in the element.
ONLOAD	*Opt*	Script	BODY	When the document is finished loading.
ONLOAD	*Opt*	Script	FRAMESET	When all the frames are finished loading.
ONMOUSEDOWN	*Opt*	Script	*All elements except:* APPLET/BASE BASEFONT/BDO BR/FONT/FRAME FRAMESET/HEAD HTML/IFRAME ISINDEX/META PARAM/SCRIPT STYLE/TITLE	When a mouse button is depressed on the element.

Alphabetical List of All HTML 4.0 Attributes *continued ...*

Attribute	Required	Value(s)	Parent Tag	Description / Notes
ONMOUSEMOVE	*Opt*	Script	*All elements except:* APPLET/BASE BASEFONT/BDO BR/FONT/FRAME FRAMESET/HEAD HTML/IFRAME ISINDEX/META PARAM/SCRIPT STYLE/TITLE	When the mouse cursor is moved over the element.
ONMOUSEOUT	*Opt*	Script	*All elements except:* APPLET/BASE BASEFONT/BDO BR/FONT/FRAME FRAMESET/HEAD HTML/IFRAME ISINDEX/META PARAM/SCRIPT STYLE/TITLE	When the mouse cursor moves out of the element's display space.
ONMOUSEOVER	*Opt*	Script	*All elements except:* APPLET/BASE BASEFONT/BDO BR/FONT/FRAME FRAMESET/HEAD HTML/IFRAME ISINDEX/META PARAM/SCRIPT STYLE/TITLE	When the mouse cursor moves into the element's display space.
ONMOUSEUP	*Opt*	Script	*All elements except:* APPLET/BASE BASEFONT/BDO BR/FONT/FRAME FRAMESET/HEAD HTML/IFRAME ISINDEX/META PARAM/SCRIPT STYLE/TITLE	When a mouse button is released over the element.
ONRESET	*Opt*	Script	FORM	When the form is reset.
ONSELECT	*Opt*	Script	INPUT/TEXTAREA	When text is selected within the widget.
ONSUBMIT	*Opt*	Script	FORM	When the form is submitted.
ONUNLOAD	*Opt*	Script	BODY/FRAMESET	When the document is unloaded (e.g., another document has been called for).
PROFILE	*Opt*	URL	HEAD	A meta-data profile.
PROMPT	*Opt*	Text	ISINDEX	An optional prompt for ISINDEX.

Alphabetical List of All HTML 4.0 Attributes *continued ...*

Attribute	Required	Value(s)	Parent Tag	Description / Notes
READONLY	Opt	None	TEXTAREA/INPUT	Data can be selected, but not modified.
REL	Opt	Rel	A	The forward relationship for the linked resource.
REL	Opt	Rel	LINK	The forward relationship for a LINK element.
REV	Opt	Rel	A	The reverse relationship for the linked resource.
REV	Opt	Rel	LINK	The reverse relationship for a LINK element.
ROWS	Req	List	FRAMESET	Comma separated list of heights for the rows of frames. The number of rows in this list will be used to determine the number of frames in the document.
ROWS	Req	Number	TEXTAREA	The number of visible rows in the text area.
ROWSPAN	Opt	Number	TD/TH	Causes the cell to span a number of rows.
RULES	Opt	NONE/GROUPS ROWS/COLS/ALL	TABLE	Specifies which rules to display between table cells. Defaults to NONE. Depreciated.
SCHEME	Opt	Text	META	The scheme to be used in interpreting the content. Depends on context.
SCROLLING	Opt	YES/NO/AUTO	FRAME/IFRAME	Controls the display of scrollbars. YES: Always display scrollbars; NO: Never display scrollbars; AUTO: Display scrollbars if warranted. Defaults to AUTO.
SELECTED	Opt	None	OPTION	Indicates that this option is selected by default.
SHAPE		RECT/CIRCLE POLY/DEFAULT	A/AREA	Declares the shape of the area. DEFAULT indicates the entire image (use DEFAULT first to overlay the other shapes on top of it). May be used with the A element only within OBJECT.
SHAPES	Opt	None	OBJECT	Object has shapes for a client-side imagemap.

Alphabetical List of All HTML 4.0 Attributes *continued ...*

Attribute	Required	Value(s)	Parent Tag	Description / Notes
SIZE	*Opt*	Number	FONT/BASEFONT	A number in the range 1–7 that specifies the size of displayed text. As an attribute to the FONT element, SIZE may be a relative number in the form +*n* or -*n*, where the resulting size will be relative to the default size or BASEFONT size.
SIZE	*Opt*	Number	HR	The thickness of the rule.
SIZE	*Opt*	Number	INPUT	The amount of space assigned for this input field. Valid only for types TEXT and PASSWORD.
SIZE	*Opt*	Number	SELECT	The number of items visible at a time in the list.
SPAN	*Opt*	Number	COLGROUP	Default number of columns in group.
SPAN	*Opt*	Number	COL	Number of columns spanned by group.
SRC	*Req*	URL	FRAME/IFRAME	The URL of the document to be displayed in this frame.
SRC	*Req*	URL	IMG	Location of the image.
SRC	*Opt*	URL	INPUT	The location of the image for an IMAGE type widget.
SRC	*Opt*	URL	SCRIPT	Optional URL for the script.
STANDBY			OBJECT	Message to display while loading the object.
START	*Opt*	Number	OL	Starting sequence number.
STYLE	*Opt*	Style	*All elements except:* BASE/BASEFONT FRAME/FRAMESET HEAD/HTML IFRAME/META PARAM/SCRIPT STYLE/TITLE	Style information to associate with the element.
SUMMARY	*Opt*	Text	TABLE	Summary statement for non-visual browsers.
TABINDEX	*Opt*	Number	A/AREA/BUTTON INPUT/OBJECT SELECT/TEXTAREA	Tabbing sequence for keyboard use.

Alphabetical List of All HTML 4.0 Attributes *continued* ...

Attribute	Required	Value(s)	Parent Tag	Description / Notes
TARGET	*Opt*	Window name	A/BASE/AREA FORM/LINK	The target window or frame for hyper-links. The following magic target names are also supported: _blank a new blank window _self the same window as the link _parent the parent frameset _top the full body of the window
TEXT	*Opt*	Color	BODY	Color of the document text.
TITLE	*Opt*	Title	A	A title string for the hyperlink.
TITLE	*Opt*	Text	LINK	An advisory title for the linked resource.
TITLE	*Opt*	Text	STYLE	Title for the style.
TITLE	*Opt*	Text	FRAME/FRAMESET IFRAME	An advisory title, as for anchors.
TITLE	*Opt*	Text	*All elements except :* BASE/BASEFONT FRAME/FRAMESET HEAD/HTML IFRAME/META PARAM/SCRIPT STYLE/TITLE	An advisory title. May display as a *tool-tip* or be spoken or rendered some other way for non-visual browsers.
TYPE	*Opt*	MIME	BUTTON	MIME type for retrieving the button content.
TYPE	*Opt*	TEXT/PASSWORD CHECKBOX/RADIO SUBMIT/RESET FILE/HIDDEN IMAGE	INPUT	Type of widget to use for form element. Defaults to TEXT.
TYPE	*Opt*	MIME	LINK/OBJECT PARAM	MIME type.
TYPE	*Opt*		LI/OL/UL	Style of bullet or numbering style.
TYPE	*Opt*	MIME	SCRIPT	MIME type for the script URL.
TYPE	*Opt*	MIME	STYLE	MIME type for the style. Defaults to "text/css".
USEMAP	*Opt*	URL	IMG/INPUT OBJECT	URL fragment identifier that points to a MAP element for a client-side image map.
VALIGN	*Opt*	TOP/MIDDLE BOTTOM/BASELINE	TD/TH	Sets the vertical alignment of content within the cell. Defaults to LEFT.

Alphabetical List of All HTML 4.0 Attributes *continued* ...

Attribute	Required	Value(s)	Parent Tag	Description / Notes
VALIGN	*Opt*	TOP/MIDDLE BOTTOM	BASELINE/COL COLGROUP/TBODY TFOOT/THEAD/TR	Sets the vertical alignment of content within the cells of the table row. Defaults to MIDDLE.
VALUE[12]	*Opt*	Value	INPUT/BUTTON	A default value for this widget.
VALUE	*Opt*	Number	LI	Reset number sequence.
VALUE	*Opt*	Alphanumeric	OPTION	The value of the option when selected. Defaults to the content of the OPTION container.
VALUE	*Req*	Parameter Value	PARAM	Value of the parameter.
VALUETYPE	*Opt*	DATA/REF OBJECT	PARAM	How to interpret VALUE. Defaults to DATA.
VERSION	*Opt*	URL	HTML	Link to the DTD for this document. Redundant with use of DOCTYPE.
VLINK	*Opt*	Color	BODY	Color of visited links.
VSPACE	*Opt*	Pixels	APPLET/IMG OBJECT	The size of the vertical gutter space around the image. Set this to zero to suppress the vertical gutter.
WIDTH	*Req*	Pixels	APPLET	The width of the applet's display space on the screen. Used to reserve space for the applet on the page so that the page can be laid out before applet is executed.
WIDTH	*Opt*	Pixels	COL/COLGROUP	Width of the column or default width of the COLGROUP.
WIDTH[13]	*Opt*	Pixels	IFRAME/OBJECT	The width of the object's display space on the screen.
WIDTH	*Opt*	Number	HR	The width of the rule.

12 The VALUE attribute is required for RADIO and CHECKBOX type input elements.
13 Technically, the HEIGHT and WIDTH attributes are not required for OBJECT, but in practice many browsers will not display the object if HEIGHT and WIDTH are omitted.

Alphabetical List of All HTML 4.0 Attributes *continued ...*

Attribute	Required	Value(s)	Parent Tag	Description / Notes
WIDTH	*Opt*	Pixels	IMG	The height of the image. Some browsers use this to reserve space for an image so that the page can be laid out before images are downloaded.
WIDTH	*Opt*	Number	PRE	Number of characters wide for the display of fixed-width data.
WIDTH	*Opt*	Pixels or Percentage	TABLE	Sets the overall width of the table, in pixels or a percentage of the width of the page (as *n%*).
WIDTH	*Opt*	Pixels	TD/TH	Sets the width of the cell in pixels.

Section 4: *Supplemental Reference*

Character Entities (ISO 8859-1)

The 98 characters here are the character entities supported by HTML 4.0. There are other characters which may be supported in the future, including Greek, Math, and other international character sets. As of this writing, all of these characters are supported by Netscape Navigator 4.0.

Name	Number	Symbol	Description
"	"	"	quotation mark
&	&	&	ampersand
<	<	<	less-than sign
>	>	>	greater-than sign
			no-break space
¡	¡	¡	inverted exclamation mark
¢	¢	¢	cent sign
£	£	£	pound sterling sign
¤	¤	¤	general currency sign
¥	¥	¥	yen sign
¦	¦	¦	broken (vertical) bar
§	§	§	section sign
¨	¨	¨	umlaut (dieresis)
©	©	©	copyright sign
ª	ª	ª	ordinal indicator, feminine
«	«	«	angle quotation mark, left
¬	¬	¬	not sign
­	­	–	soft hyphen
®	®	®	registered sign
¯	¯	¯	macron
°	°	°	degree sign
±	±	±	plus-or-minus sign

Character Entities (ISO 8859-1) *continued ...*

Name	Number	Symbol	Description
²	²	²	superscript two
³	³	³	superscript three
´	´	´	acute accent
µ	µ	µ	micro sign
¶	¶	¶	pilcrow (paragraph sign)
·	·	·	middle dot
¸	¸	¸	cedilla
¹	¹	¹	superscript one
º	º	º	ordinal indicator, masculine
»	»	»	angle quotation mark, right
¼	¼	¼	fraction one-quarter
½	½	½	fraction one-half
¾	¾	¾	fraction three-quarters
¿	¿	¿	inverted question mark
À	À	À	capital A, grave accent
Á	Á	Á	capital A, acute accent
Â	Â	Â	capital A, circumflex accent
Ã	Ã	Ã	capital A, tilde
Ä	Ä	Ä	capital A, dieresis or umlaut mark
Å	Å	Å	capital A, ring
Æ	Æ	Æ	capital AE diphthong (ligature)
Ç	Ç	Ç	capital C, cedilla
È	È	È	capital E, grave accent
É	É	É	capital E, acute accent
Ê	Ê	Ê	capital E, circumflex accent
Ë	Ë	Ë	capital E, dieresis or umlaut mark

Character Entities (ISO 8859-1) *continued ...*

&Igrave;	&#204;	Ì	capital I, grave accent
&Iacute;	&#205;	Í	capital I, acute accent
&Icirc;	&#206;	Î	capital I, circumflex accent
&Iuml;	&#207;	Ï	capital I, dieresis or umlaut mark
&ETH;	&#208;	Ð	capital Eth, Icelandic
&Ntilde;	&#209;	Ñ	capital N, tilde
&Ograve;	&#210;	Ò	capital O, grave accent
&Oacute;	&#211;	Ó	capital O, acute accent
&Ocirc;	&#212;	Ô	capital O, circumflex accent
&Otilde;	&#213;	Õ	capital O, tilde
&Ouml;	&#214;	Ö	capital O, dieresis or umlaut mark
&times;	&#215;	×	multiply sign
&Oslash;	&#216;	Ø	capital O, slash
&Ugrave;	&#217;	Ù	capital U, grave accent
&Uacute;	&#218;	Ú	capital U, acute accent
&Ucirc;	&#219;	Û	capital U, circumflex accent
&Uuml;	&#220;	Ü	capital U, dieresis or umlaut mark
&Yacute;	&#221;	Ý	capital Y, acute accent
&THORN;	&#222;	Þ	capital THORN, Icelandic
&szlig;	&#223;	ß	small sharp s, German (sz ligature)
&agrave;	&#224;	à	small a, grave accent
&aacute;	&#225;	á	small a, acute accent
&acirc;	&#226;	â	small a, circumflex accent
&atilde;	&#227;	ã	small a, tilde
&auml;	&#228;	ä	small a, dieresis or umlaut mark
&aring;	&#229;	å	small a, ring

Character Entities (ISO 8859-1) *continued ...*

Name	Number	Symbol	Description
æ	æ	æ	small æ dipthong (ligature)
ç	ç	ç	small c, cedilla
è	è	è	small e, grave accent
é	é	é	small e, acute accent
ê	ê	ê	small e, circumflex accent
ë	ë	ë	small e, dieresis or umlaut mark
ì	ì	ì	small i, grave accent
í	í	í	small i, acute accent
î	î	î	small i, circumflex accent
ï	ï	ï	small i, dieresis or umlaut mark
ð	ð	∂	small eth, Icelandic
ñ	ñ	ñ	small n, tilde
ò	ò	ò	small o, grave accent
ó	ó	ó	small o, acute accent
ô	ô	ô	small o, circumflex accent
õ	õ	õ	small o, tilde
ö	ö	ö	small o, dieresis or umlaut mark
÷	÷	÷	divide sign
ø	ø	ø	small o, slash
ù	ù	ù	small u, grave accent
ú	ú	ú	small u, acute accent
û	û	û	small u, circumflex accent
ü	ü	ü	small u, dieresis or umlaut mark
ý	ý	ý	small y, acute accent
þ	þ	þ	small thorn, Icelandic
ÿ	ÿ	ÿ	small y, dieresis or umlaut mark

Glossary
creative html design

#

8-bit graphics: A color or grayscale graphic or movie that has 256 colors or less.

8-bit sound: 8-bit sound has a dynamic range of about 48 dB (decibels).

16-bit graphics: A color image or movie that has 65,536 colors.

16-bit sound: Standard CD-quality sound quality. 16-bit sound has a dynamic range of about 96 dB.

24-bit graphics: A color image or movie that has 16.7 million colors.

32-bit graphics: A color image or movie that has 16.7 million colors plus an 8-bit masking channel.

µ-law: µ-law is a sound file format used by UNIX platforms. These files have the .au file extension.

a

active navigation: Point-and-click navigation, where the end user guides the information flow.

adaptive dithering: A form of dithering in which the program looks to the image to determine the best set of colors when creating an 8-bit or smaller palette. *See dithering.*

additive color: The use of projected light to mix color. This is the type of color we see on video monitors.

AIFC: A sound file format. AIFC is a new spec for the older **A**udio **I**nterchange **F**ile Format (AIFF). Both AIFF and AIFF-C files can be read by this format. This format is commonly used by Apple and Silicon Graphics computers.

aliasing: In bitmapped graphics, the jagged boundary along the edges of different-colored shapes within an image. *See anti-aliasing.*

animated GIF: A single GIF file with multiple images and information for displaying them sequentially.

anti-aliasing: A technique for reducing the jagged appearance of aliased bitmapped images, usually by interpolating the color and value of pixels at the boundaries of adjacent colors.

artifacts: Image imperfections, usually caused by compression.

attribute: A modifier to an HTML tag (for example, `<TAG ATTRIBUTE>`).

authoring tools: Creation tools for interactive media.

AVI: **A**udio-**V**ideo **I**nterleaved. Microsoft's file format for desktop video movies.

b

bit depth: The number of bits used to represent the color of each pixel in a digital image. Specifically: bit depth of 1 = 2 colors (usually black and white); bit depth of 2 = 4 colors; bit depth of 4 = 16 colors; bit depth of 8 = 256 colors; bit depth of 16 = 65,536 colors; bit depth of 24 = 16,777,216 colors. (See Chapter 6.)

bitmapped graphics: Also called raster graphics. Bitmapped graphics are images that have a specific number of pixels. As such, they are fixed into a particular grid of so many vertical and horizontal lines of pixels. This grid is called a "raster," and images that are fixed to such a grid are said to be "rasterized." The GIF and JPEG images that you commonly use on the Web are bitmapped. *See vector graphics.*

browser: Also called user agent. An application that enables you to access World Wide Web pages. Most browsers provide the capability to view web pages, copy and print material from web pages, download files from the web, and navigate throughout the web.

browser-safe colors: The 216 colors that do not shift between platforms, operating systems, or most web browsers.

c

cache: A storage area that keeps frequently accessed data or program instructions readily available so that you do not have to retrieve them repeatedly.

CERN: The European Laboratory for Particle Physics (formerly Conseil Européenne pour la Recherche Nucléaire). A joint project of the European Economic Community, where the World Wide Web was first conceived.

CGI: Common Gateway Interface. The programmatic interface between a web server and other programs running on that server. Commonly used for extending the interactivity of a site.

Cinepak: Cinepak is a form of very high compression for movies. The compression type is called "lossy" because it causes a visible loss in quality.

client: A computer that requests information from a network server. *See server.*

client pull: Client pull creates a slideshow effect with HTML text or inline images. It is programmed within the <META> tag.

client side: Client side means that the web element or effect can run locally off a computer and does not require the presence of a server.

client-side imagemap: A client-side imagemap is programmed in HTML and does not require a separate map definition file or a live web server to operate.

CLUT: Color LookUp Table. An 8-bit or lower image file uses a CLUT to define its palette.

color mapping: A color map refers to the color palette of an image. Color mapping means assigning colors to an image.

color names: Some browsers support using the name of a color instead of the color's hexadecimal value.

container: An element that encloses other objects, for example, <STRONG> </STRONG>.

compression: Reduction of the amount of data required to re-create an original file, graphic, or movie. Compression is used to reduce the transmission time of media and application files across the Internet.

contrast: The degrees of separation between values.

d

data rate: The data rate is the amount of data used or captured per second of real-time media. It is commonly used for both sound and movies.

data streaming: The ability to deliver media in real-time, much like a VCR, rather than having to download all the information before it can be played.

decibel (dB): The measure of relative intensity between two signals, usually used in measuring sound. Decibels are a logarithmic measurement, where twice the power is equal to 3 dB.

dithering: The positioning of different-colored pixels within an image to approximate colors that are not in the available palette. A dithered image often looks noisy, or composed of scattered pixels. *See adaptive dithering.*

document: Any individual object (text, image, media) on the web.

dpi: Dots **P**er **I**nch. A common measurement related to the resolution of an image. *See screen resolution.*

dynamic range: The measure of the listenable range of sound—that is, above the level of background noise and below the level of distortion. The larger the number the better the quality of the sound.

e

element: An object in an HTML file.

entity: Special characters (such as ©, ®, or @) that are defined by ASCII character combinations (such as ©, ®, or @).

extension: Abbreviated code at the end of a file usually used to identify the type of file. For example, a JPEG file may have the .jpg extension.

f

fps: Frames **P**er **S**econd. A movie contains a certain number of frames per second, and the fewer frames, the more jerky the motion and the smaller the file size.

frames: Frames offer the ability to divide a web page into multiple regions, with each region acting as a nested web page.

FTP: File **T**ransfer **P**rotocol. An Internet protocol that enables users to remotely access files on other computers. An ftp site houses files that can be downloaded to your computer.

g

gamma: Gamma measures the contrast that affects the midtones of an image. Adjusting the gamma lets you change the brightness values of the middle range of gray tones without dramatically altering the shadows and highlights.

gamut: A viewable or printable color range.

GIF: A bitmapped, color graphics file format. GIF is commonly used on the web because it employs an efficient compression method. *See JPEG.*

GIF89a: The most current GIF specification.

guestbook: A type of form that enables end users to enter comments on a web page.

h

hexadecimal: The base-16 number system. Often used in scripts and code. Hexadecimal code is required by HTML to describe RGB values of color for the web.

HTML: **H**yper**T**ext **M**arkup **L**anguage. The common language for interchange of hypertext between the World Wide Web client and server. Web pages are written using HTML. *See hypertext.*

HTTP: **H**yper**T**ext **T**ransfer **P**rotocol is the protocol that the browser and the web server use to communicate with each other.

hue: Defines a linear spectrum of the color wheel.

hyperlink: Linked text, images, or media.

hypertext: Text that is linked to documents on the web.

i

imagemaps: Portions of images that are hyper-text links. Using a mouse-based web client such as Netscape or Mosaic, the user clicks on different parts of a mapped image to activate different hypertext links. *See hypertext.*

inline graphic: A graphic that sits inside an HTML document instead of the alternative, which would require that the image be downloaded and then viewed by using an outside system.

interlaced GIFs: The GIF file format allows for "interlacing," which causes the GIF to load quickly at low or chunky resolution and grad-ually come into full or crisp resolution.

ISP: **I**nternet **S**ervice **P**rovider.

j

Java: A programming language developed by Sun Microsystems that is cross-platform compatible and supported by some web browsers.

JavaScript: A scripting language that enables you to extend the capabilities of HTML. Developed by Netscape. No relation to Java (except the name).

JPEG: **J**oint **P**hotographic **E**xperts **G**roup; also the graphic format developed by them. JPEG graphics use a lossy compression technique that can reduce the size of the graphics file by as much as 96 percent. *See GIF.*

l

links: Words or graphics in a hypertext document that act as pointers to other web objects. Links are generally underlined and may appear in a dif-ferent color. When you click on a link, you can be transported to a different web site that contains information about the work or phrase used as the link. *See hypertext.*

lossless compression: A data compression tech-nique that reduces the size of a file without sacrificing any of the original data. In lossless compression, the expanded or restored file is an exact replica of the original file before it was compressed. *See compression.*

lossy compression: A data compression technique in which some data is deliberately discarded in order to achieve massive reductions in the size of the compressed file. *See compression.*

m - n

mask: The process of blocking out areas in a computer graphic.

MIME: **M**ultipurpose **I**nternet **M**ail **E**xtensions. An Internet standard for transferring nontext-based data such as sounds, movies, and images.

MPEG: **M**oving **P**ictures **E**xperts **G**roup. Also the name of a high-quality media format for both audio and video.

NCSA: **N**ational **C**enter for **S**upercomputing App-lications. A project of the University of Illinois.

o

object: Any distinct component of HTML, such as a tag, attribute, image, text file, etc.

p

passive navigation: Animation, slideshows, stream-ing movies, and audio. Basically, anything that plays without the end user initiating the content.

plug-in: Plug-ins are supported by some browsers and extend the capability of standard HTML.

PNG: (pronounced, "ping") An acronym for **P**ortable **N**etwork **G**raphics. PNG is a lossless file format that supports interlacing, 8-bit transparency, and gamma information.

PostScript: A page description language used for printing text and graphics on laser printers and other high-resolution printing devices.

PP: (also IPP) Acronym for (**I**nternet) **P**resence **P**rovider. Usually a web-hosting service.

progressive JPEG: A type of JPEG that produces an interlaced effect as it loads, much like interlaced GIFs.

provider: Provides Internet access. *See ISP*.

q

QuickTime: System software developed by Apple Computer for presentation of desktop video.

r - s

raster graphics: *See bitmapped graphics.*

rollover: A type of navigation button that changes when the end user's mouse rolls over it.

sample rate: Sample rates are measured in kilo-hertz (KHz). Sound-editing software is where the initial sample rate settings are established. Standard sample rates range from 11.025 KHz, 22.050 KHz, 44.10 KHz, to 48 KHz. The higher the sample rate, the better the quality. The sample describes its highs and lows. *See data rate*.

sampling resolution: Sampling resolution affects media quality, just like dpi resolution affects the quality of images.

saturation: Defines the intensity of color.

screen resolution: Screen resolution, measured in **d**ots **p**er **i**nch, (dpi), generally refers to the resolution of common computer monitors. 72 dpi is an agreed upon average, although you will also hear of 96 dpi being the resolution of larger displays.

search engine: A type of application, commonly found on the web, that enables you to search by keywords for information or URLs.

server: A computer that provides services for users of its network. The server receives requests for services and manages the requests so that they are answered in an orderly manner. *See client.*

server push: Server push is the method of requesting images or data from the server and automating their playback. It involves CGI and the presence of a live web server.

server side: Server side means any type of web page element that depends on being loaded to a server. It also implies the use of a CGI script.

server-side imagemap: A server-side imagemap requires that the information about the imagemap be saved within a "map definition file" that needs to be stored on a server and accessed by a CGI script.

splash screen: A main menu screen or opening graphic to a web page.

sprite: An individual component of an animation, such as a character or graphic that moves independently.

t

tables: Tables create rows and columns, as in a spreadsheet, and can be used to align data and images.

tag: An HTML directive, enclosed in "<" and ">".

texture map: 2D artwork that is applied to the surface of a 3D shape.

transparent GIFs: A subset of the original GIF file format that adds header information to the GIF file, which signifies that a defined color will be masked out.

true color: The quality of color provided by 24-bit color depth. 24-bit color depth results in 16.7 million colors, which is usually more than adequate for the human eye.

u

user agent: *See browser.*

URL: Uniform **R**esource **L**ocator. The address for a web site.

V

value: The range from light to dark in an image.

vector graphics: Images that are stored as lines and curves, instead of pixels. Vector graphics can be rendered in various sizes, resolutions, and media, without losing information. *See bitmapped graphics.*

Video for Windows: A multimedia architecture and application suite that provides an outbound architecture that lets applications developers access audio, video, and animation from many different sources through one interface. As an application, Video for Windows primarily handles video capture and compression, and video and audio editing. *See AVI.*

W

WYSIWYG: Pronounced wizzy-wig. Acronym for **W**hat **Y**ou **S**ee **I**s **W**hat **Y**ou **G**et. A design philosophy in which formatting commands directly affect the text displayed onscreen so that the screen shows the appearance of printed text.

Index
creative html design

symbols

a

Index

b

m

n

o

X-Z

<deconstructing web graphics>
Web Design Case Studies and Tutorials

Deconstructing Web Graphics profiles top web designers and programmers in order to demystify and analyze how they make decisions, solve complex issues, and create exceptional web sites. Adding her own voice and digital design teaching experience to the book, best-selling author Lynda Weinman selects from her list of favorite designed web sites. She walks you through how to read and understand the source code for each page, breaks down all of the technical elements, and describes the inside details straight from the designers and programmers who created the pages.

This conversational and information-rich guide offers insight into web design that is not found through any other means. Profiles of successful web designers, programmers, photographers, and illustrators allow them to share their tips, techniques, and recommendations. You'll bring your own web design skills to a higher level through studying their experiences and the step-by-step tutorials and examples found in *Deconstructing Web Graphics*.

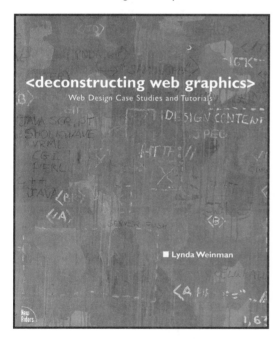

In this book, you'll learn about:

- Low-bandwidth graphics
- Scanned imagery for the web
- Cross-platform colors
- Custom Photoshop brushes & patterns
- Artwork using ASCII
- Copyright issues
- Animated GIFs
- LOWSRC animation tricks
- Tables for alignment
- Invisible GIFs for spacers
- Frames for navigation
- HTML tricks and workarounds
- Java
- JavaScript
- CGI
- Forms processing
- Server push
- Client pull
- Shockwave & Macromedia Director
- Sound & video files
- VRML

Product and Sales Information

Deconstructing Web Graphics By Lynda Weinman
Available at your local bookstore or online
ISBN: 1-56205-641-7 ▪ $44.99/USA ▪ 250 pages
Macmillan Publishing ▪ 1-800-428-5331
- http://www.lynda.com
- http://www.mcp.com/newriders

<coloring web graphics.2>
Master Color and Image File Formats for the Web

The purpose of this book is to help artists, programmers, and hobbyists understand how to work with color and image file formats for web delivery. Web browsers and different operating systems handle color in specific ways that many web designers aren't aware of. This updated second edition includes information about Photoshop 4.0, Illustrator 7.0, DitherBox, and DeBabelizer Pro.

A color palette of 216 browser-safe colors is identified and organized to help web designers confidently select successful cross-platform color choices and combinations. The book includes sections on color theory and understanding web color file formats as well as step-by-step tutorials that explain how to work with browser-safe colors in Photoshop 4.0, Paint Shop Pro, Photo-Paint, Painter, FreeHand, and Illustrator 7.0. The cross-platform CD-ROM includes hundreds of suggested color combinations for web page design, as well as hundreds of palettes and browser-safe clip art files.

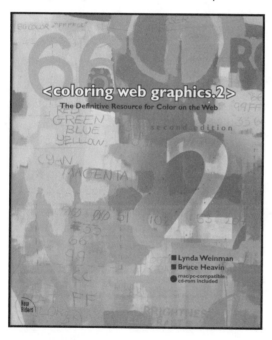

In this book, you'll learn about:

- Creating colors in your artwork that won't shift or dither across multiple platforms
- Choosing web-appropriate color schemes for your page designs
- Creating many browser-safe hybrid variations
- Using Photoshop, Paint Shop Pro, Photo-Paint, FreeHand, Illustrator, & Director to manage web-specific color

The cross-platform CD-ROM includes:

- Browser-safe color palettes
- Browser-safe color swatches for Photoshop & other imaging programs
- Browser-safe colors organized by hue, value, & saturation
- Browser-safe color clip art for web use
- Electronic versions of color swatches grouped as they are in the book
- Sample HTML pages with recommended color groupings
- Sample patterns, backgrounds, buttons, & rules

Product and Sales Information

Coloring Web Graphics.2
By Lynda Weinman & Bruce Heavin
ISBN:1-56205-818-5 ▪ $50.00/USA ▪ 314 pages
Available at your local bookstore or online
Macmillan Publishing ▪ 1-800-428-5331
- http://www.lynda.com
- http://www.mcp.com/newriders

<designing web graphics.2>
How to Prepare Media and Images for the Web

Completely updated and expanded to include the latest on file formats, file sizes, compression methods, cross-platform web color, and browser-specific techniques, *Designing Web Graphics.2* is the definitive graphics guide for all web designers. If you are already working in the digital arts, in print or video, or are looking to transfer your skills to the web, this is the book for you. Step-by-step instruction in a conversational and easy-to-read style from a fellow artist/designer will help you understand the best methods and techniques for preparing graphics and media for the web.

Written in a conversational and user-friendly tone—*Designing Web Graphics.2* has received rave reviews from both experienced web designers and newcomers to the field. It's the bestselling book on this subject, and is being used by web designers all over the world, including those from Hot Wired, Adobe, and Discovery Online.

In this book, you'll learn about:

- Creating the smallest and fastest web graphics
- Browser-safe colors for maximum cross-platform compatibility
- Comparison charts of GIFs, JPEGs, & PNGs to help you pick the best compression method
- Scanning tips (Photoshop 4.0 techniques)
- Incorporating sound, animation, and interactivity
- Creating navigation bars, rollover effects, & linked graphics
- Step-by-step tutorials for programming Photoshop 4.0 Actions Palettes
- Practical applications for JavaScript, Shockwave, CGI, & plug-ins
- Embedding inline music, animation, & movie files
- Animated GIF creation techniques (how to control size, speed, & color palettes)
- Creating GIF & PNG transparency for the web
- Web TV specs & authoring tips
- Updated typography section

Product and Sales Information

Designing Web Graphics.2 By Lynda Weinman
Available at your local bookstore or online
ISBN:1-56205-715-4 ▪ $55.00/USA ▪ 500 pages
Macmillan Publishing ▪ 1-800-428-5331
- http://www.lynda.com
- http://www.mcp.com/newriders

<preparing web graphics>

Learn to make fast, cross-platform compatible, high-quality web graphics

Understanding how to prepare web graphics properly is key to learning how to make web pages look good and perform responsibly. This lower cost alternative to *Designing Web Graphics.2* is appropriate for web publishers who aren't graphic artists. *Preparing Web Graphics* explains the mechanics of web graphics creation, preparation, and delivery. Lynda Weinman supplies the tips and tricks to create graphics that endure the irregularities of different browsers, platforms, and monitor settings.

Using Photoshop 4.0 to produce the bulk of the instructions and corresponding full-color examples, Weinman teaches web publishers how to make fast-loading images without sacrificing quality. She shares her comprehensive knowledge of web graphics engineering, including working with transparent GIFs and low-bandwidth graphics, anti-aliasing, dithering, color mapping, setting color palettes, compressing images, using browser-safe colors, creating browser-safe artwork, and working with background tiles, navigation images, typography, web animation, and more.

In this book, you'll learn about:

- Hardware and software for getting started
- Graphics that download quickly—without sacrificing quality
- What happens to graphics when viewed from mulitple platforms, browsers, & operating systems
- Successfully working with transparent images & avoiding halos & fringing
- Creating seamless tiles, efficient animated GIFs, & enhancements such as custom rules & bullets
- Follow step-by-step Photoshop 4.0 tutorials for designing web-specific images
- Working with image-based typography, using custom fonts and HTML alignment techniques

Product and Sales Information

Preparing Web Graphics By Lynda Weinman
Available at your local bookstore or online
ISBN: 1-56205-686-7 ▪ $39.99/USA ▪ 238 pages
Macmillan Publishing ▪ 1-800-428-5331
- http://www.lynda.com
- http://www.mcp.com/newriders

The CGI Book
The Complete World Wide Web Programming Reference

The CGI Book is packed with solid, well-researched information that will allow you to start writing web applications today. The first part of the book presents the basic concepts of CGI for those who need a foundation to get started right away. After reading just the first chapter, you should be able to create a simple CGI program that gets information from a user's web-browser and displays it in whatever format you choose. Then you can build on that basic knowledge and learn how to get information about a user's browser, the server you're on, version numbers, operating systems, etc.

The second part of the book has more advanced CGI topics for those who have written some CGI and want to get more out of their web services. The advanced subjects include Imagemaps, Cookies, Server Push and Browser Pull, Generating E-Mail, On-the-fly HTML, User Authorization, Security, and a section with Tips and Tricks for creating extra-sharp Web pages and services.

In this book, you'll learn about:

- Getting the maximum power & flexibility from your web site
- View examples presented in sh, Perl, C, & pseudo-code for easy migration to any programming langueage
- Explore CD-ROM bonus programs that include a mini-HTTP server and client with Perl source code
- Using multi-block GIFs for creating animated displays with no programming

The cross-platform CD-ROM includes:

- Examples from the book (in pseudo-code, sh, Perl, and C), the mini-HTTP server & client with Perl source code, plus useful utilities and references. The CD-ROM can be read with DOS, Windows, Macintosh, & UNIX.

Product and Sales Information

The CGI BOOK By William E. Weinman
Available at your local bookstore or online
ISBN:1-56205-571-2 ▪ $45.00/USA ▪ 304 pages
Macmillan Publishing ▪ 1-800-428-5331
- http://www.cgibook.com
- http://www.mcp.com/newriders

▶ Creative HTML Design

colophon

The preliminary layout design of *Creative HTML Design* was sketched on paper, and then produced using QuarkXPress, Adobe Photoshop, and Microsoft Word on a Power Macintosh 7100/80. The text was set in the Adobe Utopia family, main heads were set in Universe Bold Condensed, HTML/CODE was set in Courier New. The color was produced using CMYK mixtures, and the images were all converted to grayscale. The cover illustration was painted with acrylics and crayons, and then drum scanned. *Creative HTML Design* was printed on 55-pound Hammermill Offset, and was produced digitally using Adobe Software. Prepress consisted of Postscript computer-to-plate technology (filmless process) printed by R.R. Donnelley & Sons, Crawfordsville, Indiana.

Notes *continued ...*

Notes *continued* ...

Notes *continued ...*

Notes *continued ...*

CD-ROM LICENSE AGREEMENT

THIS SOFTWARE LICENSE AGREEMENT CONSTITUTES AN AGREEMENT BETWEEN YOU AND NEW RIDERS PUBLISHING, LYNDA WEIN-MAN, WILLIAM WEINMAN, AND JOAN FARBER ("LICENSOR" HEREINAFTER, BOTH JOINTLY AND INDIVIDUALLY). YOU SHOULD CARE-FULLY READ THE FOLLOWING TERMS AND CONDITIONS BEFORE OPENING THIS ENVELOPE. COPYING THIS SOFTWARE TO YOUR MACHINE, BREAKING THE SEAL, OR OTHERWISE REMOVING OR USING THE SOFTWARE INDICATES YOUR ACCEPTANCE OF THESE TERMS AND CONDITIONS. IF YOU DO NOT AGREE TO BE BOUND BY THE PROVISIONS OF THIS LICENSE AGREEMENT, YOU SHOULD PROMPTLY DELETE THE SOFTWARE FROM YOUR MACHINE.

TERMS AND CONDITIONS:

1. GRANT OF LICENSE. In consideration of payment of the License Fee, which was a part of the price you paid for this product, LICENSOR grants to you (the "Licensee") a non-exclusive right to use and display this copy of a Software program, along with any updates or upgrade releases of the Software for which you have paid (all parts and elements of the Software as well as the Software as a whole are hereinafter referred to as the "Software") on a single computer only (i.e., with a single CPU) at a single location, all as more particularly set forth and limited below. LICENSOR reserves all rights not expressly granted to you as Licensee in this License Agreement.

2. OWNERSHIP OF SOFTWARE. The license granted herein is not a sale of the original Software or of any copy of the Software. As Licensee, you own only the rights to use the Software as described herein and the magnetic or other physical media on which the Software is original-ly or subsequently recorded or fixed. LICENSOR retains title and ownership of the Software recorded on the original disk(s), as well as title and ownership of any subsequent copies of the Software irrespective of the form of media on or in which the Software is recorded or fixed. This license does not grant you any intellectual or other proprietary or other rights of any nature whatsoever in the Software.

3. USE RESTRICTIONS. As Licensee, you may use the Software only as expressly authorized in this License Agreement under the terms of paragraph 4. You may physically transfer the Software from one computer to another provided that the Software is used on only a single computer at any one time. You may not: (i) electronically transfer the Software from one computer to another over a network; (ii) make the Software available through a time-sharing service, network of computers, or other multiple user arrangement; (iii) distribute copies of the Software or related written materials to any third party, whether for sale or otherwise; (iv) modify, adapt, translate, reverse engineer, decom-pile, disassemble, or prepare any derivative work based on the Software or any element thereof; (v) make or distribute, whether for sale or otherwise, any hard copy or printed version of any of the Software nor any portion thereof nor any work of yours containing the Software or any component thereof; (vi) use any of the Software nor any of its components in any other work.

4. THIS IS WHAT YOU CAN AND CANNOT DO WITH THE SOFTWARE. Even though in the preceding paragraph and elsewhere LICENSOR has restricted your use of the Software, the following is the only thing you can do with the Software and the various elements of the Software:DUCKS IN A ROW ARTWORK: THE ARTWORK CONTAINED ON THIS CD-ROM MAY NOT BE USED IN ANY MANNER WHATSO-EVER OTHER THAN TO VIEW THE SAME ON YOUR COMPUTER, OR POST TO YOUR PERSONAL, NON-COMMERCIAL WEB SITE FOR EDUCATIONAL PURPOSES ONLY. THIS MATERIAL IS SUBJECT TO ALL OF THE RESTRICTION PROVISIONS OF THIS SOFTWARE LICENSE. SPECIFICALLY BUT NOT IN LIMITATION OF THESE RESTRICTIONS, YOU MAY NOT DISTRIBUTE, RESELL OR TRANSFER THIS PART OF THE SOFTWARE DESIGNATED AS "CLUTS" NOR ANY OF YOUR DESIGN OR OTHER WORK CONTAINING ANY OF THE SOFTWARE DESIG-NATED AS "DUCKS IN A ROW ARTWORK" NOR ANY OF YOUR DESIGN OR OTHER WORK CONTAINING ANY SUCH "DUCKS IN A ROW ARTWORK," ALL AS MORE PARTICULARLY RESTRICTED IN THE WITHIN SOFTWARE LICENSE.

5. COPY RESTRICTIONS. The Software and accompanying written materials are protected under United States copyright laws. Unauthorized copying and/or distribution of the Software and/or the related written materials is expressly forbidden. You may be held legal-ly responsible for any copyright infringement that is caused, directly or indirectly, by your failure to abide by the terms of this License Agreement. Subject to the terms of this License Agreement and if the software is not otherwise copy protected, you may make one copy of the Software for backup purposes only. The copyright notice and any other proprietary notices which were included in the original Software must be reproduced and included on any such backup copy.

6. TRANSFER RESTRICTIONS. The licensee herein granted is personal to you, the Licensee. You may not transfer the Software nor any of its components or elements to anyone else, nor may you sell, lease, loan, sublicense, assign, or otherwise dispose of the Software nor any of its components or elements without the express written consent of LICENSOR, which consent may be granted or withheld at LICENSOR's sole discretion.

7. TERMINATION. The license herein granted hereby will remain in effect until terminated. This license will terminate automatically with-out further notice from LICENSOR in the event of the violation of any of the provisions hereof. As Licensee, you agree that upon such termi-nation you will promptly destroy any and all copies of the Software which remain in your possession and, upon request, will certify to such destruction in writing to LICENSOR.

8. LIMITATION AND DISCLAIMER OF WARRANTIES.
a) THE SOFTWARE AND RELATED WRITTEN MATERIALS, INCLUDING ANY INSTRUCTIONS FOR USE, ARE PROVIDED ON AN "AS IS" BASIS, WITHOUT WARRANTY OF ANY KIND, EXPRESS OR IMPLIED. THIS DISCLAIMER OF WARRANTY EXPRESSLY INCLUDES, BUT IS NOT LIMITED TO, ANY IMPLIED WARRANTIES OF MERCHANTABILITY AND/OR OF FITNESS FOR A PARTICULAR PURPOSE. NO WARRANTY OF ANY KIND IS MADE AS TO WHETHER OR NOT THIS SOFTWARE INFRINGES UPON ANY RIGHTS OF ANY OTHER THIRD PARTIES. NO ORAL OR WRITTEN INFORMATION GIVEN BY LICENSOR, ITS SUPPLIERS, DISTRIBUTORS, DEALERS, EMPLOYEES, OR AGENTS, SHALL CREATE OR OTHERWISE ENLARGE THE SCOPE OF ANY WARRANTY HEREUNDER. LICENSEE ASSUMES THE ENTIRE RISK AS TO THE QUALITY AND THE PERFORMANCE OF SUCH SOFTWARE. SHOULD THE SOFTWARE PROVE DEFECTIVE, YOU, AS LICENSEE (AND NOT LICENSOR, ITS SUPPLIERS, DISTRIBUTORS, DEALERS OR AGENTS), ASSUME THE ENTIRE COST OF ALL NECESSARY CORRECTION, SERVICING, OR REPAIR. **b)** LICENSOR warrants the disk(s) on which this copy of the Software is recorded or fixed to be free from defects in materials and workmanship, under normal use and service, for a period of ninety (90) days from the date of delivery as evidenced by a copy of the applicable receipt. LICENSOR hereby limits the duration of any implied warranties with respect to the disk(s) to the duration of the express warranty. This limited warranty shall not apply if the disk(s) have been damaged by unreasonable use, accident, negligence, or by any other causes unrelated to defective materials or workmanship. **c)** LICENSOR does not warrant that the functions contained in the Software will be uninterrupted or error free and Licensee is encouraged to test the Software for Licensee's intended use prior to placing any reliance thereon. All risk of the use of the Software will be on you, as Licensee. **d)** THE LIMITED WARRANTY SET FORTH ABOVE GIVES YOU SPECIFIC LEGAL RIGHTS AND YOU MAY ALSO HAVE OTHER RIGHTS WHICH VARY FROM STATE TO STATE. SOME STATES DO NOT ALLOW THE LIMITATION OR EXCLUSION OF IMPLIED WARRANTIES OR OF INCIDENTAL OR CONSEQUENTIAL DAMAGES, SO THE LIMITATIONS AND EXCLUSIONS CONCERNING THE SOFTWARE AND RELATED WRITTEN MATERIALS SET FORTH ABOVE MAY NOT APPLY TO YOU.

9. LIMITATION OF REMEDIES. LICENSOR's entire liability and Licensee's exclusive remedy shall be the replacement of any disk(s) not meeting the limited warranty set forth in Section 8 above which is returned to LICENSOR with a copy of the applicable receipt within the warranty period. Any replacement disk(s)will be warranted for the remainder of the original warranty period or thirty (30) days, whichever is longer.

10. LIMITATION OF LIABILITY. IN NO EVENT WILL LICENSOR, OR ANYONE ELSE INVOLVED IN THE CREATION, PRODUCTION, AND/OR DELIVERY OF THIS SOFTWARE PRODUCT BE LIABLE TO LICENSEE OR ANY OTHER PERSON OR ENTITY FOR ANY DIRECT OR OTHER DAMAGES, INCLUDING, WITHOUT LIMITATION, ANY INTERRUPTION OF SERVICES, LOST PROFITS, LOST SAVINGS, LOSS OF DATA, OR ANY OTHER CONSEQUENTIAL, INCIDENTAL, SPECIAL, OR PUNITIVE DAMAGES, ARISING OUT OF THE PURCHASE, USE, INABILITY TO USE, OR OPERATION OF THE SOFTWARE, EVEN IF LICENSOR OR ANY AUTHORIZED LICENSOR DEALER HAS BEEN ADVISED OF THE POSSIBILITY OF SUCH DAMAGES. BY YOUR USE OF THE SOFTWARE, YOU ACKNOWLEDGE THAT THE LIMITATION OF LIABILITY SET FORTH IN THIS LICENSE WAS THE BASIS UPON WHICH THE SOFTWARE WAS OFFERED BY LICENSOR AND YOU ACKNOWLEDGE THAT THE PRICE OF THE SOFTWARE LICENSE WOULD BE HIGHER IN THE ABSENCE OF SUCH LIMITATION. SOME STATES DO NOT ALLOW THE LIMITATION OR EXCLUSION OF LIABILITY FOR INCIDENTAL OR CONSEQUENTIAL DAMAGES SO THE ABOVE LIMITATIONS AND EXCLUSIONS MAY NOT APPLY TO YOU.

11. UPDATES. LICENSOR, at its sole discretion, may periodically issue updates of the Software which you may receive upon request and payment of the applicable update fee in effect from time to time and in such event, all of the provisions of the within License Agreement shall apply to such updates.

12. EXPORT RESTRICTIONS. Licensee agrees not to export or re-export the Software and accompanying documentation (or any copies thereof) in violation of any applicable U.S. laws or regulations.

13. ENTIRE AGREEMENT. YOU, AS LICENSEE, ACKNOWLEDGE THAT: (i) YOU HAVE READ THIS ENTIRE AGREEMENT AND AGREE TO BE BOUND BY ITS TERMS AND CONDITIONS; (ii) THIS AGREEMENT IS THE COMPLETE AND EXCLUSIVE STATEMENT OF THE UNDERSTANDING BETWEEN THE PARTIES AND SUPERSEDES ANY AND ALL PRIOR ORAL OR WRITTEN COMMUNICATIONS RELATING TO THE SUBJECT MATTER HEREOF; AND (iii) THIS AGREEMENT MAY NOT BE MODIFIED, AMENDED, OR IN ANY WAY ALTERED EXCEPT BY A WRITING SIGNED BY BOTH YOURSELF AND AN OFFICER OR AUTHORIZED REPRESENTATIVE OF LICENSOR.

14. SEVERABILITY. In the event that any provision of this License Agreement is held to be illegal or otherwise unenforceable, such provision shall be deemed to have been deleted from this License Agreement while the remaining provisions of this License Agreement shall be unaffected and shall continue in full force and effect.

15. GOVERNING LAW. This License Agreement shall be governed by the laws of the State of New York applicable to agreements wholly to be performed therein and of the United States of America, excluding that body of the law related to conflicts of law. This License Agreement shall not be governed by the United Nations Convention on Contracts for the International Sale of Goods, the application of which is expressly excluded. No waiver of any breach of the provisions of this License Agreement shall be deemed a waiver of any other breach of this License Agreement.

16. RESTRICTED RIGHTS LEGEND. Use, duplication, or disclosure by the Government is subject to restrictions as set forth in subparagraph (c)(1)(ii) of the Rights in Technical Data and Computer Software clause at 48 CFR § 252.227-7013 and DFARS § 252.227-7013 or subparagraphs (c) (1) and (c)(2) of the Commercial Computer Software-Restricted Rights at 48 CFR § 52.227.19, as applicable. Contractor/manufacturer: LICENSOR: NEW RIDERS PUBLISHING, LYNDA WEINMAN, WILLIAM WEINMAN, JOAN FARBER, c/o NEW RIDERS PUBLISHING, 201 West 103rd Street, Indianapolis, in 46290.